Mae ★

★ *West*

Mae ★ West

An Icon in Black and White

JILL WATTS

OXFORD
UNIVERSITY PRESS

OXFORD
UNIVERSITY PRESS

Oxford New York
Auckland Bangkok Buenos Aires
Cape Town Chennai Dar es Salaam Delhi Hong Kong
Istanbul Karachi Kolkata Kuala Lumpur Madrid
Melbourne Mexico City Mumbai Nairobi São Paulo
Shanghai Taipei Tokyo Toronto

First published by Oxford University Press, Inc., 2001
First issued as an Oxford University Press paperback, 2003
198 Madison Avenue, New York, New York 10016
www.oup.com

Oxford is a registered trademark of Oxford University Press

Library of Congress Cataloging-in-Publication Data
Watts, Jill.
Mae West : an icon in Black and white / Jill Watts.
p. cm.
Includes bibliographical references and index.
ISBN 0-19-510547-8 (cloth) ISBN 0-19-516112-2 (pbk.)
1. West, Mae.
2. West, Mae—Relations with Afro-Americans.
3. Motion picture actors and actresses—United States—Biography.
I. Title.
PN2287.W4566 W39 2001
791.43'028'092—dc21 [B] 00-023182

1 3 5 7 9 8 6 4 2

Printed in the United States of America
on acid-free paper

★ *To* ★
Thomas and Doris Watts,
Donald, Rebecca, and Sarah Woo,
and
Wally

Contents

Acknowledgments

This project came toget.   generous support of Cornell University's Society for the Hum.   .s Fellowship. My thanks to the society's director, Dominick LaCapra, and the fellows, including Linda Alcoff, Gary Okihiro, Nellie Furman, Martin Bernal, and, especially, Lois Brown. Grateful acknowledgment goes to others in the Cornell community including Linda Allen, Joan Brumberg, Jackie Goldsby, Michael Kammen, Mary Beth Norton, Cybele Raver, and Rachael Weil.

I have also benefited from guidance from Ed Reynolds, Alex Saxton, Richard Yarborough, Richard Weiss, Vivian Sobcheck, and Edward D. C. Campbell. I owe much thanks to Margaret Washington for her support throughout the years. Richard Newman has been a consistent champion and mentor. I am grateful for the support and advice from Diana Brooking, Gary Campbell, Michael Fitzgerald, Lynne Harvey, Bob Kaplan, Monte Kugal, Judy Kutulas, Valerie Matsumoto, Monica McCormick, Regina Morantz-Sanchez, Peggy Pascoe, Ellen Slatkin, and Nan Yamane.

Support from California State University, San Marcos, has also been instrumental. I am grateful to David Avalos, Nancy Caine, Jeff Charles, Ann Elwood, Glee Foster, Joan Gundersen, Peggy Hashemipour, Linda Shaw, and Zhiwei Xiao. I am thankful for the support of the students in my classes at California State University, San Marcos; Weber State University; and Cornell University. Those who have worked as research assistants include Pam Cronkhite, Shane Ebert, and Bertha Walker. Jillian Martin helped me complete research (in freezing weather) in New York City.

I owe a special thanks to the following: Howard Prouty, Margaret Herrick Library of the Academy of Motion Picture Arts and Sciences; Ned Comstock, Performing Arts Archives at the University of Southern California; Matt Ker, British Film Institute; Robert A. McCown, Special Collections, University of Iowa, Iowa City; Elizabeth Dunn, Hartman Center for Sales, Advertising, and Marketing History; Maryann Clach, Shubert Archives; and Simon Elliot, Special Collections, University of California, Los Angeles. I am also thankful to the librarians at Califr   State University, San Marcos, and Cornell University's Olin Library.

Additionally, I am grateful to my former editors Liz McGuire and T. Susan Chang. This manuscript was initially much longer, and those who saw it through the final process include Joellyn Ausanka, Ellen Chodosh, Elissa Morris, and Russell Perreault. I also owe much thanks to India Cooper for her excellent copyediting and kindness.

I have been fortunate to have unfailing support from my family as I have worked on this project over the last eight years. My parents, Tom and Doris Watts, and my sister and brother-in-law, Becky and Don Woo, gave many hours of their time to helping me complete this book. (Wally, the shelter dog, came into the project about halfway through and has spent many patient hours under my desk.) But this book would not be what it is without my father's influence. He passed away just after the book went out for copyediting. Our family will forever mourn his loss. However, just as the copyediting came back, we were blessed with a new member, Sarah Marie Woo. Sarah, my father's first grandchild, reminds us that, like the bountiful vegetable garden he loved to tend, the future always holds something beautiful.

Mae ★

★ West

They Were Too Smart

Mrs. Crane Brittany: Have your ancestors ever been traced?
Cleo Borden: Well—yes. But they were too smart. They
  couldn't catch 'em.
                    —Mae West as Cleo Borden, *Goin' to Town*, 1935

I n the early 1970s, rumors circulated that after Mae West's death, her
  deepest secret would be revealed publicly for the first time. A few wagered someone would finally verify that the celebrated symbol of
  brazen female sexuality was not really a woman but a man. Others
speculated that a source would confirm that West had African-American
roots, that one of her ancestors had passed for white. Mae toyed with those
bolder journalists who confronted her with the persistent rumors that she
was a man, and when one writer, John Kobal, questioned her on her racial
background and preference for the blues, she admitted only that "her affinity
for black music was because it's the best there is." But all those who anticipated a bombshell at her death were to be eventually disappointed. In 1980,
at the age of eighty-seven, Mae West died and was buried with the secrets
that she was believed to have so carefully guarded throughout her life.[1]

Mae West's death certificate, signed by a physician and an undertaker,
confirms that she was all woman. It is more difficult to rule out the possibility that she had African-American ancestry. While three of her four grandparents were undisputedly European born, the ethnicity of her paternal
grandfather, John Edwin West, is harder to pinpoint. He first appears in
public records only after the Civil War, in 1866, when the Manhattan city directory shows him living on the Lower East Side, one block from the notorious Bowery.

The one sure fact about John Edwin West is that he had been a seafarer—
a rigger who worked on whaling ships. The rest of his background remains a
mystery. His recorded birth date varied between 1819 and 1830; his birth-

places diverged widely and included New York, Maine, Newfoundland, and even England. His death certificate indicated that he arrived in New York in 1821, at the age of two, and that his parents were named John and Edith, but there is nothing to corroborate this or to confirm where John Edwin West really spent his young life. Perhaps, like other working-class people, he remained undocumented by a society focused on the elite and privileged. But he may have also evaded record keepers, purposefully obscuring his background.

Mae West often declared that her grandfather had come from a long line of John Wests. For visitors, she proudly displayed a genealogy of a West family, mainly from Virginia and purported to have descended from Alfred the Great. This impressive lineage may have been more a public projection than a private admission; West often exaggerated or embellished her personal history. Still, these accounts not only offered glimpses into her self-perceptions but almost always were grounded in an element of truth. She frequently provided significant verifiable information on her family—with the exception of John Edwin West, the only grandparent for whom she volunteered no information on background or origins. Perhaps this vagueness was intentional, explicable if John Edwin, or one of his forebears, had escaped bondage and passed for white. Many enslaved African-American sailors took advantage of their mobility and escaped north; some of those who were light-skinned passed. While no documents substantiate that John Edwin did, similarly none prove that he did not. But his nebulous background, the reality that 50 percent of those serving on whaling vessels were black, and his absence in public records until slavery's end suggest that it was possible. Even his wife and children were uncertain about or unwilling to discuss his origins, often giving conflicting information about his past.[2]

Whatever his background, of all of her grandparents, John Edwin made the strongest impression on Mae, who found him a fascinating storyteller of maritime adventures. Mae remembered him as healthy and vigorous. He must have been, for only the most able-bodied seamen had the strength and agility to work clipper ships' towering masts and endure gruelingly long whaling voyages. She also insisted that despite his long career on the rough seas, John Edwin was a pious man. A devout Methodist, he fell to his knees in prayer at each meal and at the end of family visits. She also told how in his advanced years he proudly showed off a near-perfect set of teeth, missing only one that he had decided to pull himself.

Despite his enigmatic early years, later records show that in 1852 John Edwin took a wife, a twelve-year-old Irish Catholic immigrant named Mary Jane Copley. The daughter of Julia (née Copple) and Martin Copley, Mary Jane had come to the United States in 1848, joining thousands who fled Ireland during the potato famine. At the age of fifteen, she bore a daughter, Edith, who was probably born in Brooklyn.[3]

The West family initially remained small. Although Mary Jane eventually bore eleven children, she lost five in infancy. Her second healthy child was the hearty and spunky John Junior, who was born in March of 1866, over ten years after his older sister. Known as Jack, he was born in his parents' home on the Lower East Side. An early photograph of him shows a determined toddler with wavy black hair and steely eyes gazing steadily into the camera.

Jack West came into a turbulent world. A year before his birth, the Civil War ended and President Abraham Lincoln was assassinated. His father did not serve in the conflict; sailors were needed to keep northern commerce flowing. But everyone in Manhattan was affected by the war, which left the city's economy in ruins. Particularly hard hit were impoverished sectors like the Lower East Side, where residents, ravaged by smallpox, cholera, typhoid, tuberculosis, and pneumonia, were crowded into dilapidated tenements. Between 1866 and 1870, the Wests lived in several locations in this area, finally settling in a tenement with eight other families near Tompkins Square Park. They subsisted on John Edwin's wages and whatever Edith, the oldest daughter, now working as a seamstress, could earn.

Jack West spent his formative years on the Lower East Side's rough streets surrounded by poverty, despair, and crime. Powerful gangs controlled the neighborhoods; their influence became so strong that it eventually extended over the city government and police. Their violent exploits were legendary, and many Lower East Side boys regarded notorious gang leaders as heroes. At some point, Jack must have joined a gang, for as writer Luc Sante observes, they were "the basic unit of social life among young males in New York during the nineteenth century." Beginning in childhood, Jack found himself suspended between the honest hardworking poor and the unruly Lower East Side gangs.[4]

Mae remembered her father as outgoing and, at times, gregarious with a wide assortment of friends and acquaintances. But slum life's insecurities and poverty hardened him. A small, wiry youth, he was feisty and strong, and on the streets and in the alleys, he learned to fight. Mae remembered her father boasting that even as a child "he'd rather fight than eat." While he could be personable, according to Mae, he was "always ready to do physical violence when the urge was on him." Easily angered, he had a fiery temper. "Oh, my father was cruel, you know," she recalled in 1969. "But later, I realized all his fighting was done doing other people's fighting for them."[5]

In addition to his immersion in a culture of violence, Jack also confronted festering ethnic and racial bigotry. Nineteenth-century New York City became home to peoples of many races, ethnicities, and nationalities. Deep divides developed, and hostilities sometimes spilled over into violent clashes. These tensions were promoted and augmented by the dominant culture's denigration of anyone who failed to fit the mold of white Protestant Victorian America. Jack West, even if his father was not African-American, must have experienced some of the bruising effects of the ethnic prejudice directed at Irish Catholics. White Anglo-Saxon Protestants defined the Irish as a separate, nonwhite race, disparaging them as "savage," "bestial," and "lazy," degrading stereotypes strikingly parallel to those thrust upon African Americans. And while Irish Americans attempted to claim whiteness, throughout the nineteenth century and into the twentieth, prejudice against them remained constant. In a sense, the dominant culture pressured Jack West and his family to "pass," to deny their heritage and seek inclusion in the white and Protestant Victorian middle class. This struggle with white identity combined with poverty's entrapment could only have served to heighten Jack's frustrations and combative spirit.[6]

In 1873, when Jack was seven, the Wests left the Lower East Side for Brooklyn. They may have been drawn there by Martin Copley, who with a brother, William, operated a gardening and floral business. By this point, John Edwin and Mary Jane's family included two more daughters, Julia and Emma. They first settled in Red Hook, on the waterfront, but within a year they moved again, this time to Brooklyn's Greenpoint district. In direct contrast with the Lower East Side's impacted slums, Greenpoint in the 1870s remained somewhat rural, and open fields surrounded houses and businesses. There Mary Jane gave birth to two more boys, Edwin and William. By 1882, the Wests were able to rent their own home. But heartbreak soon followed: the next year, Emma, aged twelve, was lost to rheumatic fever.

Although the quality of life in Greenpoint may have been better overall, the Wests always struggled. Steam power rendered John Edwin's skills as a rigger obsolete; he eventually found work as a janitor. To make ends meet, the family took in boarders; as the oldest son, Jack was expected to help out. Mae often bragged that he owned a livery stable, but more likely as a youth he drove rigs for the local transit company whose stables and car barns were directly across the street from his home. By 1880, his father had apprenticed him to learn boilermaking, a hard but honest trade.[7]

But John Edwin's spirited son had already set his sights on another calling. At the age of eleven, the sturdy youth fought in his first boxing match. From that point on, Jack aspired to become a bare-knuckle prizefighting champion. It was a dangerous ambition, for boxing of this era was a deadly sport with unlimited rounds that ended only with a concession or knockout. Although small, Jack was muscular and fierce, fighting as a featherweight. Reportedly, after he retired from the ring, he entertained Coney Island crowds by fighting and beating any challenger.

Mae insisted that her father was known around Brooklyn as "Battling Jack." His moniker probably derived more from victorious street brawls than triumphs in the ring, for Battling Jack never held a title, at least not an official one. New York strictly regulated prizefighting, and championship bouts were difficult to secure. This drove unknown pugilists, like Jack, to fight underground, in illegal matches secretly arranged by local racketeers.[8]

Sometime in the late 1880s, however, Jack was sidetracked from his ambitions by a young German immigrant, Matilda Delker. Known by her friends as Tillie, she was the daughter of Christiana and Jacob Delker, who were married in Germany in 1864. She was born in 1870, probably in Württemberg, where her father had worked in a sugar refinery. She arrived in the United States in 1882 with her mother and five siblings, following her father, who had immigrated the year before.[9]

Several factors probably compelled the Delkers to leave Germany, which at the time was experiencing extreme social, political, and economic upheaval. Anti-Semitism may have driven them out—Mae had even the most discerning observers convinced that her mother was Jewish—but by the time the Delkers reached America, they were Lutherans. It is more likely that they were drawn to the United States by economic success enjoyed by relatives who had already settled in New York. Mae often claimed her grandfather was a cousin of Peter Doelger, who had arrived in the States penniless but had earned a fortune as one of Manhattan's most successful brewers. Certainly the families shared some kind of relationship. In later years, Mae publicly claimed Henry Doelger, a San Francisco developer and Peter Doelger's nephew, as her cousin.

However, Jacob Delker was, at best, a poor relation to Peter Doelger. In 1884, Jacob settled his family in Bushwick, a working-class Brooklyn neighborhood that was the center of the city's German brewing industry. He struggled to support his wife and children as a laborer, painter, and coffee peddler. In the 1890s, he served with the Brooklyn Fire Department, indicating he had established some connections with his local political boss; such opportunities usually came as reward for support from loyal constituents.

Still the Delkers remained poor: The American dream as lived by Peter Doelger eluded them. When Tillie was fourteen, her family rented rooms behind a bakery, next to the blazing outdoor oven. After several more moves, the Delkers settled near bustling Bushwick Avenue, along a street of tenements sandwiched between businesses, factories, and stores. Most likely, Tillie had to help support the family. A skillful seamstress, she could do piecework, sew for private families, or even work in one of the local garment factories.[10]

Like other immigrant daughters, Tillie was caught between old-country traditions and the enticements of her new American home. According to Mae, Tillie's ambition was not to sew but rather to become an actress on the American stage. Popular culture, specifically theater and vaudeville, provided Tillie, and many other immigrants, with an introduction to American society—its norms, values, stereotypes, and ideals. These amusements were leisure-time mainstays for Tillie's generation. From a poor immigrant girl's perspective, they were more than just diversions. The glamour of show business, in a country reputed to be the "land of opportunity," seemed to promise escape from impoverishment, dreary tenements, and a life of hard labor.

Tillie's dreams were epitomized by a single American actress—Lillian Russell. Celebrated as "a truly remarkable beauty of face and form," Russell projected the Victorian female ideal of white womanhood: blond hair, blue eyes, a heavily corseted figure, and a "peaches and cream" complexion. Tillie worshiped Lillian Russell and envisioned herself in the actress's image. Mae insisted that people often mistook her mother for the beloved actress. However, no matter how beautiful the young Tillie Delker was, Russell's WASPish qualities contrasted greatly with Tillie's dark brown hair and eyes. These attempts at remaking herself evidence Tillie's own struggle with identity. Although not subjected to the vehement discrimination unleashed against the Irish, Germans were also considered inferior, outside the realm of acceptable white norms; they were stereotyped as drunken and violent or silly and ignorant with laughable accents. Tillie battled these negative attitudes by adopting Russell's image. Mae proudly displayed a picture of her mother, anonymously retouched to make her look more like Lillian Russell and less like Matilda Delker.

Tillie met resistance as she aspired to follow in Russell's footsteps. An acting career for a newly arrived German girl who was just learning English was a remote dream, especially with parents who forbade the pursuit of such a disreputable profession, but Tillie, as many remembered her, maintained a quiet resolve. Mae claimed that Tillie secured a position as a "corset and fashion model," a profession accessible to an immigrant seamstress with unsteady English. If true, Tillie pursued this without her parents' consent. It was far from respectable; buyers were known to make sexual advances, and she could not have rejected their demands and kept her job long.[11]

She may well not have rejected them. Historian Kathy Peiss has found that young working-class women of Tillie's generation, known as "tough girls," commonly rebelled against their parents' standards and experimented with premarital intimacy. In Tillie's adolescent world, crowded tenements and eroded parental supervision allowed young people to experiment with sex. The ritual of working-class dating, in which young male suitors footed the bill for their impoverished dates, often resulted in an exchange: cultural amusements for sex. Ultimately, it would be Tillie who nurtured Mae, shaping her attitudes about sex, men, and money. Mae recalled her parents battling over her early flirtations with the boys. "My father used to want me to come home and all that, but my mother used to say, 'Oh, let her go, she can take care of herself,'" Mae recalled. "I guess she wanted me to learn all that right at the beginning." In many ways, Tillie was not only the motivator for Mae West's libertine ideals but the prototype for her sexually transgressive persona.[12]

Tillie's youthful defiance soon met its end with Jack West. Initially, the couple formed a passionate bond. Mae insisted that Jack was so jealously obsessed with Tillie that he once attacked a group of men after one had dared to flirt with her. Tillie was equally infatuated. "You see," Mae told an interviewer, "my father had swept her off her feet."[13]

Jack and Tillie appeared an odd match. He was loud and talkative with a quick temper and a love of horse racing; she was reserved and, as one journalist described her, "plain, comfortable," and "kindly." According to Mae, Jack craved bloody and bruising battles, while her mother "loved pretty things about her." Tillie adored the theater and never drank, except a rare glass of champagne—for which Jack nicknamed her "Champagne Til." At the same time, Jack and Tillie had much in common. Both rebelled against parental expectations, Jack through sports and Tillie through her dreams of a theatrical career. They both also made their livelihood, at least in part, through the exploitation of their bodies. Jack and Tillie shared a stubbornness and willingness to test tradition. And, importantly, both knew very well the underside of working-class life, its difficulties, its disappointments, and its challenges.[14]

On January 19, 1889, in Greenpoint, Battling Jack West and Tillie Delker took their wedding vows before a local minister with Jack's sister Julia acting as maid of honor. Jack was twenty-four and Tillie was nineteen. He quit boxing, and Tillie abandoned both corset modeling and, at her husband's insistence, her hopes of becoming an actress. The couple moved in with Jack's parents. In August 1891, Tillie gave birth to her first child, Katie, in Jacob and Christiana Delker's Bushwick home.

Sadness soon befell Jack and Tillie. Only a few months after her birth, Katie died, probably a victim of cholera, common in such working-class enclaves. According to Mae, Tillie was devastated and grieved deeply.

For almost two years after Katie's death, Jack and Tillie remained child-less. For Tillie, stifled in her aspirations for a stage career and suffering from the loss of her first child, married life proved to be disappointing and un-happy. Her pain was compounded by Jack's temperamental outbursts. Mae recalled that his impatience was so intense that "when he couldn't find what he wanted, he'd pull the whole drawer out and dump it on the floor and swear and everything—and my mother would have to come and find things for him." She maintained that her mother "always felt she had made a big mistake marrying him."[15]

But in 1893, life changed for Tillie. That year, she and Jack moved into a Bushwick tenement on Willoughby Avenue where, on August 17, she gave birth to a healthy baby girl. Named Mary Jane for her grandmother, but called Mae by family members, she was delivered by an aunt. (The Wests spelled it May; Mae later changed it herself.) Mae immediately became her mother's greatest treasure. Tillie doted on her, indulged her every whim, and lavished her with praise and attention. Although there were more West children to come, Tillie, according to Mae, always considered her special and handled her differently. "I was her whole world," Mae recalled. "She treated me like a jewel." Mae's first memory was of "Mama" gently rubbing her with baby oil after a bath.[16]

A firm and loving, as well as often consuming and obliging, bond devel-oped between Mae and her mother. Mae always credited Tillie as her driving force; Tillie's impact on Mae was profound. "She tried in every way to un-derstand me," Mae wrote. As evidence, Mae often recounted three episodes from her childhood, all occurring at age four. In the first, Tillie indulged Mae in her refusal to be photographed without a particular black and white dog. The second incident took place in a busy department store where her mother insisted harried clerks fetch a doll that Mae had spotted on an im-possibly high shelf. The third transpired in an elderly "spinster's" home. When little Mae, admiring some glass flowers, touched them, the old woman harshly reprimanded her. Reportedly, Mae marched out of the room, collected her coat, as well as Tillie's, and returned commanding, "We go home, Ma." They did.

While Mae offered these incidents to demonstrate her inborn determina-tion and temperament, they also reveal much about Tillie. She insisted that her daughter be "humored" and coaxed, never harshly disciplined according to standard Victorian childrearing practices. Mae attributed the evolution of her unique personality to this special treatment. "She is not like other chil-dren," Tillie cautioned John when he tried to discipline Mae. "Don't make her like the others." Tillie shaped her daughter not only with an unconventional upbringing but also by fashioning her memories. Mae did not directly remember any of these early incidents; all had been told to her by her mother. By imprinting memories on Mae, Tillie constructed her daughter as willful, strong, and innately resistant to authority. Tillie emerged as equally unyielding, tenaciously insisting that her daughter's demands always be satisfied.[17]

Tillie concentrated on nurturing Mae into her ideal image, instilling self-assuredness and pride in her daughter. According to Mae, her mother stressed the importance of physical appearance and beauty. Mae recalled strolling past Brooklyn storefronts, admiring her reflection in the windows and refusing to carry packages, believing they marred her appearance. Tillie also excused Mae from the household chores normally imposed upon young girls of her generation. Tillie had a vision for her daughter, and it had nothing to do with domesticity.

Reportedly, neighbors were critical of Tillie's parenting techniques. Those who remembered the West family later described Tillie as "too easy" and criticized her for allowing her little daughter to "push her around." Mae, like her father, had an explosive temper, lashing out angrily at other children. Reportedly, she was just as likely to "smack a boy on the nose as she would a girl." Behind the fearsome Battling Jack's back, the neighbors described "that West kid" as a "brat" and "holy terror."[18]

Mae's outbursts, easy frustration, and propensity to strike out indicated that, despite Tillie's efforts, she was hardly a secure child. Some of Mae's problems came from Jack West; she often admitted as much. She frequently compared herself to Jack, claiming she possessed not only his tireless energy and strength but also his extreme temperament. She never once cited similarities between herself and her mother, whom she worshiped.

While Mae and Tillie shared a deep bond, her relationship with "Papa" was difficult, complex from the beginning. She told one interviewer that her father had wanted a boy, not a girl. Reportedly, Jack alleviated his disappointment by teaching little Mae the manly arts of boxing, acrobatics, and weightlifting. He immersed her in his world of physical brutality, taking her to the gym and to prizefights. She claimed she enjoyed it and was fond of his boxing pals, but her introduction to violence went even deeper: Mae remembered battling her father in one-on-one boxing matches. Pitting a grown man, a trained boxer, against a small child was not mere play; it was abusive. The relationship between violence and power consumed Mae as an adult, and she often associated it with her father. Her fondest memory of him was of a trip they took to a Coney Island circus. Mae, entranced by the famous Bostick and his lions, was captivated by the struggle between animalistic brutality and human intellect.

Mae's contact with her father was limited. In the evenings, he came bounding home, ate dinner, and, before long, was off for the night. While Tillie worked at making home life pleasant and stable, Battling Jack made it difficult. In addition to his hair-trigger temper, he was restless. In the first seven years of Mae's life, the Wests lived in at least five different locations in Bushwick and Greenpoint. By 1895, Jack had abandoned boilermaking to become a night watchman, guarding local warehouses and businesses. He also worked as a bouncer at local theaters and dance halls. In the 1900 census, he identified himself as a "special policeman"; most likely he was providing muscle for local businesses and crime bosses. That year, he was making enough money to lease a home for his wife and children. Shortly afterward, he went into business as a private eye and organized a "private police force" that he hired out to those seeking help and protection. He could have only undertaken such an endeavor in connection with the New York underworld. It was common for businesses, theaters, and saloons to rely on local crime syndicates to guard their establishments. According to one source, Jack was also respected by the local police, not surprising given their own ties to gang bosses.[19]

As Jack and Tillie settled into the criminal underworld's subculture, their family began to grow. In December 1898, Tillie gave birth to another baby girl, Mildred. Soon afterward, in February 1900, came a son, named John Edwin for his father and grandfather. Although the new babies diverted some of Tillie's energies, Mae believed that her mother favored her over the other children. Tillie's permissive nature did not extend to Mildred and little John; she disciplined them harshly and even permitted an occasional switching; Mae claimed she always escaped such punishment. Tillie became increasingly convinced that Mae was exceptional.[20]

According to Mae, even before her siblings arrived, she had begun to fulfill her mother's expectations. She claimed that by the age of three she exhibited an extraordinary talent for mimicry, routinely impersonating family, friends, and acquaintances. It set the Wests howling with laughter. In an era when children were to be seen and not heard, Mae won attention and approval while commenting on a world in which she was powerless. She was too young to realize it then, but she had discovered something mighty.

A steady diet of mass culture fostered Mae's special abilities. Tillie took her along to plays and vaudeville, and Mae was enthralled. In her later years, she reminisced about long-forgotten singers, jugglers, acrobats, and dialect comedians. "I laughed with the Yiddish, Dutch, and Italian comics," she recalled. "I listened all ears to the patter of the song and dance men." While she remembered numerous entertainers fondly, one stood out as her favorite: the African-American performer Bert Williams. For most of her professional life, Mae West credited him as her earliest influence.[21]

The young Mae West was not alone in her adulation. By the early 1900s, Williams and his partner, George Walker, had become two of America's most popular entertainers. Famous for their cakewalk, an elaborate, high-stepping African-American dance originating in slavery, they were among the first blacks to break into white vaudeville and Broadway. Williams's clowning made him the favorite of the duo. Light-skinned, he borrowed from white American minstrelsy, performing in burnt cork makeup with a large white greasepaint grin. His stage persona was dim-witted and silly; his timing was calculated to be excruciatingly slow.[22]

While on the surface Williams's performances reified racism, he subtly challenged it by grounding his performances in black comedic tradition. Williams's stage presence emerged from the African-American practice of signifying, a subversive rhetorical device that uses multiple and conflicting messages to obscure rebellious meanings. Black signifying rests in double-voicedness and encompasses innuendo, double entendre, parody, pastiche, cajoling, rapping, boasting, insulting, and many other verbal, visual, and/or literary forms. Importantly, as scholar Henry Louis Gates Jr. has demonstrated, black and white signification are distinct practices. In the white community, signifying refers to implying meaning. But among African Americans, signifying involves the *act* of implying meaning. Hence the process of creating double meanings is as important as the double meanings themselves.

Gates has traced the origins of black signifying to African and African-American trickster-heroes whose double-voicedness operates as a playful but deadly serious rebellion. These tricksters engage in language games, or signification, that impart multiple and contradictory meanings. By generating a dizzy spectacle where everything is subject to constant repetition and revision, trickster-heroes, or signifiers, reorder the world through disorder. Gates describes black signifying as "a bit like stumbling unaware into a hall of mirrors: the sign itself appears to be doubled, and at the very least, (re)doubled upon ever clear examination." But, he writes, "It is not the sign itself . . . which has multiplied. If orientation prevails over madness, we soon realize that only the signifier has been doubled and (re)doubled." In the end, meaning evaporates and all that remains is the messenger, the signifying trickster.[23]

Williams embraced the trickster's role and, empowered by signifying, interrogated white oppression. He viewed his fictional character as a satire of a white man; it functioned as a mirror that compelled unsuspecting whites to peer into their weaknesses and insecurities. With the cakewalk, he resurrected a practice originally used by slaves to mock their masters' dance rituals, compelling unwitting white audiences to laugh uproariously at themselves and their outrageous behavior. His hit song "Nobody" captured not only the frustration of the tattered blackface clown who experiences "hunger and cold feet" but also the alienation of exploited African-American people who "never got nothin'." Its summation was a forceful statement of resistance. "Until I get something from somebody, some time," Williams sang in his languid, half-spoken style, "I'll never do nothin' for nobody, no time."[24]

As writer Mel Watkins observes, Williams's humor and subversion "depended on word play or lampooning usually solemn institutions." This was one of his most enduring contributions to little Mae West. She claimed that even as a small child she was fascinated by language and its potential for multiple meanings. "I had acquired the manner of speaking that has become identified with me," she maintained. "It came from my refusing to say certain words." She remembered begging her mother to read out words until she found one that when pronounced assumed an "individual connotation." Beginning with her exposure to Williams, Mae would borrow heavily from signification. By adulthood, she was well aware that she had adopted it, often explaining, "It isn't what I do, but how I do it. It isn't what I say, but how I say it, and how I look when I do and say it."[25]

Mae West's connection with Bert Williams and signification was both deeply strong and personal. She maintained that somehow her father was introduced to Williams. (Perhaps it was through their common love of boxing; Williams was an avid fan.) One of her most treasured, and seemingly traumatic, childhood memories was the night her father arrived home and announced:

> "Mae, I have a big surprise for you. Bert Williams is here. I've brought him home to have dinner with you." I rushed in, looked at this man and screamed, "It's not! It's not!" I went up to my room and cried. . . . My mother told me my father wanted to go up to me, but Bert Williams stopped him. He said, "I'll do it." He stood outside my door and started to sing. Then I knew and came right out of my room and we all had dinner. Do you know why I didn't recognize him? He was too light. He was a black man but he was too light, so on stage he wore blackface.

Like many others, Mae imagined Williams as she had seen him onstage. Even so, she attributed her outburst not to his unexpected appearance but rather to her fear that her father had deceived her. "I cried," she explained, "because I couldn't bear the thought that my father had lied to me."[26]

While this incident revealed Mae's anxieties about her father, Williams's presence also forced her to grapple with much larger issues—those of racism and identity. In interviews Mae, always attempting to project strength, admitted to crying only twice in her life, and this was one of those times. It jolted her into a realization that the performer was quite different than he or she appeared onstage. In many ways, Williams compelled her to confront, at a tender age, the falsity of blackface. It was a traumatic awakening to the societal lies regarding race, which eventually resulted in a distrust of the racist image created by white society to ensure superiority, dominance, and predictability. Williams was not a buffoonish clown but rather, as Mae observed, "looked more like a businessman." She learned that appearances were illusions, obscuring other realities that could still be conveyed through language. After all, it was the sound of Bert Williams's voice that restored order to the West household and compelled Mae to leave her hiding place and accept reality.[27]

Despite Mae's stunned reaction to the truth of blackface, she maintained that her parents held progressive racial attitudes. Certainly their willingness to entertain an African American in their home, even if it was the famous Bert Williams, indicated that they deviated from most white Americans. (Williams's own white co-stars often shunned him.) "I knew black people from the beginning," Mae would insist. "So I realized they weren't stereotypes, they were people like me, but darker." Although Mae's statement presumed whiteness as a baseline, it also awkwardly expressed identification with African Americans. Without a doubt, Mae believed she shared a marginalized status with them. "I thought white men had it their own way too long," she later remarked, "and should stop exploiting women and blacks and gays." Throughout her career, in her performances and in her interviews, she would act out an ambivalence over racial identity, pivoting between embracing and rejecting whiteness. Was Mae West passing? It is hard to determine. But it is clear that the character she would create, her fictionalized persona, certainly was.[28]

While she may not have had any African-American genetic ties, the turn of the twentieth century provided the little Mae West with a wide sampling of African-American cultural forms. The most popular music of her youth was ragtime, rooted in the African musical tradition. The cakewalk became a craze throughout the nation. Other forms of black song and dance were also popular. This process of cultural appropriation and white society's struggle to cling to its fantasy of whiteness revealed that the racial identity of European Americans was never clear-cut. If anything, much of the mass culture of Mae West's youth, with its African-American ties, challenged racial fixedness. It was within this turmoil that Mae began her search for an identity and a voice.

Race was not the only contested element of the American identity confronted by young Mae West. She had to balance her mother's world of "tough" working-class girls who defied middle-class Victorian prudishness with mass cultural forms that reinforced it. She remembered *Florodora* sextets—Broadway's singing Gibson Girls, the embodiment of whiteness and submissive femininity—being held up as role models for little girls to emulate in her youth.

Mae rejected this standard early. Much to her mother's delight, by age four she began imitating famous performers, and Florodora Girls never appeared in her repertoire. Rather, her impressions were of men—singer and dancer George M. Cohan and comedian Eddie Foy. Later Mae forcefully insisted that she did not seek to copy men but rather to mimic them; she was not striving to replicate maleness but to comment on it. At the same time, she also began imitating Bert Williams, an even more rebellious act. When impersonating him, she became a white female child pretending to be a black male signifying on and mocking white society. This was a critical step in the construction of her stage personality during a formative period of her development.

Overjoyed, Tillie encouraged Mae, believing that her daughter's energy and outrageous behavior could be redirected into performance. She hoped Mae would learn to rein in her temper by deflecting "it into channels where control would become automatic." When her vivacious little daughter reached five, Tillie arranged for her to entertain at a church social. Mae, by her own account, was the hit of the program. Immediately, Tillie booked Mae to sing, dance, and do impersonations at other local events. But Tillie's zeal produced more friction within the family. Jack protested Tillie's ambitions for Mae. Like Jacob Delker, he did not want his daughter onstage.[29]

Despite her husband's opposition, Tillie continued to promote their daughter's talents. Mae recalled that at age seven her mother enrolled her in a dancing school. Mae claimed she was such a natural that the instructor soon entered her in an amateur contest at Brooklyn's Royal Theater.

Sponsored by vaudeville houses or theater companies, Saturday night amateur contests were common in this heyday of variety entertainment. Winners received as much as ten dollars, a welcome supplement to any working-class income. But these contests could also be brutal. Audiences booed, heckled, and egged greenhorn performers; those who really flopped got the hook. Mae remembered her mother as uncharacteristically nervous on the night of her debut. Jack had opposed Mae's participation, insisting that she was too young and would suffer stage fright. Indeed, Tillie had her hands full. Mae showed no fear but was in an extremely obstinate mood. When the emcee called out, "Baby May, Song and Dance," Mae, seeing the spotlight fixed on the other side of the stage, refused to budge. After another introduction, the spotlight began to swing to center stage. "When I saw it comin' for me," Mae recalled, "I ran out to meet it, not a bit scared."[30]

Baby Mae epitomized Victorian innocence and sentimentality. Tillie had carefully assembled a costume of "a pink and green satin dress with gold spangles [and] a large white picture hat with pink buds and pink satin ribbons," accentuated by pink slippers and stockings. Mae recalled performing several popular songs (although the ones she later named were written when she was in her teens) and, after finishing with a dance, bowing to the applause. That night Mae took first place, winning a gold medal and ten dollars. Her father, who had sat smugly in the audience, was convinced. His daughter would perform again. He was going to take her himself.

Mae claimed that over the next year her parents entered her in numerous amateur contests. Soon it became a family affair. Tillie drilled her on her act, designed her costumes, and brokered bookings. On performance nights, Jack hauled Mae's suitcase to the theater and then took his place in the audience as Tillie prepared their daughter backstage. Mae's act consisted of impersonations, dances, and, eventually, a selection of double-entendre songs inflected with adult bawdiness. Her sister, Mildred, later credited the ribald nature of Mae's earliest performances to Tillie. "Even as a little girl," she remembered, "Mae's character songs were risqué."[31]

While the sight of a little child performing songs with sexual undertones may have been shocking, Tillie was borrowing from trends popular in variety entertainment of the period. Despite the prevailing rigid Victorian attitudes regarding sex, American mass culture became increasingly saturated with salacious references. In some circles, suggestive songs became the rage, and performers made their mark as double-entendre singers. Certainly no vaudevillian was more popular than singer, dancer, and comic Eva Tanguay. Billed as "the I Don't Care Girl," she emerged as one of the era's most famous stars just as Mae West first hit the amateur circuit.

Tanguay provided an alternative image to the *Florodora* sextet. Of French Canadian descent, Tanguay was short and curvy, hardly the classic American WASPish beauty. But, by her own admission, she knew how to manipulate male spectators and enact desirablity. Not a trace of Victorian sentimentality or propriety could be found in her act. Her monologues and spicy songs were indelicate; she danced with electrified abandon. Although she vigorously battled censorship, she became known as "Vaudeville's Biggest Drawing Card" and at her peak earned $3,500 a week.

Tillie joined growing legions of Tanguay admirers and became satisfied that she was the perfect role model for Mae. Tillie urged her daughter to closely study vaudeville's biggest headliner. According to Mae, her mother "was always talkin' to me about bein' an actress. Eva Tanguay was a big shot then. Everybody was crazy about her. Mother took me to see her again and again and told me I could be important like that. We went to all the shows and we talked about nothin' but what I was going to be." Eventually Tillie became acquainted with the star. It appeared to be an unlikely pairing—the working-class stage mother and vaudeville's most celebrated diva. The two did have a connection, however: Tanguay knew Bert Williams and was romantically involved with his partner, George Walker.[32]

Mae soon incorporated a Tanguay imitation into her act, her first and only impression of a woman. Ironically, Mae spent a fair share of her youthful innocence impersonating the "bad girl" of the American stage. Inspired by Tanguay and cheered on by her mother, Mae eventually came to understand the process of manipulating the audience's imagination and simulating desirability. The impact of this pint-sized performance with its sensual undercurrent was significant. Purposefully or not, Tillie exploited her daughter by playing with erotic allure. While Mae was too young to understand, it had a lasting effect. Eventually her performance would center on sexuality and seduction.

Mae boasted that her act won high acclaim and that she usually came in first at local talent contests. At the age of eight, she got her first big break with an appearance at the amateur show at Brooklyn's Gotham Theater. That evening, she claimed, her impersonations of Bert Williams and Eddie Foy netted first place. Seated in the audience was actor Hal Clarendon, a handsome leading man who often appeared with Brooklyn's most respected stock companies. According to Mae, he was so impressed by her performance, he rushed backstage to congratulate her parents and invite their little ingenue to join his troupe. "I accepted," she claimed, "even before Papa did it for me."[33]

Later Clarendon confirmed he had discovered Mae West, but his account differed somewhat. In 1933, he told the *New York Daily News* that a "Judge Rosenthal," a friend of the West family, had strongly suggested he bring Mae into his theatrical ensemble. Although Clarendon could not exactly say who Judge Rosenthal was, he claimed that he "respected" Mae's connections and, as a result, agreed to take on the child. Curiously, when the *Daily News* reporter began poking around, it seemed no one could remember Judge Rosenthal, the figure so helpful in getting Mae West her first real acting job. Clarendon's admission that he had been coerced into accepting her and everyone's caginess regarding Rosenthal's identity suggest that he was an underworld figure, most likely the colorful racketeer Herman Rosenthal.

Just as the young Mae West made her professional debut, Herman Rosenthal was moving up the ranks of New York's criminal underworld after operating for several years as a racetrack bookie and a pimp. He enjoyed support and protection from the Bowery's most powerful leader, the Tammany Hall boss Big Tim Sullivan. In fact, Sullivan, who owned saloons and theaters as well as dabbling in betting and prostitution, looked upon Rosenthal as a favored protégé.

For small-time gamblers, down-on-their-luck performers, minor gangsters, and aspiring boxers, Rosenthal became a folk hero. He was extremely generous, liberally sharing his money with friends and acquaintances. He also had close ties to Brooklyn; his mother lived there, and some even called it "Herman's Homeland." With his connections to the underworld and horse racing, Jack West had plenty of opportunity to become acquainted with the racketeer. It would have been characteristic of Rosenthal to open doors for Mae. He liked children and often assisted friends with his ties to theater people.

Many of those who benefited from Rosenthal's generous spirit were later reluctant to admit their association with him. In 1912, after publicly exposing ties between the police and crime bosses, Rosenthal was gunned down outside his favorite Manhattan restaurant. During his funeral, mourners filled the streets outside his residence, but, fearing retribution from both the police and gangs, no one was willing to serve as a pallbearer. Only family and a few close friends, including attorney Harold Spielberg, who would later represent Mae in legal battles, followed the casket to its Brooklyn resting place. Rosenthal's controversial reputation may explain why Clarendon and everyone else was so reluctant to specifically credit him.[34]

Until this point in her life, Mae had enjoyed a fairly typical turn-of-the-twentieth-century childhood. She roller-skated, played with dolls, and attended public school. Although she had several playmates, she was closest to her cousins. When the family discovered that she was left-handed, they discouraged it, forcing her to practice penmanship with her right hand for hours on end. Mae pretended she was signing autographs.

The demands of the stock company drastically cut down on Mae's youthful diversions. Initially, Clarendon used her as a preshow or between-scenes filler act, allowing her to sing, dance, and perform impersonations. Within the first week, however, she had so infuriated him that he considered dismissing the well-connected little performer. "She was a terror all right," he confirmed. Clarendon demanded that he never be disturbed in his dressing room. Mae completely ignored his edict, constantly interrupting him. According to the actor, once, while he slept soundly, she slipped in and lacquered his face with greasepaint.

Although Clarendon was, as he described it, "furious," there was probably little he could do to get rid of the West child. After suffering with her for a while, he contended, "she got me down . . . I finally got to like her." Eventually, he even eased her into children's roles in the company's plays. By Mae's account, her weekly salary climbed from eighteen to thirty dollars, an impressive sum that, if true, certainly must have helped the Wests. At best, working-class tradesmen earned between ten and sixteen dollars a week.[35]

While it was a great opportunity, stock company work was grueling. Monday through Saturday, the troupe offered two shows a day, starting rehearsals at ten in the morning and finishing with the final curtain at eleven at night. Each week, the company offered a new play, so new lines had to be learned. In the summers, Clarendon took a troupe on tour, and Mae went along with an aunt to chaperone. Back home, when Clarendon could not use her, she played with other stock companies or, at her mother's insistence, attended rehearsals to study experienced actors and actresses. Mae was always eager to please her mother, but she remembered this time as "hard days of work and more work, when I practiced dancing and singing until my feet ached and my throat felt as though I had been massaged with a marlin spike."[36]

As a result, Mae's schooling became sporadic. For a time, she had a private tutor, apparently a fellow who owed Jack money, very likely from a gambling debt. Overall, though, her formal education was limited. Although those who later knew her commented on her keen intelligence, book learning was never her strength. It did not hinder her much. Costume designer Edith Head, who later became a close friend, observed that Mae "may not have been literate, but she was utterly articulate."[37]

Now young Mae West had little time for playmates or childhood amusements. She was almost totally immersed in the adult world. Her early years onstage forced her to grow up quickly. Mildred later remembered that her sister "never did care to play with other children; they seemed silly to her."[38]

While her peers spent their days in school, Mae received her education from the stock company. "No actress ever had a better school," she maintained. Hal Clarendon cast her in a variety of roles ranging from Shakespearean classics to popular "blood and thunder" melodramas. All the plays influenced her, but she was most intrigued by melodrama. With plots pitting good against evil, this genre required distinctive acting techniques. Performers ranted their lines, underscoring their delivery with exaggerated body language. Dialogue was spartan, and players wrung the most from each word. Mae recalled that "we played it earnestly and swiftly, and we did what we could to learn our parts better and make our acting say more than the lines could." Although she was a hellion, Mae was a perceptive child and a prodigious mimic. Under Clarendon's guidance and by observing the troupe's other members, she began to refine what would become one of her most heralded talents, her ability to infuse complex meanings into her dialogue with carefully articulated gestures and intonations.

Playing with the stock company also carried its ironies. The little girl who surrendered her youth to the theater now spent most of it enacting childhood on the stage. In her first role, she starred as "Angel Child" in the temperance drama *Ten Nights in a Barroom* and pleaded with a fictional father to stop drinking. Mae also played Little Red Riding Hood, girls of the hardened urban slums, and Little Eva of *Uncle Tom's Cabin*. On occasion, Clarendon used her in male roles; she played Little Lord Fauntleroy, Shakespearean boys, and *East Lynne*'s Little Willie.[39]

Although Mae developed a variety of characterizations, she usually played little girls cut from a similar mold. Melodrama's female children were pure and virtuous but also resourceful and determined. Triumphing over danger and adversity, they were often heroines who saved the family farm or, at least, tried to rescue their dissipated alcoholic fathers. On the one hand, their exaggerated moral virtue affirmed Victorian notions of womanhood. On the other, their superiority over male villains and evil forces allowed them to transcend traditional gender boundaries. Not surprisingly, many melodramas were written by female playwrights, and the genre's biggest fans were women, who could identify with the female protagonists. For Mae, it was an even more empowering experience. She was not just a spectator; as an actress she ascended directly into the story. She became part of a staged reality in which little girls both affirmed and rejected white Victorian womanhood.

Mae quickly learned important, yet paradoxical, lessons during these formative years. She claimed that early on she became aware that women could manipulate men—that women could exploit their subordinate status to gain power. "Ever since those days," she remarked on her years with the stock company, "I realized there was a difference between the sexes. I found that as a little girl I could get my way easier than could little boys."[40]

Mae also discovered that while gender roles confined women to a rigidly subservient status, at the same time, identity could be flexible. As a child actress, she was encouraged to "be" different people and even change genders. Fundamentally, for Mae, identity became something that could be constructed and reconstructed to suit a time, place, or situation. Essentially, an actress made "passing" into a profession, always playing out a false identity. In some ways, the assumption of a variety of personas was liberating. But it also robbed Mae, at a critical period of emotional growth, of the chance to define her sense of self. No doubt, it masked, as well as accentuated, Mae's insecurities and deep wounds. If later it appeared that Mae West, the star, had no personal dimension, it was because in early childhood she was compelled to be everyone else but herself.

Mae trouped on as a stock company player until about 1905, when, at the age of twelve, she was forced into early retirement. She claimed that she had physically matured and was no longer able to carry off children's roles, but it is likely that the actions of the Society for the Prevention of Cruelty to Children contributed to halting her career. This watchdog group had successfully agitated for stricter child labor laws, especially targeting the "child slaves of the stage." The Society busily ended the careers of several noted child performers, including Buster Keaton, whose parents attempted to conceal him in some luggage during a raid. "I was to have my trouble with them," Mae confessed, "but I never hid in a trunk."[41]

Although Mae's career had stalled, Tillie remained confident that her daughter was destined for stardom. During this time, she arranged for Mae to attend Ned Wayburn's Studio of Stage Dancing in New York City. Wayburn was a former blackface performer who opened a free dance school where he not only offered instruction but also scouted acts for vaudeville. While Mae may have gained some tips from Wayburn, her apprenticeship produced little more. So she returned to performing at amateur nights, community events, and church socials, where she offered recitations, danced, sang, and did impersonations. Perfecting her Bert Williams routine, she added a rendition of "Nobody." "That was a big hit for me," she told an editor from the African-American magazine *Jet* in the 1970s.[42]

Entering her mid-teens, Mae worked up a routine as a "coon shouter." A remnant of the minstrel stage, coon shouters were whites in blackface who performed rag-style tunes, with lyrics that often perpetuated degrading black stereotypes. In the early twentieth century, they were some of America's most successful stars. One of the most celebrated was Sophie Tucker, known as the "Last of the Red Hot Mamas." It is not surprising that Mae experimented with this popular entertainment genre. Since the early nineteenth century, blackface performance had had a successful history with white audiences. With its long track record, blackface may have seemed a promising vehicle to a hopeful like Mae West.

Blackface was a complicated white performance ritual that rested, as many have argued, on contradictory impulses. On one level, blackface functioned as an assertion of racism. With grotesque exaggeration, blackface performers enacted key components of racist ideology, reinforcing prejudicial notions that African Americans were simpleminded, foolish, often violent, and sometimes dangerously sexual. While it ultimately reflected white self-doubts and insecurities, it also reinforced racial hierarchy and white supremacy. Several scholars have contended that on another level, however, it occasionally challenged key elements of racialist ideology, particularly the

immutability of race. As literary critic Susan Gubar argues, in many instances blackface performers "test[ed] the boundaries between racially defined identities." Within the space created by blackface, white performers
often unleashed potent critiques of American society, its power structure,
and sometimes even racism.[43]

Mae West's blackface performance, unlike that of other coon shouters,
rested on a volatile foundation. Their inspiration came from white min-
strels, but her adoption of blackface extended back to her early impersonations of Bert Williams. He continued to influence her performance
strongly, so much so that his style remained apparent even many years later
in Mae's half-spoken manner of singing. But his presence went beyond her
surface delivery and permeated the substance of her performance, providing
the sustaining subtext for it. For Williams each performance was a battle,
and from him Mae learned her most valuable lesson, that the performative
was the political. Up until her death, Mae continued to praise him as a "fine
artist" who challenged white society's racist stereotypes.[44]

In addition to borrowing from Williams, Mae incorporated a generous
share of Eva Tanguay into her new act. By this point, Mae had thrown off the
constraints of idealized melodramatic womanhood. In exchange, she increasingly assumed Tanguay's technique of staging desirability while challenging
restrictive Victorian expectations of women. Combining Tanguay's powerful
manipulation of the female illusion with Williams's signified rebellion, Mae
began formulating her stage persona as a coon shouter. Masked and paradoxical, it carried with it a reification of racism and sexism as well as a rejection
of whiteness and male authority. Mae's coon-shouting years were significant
in her own evolution into a trickster, an important step in her transformation into a performer who strove not only to affirm and entertain but also to
challenge and provoke through calculated wit.

These transitional years were difficult for the teenage Mae West. As a
stock performer she had led a life apart from her peers for almost four years.
Now she had to integrate into the working-class adolescent world. She briefly
returned to public school but quit at age thirteen. Outside of her cousins and
immediate family, she made few friends, having an especially hard time relating to girls her own age. Mae later claimed that Tillie had discouraged such
friendships — they were not expedient. "Girls seemed a foolish investment of
my time," Mae remarked, insisting that she felt attention was better spent on
boys. "I liked all the boys," she bragged, "and kissed them all."[45]

Despite Mae's boasting, she also expressed mixed feelings about sex. She
maintained that she first learned about it at the age of nine by sneaking a
peek at a medical book. Surprisingly, the woman who became the celebrated

"Queen of Sex" was, at first, repulsed. "After I had read it, I had a funny feeling about my parents," she confessed, "a particular feeling—disgust, you might say. It took me a long time to get over it."[46]

On many occasions, Mae alleged that she had become sexually active early, wanting to experiment before puberty to avoid pregnancy, but she gave several different accounts of her first sexual encounter. In one, a young music teacher, who gave her lessons while she sat on his lap and he kissed her, initiated her on the front steps of her parents' home. In another, she claimed to have seduced a retired actor who was ignorant of her extreme youth. She also told of a schoolteacher who introduced her to sex when she was only thirteen. "He got me to stay after school. I helped to correct papers and things," she remembered. "I was too young to feel anything, you know. But I liked it because he was paying me attention. I always wanted attention."[47]

It is possible that all of these early sexual encounters took place. Much of Mae's youth was spent among adults, and enacting sensuality made her a likely target for abuse. Despite her later insistence that she was the aggressor in these affairs, she also indicated that she felt exploited. She related her earliest sexual encounters dispassionately, with a curious detachment that would always mark her attitude toward intimacy. This ambivalence reflected the reality that Mae West's first exposure to sex was traumatic; she was a victim of what now would be recognized as child molestation. In each case, adult men used her for gratification. Her rationalization that her teacher's special attention was reasonable compensation was belied by her decision to quit school at exactly the same time. She did not really seem to covet the attention he offered.

Clearly, Mae West's earliest sexual experiences were emotionally damaging. Late in life, she discussed what she identified as her first sexual dream. She claimed it occurred sometime between the ages of ten and twelve. Although she insisted that she was not frightened by it, her account conveyed a nightmarish tone. In it, a "giant male bear" entered her bedroom, walking on his hind legs. "He came forward, toward me, and stepping up on the foot of the bed, he leaned his paws high on the wall against which my bed rested." He then proceeded to have sex with her. She often insisted that the dream was pleasurable, but to one female interviewer she confessed that it "worried me for a long time." Indeed, she revealed to a close associate that when she reached adulthood, she was plagued by such intense dreams about sex that she required sedatives so she could sleep.[48]

Some have presumed that Jack West sexually abused Mae, but she always stridently maintained that her father had never even laid a hand on her. Regardless, by her teens, she had come to detest him. "I didn't want him to touch me," she explained. "I didn't want to be in the same room with him." She attributed her reaction to Jack's pungent cigars, strict paternalism, and unpredictable temper—except in her autobiography, where she offered a curious assessment of her increasing animosity, lamenting that "Freud wasn't there to explain it to me." This odd aside is unclear but indicates that she vaguely linked her resentment to something sexual. It is possible that she may have been redirecting her anger at her father for failing to protect her from sexual exploitation. Still, while she continued to insist that Jack had never hurt her, she was definitely scared of him. She remembered fearfully hiding in her parents' bedroom, armed with an iron curtain rod, to avoid her father's wrath after he learned that she was staying out late with neighborhood boys. Jack's rage quickly passed, and apparently nothing came of this episode, but Mae's reaction implied that she was terrified of her father.[49]

The West household was hardly a happy one. When Jack was home, which was seldom, the atmosphere was tense. According to Mae, Tillie kept the peace, coolly reasoning with him. To make matters worse, the family's income declined with her career's downturn. By 1909, the Wests had relocated to a brownstone that they shared with two other working-class families. In the preceding years, death had repeatedly visited both sides of the family, all still living in Brooklyn's impoverished sections. Jack's sisters Julia and Edith died of tuberculosis, leaving their young children to be raised by relatives. Tillie's mother, Christiana Delker, died in 1901 from diabetes. Jacob succumbed to hepatitis a year later. After suffering heart problems, the colorful John Edwin West passed away in 1906 at, by any account, an advanced age. Grandmother Mary Jane moved in with Jack and Tillie, where she wasted away, afflicted with kidney failure. She died in August 1909, just days after Mae's sixteenth birthday.[50]

Tillie seemed determined that Mae would not be trapped in the dreary life of a working-class woman, destined to serve as wife and mother. She applied tremendous pressure on her daughter, insisting that Mae focus solely on her career. While Mae apparently had her share of teenage escapades, she remained a homebody, thoroughly tied to Tillie. Seemingly this was true even when Mae was in her twenties. After she reached stardom in the 1930s, journalists sought out former acquaintances for juicy tidbits on the young Mae West. All that one neighbor, who had lived near the Wests in the late 1910s and early 1920s, could say was, "It always seemed strange to me that such a vivacious and beautiful girl would prefer to stay home with her mother."[51]

Throughout her early life, Mae had little time to spare. She devoted herself to studying other performers and attending theater and vaudeville. But she would also remember that by mid-adolescence she had become aware of her position within the larger world. "When I was about 14–15, I resented that men could have sex, do anything they wanted, run around. . . . I resented being held down," she explained. "A woman couldn't pick the man she wanted. Then she was talked into a guy by her family, maybe for money or something else. If she went after a man she was marked a bum, a tramp." She would become increasingly determined to use her performance to challenge society's hypocritical attitudes toward sex and male privilege.[52]

Despite her growing resentment of gender inequalities, Mae claimed that her interest in boys intensified. Tillie attempted to control even this aspect of her life, urging Mae to experiment but avoid commitment. Tillie knew that romance led to marriage and babies, a death blow to a woman's theatrical career, but she also had to confront Mae's budding curiosity about the opposite sex. "Mother preferred that I divide my attention among several boys," Mae recalled. "She encouraged it." And Mae was not the type of girl to say no, especially to her mother.[53]

The Way She Does It

Miss West can't sing a bit but she can dance like George Cohan, and personality just permeates the air every minute she is on stage. In other words, it isn't what Miss West does, but the way she does it that assures her a brilliant career on the stage.

—*New York Morning Telegraph*, October 11, 1913

Around 1909, Mae West finally got a chance to return to the professional stage. Her break came when William Hogan, small-time vaudevillian and friend of the family, invited her to join his act. He needed a partner to play his girlfriend in a Huckleberry Finn routine. It was not a particularly original or creative act; for years, vaudeville bits based on rural, Twain-like characters had been common. With it, Mae found herself in a position similar to her experience in stock companies, playing a Becky Thatcher–type character—a white male fantasy of white femininity. Not surprisingly, the act soon underwent revision, and Huckleberry Finn was discarded in exchange for a Bowery skit. Another popular format, Bowery skits centered on the antics of a Bowery boy and his "tough girl" counterpart. Now Mae's character would become a poor but spunky, assertive, and optimistic street-smart urbanite. In other words, this was no Becky Thatcher.

With Mae's willful and independent streak, it is likely that she exerted considerable influence over the act's new direction. The urban setting was familiar to her; she had been nurtured in it. Although performing furnished an escape, every night she returned home to the reality of her working-class Brooklyn roots. She told of one early beau, among many others, whose gang affiliation resulted in bloody warfare in front of her parents' home. (Her father eagerly plunged in.) The stage offered Mae an opportunity to reenvision the old neighborhood and her position within it. It became an idealized world in which she eventually would assume complete control. Later she confessed, "I've never been more secure than when I'm on stage."[1]

While Hogan and West were eventually successful enough to secure a manager, they failed to break into the big time. Vaudeville was a precarious profession. Work was sporadic; performers were often laid off for months at a time. Reportedly, during downtime, Mae continued to hone her skills in another venue—burlesque. One Brooklynite remembered seeing the teenage Mae West performing a fan dance, her body covered with powder. "The fan was big and red and she shook her bare body behind it. . . . When she shook herself the powder would fly all over the stage, down onto us in the front rows," he remembered. "We loved that."[2]

Generally, burlesque was considered the place for performers and acts too declassé for polite middle- and upper-class society. Its audiences were predominantly working-class men. Traditionally, shows featured women in tights and revealing costumes performing musical numbers interspersed with jokes and skits by ribald male comedians. Most female burlesquers specialized in the cooch, a grinding, European-inspired belly dance. Early on, Mae became an adept coocher. While burlesque represented the ultimate in commodified and exploited female sexuality, it probably provided the West family with a more steady income than Mae's engagements with Hogan in lower-tier vaudeville.[3]

Sometime in 1909 or 1910, Hogan and West played the Canarsie Music Hall, where they shared the bill with Frank Wallace, a nineteen-year-old song-and-dance man. A resident of Queens and son of Lithuanian immigrants, Wallace had changed his name from Szatkus. Thin and modest looking, he was nonetheless a crowd pleaser; his snappy dancing and ragtime singing wowed audiences. Wallace claimed that "one day after my performance a swell-looking woman with a German accent came around back stage and said she had a daughter who was a comer. She had seen my act, she said, and thought I could help her kid." While Wallace was no vaudeville headliner, he appeared to have a promising future. According to him, Tillie suggested that he team up with Mae, which he did, he claimed, after some coaxing. But he also later confessed that he had earlier spotted Mae at an amateur competition and was impressed by her unique coon shouting. Mae always claimed that *he* had begged her to be his partner.[4]

Frank and Mae began rehearsing in the basement of the Wests' rented brownstone. He was soon captivated by Mae. She was hardworking and talented as well as attractive, with a petite figure and thick, dark, curly hair. In a few short weeks, they put together a sleek act borrowing liberally from black music and dance. They opened with Mae's ragtime rendition of

"Lovin' Honey Man" and followed with a song-and-dance number called "I Love It." Occasionally, she performed "When My Marie Sings Chidee Bidee Bee" in Italian dialect, and Wallace offered specialty dances. With Wallace's connections, the duo secured bookings on the Fox Circuit. They must have enjoyed some success, for in the summer of 1910 the census reported that she had been fully employed the past year.

In early 1911, Wallace and West landed parts in *A Florida Enchantment*, a road show on the Columbia Burlesque Circuit. While it was not the big time, Columbia was the most powerful and prestigious of the burlesque circuits. Hoping to broaden its audience, it had incorporated Broadway-style touring musicals, like *A Florida Enchantment*, staged along with the risqué comedy acts and hip-grinding Gayety Girls. Columbia's efforts at respectability were met with criticism from the more legitimate sectors of the industry. Show business's most esteemed publication, *Variety*, admonished Columbia and other burlesque circuits for drifting from "the burlesque idea," warning them to stick to "girls in tights and comedians who prefer to make burlesque fun rather than a name for themselves." In show business, burlesque was third-rate, its performers appropriately consigned to anonymity.[5]

Still, the more elaborate burlesque road shows were popular with audiences not only for their daring content but precisely because they applied the "burlesque idea" to stage traditions. Through the musical theater format, these burlesque productions poked fun at society's most sacred institutions, using comedy as a backhanded commentary on American values and class divisions. While these productions were far from revolutionary, they did serve both as a reflection of and a channel for the discontent of laboring classes and the poor—an important training ground for the maturing Mae West.

A Florida Enchantment embodied such a subversive spirit. It focused on the travails of Meyerwurst, a German "woman hater" who is seduced by a "little French adventuress" played by West. It not only lampooned high society with two aristocratic characters named Lord Bonehead and Cheathem but also mocked entertainment industry elite with a burlesque chorus spoof of the era's most famous stars, including the theater's queen of high drama, Ethel Barrymore. In addition to pursuing Meyerwurst and Cheathem, Mae delivered the song "Tiger Love," backed by the burlesque chorus. Wallace, who played a Jewish character, Young Goldburg, also had a number. During the show's olio, Wallace and West reprised their vaudeville act, receiving praise as "clever" and for their "coon shouting." One reviewer reported that they "score[d] heavily with a novel dance," and another noted that Mae made "several changes down to full tights with good effect."[6]

Enchantment's road tour took Wallace and West into the heart of the Midwest, well beyond Tillie's protective supervision. Tillie had continued to attempt to direct both Mae's personal and professional lives, cautioning her away from romance. "My mother never approved of a single boy friend I had," Mae later told a reporter. "Whenever I showed up with one who wanted to take me to the altar, my mother didn't like him and when I saw that, somehow or other I soured on him, too." While Tillie must have been proud of her daughter's favorable reviews, she would undoubtedly have been alarmed to know that, once on the road, Wallace proposed marriage. Mae claimed that she turned him down repeatedly and continued affairs with other cast members, members of the crew, men she met in hotels, and male fans from the audience. "Marriage was the furthest thing in my plans," she recalled.[7]

By the time the tour reached Milwaukee in early April 1911, West's attitude had changed. She contended that Etta Wood, an older cast member who coincidentally played Mother Goldburg, took her aside, insisting that her promiscuity would only get her into "trouble." "Sooner or later something's going to happen to you," Wood reportedly warned. "Marry Wallace and be respectable." Mae claimed that Wood's advice forced her to think hard. She concluded that she "could get married and still see other guys." Then if she got pregnant, she would "have somebody to blame it on."[8]

So on the morning of April 11, 1911, Mae West and Frank Wallace were married by a justice of the peace in Milwaukee. Only seventeen, she lied on her marriage license and stated that she was eighteen, Wisconsin's legal age for marriage. She also claimed that her mother was French, stereotypically a more "exotic" legacy than her Germanic roots. Immediately after the ceremony, she made Wallace swear not to tell her parents and to keep the marriage secret once they returned to New York. He claimed the troupe's manager gave them the night off for a honeymoon, but Mae remembered that she spent it alone in her room in a noisy hotel. She later vehemently insisted that they had never lived together as man and wife.

In light of her steadfast devotion to her mother, who would have been horrified to learn that Mae had taken wedding vows, her marriage to Wallace seems uncharacteristic. As her mother knew, marriage could severely jeopardize Mae's aspirations. Married couples struggled in show business, and matrimony often terminated the career of one or both partners. Throughout his life, Wallace insisted that West had married him out of love, but she always characterized it as a marriage of convenience. Years later her attitude toward matrimony was apparent. "I don't suppose you believe in marriage," queried a suitor in her 1933 film *I'm No Angel*. "Only as a last resort," Mae replied.

It is possible that West may have been, or feared she was, pregnant. When later responding to questions about her marriage, she always ventured into the topic of pregnancy. "Getting pregnant was a great disgrace in those days," she told one probing interviewer. "I did it [got married] because I was scared," she confessed to another. But Mae also had great faith in her birth control method—a silk sponge, regularly washed out, tied to a string. She bragged she had shared this secret, which was really quite commonplace, with comedienne Fanny Brice, claiming Brice had several abortions before she adopted Mae's method.[9]

West usually chalked up her early marriage to youthful carelessness. For the first time, Mae was cut off from her mother, and Wallace's tenacity combined with Wood's ominous admonitions may have forced her into a rash decision. Wallace admitted that she agreed to marry him only hours before the ceremony. A contemporary photograph of West and Wallace shows her flashing a wedding ring, but she claimed her regrets were immediate.

The tour ended in the summer of 1911. Mae returned to her family in Brooklyn, and Wallace went back to Queens. Although he kept his promise and remained silent about their marriage, he began to badger Mae to settle down with him. She clearly felt no attachment to him. "It's just this physical thing," she remembered telling him. "You don't move my finer instincts." But he persisted. Soon Mae realized that to preserve her career and her relationship with her beloved mother, she had to get rid of Frank Wallace.[10]

Mae broke the news to Wallace that their professional partnership was over, insisting that her mother had demanded that she go solo. Next, she arranged, or so she claimed, for him to join a road show booked for an extended tour. Wallace departed reluctantly, and with that, he was out of her life. "Marriage is a career and acting is a career and you can't mix two careers," West later rationalized. "An actor's marriage isn't like other marriages. . . . We don't think about marriage as something going on and on, with children from generation to generation. It's often just a passing whim."[11]

With Wallace out of the way, West worked up a new a song-and-dance act. She quickly secured a one-night booking at Manhattan's Columbia Theater, a popular scouting venue for Broadway producers as well as agents for vaudeville's prestigious Keith Circuit. On this particular night, Ned Wayburn was there. But so were the powerful Florenz Ziegfeld and his wife, actress Anna Held. Some claim that West's turn so captivated them that they showered her with roses during her finale.

Astonishingly, West maintained that she turned down a subsequent offer from Ziegfeld. She insisted that his New York Roof Theater was too large to capture her "facial expressions, gestures, [and] slow, lazy comic manner-isms." But her claim that Ziegfeld's theater was too large for her seems sus-pect, for the Columbia Theater was just as big. Rather, according to other sources, Ziegfeld tried to recruit her for his famous Follies chorus. Cer-tainly, West had no desire to be just another chorus girl, even if it was for Ziegfeld's Follies.[12]

Next, West auditioned with Ned Wayburn for *A La Broadway,* a comedy revue for Jesse Lasky's Folies Bergere. *A La Broadway* was an elaborate en-deavor created by writer William Le Baron as "a satirical burlesque on all musical comedies." Le Baron later recalled that Mae, who showed up with her mother, possessed an overwhelmingly strong voice. Le Baron and Way-burn decided to use her in a small but significant role as an Irish maid, Mag-gie O'Hara, a quiet lass planted in a wealthy home to report on the curious habits of New York's high society. West accepted the role but, she main-tained, with a warning that she intended to make some changes.

Although West remained confident, rehearsals went badly. She was un-able to practice her first song, a ballad called "They Are Irish," because Cook and Lorenz, a comedy team that accompanied her, could not master their props for the number. Additionally, Jesse Lasky was unimpressed and wanted to drop her from the production. But Wayburn prevailed and in-sisted that they give the newcomer a chance. West blamed her problems on the role. On her own, she recruited a songwriter to rework "They Are Irish" and transformed the mousey and hardworking Irish maid into a brash and in-solent Maggie O'Hara. "I played it as a fresh, flip lazy character who acted as a maid shouldn't," she recalled.[13]

A La Broadway opened on September 22, 1911, and, according to Mae, she plunged into her first Broadway show with the verve that marked her entire career. Her first scene came just after the chorus, costumed in military uni-forms, finished a burlesque of elaborate Broadway drill numbers. Cook and Lorenz were still unprepared, and at the last minute Wayburn sent West on without them. As the chorus stood at attention, she entered and, in a broad Irish brogue, delivered a sassy version of "They Are Irish." Probably no one was more surprised than Wayburn and Le Baron when she followed it up with nine more choruses, each more risqué and each in a different dialect. West's gamble paid off. She scored several encores, right in the middle of the revue.

While most critics panned *A La Broadway*, concluding that it was "very poor stuff" devoid of "variety and features to make it a great success," West received accolades. One reported that she dazzled the audience with "The Philadelphia Drag," a ragtime parody. The *New York Sun* noted that "she danced with considerable grace and originality," and the *New York Tribune* praised her as possessing "a bit of a sense of nonsense, which is the very latest addition to wit." Mae's triumph rested with her style, which was well matched to Le Baron's satirical intentions. She attributed her success to the blending of her early influences: "I used all the stage tricks I had learned in stock training and vaudeville." Indeed, her performance's complexities were beginning to coalesce. With Maggie O'Hara and her new lyrics, West explored the malleability of ethnic stereotypes, becoming all and none of them at the same time. Furthermore, her revision of her part was both overtly and covertly rebellious. She not only improved the production but also brazenly asserted control over a role created by a man. West was unique and confounded critics, who began to interpret such boldness from her as masculine. "She seems to be a sort of female George M. Cohan," the *New York Evening World* explained, "with an amusingly impudent manner and individual way of nailing her points."[14]

West was just eighteen, and her first Broadway appearance was a hit. But *A La Broadway* was not, folding after eight performances. Fortunately for West, two of New York's most successful entertainment impresarios, Lee and J. J. Shubert, were in the audience opening night. Impressed, they cast her in *Vera Violetta*. It was a complicated production, part comedic operetta and part variety show, with appearances by blackface comedian Frank Tinney and suggestively clad swimmer Annette Kellerman. It also featured, at an astonishing $4,000 a week, Parisian superstar Gaby Deslys in her first English-speaking performance in the United States.

To share the stage with Gaby Deslys, an international celebrity, was a privilege for the young Mae West. Deslys reigned as the French music hall queen and had revolutionized that venue with her suggestive costumes and her outlandishly oversized feather headdresses, which became a standard for chorus girls everywhere. Her voice was weak, but critics celebrated her breathtaking beauty and accomplished dancing. She was known as the actress who "made her reputation by losing it," and a U.S. newspaper dubbed her "the Most Talked About Woman in the World"—both phrases that West would later borrow for herself. Deslys became the prototype of a temperamental and eccentric star. The media chronicled her extravagant fondness for furs, pet marmosets, emeralds, diamonds, orchids, and pearls. Photographer and writer Cecil Beaton observed that she "realized the value of overdoing everything." It was a lesson not lost on Mae West.[15]

Although Deslys was phony, egotistical, and arrogant, she also controlled her career wisely, personally negotiating top-dollar salaries and always insisting that shows be built entirely around her. Her assertiveness and conceit created problems for her co-stars. In addition to run-ins with other featured performers, Deslys immediately clashed with a then unknown blackface comedic singer named Al Jolson. His contempt for her was obvious, and in each scene they shared, Jolson upstaged her with wild antics and mugging.

To make matters worse, *Violetta*'s racy and convoluted plot predestined the show for problems. It told of two couples who flirt with the idea of swapping partners but instead rediscover their love. West appeared as Mademoiselle Angelique, a dancer who offers tutorials on the art of lovemaking. Although the part was modest, it was significant enough for her to rate mention (as "May West") in ads for *Violetta*'s opening.

The Shuberts scheduled *Vera Violetta* for a tryout on November 17 and 18, 1911, at the Hyperion Theater in New Haven, Connecticut. Notorious for booking bawdy shows, the Hyperion was a favorite among the football crowd. And that particular weekend was the Yale-Princeton game, an intense rivalry made more so since the two teams were vying for a championship. *Violetta,* with its scintillating humor and Parisian star, seemed a fitting celebration for Yale's almost certain victory. Friday's opening night proved it so. One New Haven reviewer commented that "the Hyperion management could have chosen no more suitable show to brave the streamers, the catcalls, and the implacable applause of football night." He especially praised Deslys: "She has come; she the little French dancer who dances kingdoms to destruction like Nero fiddling at the burning of Rome." According to another she was "cheered from the time she first appeared on stage until after the fall of the last curtain." Sure that they had a hit, the Hyperion management doubled ticket prices for Saturday night's postgame performance.[16]

Saturday afternoon, however, several New Haven residents complained to authorities that *Violetta* was "vulgar and suggestive." That evening the police chief informed the Hyperion's manager, E. P. Eldridge, that he was closing the show. Eldridge protested and the show went on, after the manager promised to downsize Deslys's and West's roles. The chief warned him that officers would be stationed in the audience and would arrest everyone associated with *Violetta* if players did or said anything risqué. Squeezed for time, Eldridge decided to cut out all of *Violetta*'s dialogue and restrict cast members to performing only their musical numbers. The controversial star attraction, Deslys, would go on last.

When the curtain rang up, the Hyperion was packed with Yale fans, fresh from an afternoon of football and drink, smarting from their disappointing loss to Princeton. The show began late and then moved rapidly through *Violetta*'s songs and dances. Everything went smoothly—until West's entrance. For her turn, she had obtained an imitation Deslys gown with an outrageous headdress. When West took the stage, the audience, initially mistaking her for the star, "clapped, roared, and practically stood on their chairs." She then proceeded with a "little impromptu singing" that, while rated "objectionable" by one reviewer, drove the crowd wild. Deslys had been upstaged. When she made her entrance at the show's end, confused fans "didn't know whether to applaud or not." West claimed that, in the end, the woman celebrated as the "sensation of two continents" was given only a lukewarm reception.[17]

Anticipating at least another hour of entertainment, the already restless audience remained in their seats. Then the orchestra rose and departed, and a call went up for Eldridge. When the manager did not appear, several angry students jumped onto the stage and began ripping down the curtains. Others started to tear up the orchestra seats and throw chairs out of the boxes. The production crew pushed onto the stage and turned fire hoses on the audience. According to the press, several women, infuriated at having their gowns ruined, joined in the mayhem. One even ripped out an entire row of seats, hurling them to the floor. Eventually the crew forced the audience into the streets, where the mob continued its rampage, breaking windows, throwing rocks, and smashing the theater's sign. Police reinforcements arrived and "rushed pell mell into the crowd and began clubbing the students right and left." At the end of the melee, the Hyperion had sustained over $1,000 in damage, and authorities had arrested several popular student athletes.

For months following *Violetta*'s visit, New Haven fought over who was responsible for the uprising. The theater blamed the police; the police blamed the theater. Yale students and administrators blamed both the authorities and the theater. Several community leaders attributed the disturbance to American theater's degenerate state and called for censorship of New Haven's stages. In New York City, the entertainment community laid some of the responsibility at the feet of a young, brash, virtually unknown actress, Mae West. *Variety* commented, "It is said that May was right in the middle of that fray, if she did not start it."[18]

On the train back to New York City, an infuriated Deslys threatened to quit the show and return to Paris. The Shuberts panicked. She represented a considerable investment and promised healthy box office returns. Almost immediately, *Variety* announced West's sudden departure from *Violetta*, reporting she was suffering from pneumonia. While West may have been ill, Deslys definitely would not have tolerated her upstaging antics.

West's stunt could have been simply youthful high jinks; certainly her actions were foolish for an actress so obsessed with her career. Yet, while it may have been bad judgment, her mockery of Deslys, in many ways, was predictable. Since childhood she had used mimicry as a tool for criticism. Deslys was a vain, disingenuous, and pretentious star, a perfect target for

Mae's rebellious trickery. At some level, she must have known that upstaging Deslys would have disastrous effects, but her desire for attention and her inclination to challenge authority won out. Mae apparently had only one regret about the incident—her timing. In retrospect, she lamented because she had not held back until the show reached Manhattan.[19]

However, the short time West spent with *Vera Violetta* did pay off. The Parisian entertainer provided her with a role model for celebrity. It was Deslys's posturing that West both rejected and embraced as the basis for her stardom. She had already been drawn to stereotyped French allure, and Deslys reinforced that mystique. Throughout her career, she borrowed from Deslys for her performance as a public figure. Mae West would become both a star and a parody of a star.

After *Vera Violetta*, West returned to vaudeville. By January 1912, she had put together an act with two friends from *A La Broadway*, dancers Bobby O'Neill and Harry Laughlin. They played as "Mae West and Her Boys" and later as "Mae West and the Girards." Mae was the act's centerpiece, the "boys" decked out in elegant evening dress functioning only as a backdrop. The trio sang and danced to ragtime. West soloed with a cooch dance, described by one reviewer as an "enchanting, seductive, sin-promising wiggle" made even more tantalizing by a dress with a breakaway shoulder strap. For their finish, the three performed a ragtime song and a novel dance routine while seated in chairs.

Variety found the act coarse, one correspondent commenting that for West "the burlesque stage is her place and she can make a name there." Sime Silverman, the publication's founder, declared the chair routine "a peach and funny," but he warned that the act was too risqué for audiences outside Manhattan. Writing under the byline Sime, he declared West a "rough soubrette"—in entertainment lingo, a woman who attempted songs, dances, and jokes that were considered the domain of male performers. His pronouncements were critical, for *Variety* often influenced bookings for new acts. Sime's tastes were extremely conservative; he expressed not only traditional gender expectations but also strong class biases. Performers who were a little too raucous properly belonged in entertainment venues patronized by the working class. Sime insisted that vaudeville and Broadway be the preserve of tasteful amusements that drew the better people.

While influential, Sime did not always reflect popular trends. In fact, Mae West and the Girards won accolades from other critics. One praised the act as "clever" and "novel," noting that "the audience took more than kindly to them and gave them the unanimous stamp of approval at the end of the act." Another reviewer noted that West "with a Gaby Deslys costume and Eva

Tanguay line of business brought down the house." In fact, the act was so promising that they quickly secured a contract with Frank Bohm, one of vaudeville's most successful agents. Bohm was twenty-nine, smart, and aggressive. He booked acts for the Loew Circuit, reputable second-tier vaudeville and considered a good opportunity for new talent. With his help, Mae West and the Girards obtained some choice bookings, even performing at Loew's best theater, the American Roof.[20]

Under Bohm, Mae West and the Girards did well for vaudeville newcomers. In addition to good and steady bookings, he also arranged for the team to plug a song, "Cuddle Up and Cling to Me," and appear on the cover of its sheet music. West credited Bohm with helping her to channel her talents productively. "I was a hard boiled, wise-cracking kid, doing anything to get a laugh," she insisted. She remembered Bohm pointing out his office window to a comedian on the street below surrounded by acquaintances laughing heartily at his jokes. "You don't see Frank Tinney or Ed Wynn throwing it away like that," he admonished her. "Don't be a sidewalk comedian; save it for the public." She also claimed that before long Bohm began pressuring her to go out on her own. He convinced her that she could make more money in a single act, and by the end of March she dropped the Girards. She claimed they took it well, one remarking to her, "You're a great girl and a great act. It isn't what you do—it's how you do it." Mae incorporated his appraisal into a speech during her finales.[21]

Next, Bohm negotiated for West to appear in Ziegfeld's *A Winsome Widow*, slated to open in early April 1912 at the Moulin Rouge Theater. A revival of a popular 1890s musical comedy, Ziegfeld's latest show featured a stunning cast, including Fanny Brice, dancer Leon Errol, and vaudeville's famous Dolly Sisters. In *A Winsome Widow*, the central character falsely believes that he has only a few weeks to live. He decides to spend his remaining days enjoying the high life and chasing young women. In the show, West had a minor role, Le Petite Daffy, and performed a ragtime tune and a cooch.

Although anxiously anticipated, *A Winsome Widow* received mixed reviews. While the *New York Clipper* deemed it "a spectacle of gayety and gorgeousness," the *New York Times* complained about its "sameness." Sime panned it, insisting it was "at least forty minutes too long, draggy with superfluous people." One of those was West, whom he reprimanded for doing "Turkey," show business slang for the cheapest and bawdiest of burlesque acts. "Just a bit too coarse for this $2 audience," Sime concluded.[22]

A Winsome Widow lasted a respectable 172 performances. But West was not there to see the production to its end. Only five days after the premiere, she announced she was quitting the show to return to vaudeville. She gave no explanation, but her sudden departure coincided with a significant change in Bohm's situation. He had just accepted a position as an agent for the big-time Keith Circuit. Bohm's good fortune opened the door for West to appear at vaudeville's most prestigious theaters. Leaving a Ziegfeld production was risky, but working the Keith Circuit promised much more than a small part in a musical revue rated so lukewarmly. Sime actually praised her for bailing out: "That she escaped . . . [the Ziegfeld show] evidences some strength of character."[23]

Bohm must have considered West one of his best acts. That spring he took out a half-page ad in *Variety*, announcing that Mae West, the "Scintillating Singing Comedienne," had been booked at Hammerstein's Victoria Theater, one of Keith's best houses. For her debut as a single act, he encouraged Mae to splurge on two new, eye-catching gowns. She chose not only the most luxurious but, reminiscent of Deslys, also the most unusual. One gown was made of rhinestones, and the other was tight and slit from toe to thigh. She purchased a brocade coat, its train lined with white fox. It was a pricey wardrobe, and Bohm, who was rapidly becoming wealthy, may have helped her out in some way.

West's solo debut was only eleven minutes long. Her act consisted of dances and songs that she delivered, like Bert Williams, in a "talkative fashion." She opened with "Parisienne" and followed with two dance tunes, "Personality" and "Dancing-Prancing," maintaining a black presence by ragging them. The act climaxed with "Rap, Rap, Rap," which she delivered seated and playing "the bones," an African instrument that had become a minstrel show staple. She then ended abruptly, rising and launching into a cooch.

The competition was stiff on the night of West's debut. The bill contained fourteen acts, an unusually large number, with several single female song-and-dance turns. Overall response to Mae's act was tepid. Sime labeled her a "freak," charging that she lacked "that touch of class that is becoming requisite nowadays in the first class houses." The *New York Clipper* alleged that "the very palpable aid of a number of 'friends' in the audience" helped her along. But she did win praise from some reviewers and the audience for "Rap, Rap, Rap." *Billboard* commented, "Miss West sits and uses the 'bones' in a manner that might be envied by a minstrel end man."[24]

Significantly, the African-American cultural presence echoed throughout most of West's debut. Freed from male partners, she asserted increasing control over her performance and began borrowing more heavily from both original and corrupted forms of African-American performance. Her appropriation of black culture was furthered by its ever-growing popularity during the 1910s. Although still facing racism and discrimination, several

African-American performers had broken through to become stars. Tap
dancer Bill "Bojangles" Robinson and Aida Overton Walker, wife of the recently deceased George Walker, had thriving careers on the Keith Circuit.
James Reese Europe, founder of the Clef Club, a union of African-American
musicians, was in wide demand, scoring music for and accompanying the
white dancing duo Vernon and Irene Castle. Songwriters like Sheldon
Brooks, who composed Sophie Tucker's "Some of These Days," also enjoyed
success. While degrading stereotypes still abounded, white performers and
the public clamored for more African-American entertainment.

Although African-American culture subversively undermined the dominance of European-American culture, most whites never went beyond the
mere consumption of black music and dance. But West had a deeper appreciation for the power of African-American performance. She viewed it with
great respect and as an evolving art form. She recalled that her early inspiration came from "the black man's sound and we copied it because it was the
greatest. They'd been developing it for years." West was striving to enact
blackness as she comprehended it, no longer in blackface but rather in what
could be called whiteface. The ragtime-singing, bones-playing "Parisienne"
cooch dancer was just beginning to project an indeterminacy that challenged
the whole idea of racial fixity so critical to the ideology of white racism.[25]

West tinkered with her act, revising it throughout the summer and into
the fall of 1912. Most vaudevillians sought a single, steady act; change was
costly not only in time but also in money, since new material was often purchased. But the energetic nineteen-year-old Mae West sought perfection,
adding and subtracting from her routine, sometimes just to suit specific audiences. In Philadelphia, possibly to placate family-time theater managers in-
tolerant of cooching, she finished the act with a "muscle dance in a sitting
position." Bohm promoted her appearance there with handbills proclaiming,
"It is all in the way she does it and her way is all her own." Later, she added
two new songs, "Good Night Nurse" and "It's an Awful Way to Make a Living," by popular vaudeville skit man Thomas Gray. (On the cover of "Good
Night Nurse" she posed half-smiling in a nurse's frock.) By December 1912,
when she played Keith's Union Square Theater in New York City, she had
resurrected her impersonations. The audience reaction was favorable. *Variety*
noted that she had grown "taller and stouter" and observed happily that she
was no longer "tearing loose the theater foundations."[26]

As a whole, it had been a good year for Mae West. While her Broadway
career petered out, she had successfully broken into first-class vaudeville and
played engagements in some of the country's premier houses. She was not a
headliner, often occupying the bill's second spot—traditional for single, un-

known female performers. But she also occasionally played fourth or sixth in the lineup, respectable positions for a novice. At a young age, she was doing well; she claimed that Bohm eventually negotiated a salary of $350 to $500 a week for her. This may be inflated, but Bohm also provided her with some surreptitious income. During their weeks off, he secretly booked his Keith performers in small-time vaudeville. Writer Dana Rush remembered seeing West at Pittsburgh's Family Theater, a small-time house owned by Clarence W. Morgenstern. Rush described her as "one of the best ragtime singers that ever hit the Family Theater." Small time was a grueling five performances a day, and Bohm's practices were flagrant violations of Keith's exclusive control policy, but the added bookings provided the West family with even more income. It appears that Mae dutifully sent some of her earnings home. Apparently, her parents decided to invest it in property; West claimed that her father went into real estate the very year she signed up with Bohm.[27]

Over the next two years, West bounced between the Keith Circuit and small-time houses. Much of this time she spent on the road, playing in cities and towns nationwide. While having steady work was considered a blessing by any vaudevillian, tours were punishing. Performers played a different town every week and often did not know until the last minute where they were going next. Circuits provided only cheap transportation, reserving crowded and uncomfortable coach cars on the trains. Since payday was not until the week's end, vaudevillians lived on credit. Hours were long, hotels were noisy, and some theaters even charged performers extra to use dressing rooms.

Although vaudeville tours were exhausting and lonely, they allowed Mae to observe a wide range of entertainment styles. Of course, there were jugglers and dog acts. But she also shared the bill with some of the era's biggest names, including comedian Eddie Foy and the beautiful Evelyn Nesbitt Thaw, whose jealous husband, Harry, had killed her lover, the famous architect Stanford White. Once Mae became famous, she occasionally boasted that Harry Thaw, whose mother's maiden name was Copley, was a cousin. However, the wealthy Thaw family never claimed her.

Billed as "America's Youngest Temperamental Comedian" and "the Firefly of Vaudeville," West was usually well received by both critics and audiences, although, as one Keith manager observed, "the men liked her better than the women." On occasion, some critics found her too brazen for polite vaudeville. While touring in 1913, she plugged a song titled "And Then" that she delivered carefully, she said, to allow the audience to use its "imagination of course." One reviewer did not like the picture his imagination conjured up and declared Mae West "plainly vulgar. This woman is all that is coarse in

Eva Tanguay without the player's ability." Even though he admitted that "the audience howled for more," he called for censorship of West's act. And while she continued to encounter resistance—one Keith representative forced her to cut her line "The manager said he would take me out to lunch and see what he was doing for me"—almost everyone agreed she was unique. A Columbus, Ohio, Keith agent described her as "possessing unusual individuality and style that is peculiarly her own. She is distinctively different from any single woman I have ever seen."[28]

Some of this derived from her fearless exhibition of blatant sexuality that, when combined with her pastiche of impersonations, ragtime tunes, and unusual dance steps, produced an act that while engaging was sometimes bewildering. In late 1913, a Keith manager in Philadelphia commented that "the audience did not at first understand but finally approved" of Mae. Interestingly, on several occasions, reviewers characterized her, even after she had toned down, as a "nut act," a term for wild and clownish performers. But several reviewers also reported that West did not "go crazy" à la Tanguay or others: "She is not volcanic in style and manifests no inclination to whoop things up." Apparently, West's subtle zaniness was simply so different that it defied categorization.[29]

Throughout 1913 and 1914, West further refined her style and continued to move up on the bill. In October 1913, she had one of the top spots at Proctor's Fifth Avenue Theater in Manhattan. The *New York Clipper* praised her as "one of the most vivacious soubrettes that has graced the vaudeville stage in many moons." Another critic remarked on the changes in her act, noting she had reduced the songs and increased the patter. "She put it over in a manner to unmistakably indicate that this is her forte," he commented. She also further slowed her pace. In Ohio, a house manager protested against Keith's recommendation he bill her as "Harem Scarum," suggesting "the Nonchalant, Unique Artist" instead. "I used to have to work on the audience, appeal to them with little private gestures, twists of my head, the way I spoke a word, or winked over a song line. . . . I had an easy, nonchalant manner, an air of indifference," she remembered. "That was my style and I couldn't change it."[30]

West's syncretic style, which drew from vaudeville, burlesque, melodrama, minstrelsy, and African-American culture, continued to befuddle critics. They persisted in their attempts to define her within some common tradition. Some continued to attribute a maleness to her performances. One theater manager insisted that West used a "boyish, careless method of getting her stuff over," and others still compared her to George M. Cohan, one noting that she had adopted his unique manner of dance. But that only rein-

forced her links to black performance; Cohan's distinctive steps were borrowed from the cakewalk. On one occasion, a theater manager even equated
West with blackface comedian Frank Tinney.

Yet West also evoked comparisons to Eva Tanguay. In 1913, the *New York
Tribune* remarked that West made "herself popular by singing a repertory of
'I Don't Care' songs and appearing in a dazzling series of low and behold
gowns." That year, after a competitor lured Tanguay away from Keith, Bohm
began pushing West as her replacement, billing her as "the Eva Tanguay of
Vaudeville." But critics, theater managers, and West herself also repeatedly
emphasized that she had "a style all her own." In fact, she even incorporated
into her act a song called "I've Got a Style All My Own."[31]

By late 1913, West was also promoting herself as "the Original Brinkley
Girl." Based on a character created by artist Nell Brinkley, the Brinkley Girl
was the successor to the Gibson Girl, illustrator Charles Dana Gibson's image of youthful womanhood. The Brinkley Girl cast off the previous generation's corseted shirtwaists in favor of lightweight, flowing gowns. Visually,
she epitomized idealized white femininity with distinctively WASPish features. Brinkley's illustrations, serialized with her commentary in the nation's
newspapers, urged women to use their charms to control men but warned
them never to lose their hearts. It was a mixed message, but, rendered by a
woman, it spoke to West's sensibilities.

West's absorption of Brinkley's creation contributed to her continuing
construction of a racially ambiguous stage persona. On the one hand, she
embraced whiteness, borrowing so much from Deslys that a reviewer in
1914 raved as if she were the French music hall queen herself:

> Mae, chic, dainty, a Parisienne from the heels of her tiny slippers to the
> crown of her golden head, has truly as she claims "a style of her own." Fresh
> from the hands of Parisian modistes, merry Mae sings her songs and deliv-
> ers her impromptu dialogue with a pleasing individuality that marks her
> for an even higher place in the professional field than she occupies now.

Yet she did not let her whiteness go uncontested. She continued to perform
ragtime and, that year, organized a band, the Mae West Syncopators. As she
matured, she was becoming more skillful at playing with extremes, toying
with society's construction of both gender and race.[32]

On stage West was unconventional; offstage, too, she struck her fellow
vaudevillians as daring and eccentric. Charlie Abbott, who toured with her,
observed that she "kept to herself but she gloried in the stir she caused wherever she went. Sometimes she played next to closing, the best spot on the

bill, but even so traditional vaudevillians made her feel like an outsider." Vaudevillians were highly competitive as well as cliquish, and West's suggestiveness combined with her aloofness induced others to regard her cautiously. However, she did not lack company. Her autobiography implies that on tour she received plenty of attention from male townsfolk and choice male performers.[33]

One of these was Guido Deiro, "the Wizard of the Accordion," whom she met when they shared a bill in Detroit in August 1913. An international celebrity, he and his brother, Pietro, introduced the piano accordion to America. Deiro was handsome and dashing; according to some, he possessed "a magnetic personality." In white tie and tails, he performed classical and popular music, always winning ovations from the crowds. "Temperamental, talented, he loses himself in his own melodies, becomes oblivious of his audiences," one critic reported. Deiro was gregarious and flamboyant. Waiters who pleased him received huge tips, portions of which Mae and Pietro pocketed behind his back.[34]

Mae confessed that she fell passionately for the charming accordionist. True, Deiro was a headliner and could easily help her, but her attraction to him was not entirely careerist. For the first time, she later claimed, she was in love. By her account, Deiro was equally infatuated. Indeed, after playing Detroit, he arranged to be booked with her in Rochester, New York, the following week. Over the next two seasons, West and Deiro attempted to be together as much as possible. At first, joint bookings were difficult to schedule. In the summer of 1914, it became even more challenging: Keith fired Bohm for double-booking his acts in small-time vaudeville. He returned with Mae to Loew's. Things improved when Deiro followed, his Loew contract specifying joint bookings with Mae.

Between July 1914 and February 1915, West and Deiro appeared on the same bill in theaters throughout the Loew Circuit. Reportedly, Mae even worked the accordion into her act, pretending to play as Deiro stood in the wings supplying the real music. (It was Pietro's instrument, and he later found it for sale in a pawnshop.) West and Deiro became so closely identified that many in the business mistook them for a married couple. Although some later remembered that they both carried on other affairs, Mae insisted that, for the first time in her life, she felt jealous.

West, who had remained detached from previous lovers, was consumed by Deiro. She found him exciting, passionate, and indulgent; while on the road, she contracted the flu, and Deiro nursed her back to health. But Mae's happy recollections of Deiro's tenderness were countered by her admission that he had an extremely volatile side. He was possessive and flew into jealous rages, verbally and sometimes physically assaulting other men who expressed even passing interest in Mae. He spied on her, listened in on her calls, and loomed over her constantly. She told of tireless efforts to keep him ignorant of other men, even those who were simply acquaintances, fearing his reaction.

Deiro's behavior had gotten him into trouble in the past. In 1912, to avoid prosecution on a statutory rape charge, he agreed to marry Julia Tatro, also a performer. Whether or not Mae knew of Deiro's marriage before, she certainly learned of it in February 1914 when the police arrived at Chicago's Palace Theater, where the couple was performing, and arrested Deiro on a warrant issued by Tatro, who was seeking financial support. It seemed to have little impact on his relationship with Mae. He immediately paid his bail and returned to the road with her, and Mae claimed that he began to propose they marry. Deiro even sought out her parents, asking their permission. (Of course, none of them knew that *she* was already married.) Tillie stiffly refused. She wanted her daughter to remain focused on her career.[35]

Mae complied with her mother's wishes, as usual, but also continued her affair with Deiro. At Christmas 1914, Bohm featured the two in a joint ad bragging of their forty weeks of bookings for Loew's. Shortly afterward, Mae's hard work and sacrifice finally paid off. In January 1915, she returned to the American Roof Theater, this time as the headliner. For this appearance, in addition to her trademark "I've Got a Style All My Own," she performed several characterizations and Sheldon Brooks's "Ballin' the Jack." The *New York Clipper* rated it Mae's best number, noting that it "won her the desired applause." Sime remained unconverted. He felt that Deiro, also on the bill, should have occupied the featured spot, noting that Mae had "repressed her exuberance somewhat, but could stand a trifle more repression."[36]

West was twenty-one and had reached a pinnacle in her early career. After the American Roof date, she spent the next several weeks with Deiro on tour in the Northeast. Then suddenly, in early March, the couple vanished from the vaudeville routes. In April, Deiro reappeared briefly back on the Keith Circuit. But West was nowhere to be found. That summer *Variety* reported that she was on her way to California with a Universal Pictures contract; nothing resulted from this trip. That fall, Deiro resurfaced, playing some of Keith's best theaters.[37]

This lull in West's career corresponded to a general downturn in vaudeville, for the burgeoning film industry was luring audiences away. Additionally, two of vaudeville's pioneers, B. F. Keith, founder of the Keith Circuit, and Willie Hammerstein, passed away. As others jockeyed for power, circuits cut salaries, increased workloads, and laid off performers. The White Rats, the vaudevillians' union, protested the changes, inducing a standoff between theater management and performers. White Rats activists were blacklisted and their contracts canceled; the union hired gangsters to protect its members. Although excluded from membership in the all-male White Rats, West may have found her career impeded by her support for the group. In the summer of 1916, *Variety* reported that she had appeared in a special benefit show organized by the White Rats for the prisoners of Sing Sing. It was a very public link to the activist entertainers' union.

West may also have been adversely affected by changes in Frank Bohm's situation. In March 1915, just as she disappeared from vaudeville, Bohm signed up Singer's Midgets, a miniature circus with a troupe of over thirty little people. Bohm must have felt they had a spectacular future. He invested his entire savings in the act and dedicated all of his energies to promoting it. As a result, his stable of performers floundered. Deiro, a widely celebrated talent, easily returned to big-time vaudeville. West was not so lucky. She spent Christmas 1915 in Pittsburgh, celebrating with the players of the Victoria Burlesque Theater, a small-time house on the American Circuit, distinctly raunchier than her former burlesque employer, Columbia. Before long, the situation looked even more grim. On March 7, 1916, Bohm died of tuberculous of the spine. A few weeks later, West surfaced again at Pittsburgh's Victoria Theater, which was presenting a musical review called *A Jaunt in Joyland*. Without Bohm's careful attention, she had, in one year, gone from being a headliner in big-time vaudeville to performing in cheap, third-rate burlesque.[38]

Exactly what impact this had on her relationship with Deiro is unclear. However, although Frank Bohm's distractions led to Mae and Deiro's professional separation, nothing else suggests that their affair ended. The changes in their circumstances may have compelled Deiro to become even more possessive and determined to marry Mae regardless of prior entanglements. According to West, at some point Deiro, like Frank Wallace, began to pressure her to abandon her career and settle down. She claimed she loved him, and his proposal, which was impossible to accept, caused her deep distress. Although she attempted to hide her feelings from her mother, Tillie had grown increasingly suspicious. It was not long before her worries were confirmed. Mae maintained that one night Deiro, after a jealous confrontation with Joseph Schenck, a Loew Circuit boss, stormed over to the Wests', demanding Mae's hand in marriage. The Wests firmly rebuffed him. Tillie was blunt: "I'm afraid you'll harm Mae in a fit of jealous temper." While her concerns over his abusive disposition were valid, she was also committed to seeing that Mae's career always came first.

Tillie became determined to undermine Mae's relationship with Deiro. Knowing her daughter's stubbornness, at first she approached it indirectly.

"Mother pointed out other married couples to me," Mae remembered, "showed me how their lives were wasted. She didn't nag me. She never did." But Mae remained conflicted and spent months sorting out her feelings, discussing them for hours with her mother. Finally, Tillie directly expressed disapproval of Deiro, telling Mae he was not "good enough." "She explained that I was young and awful full of emotions. She said *that* was natural but that I could use them to be very famous or waste them on the *first* man."[39]

How long the relationship survived under Tillie's enormous pressure is not certain. One source remembered that the affair lasted about four years, commenting that it was "a record for Guido."[40] But Tillie was determined to distract Mae. She may have even used Mae's sister, Mildred. Tillie had pushed Mildred into performing as an amateur under the stage name of Beverly West. In the summer of 1916, Tillie insisted that Mae and Beverly develop a sister act. Perhaps she hoped the two would keep an eye on each other, for Beverly had problems too. She was spirited, fun-loving, and free-spoken—and at seventeen already a hard drinker.

"Mae West and Sister" opened with a duet, "I Want to Be Loved in an Old Fashioned Way." Next came a musical skit—ironically, on marriage—two more songs, and Mae's cooch. Then, while Beverly sang, Mae exited, changed, and returned in male attire. For their finish, they performed Sheldon Brooks's "Walkin' the Dog." Mae closed with a speech: "I am pleased, ladies and gentlemen, you like my new act. It's the first time I have appeared with my sister. They all like her, especially the boys, who always fall for her, but that's where I come in—I always take them away from her."

The sisters tried out their act at Proctor's Fifth Avenue Theater in Manhattan. Sime remained contemptuous. "Unless Miss West can tone down her stage presence in every way," he wrote, "she just might as well hop right out of vaudeville into burlesque." He suggested that if she continued to be so bold, she consider appearing in "men's dress altogether."[41]

Although trade papers fail to confirm it, West maintained that the sister act secured a twelve-week road tour. She also remembered it as a painful experience. The sisters shared an uneasy relationship, Beverly resentful of living in her sister's shadow. Additionally, she did not subscribe to Mae's work ethic and took advantage of the freedoms offered on tour. After performances, she disappeared with male admirers, sometimes staying out all night and showing up, still drunk, just before curtain time. Virtually a teetotaler, Mae grew impatient. She scolded Beverly and lined their hotel room floors with crumpled newspapers, bellowing, "I hear you," when her sister attempted to sneak in early in the morning. Eventually, she summoned Tillie to take Beverly home. Mae remembered finishing the tour alone, using a

dummy as her partner. Whether or not that was true, Mae had failed to re-
gain momentum. In the fall of 1916, *Variety* announced she would appear as a
man in an act under an assumed name. Mae then vanished from the New
York entertainment scene for almost a year and a half.[42]

It is likely that Mae had acquiesced to her mother's wishes and decided to
make a final break with Deiro. Fearing violent retaliation, she slipped out of
town without a word to him. The Wests foiled his attempts to contact her,
keeping her location a secret. On her part, she was relieved to have escaped
him but fought her urge to rekindle the affair, remembering her obligation to
her mother.

It was a difficult time for the twenty-three-year-old Mae West. "If I have
made myself seem hard and casual," she wrote candidly in her autobiography,
"it was a defense I raised against all the world." Mae may have experienced
difficulty with men before, and her selection of the abusive Deiro revealed
her ongoing insecurities, but after the demise of their relationship, she grew
ever more detached. This failed love affair was a turning point in her life; she
was prepared to take her mother's philosophy to the extreme. "From that
time on, I have only thought of Mae West," she told one journalist. "I have
thought only of myself. Nothin' else mattered. Men have been important only
as they could help me help Mae West." While Mae's public and private selves
would always be somewhat intertwined, at this juncture she had come to regard the performer, the career actress Mae West, as a distinct persona, often
referring to that component of her identity in the third person. But in some
ways, Mae West the real person no longer counted; personal wants and needs
had to be submerged. It was only the performance that mattered.[43]

West spent most of the next eighteen months based in Chicago, performing on the Orpheum vaudeville circuit's western routes. She may have even
worked for a short time as a male impersonator, but before long she was
back to her standard routine of songs, dances, comedic monologues, and the
cooch. While being stuck outside of New York City, the era's entertainment
capital, impeded her career, she recognized her time in Chicago as one of the
most critical periods in her professional development. Her exile in the
Windy City became a furious phase of reinventing herself and her performance. Here, she discovered the key components of her stage persona; not
surprisingly, all were rooted in African-American traditions.

West's arrival in Chicago coincided with the Great Migration, a time of
growth and change for the African-American community. African Americans were leaving the South for the North by the hundreds of thousands,
pushed by virulent racism and pulled by job opportunities in industries gear-
ing up to support the First World War, which had broken out in Europe in

1914. Chicago was one of the most popular destinations; African Americans from all regions of the South gathered in the Windy City, bringing with them different varieties of black culture. When West reached Chicago, the city's African-American community already boasted a lively nightlife with clubs and theaters where black entertainers from across the country performed. She patronized these nightspots and was influenced by this explosion of black culture. Out of this milieu, she adopted three components of African-American music and dance to serve as the foundation of her stage presence.

The first of these was jazz, which was quickly displacing ragtime as the African-American community's dominant musical form. By the time West arrived in Chicago, the city had become a jazz mecca, and this new, energetic musical form was so popular that it permeated white as well as black nightclubs. Improvisational in nature, jazz depended on a series of revised riffs that some have linked to the African-American practice of signification. West was immediately attracted to jazz; it fit well with her impromptu manner and her subversive nature. "Jazz suited me," she remarked. "I liked the beat and emotions." She organized another band for her act—this time a full-fledged jazz band composed of musicians she recruited from Chicago clubs.[44]

Second, and just as important, she appropriated heavily from the blues, beginning her evolution into a blues singer. Like jazz, the blues had arrived in Chicago with African-American immigrants fleeing the South. Descended in part from the African-American tradition of spirituals, the blues carry double, sometimes triple meanings conveying messages of resistance and rebellion. Since childhood, West had been attracted to the flexibility of and the multiple messages in language, but the blues' appeal ran even deeper. Not just laments of lost love, the blues interrogate existence, probing life's passages and meaning. As scholar Houston Baker asserts, the blues explore "experiencing the experience." They go beyond simply relating life's events and express the feelings and emotions of how life is understood and apprehended. Baker contends that blues singers become "translators" who furnish a variety of interpretations of a life story and its circumstances. As a result, the blues singer becomes a mediator, and the blues become "a mediational site" where conflicts are initiated, explored, and resolved, only to be initiated again. In a sense, then, the blues singer acts as a trickster and the blues function as the trickster's language. It was precisely the vehicle that West had been seeking. The blues provided her with a voice that reaffirmed but resisted the dominant culture. She understood the dualism of the blues and embraced it as her musical signature.[45]

Just before she left Chicago, West stumbled onto a third compelling African-American cultural manifestation. One night she joined some friends at The Elite No. 1, a nightspot located in the heart of the black entertainment district on Chicago's South Side that also drew many white patrons. It was here, while the band played "Can House Blues," that West witnessed African-American couples dancing the shimmy. She was captivated. "They got up from the tables, got out to the dance floor, and stood in one spot with hardly any movement of the feet, just shook their shoulders, torsos, breasts, and pelvises."

The shimmy was not new. Scholars trace its origins to West Africa, contending it evolved into its celebrated form in African-American "jooks," or dance halls, just after 1900. By the 1910s, it had made its way into vaudeville through a few white female shimmy dancers. Certainly West must have encountered it before visiting The Elite No. 1. But for some reason, seeing it done by African Americans gave her a new awareness of the shimmy. She was mesmerized, finding both humor and "a naked, aching, sensual agony" in the dance.[46]

While West's recollection that she and her companions "were terribly amused by it" smacked of racism, she also correctly deciphered the shimmy's dualistic nature. On the one hand, it was a dance that exuded sexuality. On the other hand, African Americans also perceived it as comedic. The shimmy contained an "in-group satire" for African-American spectators. The sight of African-American men doing a shake dance, something performed only by women in white American culture, was considered hysterical. Indeed, several African-American comedians, including Bert Williams, performed a shimmy as a parody of a white female cooch dance.

For Mae West, the shimmy proved irresistible; it was both serious and funny, underscoring and parodying sensuality. The day after her visit to The Elite No. 1, she substituted a shimmy for her standard cooch finale. "The theater began to hum," she remembered. "It was amazing and daring and it started a huge round of applause and whistles from the balcony." The following week, she departed Chicago on tour and continued to perform her shimmy, receiving equally enthusiastic encouragement from audiences. Mae West's days as a cooch dancer were over. Her European grind had been displaced by the African-American shake. West had discovered a satisfactory combination of African-American music and dance for her act, for her stage identity. It provided her with a voice and a language to speak in. Finally, in Chicago, during the Great Migration, Mae West, the stage persona, was born.[47]

Shimadonna

The shimmy idea seems made to order for an entertainer of
Mae's type. . . . Honest to goodness, that shimmering, black
outfit she displays during her turn is of a gelatine design. . . .
And when Mae swings into the shimmying thing the orchestra
leader feels like quitting his post and shouting "Atta girl, Mae."
———*New York Dramatic Mirror*, September 25, 1919

B y the time Mae West resurfaced in New York in the spring of
1918, the world had changed drastically. The United States had
entered World War I, and several of her friends and relatives had
gone off to fight. West pitched in, displaying her patriotic efforts
in a series of publicity photos. Shots showed her, outfitted in straw hat, over-
alls, and high heels, planting a victory garden or perched on a ladder with a
caption reading: "While the men go to the trenches, Mary [*sic*] West paints
the old barn." She also helped entertain the troops and, after the war's end,
was among those honored by the U.S. military for giving benefit performances for the fighting men.[1]

West's homecoming also marked another significant change in her life.
Her mother was anxious for her to meet a thirty-three-year-old attorney,
James A. Timony, whom Tillie had retained for some legal business. Mae
never specified what affairs Timony had handled, but in January 1917 he escorted Beverly, now working as a cabaret singer, to Brooklyn's City Hall to
be married to Serge Treshatny, a munitions expert and Russian immigrant.
Timony even signed her marriage certificate——in the spot typically reserved
for the maid of honor.

No matter what services he had performed for the Wests, Timony was an
important contact. The Brooklyn-born son of an Irish immigrant who was a
successful contractor and developer, Jim Timony had practiced law since

1905. He specialized in entertainment and real estate law, offering his services as an investment counselor in show business trade journals. He was closely tied to entertainment leaders and served as counsel to the Showmen's League of America, the Actors' Guild, and the White Rats. Many believed that he had strong ties to New York racketeers and the Democratic political machine, Tammany Hall. Mae claimed that he was well-off and that he owned a plane and a baseball team. It is clear why Tillie wanted her talented daughter to meet such a prosperous and well-connected lawyer.

Mae claimed that she shared an immediate chemistry with Timony. Like her, he was a risk taker—uncompromising, flamboyant, and extremely determined. A former football player, he had an overwhelming physical presence; he was large, favored flashy dress, and always sported a diamond ring on his pinky finger. "His suit was a loud black-and-gray checkered pattern," one journalist reported. "He wore a wing collar and a puffed Ascot tie, in which a diamond horseshoe tie-pin flashily reposed; his hat was a derby, and his cane had an elk's tooth imbedded in the handle." He smoked oversize cigars, wheezing while puffing away vigorously. He walked with a limp that some ascribed to a football injury but others whispered was from an old gunshot wound.[2]

Timony was smitten with Mae. He called her daily and squired her around Manhattan, where he maintained his office. In many ways, he was similar to her previous paramours—domineering, growing jealous easily, fighting both Mae and other men to keep her to himself—but one quality set him apart. His devotion extended beyond romance; he was also willing to dedicate himself completely to championing her career.

Timony's adoration, connections, and expertise were immensely beneficial. Mae trusted him, and he became one of the few people outside her immediate family that she took into her confidence. Her faith in him was so thorough that she shared with him her most closely guarded secret—she had married Frank Wallace. She had not seen her husband, still a struggling vaudevillian, for years. Then one day, as she sat with Timony in his elegant car on Broadway, Wallace strolled past. Timony confronted him. "He said I ought to realize my marriage to Mae West was a fizzle and that she could not afford to be married because there was a future waiting for her in show business," Wallace recalled. When Beverly, who now also knew Mae's secret, arrived at Wallace's hotel room to deliver divorce papers, she found him in a state of shock. "I had a nervous breakdown," Wallace later claimed. However, his reaction may have resulted more from panic than heartbreak, for in 1916 he had married another woman. When Timony later called claiming the divorce had been finalized, Wallace destroyed the papers without signing them.[3]

What Wallace did not know was that Timony had never initiated any official divorce proceedings. Mae might have convinced him to stop, fearing that
her mother might somehow learn of her marriage. But Timony had also
hoped to marry Mae; perhaps he realized that she was going to refuse him and
made sure she could never become any other man's wife. Mae West and Jim
Timony shared a complicated relationship. While Mae maintained close emotional ties to Timony, she refused to be faithful to him. His desire to possess
and control her only drove her to rebel against him even further. But she always acquiesced to him in some form, for he provided her with unconditional
loyalty and friendship as well as critical professional support and guidance.

With Timony's help West restarted her New York career. In the spring of
1918, she obtained a plum role in Arthur Hammerstein's *Sometime*. The play
chronicled the adventures and heartaches of a touring theatrical troupe. The
cast also included popular comedian Ed Wynn, who starred as a hapless
property man. West played the "flip chorus girl" Maymie Dean, "in search of
temptation but never finding it." She had the privilege of opening the production with a musical lament, "What Do You Have to Do?" In addition, she
was featured in "All I Want Is Just a Little Lovin' " and "Any Kind of Man,"
which she delivered with a shimmy.

Sometime opened on October 4 with West receiving excellent notices. The
New York Clipper rated her performance "capital," and *Variety*'s Sime, although
complaining that her shimmy was inappropriate for Broadway, agreed that she
"bowled them over." Leonard Hall, a young soldier just returning from war,
later recalled her as a "slender, beautiful ball of fire who performed as a specialty dancer in high kicks, cartwheels, and fast taps. She was a tasty tornado."
West was the show's hit. While Sime attributed some of her enthusiastic reception to a "well placed claque," he praised West's "rough hand on the hip"
characterization as perfect for the vampish Maymie Dean.[4]

West took most of the credit for Maymie Dean's success and popularity,
again alleging that she asserted control over the direction of her character
and enhanced her role significantly. She claimed that she spiced up "All I
Want Is Just a Little Lovin' " with new lyrics, and rather than working with
the show's choreographer, she sought help from Joe Frisco, a Chicago friend
and popular white jazz dancer who had carefully studied black technique.
Maymie Dean was originally conceived of as somewhat pathetic, but West
portrayed her as proud and determined; critics lauded Maymie as "tough"
and a "wise dame."[5]

Of all her contributions to *Sometime*, the most important, as well as successful, was West's shimmy dance. It was a crowning achievement, for while
the shimmy had made the rounds in vaudeville, until this point it had been

considered too raunchy for the Great White Way. Introducing the shimmy to Broadway, Mae stopped the show, then made a speech and, as Sime testified, "then made another." It propelled a shimmy craze that swept Manhattan, driving the city's moral guardians to ban it from nightclubs, dance halls, and restaurants.

West was immediately linked with the shimmy and appeared on the sheet-music cover of the popular hit song "Everyone Shimmies Now." Shortly after she debuted her shimmy on Broadway, several shimmy imitators, most notably Gilda Gray and Bee Palmer, followed in her footsteps. Later West adamantly asserted her claim to the title of Broadway's shimmy pioneer but carefully credited African Americans as its creators. West specifically resented Gilda Gray for declaring that she had originated the shimmy. "She started telling the story that it was a native dance," West later ranted to a reporter, "and she's *Polish!*"[6]

In *Sometime* West sharpened her performance style. She discovered fresh inspiration in Ed Wynn, who was at the peak of his stage career. Wynn had moved comedy away from slapstick toward conversational humor. His timing was impeccable, and he was a master scene-stealer. West deeply admired Wynn, but she quickly grew weary of being overshadowed by him and of serving, as she described it, as "something which could be draped in the background to make the stage look a little less empty." She recalled, "All I had to do, I discovered, was to wander around that stage like so much bait while the boys kept the audience happy with laughs." Soon she devised a plan to upstage Wynn. Realizing that his power rested in his timing and rhythm, she decided to turn the tables on him. One matinee, during a scene where she normally traversed the stage behind him, she altered her gait, adopting what later became her famous walk. Her slow and studied strut clashed directly with the pace of Wynn's rapid wisecracking. As she swaggered across the stage, "the audience forgot the comedians. They forgot the patter. . . . They just looked."[7]

With her unique walk, West had successfully stolen the moment—as well as the power—from the male star Wynn. It was a brazen move and, not surprisingly, originated from the African-American presence in her performance; the shimmy opened the door for her subversive trick. The infamous Westian gait, radiating from the shoulders downward, was a slow, strolling shimmy. A few years later, a reviewer immediately made the connection, declaring that West's "peculiar slouching about the stage" proved that "she originated the shimmy dance." West's actions were becoming more purposeful. "Even though I must have always talked like I do, and used my eyes like I do and . . . sort of naturally walked like I do today," she remarked in the 1930s, "I wasn't really

conscious of it then. But I was always a good one for trying to analyze things."
West was increasingly aware of how timing empowered her performance in
the male-dominated stage world. She credited Wynn and *Sometime* as major influences, explaining, "Everything I do and say is based on rhythm."[8]

Sometime earned a chilly reception from New York critics, but after a
rough start and a move to a smaller theater, it became one of the 1918–1919
season's biggest hits. Twenty-five-year-old Mae West was so popular that
Hammerstein had to fight off a rival producer's attempt to lure her away. She
was such a shimmying sensation that in February 1919 *Theatre Magazine* featured her in "Players of Talent and Personality," raving that "her clever dancing is one of the bright spots of the piece."[9]

After a triumphant season, *Sometime* closed in June 1919 and prepared for
a road tour—but without West. She had returned to vaudeville, billing herself as "Shimadonna" and "the Girl Who Made the Shimmy a Classic" in a
new act that included a piano accompanist and a jazz trumpeter. When she
debuted it at the end of September 1919, *Variety*'s Bell pronounced her "an
unqualified hit." Noting her extended hiatus from New York's vaudeville
stages, he praised her "marked improvement in method and delivery." Ironically, her new routine differed little from earlier acts. She opened with a
"vamp medley" that included a French dialect tune ("The Yankee Boys Have
Made a Wild Woman Out of Me"), a "comedy Indian song," and a ragtime
number. But for her finish, she sang and shimmied to "All I Want Is Just a
Little Lovin'," slightly lifting her black evening gown for a daring peek at her
black silk stockings.[10]

Although West had played a central role in introducing the shimmy to
Broadway, she had difficulty cashing in on it in vaudeville. *Variety* assessed her
version as "a bit broad for vaudeville." In contrast, the same week that West
debuted her latest routine, rival Bee Palmer premiered a new act complete
with an entire jazz band and a shimmy encore. The WASPish Palmer won
overwhelming praise; one reviewer rhapsodized that her "golden hair shoulder shaking" would "find a big welcome in vaudeville." Indeed, Palmer
quickly scored a contract with Keith and a date at New York City's Palace,
the nation's most prestigious vaudeville house. Despite her solid reviews,
Mae West again found herself searching for another break.

Why did Bee Palmer succeed where Mae West failed? Most likely it was
because Palmer's shimmy was simply less threatening to white audiences.
Blond-haired and blue-eyed, Palmer possessed the classic looks of the idealized white woman. Although Palmer, with her jazz band, also linked her performance to black culture, she performed the shimmy as an exhibition of
white female sensuality. West's shimmy was much more dangerous. Further-

more, distinct from Palmer, West was a comedian, and her shimmy contained multiple meanings. It thrilled, just like a good old-fashioned bump and grind, but also mocked that thrill. Appropriately, when Mae debuted her shimmy in *Sometime*, *Variety* announced that it was "the rawest 'shimmy' that New York has thus far seen in public." But shortly afterward, it also declared that shimmying Mae was just "too funny." It was hard to pin West down— was she serious or joking? In reality, she was both. Unlike Palmer, West attempted an authentic signifying shimmy. It was simply too real and too unreal, too serious and too humorous, for many whites.[11]

Although big-time vaudeville passed West up, that October she was booked at $500 a week for Ned Wayburn's ambitious new project, *The Demi Tasse Revue*. Scheduled to open the new Capitol Theater, the largest movie palace in the world, *Demi Tasse* mixed first-run films with skits and musical routines. For the inaugural show, West reprised her vaudeville act, used some of Wayburn's material, and delivered "Oh What a Moanin' Man" for her shimmy finale. It proved disappointing. While *Variety* hailed her, other reviewers were not kind. She abruptly exited the show, claiming a case of tonsilitis. Rumors circulated that a dissatisfied Wayburn had released her.

Shortly afterward, West signed an exclusive contract with the Shuberts and played a Sunday night concert at their Winter Garden Theater. With that she came under the control of one of show business's most successful production organizations. It seemed to pay off. In December, she appeared on the *New York Dramatic Mirror*'s cover, an honor accorded to major stars and up-and-coming talent. Identified as a "popular Broadway Comedienne," Mae's portrait was fitting, a head shot revealing little but a sultry stare peering out beneath a mass of dark curls.[12]

Despite West's association with the Shuberts, her rise to stardom came to a halt. She lay low until August 1920, when she reemerged with still another act. Scripted by Thomas Gray, it again featured ragtime music, dances, jokes, and a skit: "The Mannikin," in which she played three different characters. Of course, she wrapped it all up with a shimmy.

The *Clipper* denounced West's shake dance, commenting, "The men liked it and it stopped the show, but there were women and children present who did not." But *Variety* raved: "Thanks to Tommy Gray and her own comedic ability, Miss West looks set as a big-time feature." (This enthusiasm probably derived from Gray's ties to the publication; he contributed a popular weekly column.) Despite *Variety*'s endorsement, she failed to break into big-time vaudeville. In fact, illness prevented her from finishing her dates in New York City. She surfaced in upstate New York that October but soon vanished again from vaudeville.[13]

Although Mae's career had taken a dip, the West family's fortunes had improved. Mae's income was intermittent but still respectable for the era. Timony, no doubt, helped Tillie invest her daughter's earnings wisely. By 1920, the Wests had purchased a family home in Woodhaven, Long Island, a middle-class neighborhood conveniently close to the Aqueduct racetrack. Beverly had returned home, separated from her husband after accusing him in a New York tabloid of treating her like "a bird in a gilded cage." Nineteen-year-old John Junior worked as a clerk for a local newspaper. Jack had become a masseuse and later, after taking a correspondence course, began practicing chiropractics. Tillie had earned her American citizenship and remained devoted to cheering Mae on.[14]

After a slow year, Mae's situation began to brighten. In February 1921, she secured a role in a Shubert musical revue, *The Whirl of the Town,* staged by the popular vaudeville comic Jimmy Hussey. That winter, it set out on an extended tour as Hussey reworked it, adding and subtracting routines. By the time it arrived in Washington, D.C., in March, the revue consisted of two acts and twenty-five scenes. Hussey featured West in several skits. As Shifty Liz, she conned a society matron. She also played an unfaithful wife and Jewish and French dialect characters. But the hit of the road show was "The Trial of Shimmy Mae," in which she stood trial in Hussy's chaotic courtroom for doing the shimmy. As evidence, West shimmied, which, according to one critic, "caused a riot—men actually stood up and yelled. . . . Mae West simply shook that house from its seats as well as shaking herself from her neck to her toes and then back again." When the show played Boston, a city known for rigid censorship, with West's first ripple the crew cut the lights, plunging the stage into darkness.[15]

After months of tryouts, Hussey's revue, retitled *The Mimic World of 1921,* finally debuted on Broadway on August 15, 1921. But just hours before the premiere, when Hussey learned the Shuberts had cut the production, limiting him to two scenes, he walked out in a rage. The Shuberts rearranged skits, deleted those dependent on Hussey, including "The Trial of Shimmy Mae," and recruited new acts. They even called boxer Jack Dempsey out of the audience to play Hussey's part in a popular prizefighting skit.

Despite the shake-up, West remained prominently featured. The Shuberts retained Shifty Liz, but she now turned her tricks on a Salvation Army officer. West also reprised her impression of a French coquette, played Cleopatra in "Shakespeare's Garden of Love," and, as "Jazzimova," parodied the queen of all movie vamps, Nazimova. "Yes, Miss West certainly wiggled," proclaimed *Billboard.* "And Wiggled. AND WIGGLED." While most critics panned *The Mimic World,* one sniffing that "the comedy is nothing to laugh at,"

West definitely got noticed. *Variety* acknowledged the crowd's enthusiastic reception and rated her performance "snappy," although it still asserted that she was more suited to burlesque, insisting that "in a tent [her shimmy] would have been a riot."

The dance had become a Broadway staple, but West's version continued to threaten even New York critics, who were growing more blasé with the increase of risqué material directed at jazz-age audiences. Mae was dangerous; by playing between the extremes of whiteness and blackness, she made her performance subversive and disquieting. *Theatre Magazine*'s 1921 photo tribute to *The Mimic World*'s shimmying star unintentionally celebrated her revolutionary dualities. West's whiteness was highlighted—locks lightened to blond, her head tipped to create the impression of an upturned WASPish nose, and a dark drape clutched to her bare chest accentuating her white skin. At the same time, the magazine proclaimed her "the leading woman of many musical comedies whom those who do not know African tribal customs credit—or damn—with the invention of the shimmy."[16]

Despite West's celebrated shimmy, poor attendance forced *The Mimic World of 1921* to close after a month. But she had used the year productively. In addition to her appearance in Hussey's revue, she had worked on writing her first piece, a short playlet, *The Ruby Ring*. She relied on Jim Timony's secretaries to transcribe ideas and dialogue she had jotted down. It was brief and simple but offered important insights into the evolution of Mae West the author and Mae West the character.

The Ruby Ring took place at a grand ball where the enchanting Gloria (West's role) instructs two female friends on the art of flirtation. Gloria bets her bracelet against a ruby ring that she can get five men to propose to her, each in less than five minutes. By assuming a different personality tailored to the unique qualities of each man, Gloria successfully seduces a college boy, businessman, rich elderly gentleman, cowboy, and psychology professor. All return at the same moment to whisk her to the altar but discover that Gloria has duped them. Not only has she accepted proposals from all of them, but she is already married. She collects on her bet and, as the skit closes, remarks to her unwitting husband, "Look dear—how do you like my new ruby ring?"[17]

The plot of *The Ruby Ring* was certainly not unique. Constantly in the process of appropriation and revision, West synthesized it from a variety of sources including Gray's "Mannikin" skit. Regardless, *The Ruby Ring* allowed West to channel her tricksterism by adopting the role of a shapeshifter. For Gloria's collegiate beau, she became a well-read society maiden. To the powerful businessman, she appeared as a devotee of "pep" and "ambition."

She insisted on her fondness for gingham to the cowboy, and her youthful innocence bewitched the wealthy older man. In the end, she transformed into a deadly temptress to ensnare the bookish psychology professor.

Although she relied on traditional gender roles, West used *The Ruby Ring* to upend conventional expectations regarding men and women. By wearing masks of fantasized womanhood but remaining self-determined underneath, Gloria dominated men and robbed them of their authority. She did not pursue romance, or even sex, but rather material fulfillment. Her prize, the ruby ring, evidenced West's belief that male lust could and should be exploited for profit; jewelry symbolized success. A rejection of love and even sex, *The Ruby Ring* was a product of Mae's abusive past, broken love affairs, and relationships with controlling men; it also reflected her mother's working-class world, where male-female relations were based on material exchange.

The Ruby Ring also reveals West's growing interest in wordplay. Gloria's masquerades all rest on conversation; she makes no costume changes. Throughout the dialogue she retains complete control, setting the pace and rhythm, asking the questions, and supplying the answers. "Do I look so wicked—so immoral?" she asks the psychologist. "My dear young lady," he replies, "morality is merely a question of distance from the Equator." Gloria slyly responds, "Whose equator?" The exchanges between Gloria and her suitors contain humor but are also serious challenges to male privilege. Romancing her cowboy, she exclaims, "There's the blue of the skies in your eyes—the thunder of the mountain is in your voice. . . . I can see you—so noble in your shape, with a lariat around your neck." Significantly, the psychology professor, a student of Schopenhauer, understands her the best, declaring Gloria "a paradox." During his verbal battle with her, he observes, "You merely play with words." His assessment indicates that West had not only absorbed signification's language games but also knew exactly what she was doing with them.[18]

The Ruby Ring was never produced, but West used a portion of it in a new act that she assembled in the spring of 1922. It was elaborate and ambitious, almost twenty minutes long, and required a male piano accompanist. Mae commenced a talent search; Jim Timony carefully screened male performers for auditions. He favored a homely but talented jazz pianist named Jimmy Durante. Mae much preferred another candidate, the tall, sophisticated, and handsome Harry Richman. She won out. But Timony sternly warned Richman, "If you ever have a romance in any way with Mae West, you're finished."

Richman later contended that he carefully heeded Timony's admonition. However, Milton Berle, then a young Broadway initiate, recalled that Richman bragged of a torrid affair with Mae West. By then, Berle claimed, West's libertine reputation was widespread in entertainment circles. Although Richman was equally renowned for his sexual escapades, he met his match with Mae. For her, sex revolved around control, personal advancement, and sometimes revenge. Richman told Berle of an afternoon sexual rendezvous when West insisted the radio be tuned to a baseball game so she could stay awake. Despite Richman's legendary lovemaking, West remained more interested in the power than in the passion that could be derived from sex.[19]

While their intimate relationship may have lacked spark, onstage the pairing of Mae West with Harry Richman was electric. Their act, billed as "Bits of Musical Comedy—Mae West assisted by Harry Richman," was flashy and sophisticated, much of it written by Mae and moving quickly through the songs and skits. It opened with the abbreviated version of *The Ruby Ring*, allowing West to show off her versatility in a series of characterizations. After that, she returned to older material. Reminiscent of Deslys, she played an arrogant French prima donna who unleashes outrageous temper tantrums on her beleaguered manager, played by Richman. She then appeared as a suggestively clad Roman empress in search of a new gladiator to wear an equally skimpy uniform. For her finish, she often used the folk tune "Frankie and Johnny," which she sang in blues style. Occasionally, when the house permitted it, she offered an accompanying shimmy.

The act premiered, without the shimmy, in Manhattan in June 1922 to an enthusiastic reception from critics and vaudeville fans. One reviewer gushed that West "made the half a houseful of patrons forget the heat Monday night." Richman recalled that at the end of the gladiator skit, men jumped to their feet, cheering and applauding. *Variety* hailed Richman as "an ideal opposite" and heralded Mae's coming of age on the stage: "She rises to heights undreamed of for her and reveals unsuspected depths as a delineator of character songs, a dramatic reader of ability and a girl with a flair for farce that will some day land her on the legitimate Olympus." The turn won the duo a date at the coveted Palace, and *Variety* extolled her again: "How the show-makers have let that blond baby get away from them so long—in fact, why anyone has let her squander seasons as a shimmy dancer is inexplicable." The *New York Clipper* found the act uneven but praised it as Mae's best effort to date.[20]

West claimed that Keith offered her a lucrative road tour but, to Richman's dismay, she declined. Timony's possessiveness may have influenced her decision; he battled unrelentingly to keep her under his close watch. She later insisted that she had simply grown weary of travel and was holding out for a starring role on Broadway. In the meantime, she accepted engagements in the Northeast, but only at $700 a week. (Richman got a $200 cut.) Anything less, which it almost always was, and she refused to work. Richman claimed that West fell on desperate times, that she had to borrow money from him to pay her overdue utility bills. But others remembered it differently: that while partnered with her, Richman subsisted on only coffee and doughnuts. For her part, Mae was well provided for. Jim Timony's practice was thriving, and her parents maintained their respectable Long Island home.

In the meantime, West pursued her Broadway dreams. While legitimate theater impresarios passed her by, she did attract interest from a Paul Dupont. An unknown producer with lots of drive and big ideas, Dupont boasted that he could "out-Ziegfeld Ziegfeld." He laid out a proposal for West to headline a two-act variety show that he insisted would definitely land her as a star on the Great White Way. It could be done on a shoestring, he promised, and if she kicked in some money, she would reap healthy returns.

Working with an unknown like Dupont was a gamble, but it also permitted West to assert more creative control than she could have normally done. Dubbing the show *The Ginger Box Revue*, West and Dupont recruited Harry Richman as well as fourteen other acts and a chorus line of twelve Greenwich Village models, all of whom purportedly had "posed for well-known artists and sculptors." They also booked the Clef Club, New York's premiere African-American musicians, to play between the acts and feature "Pick 'Em Up and Lay 'Em Down," reportedly "the fastest jazz song on record." Although the Clef Club was relegated to a specialty position within the revue, their appearance was notable. They not only extended West's connection with African-American performance but also presented a mild defiance of the color line, for many white entertainers still refused to appear in mixed-race revues even if they did not share the stage with African-American performers.

Mae West's stamp was visible throughout *The Ginger Box*. In addition to a duet with Richman called "The Vamp of Broadway," she parodied Eugene O'Neill's treatment of working-class life, playing *The Hairy Ape*'s Yank Smith. She also planned to appear as Circe, the Greek goddess who transformed male paramours into pigs. For her finale, West scheduled three songs, "I Want a Cave Man," "I'm a Night School Teacher," and "Sorry I Made You Cry."

Rehearsals began in early July, and the production was immediately besieged with setbacks. First and foremost, *The Ginger Box* quickly incurred heavy debts. Harry Richman remembered making the rounds with Timony on Broadway attempting to raise money and "talk[ing] actors into working on 'spec.'" At the end of the month, *The Ginger Box* journeyed to Stamford, Connecticut, for a tryout. Just hours before opening, the cast learned that Dupont had failed to secure most of the wardrobe and scenery. West insisted that the show go on and played two nights to sellout crowds. *Variety* gave them a thumbs-down review.[21]

Dupont returned the cast to New York City, announcing that the scheduled premiere at the Greenwich Village Theater would be delayed for one week. He then disappeared. Outraged, the theater's manager canceled the show and threatened to sue him. Angry cast members filed complaints in city courts and with Actors' Equity. When reporters tracked West down, she "expressed a warm desire to have a settlement with him" but described Dupont as "likeable. . . . He seemed to have a lot of trouble. I think he was all right, but just couldn't get the money he needed."

A week later, Dupont resurfaced, claiming that he had taken some needed rest by yachting off Long Island. Newspapers revealed that Dupont, also known by several other aliases, was really Edward Perkins, a producer with a long, disastrous track record. He had stranded casts outside of New York City with no way home, had welched on salaries, and was even once shut down by the police. Only one *Ginger Box* cast member had received any compensation, a chorus girl who immediately returned her money to Dupont for opening night tickets and his promise he would make her a star. Clearly Dupont was a con man. Timony attempted to shop the failed *Ginger Box* around but found no takers. Dupont had left the production $10,000 in the red.[22]

West immediately announced her return to vaudeville with Harry Richman and subsequently secured a lucrative four-week contract on the Keith Circuit. But before opening, Richman defected, accepting a part in a Broadway musical, a step up from his second-string position as West's accompanist. For Mae, it was catastrophic. Keith immediately withdrew its offer, leaving her, once again, out of work.[23]

Shortly afterward, West revealed in *Variety* that she planned to write and star in her own play. For the remainder of the year, she poured her energy into that ambitious project. Teaming up with experienced playwright Adeline Leitzbach, she composed *The Hussy*, a full-length, three-act play. Mae contended that she began writing her own material at her mother's insistence. As before, her father discouraged her attempts. "Let the producers find the play and do it," he advised. "Then if it doesn't turn out too good, it will be their fault." Mae forged ahead anyway, and while she never found a producer for *The Hussy,* the play was a milestone in her evolution. It allowed Mae to further craft her fictional presence through a new means—autobiographical confession. "My ideas and my texts," she later confessed, "were from the first for the stage, through the secret doors of my personal life." Mae's identity became increasingly engulfed by the fictional sphere she created, but it was her inner self that provided the genesis of her imaginary world. Mae West's work and life were becoming completely intertwined.[24]

The Hussy centers on the notorious vixen Nona Ramsey, who lives with her financially struggling parents in a recently gentrified Long Island neighborhood. The community's residents are aghast: Every day Nona steps out with a different man. She supplies her family with extravagant gifts and money, fueling neighbors' speculation that she is a prostitute. Even her father, Tom, an ill-tempered private eye who gambles away his meager earnings at the racetrack, believes it. Tom and Nona repeatedly clash, with Jen Ramsey, Nona's mother, frequently mediating. Although Nona insists that she only acts as companion and gives betting advice, her father threatens to "break her neck" for bringing shame upon the family. Nona herself sees nothing wrong in accepting the gifts that her male admirers provide and assures her family that she will marry — someday.

Later, Nona attends a high society ball. Reprising *The Ruby Ring,* she offers vamp lessons to a group of young women, wagering that she can entice any man into marrying her by assuming a compatible persona. She succeeds with a rugged outdoorsman and an economics professor, but she stops short with the next man, the wealthy Robert Van Sturdivant. She calls off the bet and announces that she has found her true match, intending to secure a legitimate proposal from him.

Fearful that Van Sturdivant will reject her when he learns of her true background, Nona rents a mansion and convinces her family to pretend that they are its usual tenants. But her conscience overcomes her, forcing her to admit to him that she has lied and has no money or social standing. Van Sturdivant reveals that he already knows she is not a blue blood and whisks her off to be married anyway.

Even though *The Hussy* appears contrived and amateurish, this early piece indicates that Mae West had begun to think about and structure her performance in very specific ways. Several important elements had converged to form a base for her future work. First, she not only developed a prototype for her stage persona but was also continuing her experimentation with the power of language. The Ramseys' neighbors engage in considerable discussion of Nona before she actually appears. "The hussy! Every day a different man," cries one; another coos, "Look at the gown!" Through dialogue West controlled her audience, telling spectators what to look for and how to read her image. In Nona's case, she becomes irresistibly beautiful, scorned by proper women but adored by men, who are, according to one high society maven, "twisted around her little finger."[25]

Next, West pits her character in a contest against men. Again, she demonstrates the mutability of identity, the transformative power of her tricksterism, which allows Nona to conquer male privilege through guile and wit. Out of this battle, West's character always emerged the victor. Mae West would always get her man.

Nona succeeds because she understands how to manipulate men to get what she wants and needs. For her, men are not a source of sensual pleasure; they serve utilitarian purposes. She shares her distinct philosophy with her admiring peers during her vamp lessons. She cautions them to mask their female superiority. "Men never like to feel that you think you are superior to them," she insists. "Oh, they want you to be and if they don't think you are—it's a lost cause where you're concerned, but they don't want you to know you are!" She contends that all male-female relationships center on capital; men will generously offer gifts and cash in exchange for female attention. These material awards depend on a woman's appreciation of the male ego. A successful woman knows how to control men by molding herself to their individual traits and expectations. But, Nona warns her pupils, their male "victims" should never be too certain of the relationship: "Never let a man see you care for him—keep him guessing. Don't be too nice to him; never let him be sure of you."[26]

Nona's principles were a mixed bag of conservative and rebellious principles. While the Westian character only found satisfaction in relationships with men, at the same time, she contested their power and authority. Within this confusing array of attitudes, West challenged women's subordination by inverting traditional roles. She constructed male characters as weak; many are easily fooled and even a little dim-witted. Additionally, the Ramsey home was hardly a testimony to the "Cult of Domesticity." The Ramseys' gender roles are out of kilter: The daughter supports the family, and the father is completely dependent on her income; Nona constantly berates her father for failing to fulfill his traditional obligations to support his family.

The Hussy's autobiographical undercurrent indicates that it functioned as a cathartic for Mae's frustrations with her personal life. Thomas Ramsey clearly represented Jack West. Like Tillie, Jen, a seamstress who is completely devoted to her daughter, constantly intercedes on Nona's behalf. *The Hussy* may offer one of the most honest glimpses into the West family life—the constant battles between Mae and her father, his explosive temper, and her resentment of him. Nona observes that her father has "never liked anything in his life" and that despite his unhappiness he has done nothing to improve himself. She lectures her younger brother, Tom Junior, predicting that "[you would] make a bum out of yourself—that's what you'd do! Marry some decent little woman and make her life like the old man's wrecked Mom's—and you'd put children into the world like you and me—And they might take after you—same's we take after Dad."[27]

The Hussy was as much a story of Nona's (or Mae's) triumph over her father as of her victory over male suitors. It paralleled Mae's perception of her life, her understanding of relations with men, and her stubborn refusal to allow her father to discourage her aspirations. Mae had begun to use her work to explore and renegotiate the realities of her existence and oppression. Nona Ramsey reigned supreme over the men who attempted to dominate her. Additionally, she was a working-class woman who slipped easily into wealth by attracting the right man.

West could not find backers for *The Hussy,* so, deciding to return to vaudeville, she began a search for Richman's replacement. She finally hired two men, singer Joseph Lertora and pianist Leon Flatow. Billed as "Mae West and Company," in January 1923 they debuted an act similar to the one that Mae had played with Richman; she did add several new musical numbers, bringing the act to almost thirty minutes. Reviewers panned this version, complaining that it was underrehearsed and too long. Sime lamented the absence of Richman, noting that without him West "had lost the little touch of finesse." The West and Richman pairing had produced a more palatable Mae, his sophistication softening her rawness. Mae had used Richman as her balance, a second voice to signify her double meanings and mixed messages. [28]

Reviewer reactions convinced West that she needed to get Richman back. By April, she had successfully convinced him to rejoin her, and together they appeared at Manhattan's Colonial Theater to a sold-out crowd. West had updated her wardrobe to include new, stunning gowns; one, in black velvet, was accented by a large, plumed, Gaby Deslys–style silver headdress. The act also included an African-American actress who played the French prima donna's maid, hauling around an overgrown German shepherd in place of the anticipated miniature poodle. For her encore, West shimmied. The house went wild, demanding several bows. Later that night, she took the stage again, joining a jazz band to sing as African-American tap master Bill Robinson danced. This time *Variety* rated her "the hit of the bill." [29]

Despite their success, this engagement was the death blow to the West-Richman partnership. Richman alleged that Timony, growing more jealous, broke up the act, but according to Richman's close friend Nils Granlund, it was Mae who decided to end their collaboration. Apparently, several of Harry's buddies attended their performance later in the week. At the act's end, after Mae took her bows, they called for *Richman* to do an encore. Richman happily obliged. West fired him immediately. [30]

Richman quickly rose as a theatrical star and opened his own nightclub. West again faded away. Fate, pride, misfortune, and bad decisions had interrupted her rise and, combined with her stubborn insistence on controlling her performance, forced her yet another time into the entertainment world's outback. She was thirty years old and had been in show business for over twenty years. Several times she had stardom in her grasp only to see it slip away.

Yet Mae trouped on. Between 1923 and 1925, she intermittently played small-time vaudeville throughout the country. In the act, she plugged and appeared on the covers of several new songs, including "Hula Lou," and "I Never Broke Nobody's Heart When I Said Goodbye." Not surprisingly, during this period she plowed through several more accompanists. While she was often able to secure good spots on the bill, she could no longer command top-dollar salaries. She played Philadelphia several times at only $125 a week.[31]

In March 1924, she accepted a four-week contract to appear on the Interstate Vaudeville Circuit. One of vaudeville's least desirable routes, it covered Texas, Arkansas, Oklahoma, and Kansas. She opened in Dallas and by the next week, in Houston, attracted the affections of R. A. "Bud" Burmeister, a publicity agent for a local theater. He applied for a marriage license, but before he could get her to the altar, she had left town for San Antonio. She wrapped up the tour with a week in Fort Worth.

The Interstate Circuit promoted West as "fresh from Broadway" and ran advertisements exhorting, "Hot Mamma! The queen of the jazz babies is here! Beautiful back—shaking shoulders, delicious spice and all!!" One critic praised her performance and her "strikingly beautiful figure," noting she was well received. But it was hardly the dazzling impression she had hoped to make. By the time she arrived in Fort Worth, management had dropped her to fourth on the bill, the same spot she had occupied in 1912. Several months later, she resurfaced on the Keith Circuit, playing theaters in Columbus and Detroit. Again Broadway's former shimmy queen found herself relegated to the fourth spot, just after "Marcel and his Trained Seal."[32]

Mae spent downtime in Woodhaven with her family. Neighbors remembered her fondness for two neighborhood toddlers, Jack Meuchner and Girard Thompson. She showered them with attention and gifts—boxing gloves and cowboy suits. "She wanted what they called boy children," Jack Meuchner's aunt recalled. "Girls never did appeal to her." Regardless, Mae was more a playmate than a nurturer. Late in life, she always insisted that she was unsuitable for motherhood. "I'm my own child. . . . I had to create myself," she explained. "I knew instinctively that I shouldn't have children. I had to have the attention all the time." And while she idolized her mother, Mae could never be selflessly devoted like Tillie. Neighbors described the intense bond between the two. Mae proudly recalled a New Year's Eve performance when she brought her mother onstage to take a bow. "She loved it," Mae related. "She lit up. I threw the audience a kiss and she did too."[33]

Tillie remained the backbone of the West family. Even though Mae's earnings had declined, between 1923 and 1925 the Wests' finances appeared to be on the upswing. In fact, in 1923, under the alias of Tillie Landauer, Mae's mother took over the operation of the Harding Hotel, leasing it from a real estate company. (Later, Mae boasted that her mother owned it.) On Broadway, near Times Square, the Harding had twelve floors and totaled $700,000 in annual rentals. It was a popular hangout for boxers, show people, and some of New York's most notorious gangsters, including Feets Edison, Legs Diamond, Arnold Rothstein, and Dutch Schultz. Additionally, by the mid-twenties, Tillie undertook the management of three Long Island roadhouses: the Royal Arms, the Blue Goose, and the Green Parrot. Like the Harding, these had questionable reputations. Roadhouses were considered wild places where patrons enjoyed bootleg alcohol to the sound of jazz and blues.[34]

Running a midtown Manhattan hotel and three roadhouses definitely required a large financial outlay. The family must have benefited from Jim Timony's wise investment strategies, but even Timony could not have so quickly propelled the Wests into such high-rolling financial endeavors. Rather, it seems that the family's underworld ties were paying off. Tillie, the kindly German housewife and ambitious stage mother, was almost certainly acting as a front for one of New York's most powerful crime bosses, Owney Madden. Later, rumors circulated that *he* owned the Harding.

Madden had good reasons for keeping a low profile. For most of his life, he had been involved in crime. In 1902, at age eleven, he migrated from England to New York's Hell's Kitchen, where as a young man he assumed leadership of New York City's most violent gang, the Gophers. In addition to theft and burglary, Madden's gang provided protection and secured votes for Tammany Hall. In 1915, Madden's rise was halted by a stay in Sing Sing for the murder of a rival gangster. After his early release in 1923, which some attributed to his political ties, Madden quickly moved in on the bootleg trade, made lucrative by the federal Prohibition laws that had gone into effect in 1920.

Madden quickly amassed a fortune. He provided the public with Madden's No. 1, one of New York's most popular beers—for both its quality and the dire consequences of rejecting it. Although it was deadly to cross Madden, he was known to be polite, gentlemanly, and cautious. He had powerful friends in both City Hall and the New York City Police Department. Some New Yorkers believed that he really ran the city. Many in the working class and underclass regarded him as a Robin Hood. He was famous for helping out friends and strangers and also for his charitable contributions to the Catholic Church.

As his wealth grew, Madden invested in other business endeavors, many of them, like the Harding Hotel, legitimate. He despised publicity and avoided the limelight, remaining a silent partner and seeking business associates who were willing to act as his fronts. As a result, the extent of his financial empire was unclear. However, as his fortune rose, his presence was detectable in New York City's sports, entertainment, and nightclub scenes. Madden backed boxers and Broadway shows. (It was rumored he even invested in Hollywood studios.) He also partnered with Texas Guinan, Manhattan's colorful nightclub hostess famous for her greeting "Hello, suckers!" He sponsored her El Fey Club and later her Three Hundred Club just down the block from the Harding. Even more important, he was the money and power behind Harlem's famous Cotton Club, which showcased the best African-American entertainers of the era. The club's clientele was exclusively white, and Madden used the place to sell his alcohol.[35]

How the Wests came to know the powerful bootlegger and gang chieftain is not certain. However, they had long maintained ties to organized crime and could have easily been acquainted with Madden even before his stay in Sing Sing. (He most likely saw Mae perform in 1916 at the White Rats Sing Sing benefit show.) Forging a relationship with Madden during the 1920s was one of the smartest moves Tillie had made thus far. It catapulted the Wests into a profitable financial arrangement; with these connections, Mae could afford to work for $125 a week. Additionally, Tillie must have hoped that Madden would open doors for her talented daughter.

West claimed that she first met Madden at the Harding and found him enticing because he was "so sweet and so vicious." One of the hotel's residents claimed that for a time West and Madden were romantically involved. In later years, when pressed about his relationship with her, Madden simply smiled fondly. Regardless, he became a close family friend and provided Mae with an entrée into the elite of gangland society. He also furthered her ties to the African-American community. Through Madden, she attended the Cotton Club's floor shows and befriended the headliners, most importantly the leader of the house band, Duke Ellington.

Mae had frequented African-American nightspots since her Chicago days and continued to do so once she returned to New York. She did visit the Cotton Club's whites-only competitor Connie's Inn, but reportedly she preferred mixed-race clubs and was even welcomed in places that excluded most whites. African-American pianist Willie "the Lion" Smith remembered black nightclub owner Johnny Carey escorting her at his club, The Nest, which offered some of Harlem's finest musical entertainment, including performances by "the Empress of the Blues," Bessie Smith. In the early morning hours, West frequented Pod and Jerry's Catagonia Club, which served Madden's No. 1 as well as the best breakfast in town. Harlem nightlife fed her creative appetite as she sharpened her performance. Most important, it thrust her into the midst of a critical moment in African-American history, the Harlem Renaissance.

Since childhood West had appropriated African-American culture, but her exposure to the burgeoning renaissance that swept Harlem in the 1920s reinforced her connections with the black community. In the 1920s, Harlem was an exhilarating place. It hosted the largest black population of any city in the world and became a magnet that drew black artists, musicians, entertainers, writers, religious leaders, intellectuals, and political activists. With this convergence came a celebration of African-American history, culture, and contributions, as well as a revitalized drive to fight racism. Jazz and the blues flourished; African-American art and literature thrived. Furthermore, white interest in black culture continued to increase, bringing it more into the American mainstream. By the mid-1920s, whites—many of them entertainers supplementing their performances by stealing bits of African-American culture—haunted the nightclubs of Harlem.[36]

By now, West had long been a practitioner of jazz and the blues. But she was in a continual process of revising her stage identity, and the Harlem Renaissance only spurred on her efforts to incorporate more African-American music and dance into her performance. She became a familiar figure at the Gaiety Theater Building and the offices of African-American composers, including the father of the blues, W. C. Handy. There West met Andy Razaf, James P. Johnson, and Perry Bradford, all highly successful African-American songwriters who had written some of the era's biggest hits.

West also looked to African-American dance masters. She worked with Buddy Bradley, who ran a Manhattan dance academy. Famous for his precise technique, Bradley mentored numerous white performers, among them Fred and Adele Astaire. West was also coached by Willie Covan, a Chicagoan celebrated for his grace and agility. Despite his exceptional talents, like many black performers, he found the rigid color line prevented him from achieving stardom. But he remembered West, who was his first pupil, as an ally. With her encouragement he opened a studio and became one of the nation's most sought-after dance instructors.[37]

Still, many African Americans who supplied white performers with material and training felt a deep resentment against the racism that stymied their own careers. Some regarded white performers who pillaged their cul-

ture with contempt. (Throughout the 1920s, whites continued to appropriate black culture, rarely acknowledging the source.) Additionally, many
Harlemites were offended by whites who made a practice of "slumming" in
their community. Several African-American club owners declared their
nightspots off limits to whites. Bessie Smith almost always refused to perform in whites-only clubs, despising those who sought out thrills at the black
community's expense.

Mae West participated liberally in this cultural theft, to such a point that
later one journalist actually compared her blues delivery to Smith's. And
while West was supportive of African Americans like Covan, in the 1920s
she remained a behind-the-scenes champion. During these years, she never
publicly protested racism or discrimination. In private, it was rumored, she
forged very personal relationships with African Americans, pursuing affairs
with black male athletes and performers. At the same time, she continued to
exploit their culture for her own ends.

Like most aspects of Mae West's life, her relationship with African-American
culture and her connections to the black community were complex. Perry
Bradford recalled West's maid Bea Jackson dropping by his office to pick up
a copy of "He May Be Your Man but He Comes to See Me Sometimes" for
Mae. Jackson was a friend of blues man Fats Waller and songwriter Sheldon
Brooks and was nicknamed "Hot Story Telling" for her colorful yarns. She
worked for West for years, and Mae became tightly bonded to her. For visitors, Mae produced photographs with her skin tone tinted brown to highlight her resemblance to Jackson. When entertainment reporter Sidney
Skolsky dropped in on Mae in 1930, he exclaimed in his column, "Mae West
has a colored maid who is a dead ringer for her." Whether or not West was
attempting to claim a real or imagined African heritage, she certainly was
challenging society's assumptions regarding the invariable nature of race.
Her actions may have also revealed, in a characteristically covert fashion,
West's deep identification with African Americans. It was extremely important that in the mid-twenties, as Mae West was just about to enter her most
productive and successful years in theater, Bea "Hot Story Telling" Jackson
became a constant presence in her life.[38]

Speaking of the Influence of the Jook

Speaking of the influence of the Jook, I noted that Mae West in "Sex" had much more flavor of the turpentine quarters than she did of the white bawd. I know that the piece she played on the piano is a very old Jook Composition. "Honey let yo' drawers hang down low" has been played and sung in every Jook in the South for at least thirty-five years. It has always puzzled me why she thought it likely to be played in a Canadian bawdy house.

—Zora Neale Hurston,
"Characteristics of Negro Expression," 1934

One day, Mae West and some friends sat stuck in New York City traffic. In a rush, she ordered her driver to take a shortcut past the waterfront, and as her car rolled past the docks she spied a young woman with a sailor on each arm. West described her as attractive but with "blonde hair, over bleached and all frizzy . . . a lot of make-up on and a tight black satin coat that was all wrinkled and soiled. . . . She had runs in her stockings and she had this little turban on and a big beautiful bird of paradise." Mae remarked to her companions, "You wonder this dame wouldn't put half a bird of paradise on her head and the rest of the money into a coat and stockings." But as her friends speculated that the bird of paradise was probably a seafaring john's recompense and that this woman of the streets at best made only fifty cents to two dollars a trick, Mae grew enraged. Certainly she was worldly enough to know about prostitution, yet she recalled, "I was really upset about that." She insisted it disturbed her to witness such exploitation of a woman—and also to realize that a woman could be so ignorant of her potential for exploiting her exploitation.

Mae continued to ponder the waterfront waif. "I kept thinking, 'Fifty cents! How many guys would she have to have to pay her rent, buy her food?'" She claimed she dreamed of the woman that night, awakening the next morning still contemplating her hard luck. "And then I said," she told *Life* magazine, "Is it possible? Is this the play I am going to write?" She realized that she had mentally "remade" this scarlet woman, envisioning her on a path that led out of the slums to a better life, a transformation easily achieved onstage. Inspired, she set out to write a new play.[1]

For some time, West had searched for a vehicle for a Broadway comeback. She had spent several years reviewing scripts, rejecting them all as unsatisfactory. But in 1924, about the time she received her waterfront inspiration, a client of Timony's, John J. Byrne, showed up with a one-act vaudeville skit called "Following the Fleet." Hearing that West was searching for a scarlet-woman vehicle, something like Somerset Maugham's *Rain*, he had composed a story of a Montreal strumpet who makes a living by seducing British sailors. On West's behalf, Timony purchased Byrne's sketch for $300. He then charged the writer $100 for acting as his agent and pressed him to invest the rest in a real estate deal.

In December 1925, working again with Adeline Leitzbach, West expanded Byrne's sketch into a three-act play that she called *The Albatross*. In it, she took a prostitute from Montreal's red light district to the mansions of Westchester County, New York. Energized by her waterfront muse, West claimed ideas spilled forth on paper bags, stationery, envelopes, and old scraps of paper that she forwarded to Timony's secretaries for transcription.

But Mae's dedication wavered. To keep her on the task, Timony began locking her in her room, refusing to let her out until she had finished writing. It not only forced her to work but prevented her from seeing other men, demonstrating the great degree of control he maintained over her. Her acceptance of this treatment indicates that the private Mae West had yet to achieve the forcefulness and confidence of her fantasized stage presence.[2]

After *The Albatross* was drafted, Timony and West set out to find backers. Their first choice was the Shuberts, and she sent them her script under a pseudonym, Jane Mast. She quickly received a curt rejection note. In fact, none of Broadway's producers, big or small, were interested, so West and Timony decided to raise the money and produce the play themselves. Timony put in a share and later convinced Harry Cohen, a Manhattan clothier, to kick in a loan of almost $4,000. As producer, he recruited C. William Morganstern, the former proprietor of Pittsburgh's Family Theater, where West had performed in 1912; his most current endeavor involved producing Broadway's *Love's Call*, one of the biggest disasters of 1924. But funds still fell short, and Tillie, with the help of Owney Madden, supplied the balance. Timony then incorporated their endeavor as the Morals Production Corporation.

Recruiting a director proved difficult. Several candidates turned down the job outright, insisting that the script was too bawdy for legitimate theater. Another prospect demanded extensive revisions. West immediately rejected him. Finally, Timony arranged for a meeting with Edward Elsner, a small-time director whose most recent undertakings had been total flops, one a comedy rated by a reviewer as "monotony." West presented her script by reading it out loud to him, since he had conveniently forgotten his glasses, and as she finished, she claimed he cried out, "By God! You've done it! You've got it! This is it!"[3]

Finding a cast was also a challenge, for West was attempting her Broadway comeback in the midst of controversy. For several seasons, the Great White Way had hosted a series of "sex plays," including *Lulu Belle*, the story of a mixed-race prostitute who slept her way to Paris, and *The Shanghai Gesture*, the chronicle of a madam of a Chinese brothel and her rage against men. These productions stirred a call for a cleanup of the city's stages. As a result, career-minded actors and actresses, fearful of negative backlash, steered clear of Mae West and similar ventures. Beyond this, the Morals Production Corporation's salaries were not competitive, forcing West to sign up a cast of unknowns. On a tight budget, she used Beverly as her understudy, acted as barber to male cast members, and borrowed old scenery from a former burlesque producer.

Securing a theater proved to be another problem. Booking space on Broadway was costly and competitive; shows had to demonstrate potential profitability. Disappointingly, all the venues in Manhattan's theater district were either occupied, not interested, or too expensive. Finally, Timony discovered one possibility: Daly's Sixty-third Street Theater, a small off-Broadway house. Daly's had a reputation for experimentation; in 1921, it hosted the successful all-black revue *Shuffle Along*. Even more important, the management agreed to waive normal up-front charges in exchange for 40 percent of the show's profits.[4]

During rehearsals West's play took final form. While she already had a completed script, at Elsner's suggestion she retooled it, urging the cast to improvise and reshape their roles. For her part, she found Elsner a catalyst for the exploration of her full range of talents, making her more aware of her performance's verbal and nonverbal nuances. As she remembered, he observed, "You have a quality—a strange amusing quality that I have never found in any of these other women. You have a definite *sexual* quality, gay and unrepressed. It even mocks you personally." While Elsner may have been a third-rate director, he understood West's strongest asset, a style that rested in signification and communicated sensuality that was both serious and satirical. With his guidance, she further honed her ability to offer conflicting messages and double meanings.

West's play continued to evolve until just before the curtain rang up on its first tryout performance in Waterbury, Connecticut. Just hours before opening, she had another inspiration. After listening for weeks to Elsner rave about her "sex quality, a low sex quality," she had a revelation. She insisted that the manager replace *The Albatross* on his marquee with a new title— *SEX*. Her first night in Waterbury produced excellent box office, bringing in several thousand dollars.[5]

Shortly afterward, the company traveled to New London, Connecticut, for more trial performances. Despite the play's bold new title, the opening night's audience numbered only eighty-five by curtain time. But, West insisted, the following day's matinee was a great morale booster. That morning, the U.S. naval fleet arrived in port, and that afternoon sailors, lured by the sign reading *SEX*, lined up around the block for tickets. Their reception was more than enthusiastic. "Believe me," West told a reporter later, "I'll never forget the Navy."[6]

SEX returned to Manhattan and, promoted with ads reading "*SEX* with Mae West," opened at Daly's Theater on April 26, 1926. The premiere was well attended, but the production still had some rough spots. One actor's collar kept springing up, a window shade refused to stay rolled down, and a loud bang offstage interrupted one scene. The sound effects for a champagne cork's pop occurred several conspicuous seconds after the bottle had been opened. But the play's blunders were minor in comparison to its "frankness." One reviewer complained, "We were shown not sex but lust—stark naked lust." Early in the program, several patrons left in disgust, and by the third act, empty seats dotted the theater. Judging by the newspapers, the opening night audience's reaction was mixed. Some sat quietly stunned, while others roared with laughter, shouting out their approval at choice moments.[7]

SEX was a little bit of *Rain*, *Lulu Belle*, and *Shanghai Gesture* thrown together with some vaudeville, old-fashioned melodrama, and burlesque. Manhattan had never seen anything like it. West conceived of it as dualistic, a "comedy-drama" oscillating between travesty and tragedy. It centered on the escapades of Margy Lamont, a lady, as one critic noted, "of the evening— and of, for that matter, the afternoon and morning too." With her pimp, Rocky Waldron, Margy works the streets of Montreal but has wearied of cheap hustling. She confesses to a friend that she now aspires "to the top of my profession." She muses, "Why not? Others do it, why can't I? . . . It's all a question of getting some guy to pay for the certain business, that's all." In the midst of planning her new life, Margy accepts a dinner invitation from a former customer, Lieutenant Gregg, a British naval officer who presents her with a gift—a bird of paradise.[8]

When Margy and Gregg later return to her flat, they discover a wealthy blue blood, Clara, unconscious. While slumming in the red light district, she has overdosed on drugs, and Rocky has ditched her, leaving her for dead. Margy brings her around, saving her life. But when a policeman arrives on the scene, Clara accuses Margy of drugging her in an attempt to steal her jewels. Margy vows revenge.

Margy decides to leave Montreal with Gregg and "follow the fleet." She ends up in Trinidad, where a young millionaire, Jimmy Stanton, mistakes her for a vacationing heiress and falls in love with her. Both Stanton and Gregg seek her hand in marriage. Gregg gets a turndown, Margy confiding:

> Why ever since I've been old enough to know Sex, I've looked at men as hunters. They're filled with Sex. In the past few years, I've been chattel to the Sex. All the bad that's in me has been put there by men. I began to hate every one of them, hated them, used them for what I could get out of them, and then laughed at them, and then—then he came.

She accepts Stanton's proposal, departing with him to meet his parents at their Westchester estate.[9]

To Margy's shock, Stanton's mother turns out to be Clara, the woman she rescued in Montreal. Privately, Clara threatens to expose Margy's true identity to her son. "Say, you've got the nerve putting yourself on a pedestal above me," Margy admonishes her. "The things I've done, I had to do for a living. I know it was wrong. I'm not trying to alibi myself. But you've done those same things for other reasons." She observes, "The only difference between you and me is that you could afford to give it away." Instead, it is the society matron's past that returns to haunt her. Rocky Waldron shows up demanding hush money. Margy stops Clara from murdering him. After turning Rocky over to the authorities, Margy confesses her wanton past to Jimmy. "Mrs. Stanton, I'm giving you back your boy," she says. She turns to Lieutenant Gregg, who has arrived on the scene, declaring her intention to go "straight—to Australia."[10]

Early on, SEX's future looked dim. The Morals Production Corporation had little money for a publicity campaign, and within the first week attendance lagged. The reviews were disappointing. The more stodgy New York dailies agreed to downplay SEX's sensationalism and blast it as inept and amateurish. One of these, the *New York Times*, branded *SEX* as "feeble and disjointed," declaring that Montreal, Trinidad, and Westchester possessed "ample cause for protest." The *New Yorker* was far less kind, declaring it a "poor balderdash of street sweepings and cabaret sentimentality unexpurgated in tone." *Variety* summed up the reaction of many, proclaiming *SEX* a "disgrace," with "nasty, infantile, amateurish and vicious dialogue." While the play was attributed to the mysterious Jane Mast, no one was fooled. All blamed Mae West for what one reviewer condemned "as bad a play as these inquiring eyes have gazed upon in three seasons."[11]

But with the help of word of mouth and several lurid reviews in the city's tabloids, curiosity began to draw New Yorkers to Daly's little off-Broadway theater. Before long, more and more came. When writer Robert Benchley attended, he noted that "at the corner of Central Park West and Sixty-Third Street we ran into a line of people which seemed to be extending in the general direction of Daly's Theatre . . . and what was more, the people standing in line were clutching, not complimentary passes, but good, green dollar bills." Within a few weeks, *SEX* was a hit, seats in the house went for top dollar, and it began to turn a nice profit. While it slipped during the hot summer, its low overhead helped *SEX* generate strong returns for the rest of the year.

SEX attracted a wide range of fans. Many rank-and-file New Yorkers, especially the men, supported West's efforts. In addition to writers like Benchley, Harlem Renaissance figures like writer Zora Neale Hurston made their way to Daly's. It also became a fashionable outing for the New York elite, who during the 1920s demanded increasingly more scintillating experiences. Benchley observed that "each night soft-purring limousines roll up with theatre parties of gentry, out 'just for a lark.' "[12]

In the 1920s, New York's rich smart set perfected "slumming," thrill-seeking excursions to poorer and rougher sections of town. *SEX* took its place next to speakeasies, nightclubs, and dens of iniquity found in the Bowery, Greenwich Village, Chinatown, and Harlem. Journalist Elizabeth Yeaman later remembered that "some of the so-called highbrows would venture to her [West's] theater in something of the spirit that they would go on a slumming tour."[13] In a sense, West presented them with a voyeur's delight, a virtual reality where the elite could immerse themselves in the world of an impoverished prostitute without ever having to leave the safety of their theater seats. Mae West made slumming easy.

Yet it was not as simple as it appeared. For while the spectators sat snugly protected in the darkened theater, they became her marks. *SEX* mocked many of its most devoted fans. West used Margy to signify on those who attended *SEX* for a titillating peek at life's seamier side. Margy deplores slumming's disingenuousness and exploitation, labeling Clara as "one of those respectable society dames who poses as decent, and is looking for the first chance to cheat without being found out." While the audience chuckled away, they became unknowing victims of Margy's, and Mae's, disdainful indictment of their behavior.

With *SEX*, West clearly began an exploration of class conflict. Margy despises the upper class and rages against Clara's dishonesty and hypocrisy. "I don't count, I suppose. Because I'm what I am. But, I'll tell you . . . if I ever get a chance, I'll get even with you, you dirty charity, I'll get even." Identifying Clara as a "charity" girl, slang for a woman who traded sex for gifts or thrills, Margy exposes the duplicity of the upper class, the perpetrators of rigid Victorian standards that even they fail to uphold. Margy never evens the score with Clara; she is above that. But West did secure revenge on Clara's kind, those pedigreed sensation seekers filling Daly's seats, who snickered not only at Margy but, through *SEX*'s mirror, at themselves. West was well aware she had created such a reflection, describing her work as "a mirror which tells the truth."[14]

In a similar manner, *SEX* criticized the male audience members who came to hoot and holler as Margy cavorted from Montreal to Westchester. Margy is not only of easy virtue but constructed as the epitome of desirability. Her irresistible beauty is constantly anticipated and reinforced. At the same time, Margy revealed West's ambivalence about men and sex. Margy's characterization of men as predators and her admitted hatred for them, blaming all that was "bad" in her on men, operates as a blunt exposé of Mae's anger with and rebellion against men. Like *The Hussy*'s Nona Ramsey, Margy views men in economic terms, seeking liaisons for material gain. *SEX* reinforced this philosophy, for with this cut-rate, off-Broadway production, West fleeced male customers who were drawn in by both *SEX* and sex.

Significantly, West established her sensuality and desirability with an image that ran counter to the popular female archetype, the flapper. In part, this was by necessity. Now thirty-three, West was full-figured and did not possess the 1920s' voguish slim, flat-chested, and "boyish" physique. It did not go unnoticed—one critic decried her as "over plump"—but West chose to exploit rather than downplay her difference. Embracing her natural body, she used it to assert herself physically over *SEX*'s male characters. "The curve is more powerful than the sword," she later maintained. Mae had begun to construct her body as both a weapon of resistance and a battlefield, a place to wage war. Again, as in *The Hussy*, she asserted that women are in reality stronger than men. Several publicity stills pictured Margy towering over her male admirers, one even helplessly sprawled under her on a chair.[15]

In addition to recycling themes from *The Hussy*, West experimented with yet another device that became a hallmark of her work—an ambiguous ending. Unlike *The Hussy*'s cross-class romance, in *SEX* Margy succumbs to Lieutenant Gregg, a man of similar class standing. At one level, it affirmed the impossibility of transcending class boundaries. However, thanks to Clara, upward mobility appears less than desirable, for truthfulness, loyalty, and courage really belong to the underclasses. Margy is not like Nona; she really does not aspire to enter the Social Register. And while Margy indicates that she will "go straight," it remains unclear whether that means she is going to marry Gregg or continue in her old ways and just follow him to Australia. The *New York Herald Tribune*'s Percy Hammond certainly read Margy's plans as more licentious, reporting that, in the end, she "abandons the precincts of respectability to return to the crimson life."[16]

Critical elements of the fictionalized Mae Westian persona were coming together. Reviewers noted her rolling walk, domineering presence, and unique timing. Margy Lamont is tough-talking and no-nonsense. Unlike Nona, she is a genuine woman of ill repute. But she does possess a good soul. Although filled with hostility for men and the rich, Margy is not singularly overcome by her rage. Rather, she also enjoys herself. A naval officer asks, "Miss Lamont, may I present Mr. Stanton?" One can easily hear the mature Mae West hum, "Yes, you may."

But who is Margy Lamont? The play says nothing about her origins. Zora Neale Hurston's observation that *SEX* owed more to the African-American jook than it did to the white bawdy house indicates that at least culturally Margy's roots lay closer to African Americans than to whites. When Margy sits down at the Stantons' piano and plays "Home Sweet Home," Gregg comments, "That doesn't sound a bit like you." She switches to the blues, remarking, "It's not supposed to be." Margy's "whiteness" is even further contested. Visiting a Trinidadian café, she joins in with the floor show. The other entertainers perform old standards, sea songs, and tangos. But, backed by a jazz band, Margy sings blues numbers: "My Sweet Man" and "Shake That Thing." For an encore, she shimmies to W. C. Handy's "St. Louis Blues." It prompted one reviewer to compare the scene to "a Harlem cabaret we have seen further downtown" and another to praise her rendition of "Sweet Man" as "very Harlem and with a jazz dance right out of the eff-sharp department."[17]

West borrowed even more deeply from the blues, using it to structure portions of *SEX*'s dialogue. When Lieutenant Gregg drops in to see Margy, he tells her, "Oh, I've got something for you. Wait until you see this, wait until you see this."

"Well, come on," Margy demands.

"You'll get it, you'll get it," Gregg promises. "I don't mind telling you I had an awful time saving it for you. Why all the women were fighting for it."

"It better be good," she responds.

"It's good alright. It's the best you could get, but you've got to be very careful not to bend it," he declares, and then offers her the bird of paradise.[18] Their double-entendre, comedic exchange was a variation—or in jazz terms, a riff—on blues man Papa Charlie Jackson's "I Got What It Takes but It Breaks My Heart to Give It Away."

> I save it up : since the Lord knows when,
> I ain't saved a thing : because of any of you men.
> I've had it so long : I'd hate to lose it
> Because ever gets broke : I'll be able to use it.[19]

Even more interesting, Jackson's song was intended for a woman. Placing a woman's words in Lieutenant Gregg's mouth, West created a reversal: The man rather than the woman "saves it up" and worries about "breaking it."

Still other blues elements appeared in *SEX*. As Houston Baker contends, trains and riding the rails provide core motifs for the blues vernacular, which records journeys and the dilemmas of reaching "junctures." He views the blues and its singer as "travelers" that are "always at this intersection, this crossing, codifying force, providing resonance for experience's multiplicities."[20]

Margy, also a blues singer, is one of those travelers who passes through a series of crossings, rambling restlessly and perpetually moving on to the next stop. She speaks not of a scarlet woman's life but of "experiencing that experience," narrating a story of anger, frustration, and determination to resist her exploitation. As the trickster, she dupes men out of their money, hating them as they make love to her but immensely enjoying her own joke. As the blues singer, she uses the blues to protest. West had reached a critical juncture herself. In vaudeville, she had become a blues singer. Now, adding another complexity to her stage identity, she was a blues singer playing a prostitute who was playing a blues singer.

In many respects, both Margy and Mae emerged as tricksters, creating chaos from order and order from chaos. How many in the audience comprehended West's intentions is unclear, but reactions, which puzzled critics, indicated that some were in on the joke. One reviewer expressed amazement at the "whooping, indeed, a little more happily in those sadder moments when the affair degenerated into the moralistic and heroic." Similarly, *Variety* noted that the "audience often laughs when it should weep."[21] But the ambiguities of *SEX*, the multiplicity of meanings and messages, and its syncretism of comedy and drama were all elements of the signification that Mae West was in the process of perfecting. *SEX*'s topsy-turvy world allowed Mae as well as Margy to emerge triumphant.

Although *SEX* became a success and rapidly transformed Mae West into a celebrity, if not a star, it also drew attention from Manhattan's moral watchdogs. *SEX* debuted just as many civic and religious leaders escalated their calls for censorship of the stage. Leading the charge was John S. Sumner of the New York Society for the Suppression of Vice (NYSSV), dedicated to ridding the country of books, newspapers, magazines, artworks, or plays the group deemed obscene. Sumner wielded a considerable power and counted John D. Rockefeller and J. P. Morgan among his supporters.

The 1920s stage, having felt the impact of the raucous jazz age, presented a particular challenge to Sumner. Under the influence of playwrights like Eugene O'Neill, Broadway had ventured into more gritty realism and controversial issues. Additionally, the jaded jazz generation's demand for more sophistication as well as more titillation fed an impulse toward new, sometimes more realistic, and often more risqué, drama. In Sumner's opinion, the public had an alarming appetite for smut, and those with weaker psychological constitutions or little education were easily addicted to the salacious. The theater, he believed, was well positioned to strongly influence society and had an ethical responsibility to play an uplifting role. Rather, he lamented, Broadway, with its focus on profits, had sought out increasingly more licentious plays.

Despite his strong feelings, Sumner initially opposed appointing a stage censor. Instead, he helped organize a less severe alternative—the play jury, empaneled by the district attorney. Twelve New York City residents were recruited to attend and vote on the appropriateness of plays. It was a fairly lenient system; a play remained open with only four affirmative votes. But Sumner had faith that the good citizens of Manhattan would close down all plays endangering the morals of theatergoers.

With *SEX*'s debut, Sumner moved quickly. In April, he paid a visit to Daly's and immediately registered a complaint with the New York City police contending that *SEX* was "filthy and obscene." But what Sumner and even drama critics saw was mild. Borrowing an old burlesque trick, West had two versions of *SEX,* a tamer one for the press and moralists like Sumner and a spicier one for the general public. In June, tipped off that the play jury was about to visit the show, she played the blander version. The jury met, and *SEX* fell one vote short of being shut down. With that announcement, attendance skyrocketed. Notwithstanding, Sumner branded *SEX* as "moral poison" and continued to agitate for its closure.[22]

Sumner's tone was echoed by many in the New York press, in particular the tabloids, who offered some of *SEX*'s harshest criticism. William Randolph Hearst's *Daily Mirror* was especially brutal, denouncing West's play as "a monstrosity plucked from the garbage can, destined for the sewer." Exposing *SEX*'s depravity served two purposes for the *Mirror*'s editors. First, since Sumner had earlier taken aim at tabloids, by attacking *SEX* they testified that they were on the right moral track. Second, by informing the public of the exact details of such vile controversy, they sold even more papers.[23]

Not everyone in the press followed suit. Alarmed by an escalating censorship movement, the *New York Herald Tribune* and *Variety* ran follow-up reviews that reversed their initial condemnations of *SEX*. Percy Hammond celebrated West's portrayal of Margy Lamont. "She is thoroughly cold and malign," he wrote, "an omen of damages that penalize foolishness and wrongdoing." Others found Mae equally compelling. One critic, complaining about *SEX*'s "pathetically frantic vulgarity," conceded that "Miss West goes on unperturbed—smooth, silky, and never at a loss." *Variety*'s Jack Conway celebrated her as "the Babe Ruth of stage prosties" and offered a prophetic assessment: "It's realistic and realism all the way. Mae's conception of Margie LaMont [*sic*] will sentence her to the scarlet sisterhood artistically for life."[24]

Any attempt to drive *SEX* offstage was going to be a battle. West had her friends. Owney Madden was not only a co-investor but also charged her a protection fee. Seemingly his ties, as well as Timony's, to Tammany Hall should have benefited Mae West, but Tammany's power had been waning for years. Additionally, the debate over censorship was tied to thorny New York City and state politics. On the local level, it appeared that key factions protected plays like *SEX*. Instrumental was New York City's mayor Jimmy Walker, a Tammany Hall Democrat with strong show business ties. A former songwriter and patron of Texas Guinan's, he was a major impediment to Sumner's campaigns. Facing this powerful opposition, Manhattan courts seemed unlikely, despite Sumner's agitation, to shut down any New York production, even *SEX*.

An even more powerful player in the debate was New York governor Al Smith, another son of Tammany Hall, who was preparing to run for president in 1928. While he did not share Walker's close ties to show business, he was philosophically opposed to censorship. Republicans, aware that censorship was a political hot potato for Smith, gladly pushed the issue to the forefront. Their efforts were assisted by newspaper publisher Hearst, an opposition Democrat and longtime Smith opponent. Using his papers to exacerbate the situation, Hearst attacked Broadway and expounded on the need for a stage censor. Ideally, the state assembly's Republican majority would pass a censorship bill forcing a Smith veto that would undermine his presidential aspirations. While Mae West rarely expressed overt interest in American politics, SEX propelled her into a vigorous battle between competing political interests.[25]

Into the fall, Sumner continued to demand that the city take action against Mae West. However, he had his hands full, for the 1926–1927 theatrical season produced two more controversial productions. First, and most successful, was *The Captive*, based on Marcel Proust's novel on female samesex love. Next came *The Virgin Man*, a story of a Yalie who struggles to retain his virtue against female seductresses. Many hailed *The Captive* as high drama, while moralists lumped it in with SEX and *The Virgin Man* as a "dirt play."[26]

SEX and the agitation against it kept Mae West occupied. Tiring of commuting from her parents' Woodhaven home, she booked a suite at the Mayflower Hotel. For the first time, Mae had left the family nest. While her circle of acquaintances grew, Timony, her family, and Madden and his friends remained her closest ties. Although work took up much of her time, she was spotted at Harlem nightclubs, upscale restaurants, prizefights, and Texas Guinan's.

West established a close rapport with Guinan, who was warm, kind, and generous. Unlike Mae, Texas was outgoing and made friends easily. Believing she was a reincarnated "wise, Oriental soul," Texas was fascinated by Eastern philosophy and spiritualism, and she may have been one of the first to introduce Mae to these religious alternatives. In late August 1926, Mae and Texas hosted a séance to contact the recently deceased Rudolph Valentino's spirit. One guest remembered Texas leading the gathering as Mae sat quietly observing. But just as they seemed to make contact with the silver screen's most celebrated lover, a loud crash broke the link. When the lights came up, entangled in a mess of folding chairs were two latecomers, Texas's brother Tommy and Owney Madden.

Madden's connections provided West with many opportunities, and during the run of SEX, she developed a close bond with his boyhood friend George Raft. A dancer and former boxer, Raft was handsome and, like Madden, dapper and low-key. Although he continued to work for the gangster, running errands and even riding shotgun on predawn bootleg deliveries, with Madden's help Raft had worked his way into the nightclub circuit, often performing at Guinan's. In 1926, Madden assigned Raft to a late-night visit to Daly's to collect his share of SEX's box office receipts. Before long, Raft began spending more time in the leading lady's dressing room. Unlike Richman, Raft was not one to brag, but many believed that he and Mae had a passionate affair. If they did, it was short-lived, for Raft soon left to tour Europe with a dance act. Regardless, he would remain one of West's few close friends.[27]

For Mae West, 1926 had been a successful year in more ways than one. Good or bad, she was the talk of Broadway as Sumner and his legions continued to wage their battles to clean up the stage. And while pressure to drive *SEX* off the boards increased, West contemplated an even more daring venture. One evening, she had Timony escort her to a Greenwich Village nightspot to attend a show put on by a group of female impersonators. Afterward, she gave each a free pass for the next evening's performance of *SEX*. Those who attended were invited to audition for Jane Mast's latest comedy-drama, *The Drag*.

This was not West's first exposure to the gay subculture; she had patronized similar establishments in Harlem. Additionally, she had known many gays during her long career in burlesque, vaudeville, and the theater. Now, though, West claimed she had become curious about homosexuality because of an actor whom she met during her run in *SEX*. She found him enchanting; he sent her flowers. But her interest waned after she learned that he had been married and fathered a child, was divorced, and was also bisexual.

West insisted that this experience compelled her to study differing psychological interpretations of homosexuality. Although she became familiar with Sigmund Freud and Richard von Krafft-Ebing, she favored Karl Heinrich Ulrich, a mid-nineteenth-century gay intellectual who advanced the theory that homosexuals represented an "intermediate" sex, possessing both male and female qualities. She also subscribed to psychologist Havelock Ellis's theory that homosexuals were "inverts," born with drives that had been turned inward. Although West stated that she believed homosexuality "a danger to the entire social system of western civilization," she also expressed sympathy for most gay men, whom she perceived as female spirits burdened with men's bodies. West bragged that she had warned police, "When you're hitting one of those guys, you're hitting a woman." However, she also divided homosexual men into two categories. The first, "born homosexuals," she found acceptable, a result of biological makeup. The second she labeled "environmental" homosexuals. In her opinion, these were secretive degenerates driven by acquired urges for unnatural sexual thrills.[28]

West's fascination with gay subculture was not unique for the era. Historian George Chauncey argues that during Prohibition, gay and cross-dressing performers experienced a heightened popularity in New York City. Extravagant drag balls where female impersonators performed for prizes were popular diversions for New York's smart set. Many Manhattan nightspots featured openly gay entertainers as well as drag queens. Two of the era's most celebrated entertainers were female impersonators Julian Eltinge and Bert Savoy. Eltinge, who presented tasteful tunes while outfitted in exquisite gowns, was hailed for his uncanny ability to replicate feminine beauty. Savoy dressed outrageously and enacted a loud, comedic, love-starved tart, famous for his/her exuberant invitation "You *must* come over." Gay performers and female impersonators were in such demand in the 1920s that observers declared Manhattan was in the grip of a "pansy craze." West, who recruited forty Greenwich Villagers for *The Drag*, was obviously attempting to cash in on this trend.[29]

West's goal was to achieve authenticity, and she arrived at the first rehearsal with only an outline for *The Drag*. She did not intend to appear in the play herself but rather hoped to write and direct it, with Elsner's assistance. Drawing on his directorial methods, she encouraged the drag queens and gay performers to ad-lib their roles; from there, she began refining her script. A journalist who later watched West at work described her technique as "spontaneous combustion . . . these players, by their physical types, suggest story and speeches to her and thus drama takes form orally in the first instance, only to become a completed script when the curtain is ready to rise on its premiere." Elsner had shown her how to get the best from her performance, and that, she became convinced, was the most effective way to develop theater. By mid-January 1927, spectators filled the seats during rehearsals at Daly's. *Variety*'s correspondent, who sneaked a preview, castigated *The Drag* as a "sex perversion exposition" but praised the players' improvisation as "natural and spontaneous."[30]

As *The Drag* was rehearsing, voices calling for censorship grew louder. When John Sumner, also a foe of the gay community, heard of *The Drag*'s pending Broadway premiere, he called more stridently for a ban of such productions from the New York stage. He joined others who now criticized the play jury, which in three years had closed only one play. The district attorney, Joab H. Banton, also a Tammanyite, defended his office's oversight of the jury. Banton argued that it was difficult to recruit jurors and that often those who accepted theater tickets later refused to file their reports. Certainly, that process, which entailed a face-to-face evaluation in his office, proved daunting, if not threatening, for those called to serve.

That January, the climate seemed to change. Under pressure from censorship proponents, Jimmy Walker met with Broadway producers, warning that if plays were not toned down, censorship was inevitable. District Attorney Banton also chimed in, declaring that it was "about time that we clean up the salacious plays." Such high-minded denunciations simply fueled public curiosity, sending even more people to see *SEX*.[31]

Despite the public's similar curiosity about *The Drag*, Timony could only secure half a week at Poli's Park, a Bridgeport, Connecticut, burlesque house. On Monday, January 31, 1927, the Morals Production Corporation stretched a banner that read, "*The Drag* by the author of *SEX*, more sensational than *Rain* or *The Captive*," across Bridgeport's main street. New Yorkers lured by gossip surrounding West's latest undertaking paid premium prices for reserved seats. West claimed it drew fans from Boston to Philadelphia. It also brought out the New York City Police Department's James Sinnott.

After tense last-minute negotiations with Bridgeport's police, that evening the curtain went up on the first public performance of *The Drag*. For the next several hours, the audience received a glimpse into gay life through the eyes of Mae West. *The Drag* centered on the heartbreak of a woman, Clair, daughter of a prominent physician, Dr. James Richardson. She is married to Rolly Kingsbury, son of a respected judge. Although Rolly is a kind husband, Clair's marriage is loveless. She is unaware of the cause, but it is clear: Rolly is gay. In fact, his spurned lover, David, seeks help from Dr. Richardson. Rolly has fallen in love with his straight business associate Allen Grayson. When Grayson, who loves Clair, learns of Rolly's affections, he explodes with anger. It is not Rolly's gayness that bothers him but his treatment of Clair. "I think that's the most contemptible thing you could do," Grayson shouts. "Marry a woman and use her as a cloak to cover up what you really are."[32]

A few days later, while Clair is away, Rolly throws an elaborate drag ball. His guests arrive, one by one, in drag finery, exchanging catty quips and insults. One drag queen, Winnie, greets another, Hell's Kitchen Kate, "My but you're getting thin." Kate exclaims, "I can at least cling to a man without wearing him out. You're terribly fat." Winnie shouts, "Fat! I should say not! I'm the type that men prefer. I can at least go through the Navy Yard without having the flags drop to half mast." But Kate refuses to concede: "I'm just the type that men crave. The type that burns 'em up. Why when I walk up Tenth Avenue, you can smell the meat sizzling in Hell's Kitchen." A police raid ends the frivolity and sends the guests scrambling. Rolly promises to fix everything with the authorities and, escaping arrest, retires to bed. Offstage a shot rings out. Rolly's butler finds him murdered.

Everyone gathers at the murder scene, and Dr. Richardson arrives with David, who confesses that his broken heart drove him to kill Rolly. Outraged, Judge Kingsbury threatens to strangle David, who passionately responds:

Strangle me, strangle me! You Judge Kingsbury—the great supporter of justice—you would crush me, destroy me—but your son was the same as I. . . . When you condemn me, you condemn him. A judge's son can be just the same as another man's son.

Detectives hustle David away. Left alone with Judge Kingsbury, Richardson pleads with him for compassion, reminding him that both families possess unblemished reputations. As the play closes, Kingsbury orders Rolly's death to be recorded as a suicide.[33]

With the exception of a drunk who wandered in and, expecting a burlesque show, began complaining loudly and a middle-aged couple who left in a huff, the audience's reception was exuberant. Many lingered after the show to congratulate the cast. One journalist reported that *The Drag* became the talk of Bridgeport; he had happened upon a group of residents listening intently to an animated description of the play by one of the few who had secured a ticket. But critics overwhelmingly condemned *The Drag*, *Variety* blasting it as "an inexpressibly brutal and vulgar attempt to capitalize on a dirty matter for profit." When newspapermen approached James Sinnott, inquiring about the play's future in New York City, he smiled and responded, "No comment."[34]

While still in Bridgeport, the production ran into a minor setback. On February 2 at five in the morning, the police arrested Beverly West and Edward Elsner after a loud fight broke out in his hotel room. Authorities found the couple alone, and Elsner was half-dressed. Although the case was dismissed, Serge Trashatny immediately initiated divorce proceedings against Beverly. Elsner moved on with the *Drag* troupe to play out the week in Paterson, New Jersey. Next, they went on to Bayonne, New Jersey, where the first performance was a sellout. But just before the second began, as over five hundred people stood in line for tickets, local authorities announced that they were closing the play and banning it permanently from Bayonne.[35]

Back in New York, Jim Timony was fighting for a Broadway berth. Opposition to *The Drag* was growing, however, and the drive for censorship was gaining momentum. Guardians of good taste pushed for a stage censor, a political appointee with broad powers to safeguard Broadway from such obscene productions. Alarmed, Broadway executives gathered to discuss the crisis, placing most of the blame for the censorship threat on *The Drag*. Fearing that *The Drag* would result in the selection of an unfriendly censor and a rash of play closures, they agreed to block its New York premiere and demanded that Timony abandon the production. Timony declared that only when *The Captive* was pulled off the stage would he even consider canceling *The Drag*.

SEX may have been controversial, but *The Drag* was dangerous. One Broadway producer, William de Lignemare, proclaimed, "*The Drag*, I believe, is the worst possible play I have ever heard of contemplating an invasion of New York. That production . . . strikes at the decency of manhood." While in many ways West may have been following a popular trend, her treatment of male homosexuality was extremely menacing to society at large. The "pansy craze" had made gay entertainers the vogue in some circles, but their forums, in general, were speakeasies, drag balls, and underground clubs. Gay performers hardly enjoyed widespread acceptance; even the upscale Manhattan nightclubs where they performed catered to a select world-weary audience. On the other hand, West's purpose was radical; she intended to bring her depiction of male homosexuality and drag queens into New York City's great theater culture. The legitimate stage had struggled to gain respectability and to rise to the status of high art. *The Drag* threatened to bring all that hard work tumbling down.[36]

Although *The Drag* was the product of a straight woman's imagination, West's attempts at genuineness made it all too real. Some have pointed out that her shrill drag queens, mentally unbalanced spurned lovers, and deceitfully closeted homosexual men conveyed homophobic messages. Yet, as Chauncey notes, in *The Drag*, for the first time, gay men played gay men. Additionally, the Greenwich Villagers, through their ad-libs, became *The Drag*'s collaborative authors. In fact, West had recruited two drag community leaders, known as the Duchess and Mother Superior. The Duchess tutored young drag queens on in-group customs of language, dress, and deportment and, along with Mother Superior, provided support and advice to new members. Both were recognized activists, frequently writing the dailies to protest discrimination against gays. Clearly, their presence must have affected the content of *The Drag*.

Yet, like West's other plays, *The Drag* offered mixed messages. Reviewers criticized the labored debate over homosexuality between Dr. Richardson and Judge Kingsbury, insisting that it was a "phony" device used to give the production a thin veneer of respectability. While West may have used it to excuse her more bawdy intentions, it also complicated the piece, offering multiple perspectives. On the one side is Dr. Richardson, who voices an Ulrich-based position that West considered enlightened. On the other is the vehemently anti-gay Judge Kingsbury, whose opinions reflect the homophobia of society's moralists and lawmakers.[37]

If the debate seemed contrived, perhaps it reflected West's internal conflicts over both men and sexuality. When questioned later about her sexuality, she claimed that she would have "recoiled in horror" to discover homosexual leanings in herself. She insisted that she spurned friendships with lesbian women because she found them "rather morbid." (It was not true, for she befriended several lesbian and bisexual women.) "I am all woman," she insisted emphatically in 1970, but, in the same interview, she also argued that everyone manifested elements of masculinity and femininity. *The Drag* was equally ambiguous, pro-gay in some moments and homophobic in others. West was aware of the internal inconsistencies. When discussing *The Drag*, she explained, "I had presented no solution. . . . One could come, see, and make up one's own mind."[38]

Despite its ambiguities, *The Drag* furthered West's experimentation with signification. She discovered a compatible tradition in the comedic verbal play of drag performers. As an act of rebellion and to promote group solidarity, the gay community evolved complex and separate linguistic practices that relied intensely on double meanings. As a result, double entendre dominated drag humor, popularly referred to as "camp." But for homosexual men, camp went beyond outlandish humor and drag's exaggerated notions of femininity, providing commentary on oppression and gay experiences. Still, West defined camp as "the kind of comedy where they imitate me. . . . Camp is bein' funny and dishy and outrageous and sayin' clever things."[39] Although she always claimed ascendancy, she found comradeship in the camping of the drag queens. Their comedic stylings made a satisfying compliment to her signification on American society.

The drag queens' presence also supported West's challenges to rigid gender roles. *The Drag* explored an issue very close to Mae, that of identity. *The Drag* castigates those who deny their true identities and celebrates those who fully embrace them. Rolly emerges as a deplorable character similar to Clara Stanton of *SEX*; he is a dishonest and selfish thrill seeker, willing to sacrifice others to protect his reputation. Identity, or false identity, was a theme that dominated both *SEX* and *The Hussy*, and it continued in *The Drag*. It reflected a personal issue for West, one of her "secret doors." Ironically, she had built a career based on the assumption of false identities. But *The Drag*, like *SEX*, revealed her disgust with such masquerades and with a society that demanded them.

The Drag and *SEX* appear drastically different, but in many ways they are companion pieces. Margy's brazenness parallels that of *The Drag*'s crossdressers. Like Margy, the drag queens sing the blues and perform to jazz. Margy Lamont shares an even closer kinship with Clem, the Duchess, Winnie, and Hell's Kitchen Kate. Like *SEX*, *The Drag* signified on men and their power in society. West linked the oppression of women, especially the poor, with that of gay men, seeing both as victims of male domination.

To those in power in New York during the 1920s, *The Drag* proved far more alarming than *SEX*. *The Drag* interrogated social norms that directed straight men to be strong, competitive, and emotionless. Male heterosexual identity rested on men's distinctiveness from women. But *The Drag* rejected what producer de Lignemare described as "the decency of manhood." The drag queens completely undermined the "cult of masculinity" by their desire not to be distinctive from women but rather to be like them.

Just as threatening were West's allegations regarding a powerful male heterosexual institution, the New York City Police Department. Well known for brutality toward the gay community, for years the NYPD had raided gay hangouts, in particular Central Park, arresting gay men and cross-dressers and often subjecting them to brutal beatings. During the 1920s, authorities, aided by new state laws, stepped up persecution of homosexual men. In a sense, Manhattan became a site for battles between rigid notions of straight masculinity and a more flexible conception of gender and, specifically, maleness.

The Drag embroiled Mae West in this clash. The NYPD had been monitoring *The Drag*, and James Sinnott's appearance at its Bridgeport premiere confirmed that authorities were concerned. What Sinnott witnessed could not have made the NYPD happy. *The Drag*'s cross-dressers discuss police raids as if they were parties, effusing desire for men in uniform. Significantly, implying that the attraction went both ways, the Duchess declares, "Say, the cops, they like me. They all know me from Central Park." West took another shot by staging a fight between drag queens arrested at Rolly's party over who would be first into the paddy wagon. One exclaims that at a previous raid he/she "had a gay time." West certainly intimated that gays had infiltrated the justice system: Rolly promises to protect his gay friend using his father's connections. In defending *The Drag* in 1929, West asserted that "many of our famous lawyers, doctors, bankers, and judges are homo-sexualists."[40]

No doubt such allegations angered New York authorities and fired up their opposition to West's work. Even before *The Drag*'s Bridgeport premiere, the police began harassing her by threatening to shut down the ever popular *SEX*. Despite *Variety*'s warning that bringing *The Drag* to New York "would be a calamity, just at this time when, more than ever before, the subject of a Broadway play censor is under national agitation," West remained determined. On February 8, she invited city officials and several respected physicians to a private midnight performance of *The Drag* at Daly's. Contending that *The Drag* served educational purposes, she believed that an endorsement from the medical community would allow her to ease the production back into the city.[41]

The next evening, just as *SEX*'s performance was getting underway, James S. Bolan of the district attorney's office arrived at Daly's with ten officers. Across town, the same scene was being repeated at *The Captive* and *The Virgin Man*. As rumors of the raids spread, crowds lined up outside Daly's with newspaper reporters and photographers poised to catch the action. The audience filed out and joined the mob. Inside, at the play's end, Bolan announced that West, Timony, Morganstern, and seventeen of the cast and crew were under arrest. Mae retired to her dressing room, removed her makeup, changed her gown, and then, reemerging, announced that she was ready to go.

As officers led Mae West and her comrades out of Daly's, cheers went up from the throng, which now numbered over one thousand. Arriving at the night court, she was welcomed by another group of onlookers and reporters. Inside, a judge was prepared to quickly arraign West and her entourage. Sitting on the bench with the judge was Acting Mayor Joseph V. McKee, who had ordered the raids in the absence of the vacationing Mayor Walker. (The mayor was conveniently in Havana with other Tammany heavyweights.) McKee claimed he had only acted after receiving approval by phone from Walker, but West blamed the raid on the acting mayor anyway, accusing him of succumbing to pressure from John Sumner. However, McKee also had other motivations. An ally of Bronx political boss Edward Flynn, who had grand political aspirations, McKee often undermined the mayor when possible. Mae would always refer to McKee as "Holy Joe."[42]

Early in the morning of February 10, the court charged *SEX*'s defendants with staging an indecent performance, maintaining a public nuisance, and "corrupting the morals of youth and others." Timony represented the group and immediately bailed everyone out. As they departed, McKee warned that if they attempted another performance of *SEX*, the police would arrest them again. Jim Timony boasted that they not only intended to continue with *SEX* but were also "seriously considering hiring Madison Square Garden for *The Drag*."

The following morning, Timony obtained an injunction that prevented the authorities from interfering further with *SEX*. That night, publicity surrounding the arrest brought record crowds out to Daly's. The next day, Banton proclaimed to the media that nothing would stop him from prosecuting everyone arrested in the February 9 raids. Walker announced that he would "expect the police commissioner to investigate any show that he hears of if told it's objectionable, and . . . make arrests if it appears the show violates the law." Tammany was selling Mae West out. In an interview with the *New York Times* on the night of his arrest, Morganstern sputtered, "What is responsible for tonight's action? The answer is politics."[43]

As the leaders of the New York stage feared, the raids opened a Pandora's box. Calls for censorship and demands to clean up public amusements swept the nation. Movie censor Will Hays received more complaints regarding in-

decency in films. Around the country, lawmakers introduced censorship legislation. In New York, a Republican assemblyman proposed a bill mandating
a stage censor, exactly the type of legislation Al Smith dreaded. Back in the
city, theater managers, owners, and playwrights continued to meet, heart-
ened only slightly by Jimmy Walker's pronouncement that "a good loud blast
of a police whistle" was just as effective as censorship laws.[44]

Police action against *SEX* had been more in opposition to *The Drag* than to
Margy Lamont's lascivious adventures. While efforts to mothball *The Drag*
succeeded, *SEX* played to capacity crowds for several more weeks. However,
by the beginning of March, attendance died off and profits shrank. Desperate
to keep the production alive, the Morals Production Corporation ordered a
25 percent pay cut for everyone. Several players handed in their notices. Finally, on Saturday, March 19, after the evening's performance, Morganstern
announced that West was physically exhausted and was closing the play. Yet
he also emphasized her determination to fight the case to its end.

Only a few days later, the New York state senate passed the Wales Padlock Bill, which required the district attorney to prosecute everyone associated with an indecent production and to lock down for one year any theater
that hosted such shows. It was less severe than mandating a stage censor and
allowed the power over Broadway to remain with the district attorney, who
in New York City was the Tammany Hall loyalist Banton. The bill now sat
waiting on Al Smith's desk.[45]

Shortly afterward, on March 28, 1927, the defendants from *SEX* came to
trial. The courtroom was packed, and the streets outside were jammed with
fans and onlookers. To represent her and her co-defendants, West hired a
team of four lawyers—two connected with Owney Madden—headed by
Herman Rosenthal's former associate Harold Spielberg. The ensuing trial
came off almost like one of Mae's comedy-dramas. As "People's Exhibit A"
the prosecution, led by Deputy District Attorney James Wallace, entered
the play itself. Next, Wallace called a series of witnesses who he claimed
could verify the immoral nature of *SEX*. Backer Harry Cohen testified that
he complained about the play's lewdness; he was particularly offended, he
said, by its strong language and the star's "kootchie." He claimed West dismissed his concerns, insisting it would generate "box office." She maintained
that audiences demanded licentiousness, telling him, "I'll give it to them."[46]

The highlight of the prosecution's case rested on the testimony of
Sergeant Patrick Keneally, who had attended three performances of *SEX*,
taking voluminous notes. An Irish immigrant with a thick brogue, Keneally
repeated what prosecutors identified as the play's most salacious lines. He
also described what he considered to be *SEX*'s more "indecent" moments,
which included Margy's "prolonged" kisses and what he characterized as a

"muscle dance." Not surprisingly, much of the prosecution's testimony focused on West's shimmy, the officer testifying that "Miss West moved her navel up and down and from right to left." On cross-examination, defense attorney Norman P. S. Schloss compelled him to admit that he could not swear he saw her navel, but he still emphatically insisted that there "was something in her middle that moved from east to west." When Schloss challenged Keneally to demonstrate the dance, Wallace objected, sneering that "everyone in the police force is not a dancer."

Wallace repeatedly emphasized that it was not SEX's dialogue alone that made it objectionable. Rather, Mae West's movements and delivery made it so indecent. As West recalled, he contended, "Miss West's personality, looks, walk, mannerisms and gestures made the lines and situations suggestive."[47]

West's defense quickly ran into obstacles. The judge, George Donnellan, blocked their attempts to introduce testimony from SEX's play jury, so Schloss called the production's stage manager. He challenged Keneally's testimony, contending that contact between Margy and her suitors was "mere touches" and that heavy theatrical makeup prevented any lengthy kissing. Another witness, Harry S. Geiss, a nightwear manufacturer, testified that he had seen SEX twice and found nothing indecent about it at all. Under cross-examination, however, he admitted that he was a close friend of Morganstern's and had been recruited to give positive testimony. Winifred Noy, a screenwriter who had seen SEX, was more help, insisting that West's much debated dance was an "ordinary jazz shimmy" commonly performed in stage shows around the nation. During testimony, Schloss stridently interjected that SEX was a morality play that educated the public on the "horror and disgust of harlotry."[48]

After a week of testimony, the case came to a dramatic end. Wallace vigorously implored the jury to rid the stage of immoral productions. He decried SEX as a slumming tour. "We have cleaned up the red light district of New York. It's a pretty clean town," he stated. "But we've got red lights on the stage." For the defense, Harold Spielberg began with recitations from the Bible and Shakespeare, arguing that, taken out of context, these great works could also be considered obscene. He conceded that SEX was not a literary masterpiece; it contained dialogue that was "cheap," "tawdry," and "in bad taste." But he also insisted that SEX should not be judged by single lines. He pointed out that it had run for almost a year without any interference but that when "a sacrifice was needed . . . the police picked SEX." With that, the court was recessed and the jury began deliberations.[49]

After deliberating for several hours, the jury voted nine to three to acquit the defendants. Then, after receiving additional instructions from the judge, who ruled that if any portion of a play was obscene, the entire play must be considered obscene, they returned to the jury room. At that point, it started to look grim for West and her colleagues. Making the most of it, Timony re-treated to a corner of the courtroom and began praying the rosary. West's leading man, Barrie O'Neill, who had appeared chipper throughout the trial, looked crestfallen. West, the pillar of strength, reassured him. "Don't worry, Barrie," reporters overheard her say, "it'll come out all right."

It didn't. On April 5, the jury returned with a guilty verdict. Barrie O'Neill and another actor burst into tears. Mae's whispered words of consolation to her leading man did little to help; O'Neill shuddered and "bit his handkerchief for several minutes." Timony and Morganstern left silently dejected, refusing to speak to journalists. But West's spirit was energized. Lashing out at Wal-lace, she told reporters, "Anybody who needs a dirty play ought to call on him for suggestions." She declared her determination to fight the conviction all the way to the Supreme Court, contending that *SEX* was "a work of art." As she left the courtroom, friends and well-wishers who lined the corridor cheered her. "You've got to fight in this world," Battling Jack's daughter told a reporter. "You got to fight to get there and fight to stay there."[50]

As Mae West and her comrades awaited sentencing, members of the en-tertainment community, confident that *SEX*'s "sacrifice" had put to rest the censorship drive, did virtually nothing to lobby against the pending Wales Padlock legislation. To their surprise, Smith, feeling the pressure to act against the indecencies of the New York stage, fearing more strident censor-ship, and thinking of his presidential aspirations, signed it into law.

On April 19, the day of West's sentencing, a mob of fans, spectators, and reporters crammed into the courtroom. As she had each day throughout the trial, Mae appeared fashionably attired, looking relaxed. Judge Donnellan was less composed. He announced suspended sentences for all involved ex-cept West, Timony, and Morganstern. Denouncing *SEX* as "obscene, im-moral, and indecent," he contended that stiff penalties for the principal defendants would not only banish unseemly productions from the stage but also help rehabilitate the sullied reputation of "the most moral city in the universe," New York City. Acting against *SEX* protected the community from threats to its moral fiber, especially sheltering susceptible youth who could be permanently damaged by such licentiousness. He placed most of the blame on Mae West, who he claimed "seemed to go to extremes in order to make the play as obscene and immoral as possible." With that he fined her and Timony $500 each and sentenced them along with Morganstern to ten days in jail. *Variety*'s courtroom observer reported that Mae, "assum[ing] the hard-boiled manner she played in the play, did not wink an eyelid when the sentence was pronounced." As a police officer led her away she told re-porters, "I expect it will be the making of me."[51]

You Can Be Had

I've met your goody, goody kind before. Why don't you come up sometime? You needn't be afraid, I won't tell—Oh, you can be had!

—Mae West, *Diamond Lil*, 1928

While Mae West's underworld connections failed to keep her out of jail, they did ease her incarceration. After a night in the bleak Jefferson Market Women's Prison, she was transferred to Welfare Island's penitentiary, where the warden, Harry O. Schleth, was known for his generous treatment of "well-connected" prisoners. Although she was strip-searched and issued the standard prison uniform of coarse cotton stockings, cotton underwear, oversize slippers, and blue-checked dress, Schleth assigned her a private room in the administration building and "light housekeeping"—making beds, sweeping, and dusting books in the prison's tiny library. She later lunched with him in his home, a privilege accorded to celebrity prisoners. She protested her prison attire, and he arranged for her to purchase new stockings from the commissary. When reporters confronted Schleth about West's preferential treatment, he responded that he viewed her the same as other inmates but had to protect her from the island's "hardened offenders."

West remembered mingling liberally with the other female prisoners and claimed that as she passed cell blocks with a matron, prisoners applauded her, shouting, "Hello, Mae," and "Glad to see you!" She received an equally warm welcome from women in the venereal and narcotic wards, where the inmates had requested to meet her, but she recalled that at the infirmary there "were not happy thoughts or sights." This experience returned her to reality, reminding her of the destructiveness of poverty, discrimination, and sexual exploitation of women. During her incarceration, West came to know several female inmates fairly well. She even summoned her attorneys to represent one, a young mother awaiting trial for petty larceny. West supported the woman's children until their mother was freed.[1]

Imprisonment generated more publicity for Mae West as dailies chronicled each detail of her stay. The *New York Times* noted she was transported in a common paddy wagon with "five fellow prisoners, two of them negroes," which in the era's segregationist view affirmed her degraded state. Reporters also gave considerable attention to her rumored dissatisfaction with the prison's "fuzzy" underwear, one claiming she composed a poem dedicated to the warden about it. Her stay excited so much attention that *Liberty* magazine, nationally circulated, engaged West to write an article on her imprisonment.[2]

After she had served eight of her ten days, Warden Schleth released Mae for good behavior. On the day of her discharge, Tillie, Beverly, Bea Jackson, and a flock of reporters showed up to escort her home. As she departed Welfare Island, photographers snapped pictures of her bidding farewell to the prison's staff. One shot showed Schleth shaking Mae's hand; he told reporters that she was "a fine woman—a great character." He had reason to praise her, for she had donated her $1,000 advance from *Liberty* to build a better prison library.

West's article, "Ten Days and Five Hundred Dollars: The Experiences of a Broadway Star in Jail," offered an account both of her imprisonment and of her "experiencing" that "experience." Throughout, she subtly challenged society's assumptions about race, class, and gender. The piece began with the moment she was led from the courtroom and delivered into the hands of "Mrs. Campbell." An officer of the court, Campbell was an African-American woman, whom Mae praised as especially knowledgeable. Soon Mae found herself sharing the holding room with three white women and two black women. While she was sympathetic to all, her depiction of the black women was decidedly more positive. She described the whites as worn, scarred, and emaciated but claimed the African Americans exhibited resiliency. One possessed a great comedic sensibility, like Mae's, similar to Bert Williams's. Another, despite her addiction to drugs, was reportedly youthful and fit.

West's preoccupation with African-American female prisoners continued throughout the article. At the warden's residence, she encountered three black women and three white women assigned to housekeeping duties. Only one of the white women, an expert shoplifter, received any specific mention. In contrast, she reported details on all of the African-American women. She found the warden's cook "very likeable" with "wonderful flashing black eyes." The laundress was a recovering drug addict with a reserved demeanor. West's favorite was Lulu, a "stick-up" woman. "I liked Lulu very much," she wrote, "for it requires a lot of nerve to 'stick-up' a man."[3]

West's commentary on prison life revealed her ongoing identification with African Americans, in particular black women. She had only pity for white female inmates, with the exception of the crafty shoplifter. On the other hand, she celebrated the black women for qualities she respected, and projected, as integral parts of her own identity. These women were funny; they were beautiful. This acknowledgment of the beauty of African-American women was a radical attack on the dominant culture's obsession with WASPish femininity. Additionally, African-American women were bold and courageous as well as physically and emotionally strong. White women were weak, a trait she despised. Although Mae's article reaffirmed some elements of racism, ultimately she used it to invert racial hierarchy. Black women became superior to their white counterparts.

More overtly, West's article criticized society's treatment of women of all races, especially the poor, and faulted the criminal justice system. She stressed that most female criminal offenders had two common experiences: poverty and exploitation. She was adamant that prisons exacerbated rather than remedied their plight. Released from jail penniless, homeless, and jobless, these women had to "go back to the old life to keep body and soul together. . . . These girls are willing to work but how can they when the law is always ready to pounce upon them and send them back to the Workhouse?" A believer in hard work and independence, Mae advocated job training and work relief, contending that female inmates, most incarcerated for prostitution and drugs, only resorted to crime out of economic necessity. Upon departing Welfare Island, she announced her intention to help some of the prisoners find work once they were freed. Indeed, almost ten years later she was still providing assistance to Welfare Island acquaintances.[4]

After her release, Mae had to find something to top *SEX*. Her incarceration had proved inspirational. She claimed that on the way to Welfare Island she had been moved to compose an exposé on corruption—in beauty pageants. Roughed out in the summer of 1927, *The Wicked Age*, as she called it, began rehearsals in September. Again, to cut costs, she hired obscure players, among them her mentor Hal Clarendon and a crusty veteran of stock and vaudeville, Marjorie Main, who later became moviedom's famous Ma Kettle. West sought financing from familiar sources, including Timony and, of course, Owney Madden. She needed it, for over the next two months she drove the production deep into debt with long rehearsals and extensive rewrites.[5]

The Wicked Age's main character, Babe Carson of Bridgetown, New Jersey, was West's study of young, rebellious flapperdom. Babe enjoys roadhouses (especially "The Blue Goose," named for Tillie's establishment), bootleg liquor, and petting parties. Despite opposition from her stern uncle and guardian, Robert Carson, she enters and wins a local beauty pageant, which was supposed to be fixed for her rival. But victory is bittersweet. Her best friend, Gloria, is murdered and another pal, Willie, stands accused of the crime. Only Babe's intervention saves him from an angry lynch mob.

Babe's title as Bridgetown's beauty queen catapults her to fame and fortune, transforming her into a vain and cocaine-addicted star. She unleashes temper tantrums on everyone, except French count Gene De Monte, who woos her with "I kiss your hand right now Mademoiselle and later I kiss you some more." She replies, "Fifty million French men can't be wrong." But the count, who has promised her Atlantic City's Miss America crown, grows jealous of Babe's many male admirers. He attacks her and reveals he is Gloria's murderer. In the end, a hometown boy saves Babe and she accepts his marriage proposal.[6]

Opening night, November 4, did not go well. Just hours before curtain, Actors' Equity, responding to a complaint from West's leading man, demanded she expand his part, which she had cut after his dissatisfying tryout performances. Additionally, the scenery, delivered only the previous day, was too large to fit through the stage door and, left outside, had been soaked by an overnight rainstorm. Working feverishly, the crew sawed it in half and reassembled and repainted it onstage. When the curtain rose, almost an hour late, the house was full. But most of the major critics were absent, and those second-stringers in attendance panned The Wicked Age. One declared it "a vulgar presentation of practically nothing at all. It is so empty that it is almost a vacuum." The New York Times branded it "the low point of the theatrical season of 1927–28," and Variety decried West's latest as "a choice piece of limburger." Percy Hammond, who had applauded Margy Lamont, now pronounced West "the worst actress in the world," a remark that compelled him to fret for his safety for several weeks. Regardless, Variety predicted that The Wicked Age's salaciousness and West's naughty reputation would make it a success.[7]

Variety was wrong. The first week's take was disappointingly low. The next week, West missed Monday night's performance, claiming severe indigestion. Her absence coincided with her inability to pay the company's salaries. The next morning, with everyone paid, the play resumed, but attendance continued to plunge, and the show closed on November 21. Although West vowed to reopen with a new leading man and new backers, all attempts to resurrect the troubled production failed.

The Wicked Age's problems were far more critical than a difficult leading man and shaky finances. Its greatest weaknesses rested in the new role West had created for herself. With Margy Lamont, she had carved out a character with a reputation as a hard-boiled woman of the streets. Babe Carson hardly had Margy's panache. The beauty queen represented a safe woman, a character who reinforced female stereotypes. Babe lacked Margy's rage and self-awareness; taking her beauty seriously and becoming unwittingly complicit in her own exploitation, she succumbed to drink, drugs, her ego, and a conventional marriage. In part, *The Wicked Age* flopped because West stepped back from her evolving stage persona and well-crafted rebellious techniques. Babe lacked a double voice, and audiences were downright disappointed.

West was still attempting a social critique but with a new method, repositioning much of her rebelliousness within lengthy debates between the play's male characters. She funneled the rest through the bathing beauty contest, dismissed sarcastically by the *New York Times* as her "pressing sociological matter"; she used it to interrogate women's exploitation, censorship, and even corruption.[8]

In *The Wicked Age*, Bridgetown's leaders are crooked and money hungry. Willing to do anything to drive up land values, they conspire to force a beauty contest on their reluctant community (a common real estate gimmick in the 1920s). Babe's uncle, Robert Carson, protests that their scheme only degrades women, placing them "on exhibition like prize cattle." But he is no match for greedy land speculators, one contending, "The basis of any industry . . . for success today is based on the exploitation of the female form." Another links this to the theater's state: "Which plays get over and make money for their producers? Those that try to uplift the public and teach it bigger and better ways of living—don't make me laugh—those plays go over that exhibit the woman's body in some way or another." West literally and figuratively laid it bare: Society's wealth was built on the commodification of women. Those men in *The Wicked Age*'s audience who had come to catch an eyeful of the voluptuous West in a bathing suit left disappointed, however. The beauty pageant scene was staged behind the wall of a tent, with the play's characters watching through a hole in the canvas. "Three cheers for Babe," the invisible crowd chants inside.[9]

Despite its flaws, *The Wicked Age* did mark an important stage in the evolution of a black presence in West's work. In this play, her interpretation of blackness materialized as distinct characters—Babe's maid and some jazz musicians who, in an almost symbolic gesture, present her with a song they have composed for her. Significantly, there was a twoness to these characters. On one level, they reinforce Babe's whiteness; she derides them and clearly views herself as superior. (Her maid misuses language, a common racial stereotype.) But they equally undermine her whiteness. Babe sings and shimmies to jazz, plays a "mean blues" harmonica, and performs several numbers with the African-American band. She also shares a closeness with her maid, seeking her advice on love. These images represent West's earliest attempt at introducing and establishing a relationship with black characters in her plays. In particular, Babe's maid was a departure from traditional portrayals. Black maids onstage were almost always silent, one-dimensional symbols of class and white privilege. Babe's maid not only spoke but enjoyed a life outside of her service to the white woman.

While *The Wicked Age* proved disappointing, West remained resilient. In the fall of 1927, she moved into the Harding Hotel and began a search for a new vehicle, interviewing several writers and producers. One of them was another victim of John Sumner, Samuel Roth, an author and bookseller who had also been imprisoned on Welfare Island. In a meeting at the Harding, he pitched several possibilities for plays, including one based on the life of Nancy Hanks, Abraham Lincoln's mother. West "sweetly" rejected the idea, telling Roth, "Don't you see, for the public I am a bad woman, and a bad woman I will have to remain: They just see me bad and imagine me worse. I can never be bad enough to please my dear public."[10] As painful as it was, *The Wicked Age* had been a good lesson. Mae had hit on a successful formula with *SEX* and had learned to stick to her original style.

Shortly afterward, West discovered a more intriguing prospect in a gay nineties Bowery script written by a vaudevillian, Mark Linder. He presented it to her in the office of his brother, Jack Linder, a vaudeville talent agent. She arrived for the appointment bedecked in $20,000 in diamonds, refused to read the script, and, after listening to Mark recite it out loud, announced that she too had been working on a play set in the Bowery of the 1890s. However, she mused, she might rework Mark's piece. Jack Linder, an aspiring producer, eagerly agreed.

It is possible that both Mark Linder and Mae West simultaneously stumbled onto a Bowery concept, for it was hardly an innovative idea. By the midtwenties, the country was in the midst of a gay-nineties revival. Several turn-of-the-century productions enjoyed new runs on Broadway. Books about the period sold well. Images of the 1890s appeared throughout American culture. A growing nostalgia for this seemingly simpler time swept the nation. Certainly it was true for Tillie, who regarded the nineties with fondness; it was the era of Lillian Russell, when stylish women wore elaborate picture hats and gowns. She urged Mae to forge ahead with the Bowery project.

Mae also insisted that a serendipitous event propelled her along. One night the Harding's front-desk night manager, admiring Mae's diamonds, began to reminiscence about his younger days in the Bowery, where he had been a police officer. He told Mae of his sweetheart, famous throughout the neighborhood as Diamond Lil. Reportedly, she had stolen not only his heart but that of almost every man of the Bowery. Mae followed him up to his room, where they rummaged through old photographs, newspaper clippings, and keepsakes as he told Lil's story. A hardened woman, she valued only diamonds provided by smitten suitors. Without remorse, she betrayed her lovers, broke up marriages, and even murdered a woman. A local political boss supported her, and she lived in elegance above his beer hall. Yes, the night manager's story was true. There really was a Diamond Lil. Others remembered her well, for her shrewdness and cold charm as well as for the sparkling diamond inset in one of her front teeth.

West found herself drawn to this "Queen of the Bowery." She admired Lil's strength, power, and cunning. Mae went into seclusion, probably with Timony's coercion, and worked steadily for a week, producing a new play that she christened *Diamond Lil*. Although she disliked the Linders, Timony knew they had money and convinced her to accept Jack as her producer and split the script's royalties evenly with Mark. She also cast Mark in the play and hired his friend Robert Sterling as company manager. Mae pawned some of her jewels and, with additional funds provided by Timony and Madden, purchased half of the show's stock. The rest was divided among Texas and Tommy Guinan, Jack Linder, Robert Sterling, and three other investors, all close associates of the Linders.[11]

During rehearsals, West reshaped the story and script. Before long, she dominated the entire production, vetoing all of the Linders' suggestions and driving out the director. She oversaw each detail, including music and costuming. Seeking authenticity, she recruited players, many nonprofessionals, who could bring a genuine Bowery atmosphere to the show. One recalled, "She didn't want actors to play the part of bums. She hired real bums. All sorts of them, flat-nosed, punch drunk prizefighters, genuine homosexuals, real alcoholics." For inspiration for her leading man, West took a drive through the Bowery, where she spotted a handsome young Salvation Army officer standing outside of a mission. "He walked out this door, right to the gutter at the end of the sidewalk," she remembered. "I said 'Uhmmmm, ahhhh, ohhh' and I suddenly felt like drivin' round the block again to take another look." That was enough for Mae. Diamond Lil's leading man became Captain Cummings, a Bowery missionary, similar to the Salvation Army officer she vamped as Shifty Liz in *The Mimic World*.[12]

In early April 1928, West was ready to break in the play. To save money, Timony secured Teller's Shubert Theater in Brooklyn for Easter week. It was cheap and considered risky because so many New Yorkers abstained from theater during Holy Week. But Mae's hometown stuck by her; Brooklynites turned out in droves. *Variety* reported the take was exceptional.

Many anxious Manhattanites trekked to Brooklyn to view West's latest creation. Among them were writer Gilbert Seldes and the *New York Evening Tribune*'s popular columnist Robert Garland. Seldes found the show wanting, complaining that Mae, "unenergetic as ever, mov[ed] sullenly about the stage as if it pained her, forgetting her lines, dropping out of character and into it again as if it doesn't matter (and it doesn't)." Conversely, Garland praised *Diamond Lil*: "From now on, I'm willing—anxious, even—to pay money to enjoy her. From now on, I intend to applaud her from the top lines of my column and the front rows of theaters in which she happens, by the grace of God and the laxity of the Police Department, to be playing."[13]

For Manhattan, Timony secured the Royale Theater, a small venue seating just over a thousand people. Although the Royale had never hosted a hit, when *Diamond Lil* opened on April 9, the house was bursting at the seams. Glowing praise like Garland's combined with smart advertising underscoring *Diamond Lil*'s underworld tone brought New Yorkers out en masse. For the remainder of the theatrical season, they packed the Royale.

Diamond Lil sent audiences back to the Bowery of the 1890s. It was set in Suicide Hall, a saloon named for its popularity among women desperate to take their lives. Its owner, Bowery boss and Tammanyite Gus Jordon, also runs a white slave ring with two Brazilian accomplices, Rita Christina and her paramour, the handsome toreador Pablo Juarez. Although Jordon is unaware of it, a rival politician, Dan Flynn, is conspiring to unseat him by exposing his illegal activities. Jordon, awaiting the arrival of Diamond Lil, who is his lover and the saloon's star entertainer, joins Flynn, Rita Christina, and Juarez in the barroom. The doors part and, amid cheers from both inside and outside Suicide Hall, Lil enters. Juarez rushes to kiss her hand. "Pablo is my assistant," avers Rita. Lil asks, "Day or night work, Rita?"[14]

In the meantime, a suicidal waif, Sally, comes in. Gus recruits Lil, who is ignorant of his prostitution scheme, to help Sally and place her in Rita's hands. Lil quickly sizes up Sally. "You probably left the old folks on the farm flat for some city slicker who done you wrong," she surmises. She immediately senses that Sally is pregnant and unmarried. "How—how did you know?" Sally asks. "Why you poor fool," Lil responds, "it stands out all over you. Well, what of it? It's being done every day." She convinces Sally to go to Rio with Rita; she can have her baby there and return without anyone ever knowing. "Listen kid, don't be fool enough to throw your life away for any man; it flatters them too much," Lil advises. "Men are all alike, married or single. It's the same game—their game. I happen to be wise enough to play it their own way."

In the meantime, the Salvation Army's Captain Cummings wanders into the saloon. Although Lil is drawn to him, she scoffs at his soul-saving; she plans to enjoy herself and suffer her fate in hell. She beckons the straitlaced missionary to join her: "Say why don't you drop in and see me sometime? Home every evening you know." He declines but invites her to worship services. Lil responds, "Oh—you can be had."[15]

Later Lil lounges in her lavish but gaudy room, replete with copies of the era's most notorious tabloid, the *Police Gazette,* and an enormous gold swan-shaped bed. She has learned from a shoplifting friend that the Salvation Army, behind on its rent on the mission, is facing eviction. She arranges to purchase the mission building secretly and have the title transferred to Cummings.

Shortly afterward, Cummings comes up to her room. But he wants Sally; her family is searching for her. Lil remains silent and he pleads, "Somewhere inside of you there must be a heart." Capitulating, Lil reveals that Sally has left for Rio and then attempts to seduce the missionary. He fends her off, stating, "Diamonds always seem cold to me. They have no warmth, no soul." Lil responds boldly, "Maybe I ain't got no soul." He disagrees. "Yes you have, but you keep it hidden under a mask." As he departs, she demands a kiss, which she receives, to her disgust, on the forehead.[16]

But Lil finds that she has plenty of men to keep her busy. Flynn has his eye on her and warns her that Jordon is under surveillance by the Hawk, an undercover police detective whose identity is a mystery. Additionally, Chick Clark, a spurned lover, has escaped from prison and trails her to Suicide Hall. Learning she has taken up with Jordon, he attacks her but then, overcome by her allure, falls before her. She shuttles him out just as Jordon enters, accusing her of indiscretions with Juarez. She calms his fears; he leaves, and Juarez shows up. He presents her with a diamond pin and a fervid kiss. Rita interrupts them. "So the minute my back is turned I find you making love to another woman," she bellows. "Well what did you think he'd be doing?" replies Lil coolly. "A boy with a gift like that should be working at it."

Juarez slips out, and Rita confronts Lil, demanding the diamond brooch, originally a gift to *her* from the bullfighter. A struggle ensues and Lil accidentally stabs Rita. Lil throws the brooch at the dead woman, shouting, "Here take the damned thing. It has no soul anyway."[17]

A trusted admirer of Lil's disposes of Rita's body as Lil rushes to prepare for her appearance downstairs, where the saloon is packed with her fans. After several song-and-dance acts, Lil takes center stage in her "flaming red" gown for two numbers, "I Wonder Where My Easy Rider's Gone" and "Frankie and Johnny." As she concludes, Chick Clark returns. Lil dispatches Flynn to intercept him, but Clark shoots him dead. The police burst in, and leading the raid is Captain Cummings, who turns out to be the Hawk. Angered by his deception, Lil brands him "the lowest kind of thief" for "stealing the confidence of people." She admonishes him:

> You making me think I was a lost soul or something; me laying off my diamonds one by one, laying off my paint and powder, laying awake nights thinking I wasn't good enough for you—and you just a common ordinary cop! God, I'm mad.

But Cummings confesses that he loves her and intends to have her to himself. As the curtain descends, Diamond Lil murmurs, "I always knew you could be had!"[18]

As the curtain fell on opening night, the audience rose to its feet with cheers and applause. Afterward, celebrities and theater critics crowded backstage to meet the star, who shrewdly remained in costume and character as she received some of New York's greatest luminaries, including columnists Walter Winchell and Heywood Broun. Texas Guinan and her family joined Tillie, who was always on hand for Mae's opening nights. Later they all retired to Texas's club for a party in Mae's honor.

Diamond Lil's reviews were mixed. A few critics condemned the play as poorly written and badly acted. Richard Lockridge rated the cast "inadequate" but assured theatergoers that West was "by no means as bad an actress as a playwright." However, others recognized that West had a hit on her hands. The *New York Times*, never a big fan of her work, praised her play as "lurid and frequently rousing," noting that it contained a healthy dose of "O yes—sex. Miss West has a fine and direct way of approaching that subject that is almost Elizabethan. If you can stay in the theatre you are likely to enjoy it." Many praised Mae for her authentic re-creation of the rowdy Bowery of the 1890s. *Variety* observed that seeing *Diamond Lil* was "like going slumming thirty years ago." This time, Percy Hammond showered her with accolades. He declared *Diamond Lil* "one of the 'hits' of the waning season" and West a "Broadway institution." John Mason Brown, who panned the show, still concluded that "her Lil is the acme of the hard-boiled and the epitome of deliberation, but of its kind it is peerless, so vivid and extraordinary, in fact, that it much more than justifies a visit to the play."[19]

The public took note. The Royale was packed every night. Before the end of April, tickets were sold out for eight weeks in advance. Slumming parties again made West a stop on their late-night prowls. Broadway figures like David Belasco and Noel Coward showed up. Carl Van Vechten, a white writer immersed in the Harlem Renaissance, saw *Diamond Lil* three times.

Every night for two hours after the show West, still in character and costume, welcomed the rich and famous. (Thursday nights the stage bar even served Madden's real beer.) One writer described her chatting away, "dropping fairly good, though somewhat trite, epigrams peppered with bad grammar and made important because of her drawl and her insinuations." After meeting West, actress Constance Collier departed the theater squealing in delight, "She's so reee-uhl!"[20]

New York's celebrities and artists were not the only ones to fill the seats at the Royale. At the Brooklyn premiere, a working-class fan proudly testified to a reviewer that Mae West was "an actress and no fooling." Additionally, *Variety* noted the presence of underworld figures, well-known gunmen, and pickpockets in the audience. One spectator bet friends "six, two and even that if some guy drops dead during the show, he'll be buried without his watch."[21]

As box office receipts soared, however, dissension festered among the show's investors. West had become more demanding, and, in response, the Linders became more resistant. Some of the investors lobbied Jack Linder to replace her, but he refused. West owned the largest chunk of the show, and he acknowledged that without her, *Diamond Lil* would fold. But the brothers also alleged to the press that West was trying to muscle them out of the show.

Tensions continued to escalate and by midsummer exploded into a public war between Mae West and the Linder brothers. Early in July, West deleted Robert Sterling's theme song "Diamond Lil," insisting that his $100 per week royalties were excessive. The Linders retaliated by filing a complaint with Actors' Equity charging her with "insubordination." The brothers were angered not only by the actress's strong hold over the play but also by her domination, without their consent, of the show's business affairs. The divide deepened when Mark Linder asserted that *he* was *Diamond Lil*'s author. Despite Timony's warnings, Mae angrily confronted him in front of a *Variety* correspondent:

"Did you write one line of the dialog of *Diamond Lil?*" asked Mae.

"No, no dialog. I said you rewrote the play," Mark replied.

"Is there a situation in *Diamond Lil* that was in your play?" shouted Mae.

"Atmosphere and locale, atmosphere and locale," yelled back Mark, "it's all mine."

"Atmosphere and locale! You can't copyright atmosphere and locale. There are a number of Bowery sketches with that same atmosphere. I own the copyright to *Diamond Lil* and I wrote every line of it. There isn't even a name in *Diamond Lil* that was in your play except that of Chick Clark and I think I'll take that out. . . ," retorted Mae.

West eventually credited Mark Linder with "atmosphere and locale," but not until she had bought out some of the Guinans' shares, making herself *Diamond Lil's* principal stockholder. Under her total control, the show continued to rake in money.[22]

Several factors made *Diamond Lil* a hit. First, the production was well funded, liberated from the financial insecurities that had marked West's earliest endeavors. Second, *Diamond Lil's* script was distinctly sharper than her past attempts. The dialogue was trimmer, indicating that West had matured and found better collaborators. Most important, she had perfected both the Westian character and her performance style. Her years in melodrama, burlesque, vaudeville, and musical comedy had converged with her realization that she could "create an illusion" and "say almost anything, do almost anything on stage if I smiled and was properly ironic in delivering my dialogue." Mae had mastered the art of signification: Her basic messages remained unchanged, but she now had refined her ability to obscure them. One reviewer congratulated her for finally discovering she could be "vulgar without being brazen." *Diamond Lil* floated by with no protest from John Sumner.[23]

That summer West celebrated her thirty-fifth birthday. It had been a long road, but *Diamond Lil* represented the culmination of years of crafting her performance, a synthesis of a variety of cultural forms into one character. In a sense, *Lil* was a composite of almost all the trends present in the previous fifty years of American popular entertainment—a pastiche of a Bowery girl, Lillian Russell, George M. Cohan, Eva Tanguay, a drag queen, Bert Williams, a shimmy dancer, and a blues singer, to name a few. The mix that became *Lil* was puzzlingly revolutionary. Critics could not decide whether the play was old-fashioned melodrama or new realism.

In a sense, West had synthesized a female culture heroine. Lil was bigger than life. Mae padded her costume and added height with impossibly high-heeled shoes that made her unique shimmying strut, which emanated from "her head to her hips," even more pronounced. And Lil's old-fashioned corset was not really so old-fashioned. Mae reshaped it by trimming the top off a standard corset and wearing it upside down. The result exaggerated her bust and shoulders over her waist and hips, giving Lil a husky and powerful look. Her speech and accent augmented the effect. She had perfected a low, reverberant, nasal working-class drawl. "She talks in a quiet monotone," observed Percy Hammond, "never disturbing her humorous lips with the noises of elocution."[24]

Diamond Lil, who was of a bygone era, appeared less threatening and more lovable than her predecessor, the seemingly hardened Margy Lamont. Unlike Margy, Lil was never actually seen peddling sex, but *Diamond Lil* continued the saga of Margy Lamont, picking up the scarlet woman after she had left the streets to become a "legitimate entertainer." Lil could not have existed without Margy. Mae needed *SEX* to establish the subtext for her characterization. It provided a foundation that allowed spectators to decode hidden layers of Lil's background. Nowhere does the play directly identify Lil as a former prostitute. The closest Lil comes to the oldest profession is when she compares her fate to that of a biblical "scarlet woman." However, audiences and critics alike would always interpret Lil as a woman of the streets.[25]

Although some have seen Lil as a milder character than Margy, mediated for mainstream audiences, in many ways she was much "badder" than her prototype. Both Lil and Margy move from man to man, deriving capital, one way or another, from men. Although critics hailed Lil's heart of gold, she commits murder and sets Flynn up to die at the hands of Chick Clark. Lil's single good deed was to buy the Salvation Army a building. Margy's only real sin was that poverty forced her to sell her body; she never took a life and even saved Clara from both an overdose and loss of reputation.

Lil ingrained herself into the mythology of America. Because her emotional life and spiritual struggles were so visible, audiences found Lil more endearing than Margy Lamont. Margy goes no further than acknowledging her anger; she has no spiritual depth. Lil not only achieves self-awareness but evolves, facing questions that cut to the core of existence and agonizing over sin and salvation. *Diamond Lil* becomes a "near-miss" conversion tale, a story of a woman who has no faith but who gains it in the end—perhaps.

Diamond Lil provided a serious exploration of the split between the secular and the sacred. No doubt the subject was much on West's mind as she continued exploring spiritualism. In *Diamond Lil*, she placed the material and spiritual into direct conflict. At the onset, Lil represents, literally, the profane. She warns Cummings that she has "no conscience," that all attempts to convert her will fail. In the earliest drafts, she is even more unregenerate, mocking Cummings in front of Suicide Hall's patrons. She snatches his hat and wears it, shouting, "I ain't afraid of nothin', God, man, or the devil; and since you come in for this prayer meeting stuff, I'll give you a Hallelujah you won't forget." In the original, the Bowery belle expresses disdain for religion and those who preach it.[26]

In both versions, Cummings's presence touches off an internal debate for Diamond Lil. She finds him attractive but unattainable; they are too far separated by their differences. "He would only look at me out of curiosity," she tells a friend. She is especially disturbed by his condemnation of her diamonds, which she considers to be the "the most valuable thing a body can have." While she finds him a challenge and aspires to seduce him, she undergoes an honest crisis in her value system. In the end, Lil rejects materialism. Rita's death, which results from a fight over a diamond (not a man), reinforces the unhappiness and shallowness of the profane—the only thing Lil believed life had to offer.[27]

In this light, *Diamond Lil* establishes its kinship with the trickster tale. According to Henry Louis Gates Jr., a trickster, who is often disguised, transmits sacred intentions, mediating between the secular and spiritual realms. Lil's attempted seduction of Cummings forces him into a dialogue about religion. Lil casts in with the devil, but the captain dismisses this as just a masquerade. When Lil enters into anguished self-evaluation, however, she is drawn nearer to the sacred and ends up actually closer than even Cummings, who is only posing as a man of faith. Her outrage when she learns Cummings is the Hawk reintroduces West's preoccupation with the denial of identity while incorporating another twist. In the end, Lil's spirituality may be just another mask. Delighted that Cummings has succumbed to her charms, Lil proclaims with worldly confidence that he has been "had," that she has tricked him and will "have" him.

Lil also revisited West's interest in power and control. In many ways, it reflected her recent battles. Despite those who insist that Mae had little interest in politics, *Diamond Lil* was politically charged and had some basis in reality. Suicide Hall did exist. No doubt many recognized turn-of-the-century Bowery boss and Tammany man Big Tim Sullivan in the character of Gus Jordon. By setting the play in the past and using Jordon to represent Tammany corruption, West poked fun at the modern-day Democratic machine that had sold her out.[28]

Furthermore, it was probably no coincidence that Dan Flynn shared his surname with Tammany rival Ed Flynn, whose lackey, Acting Mayor "Holy Joe" McKee, had ordered Mae's arrest. Through Dan Flynn, she derided the Bronx's Democratic party machine. Lil's dislike for Dan Flynn is abundant; she expresses deep distrust of him. When Dan Flynn departs for "a date in the flaming twenties," an area where gays congregated during the 1890s, Lil questions his sexuality. And while Ed Flynn maintained a sterling family-man reputation, West used *Diamond Lil* for a homophobic attack on those who had prevented *The Drag* from playing New York City. Onstage, Flynn is shot dead and Lil walks away with the spoils. Rather than being the victim of manipulating male politicians, through Lil, West dominated the men who in real life had impeded her work.[29]

Probably the most widely acknowledged message in *Diamond Lil* focuses on gender relations. West's work had long explored such issues, and *Lil* was the next logical step in the development of her character and philosophy. She claimed that Lil had been developed with women in mind: She had tired of playing only to men. Motivated probably by both profit and conviction, she constructed a character with appeal to both women and men. West insisted that *Lil* emboldened women. She accomplished this by making Lil stronger but less embittered than Margy. In the earliest drafts of the play, Lil is a much harsher figure; she even tells Juarez, "I want to forget ALL men for a few hours." A disdain for matrimony was apparent; Cummings informs Lil, "I want you—as a prisoner—but not with bracelets [handcuffs]. My idea is a plain gold ring." By the final version, Lil's resistance to male authority remains submerged within the play's undercurrents. Lil signifies Margy's anger and bitterness. As a result, Lil is even more dangerous than her brazen prototype.[30]

Some have argued that Lil, who forcefully rejects male domination, offers an early feminist role model. Others have disagreed, contending that her focus on fulfillment through men is in line with traditional norms. Indeed, while Lil is strong, she does not truly fit a feminist notion of womanhood; she plays men's games by their rules. However, feminism was an ideology that West, a working-class woman of the early twentieth century, neither publicly accepted nor rejected. In her time, middle- and upper-class white women generally dominated the women's movement, one that would have certainly disapproved of Mae and her Diamond Lil for their lifestyles and wanton celebration of their sexuality.

Yet *Diamond Lil*, like the rest of West's work, did offer a critique of male privilege that may be better described as "womanish." A womanish consciousness, or womanism, derives from the African-American expression "you're acting womanish," used when a woman defied gender norms by acting and/or speaking boldly. West had more direct exposure to womanism than to middle-class white feminist ideology. It was easily accessible through the blues, for African-American female blues singers conveyed a powerful womanish presence, rejecting female domesticity and docility. These women rarely sang of marriage, family, home, and children. Instead, their songs focused on sexual pleasure, social protest, and gender relations. Rather than denying their sexuality according to Victorian middle-class norms, they celebrated it. West imbibed womanism from the blues, adopting her rebellious voice not from white progressive feminists but from African-American female blues artists.

During the saloon's musical revue, Lil performs two songs, both owing their origins to the African-American community. The first, "I Wonder Where My Easy Rider's Gone," was an old blues standard that employed the language of the racetrack to convey sexual desire through humorous double meanings. "To win a race, he knows just what to do," Lil sings, expressing the forbidden: overt female lust. West shattered even more norms with "Frankie and Johnny." Most critics and fans considered it to be the highlight of the production, one reviewer announcing that it "alone should help keep a line at the box office." But West's dazzling performance of "Frankie and Johnny" was more than just a showstopper; it was the play's essence, signifying its most important messages.[31]

"Frankie and Johnny" told the true story of a biracial, or "mulatto," St. Louis prostitute, Frankie Baker, who in 1899 shot and killed her unfaithful lover. In St. Louis's black community, a song based on Frankie's heartbreak gained popularity, becoming a bawdy-house favorite. Numerous variants evolved; in many versions, Frankie is executed for her crime. (In reality, Frankie was set free.) By the late teens, the song had become a nationwide hit.

"Frankie and Johnny" fell into the category of folk music, but many artists, like West, delivered it as a blues song. It certainly complemented other African-American female blues tunes that told tales of women's revenge against abusive lovers. In West's version, Frankie learns of her man's infidelity. She fetches a shotgun, finds Johnny at a "hop joint," and shoots him. As he dies, he confesses: "I was your man, and I done you wrong." Frankie is jailed and, knowing her fate is death, repeats the key refrain, "He was my man, and he done me wrong."[32]

Diamond Lil's plot echoed the underlying spirit and themes of "Frankie and Johnny" but inverted its storyline. Like Frankie, Lil rebels against male privilege. Refusing to bow to any man, she repeatedly dupes those around her into providing her with physical pleasure and diamonds. But, unlike Frankie, Lil is not victimized by a womanizer, for *she* does *him* wrong. Reversing the double standard, Lil resolves to have all the men she desires. She fights men with her lack of fidelity, acting as both Frankie and Johnny. And as the males in the audience gazed upon Lil's "blazing" beauty, she signified on their power, furnishing women with a heroic voice that triumphs through intelligence and wit. "I speak a language which all women can understand in the due course of time," Lil tells Sally. Lil preaches independence and self-assurance, standing as an icon of female self-determination.[33] At its core, *Diamond Lil* is a blues play that explores women "experiencing the experience," overturning women's oppression using the blues vernacular.

Lil's ties to Frankie signified not only her illicit past and defiant agenda but also her ethnic background. While Lil appeared to be white, her kinship to Frankie reveals that, as Mae imagined her, she was really biracial, both black and white. One reviewer recognized the complexities in Lil's racial identity, describing her as "a bit of *Lulu Belle*," Broadway's controversial mixed-race prostitute.[34] Of Lil's past, the playgoer knows only that she is from Chicago, the place where West discovered her black performance roots. By transforming Frankie into Lil and making her hometown Chicago, Mae was signifying that Lil, although she looked white, had African-American heritage. Mae West may not have been passing, but Lil sure was.

West extensively used linguistic games, her signification, to undermine white society and notions of racial fixity. Borrowing from the blues, Mae fashioned a prototype for what eventually became her most famous line, "Come up and see me sometime." Lil twice invites Cummings to her boudoir, commanding, "Why don't you drop in and see me sometime?" and "Why don't you come up sometime?" Mae had used a version of this previously; in *The Drag*, a drag queen invites Grayson to "Come up sometime and I'll bake you a pan of biscuits." Several trace West's character to the campy Bert Savoy's Margy, who continually effused, "You *must* come over." No doubt West, who appropriated material from everywhere, was influenced by Savoy, but his Margy was loud, outlandish, gossipy, and love starved. Lil was worldly, secure, a bit reserved, and certainly well loved. She did not even remotely fit Savoy's conception of Margy as "the type of woman that knows everything but knows nothing, that wants to make you believe how bad she is and never gives herself a chance to be bad." Lil really was "bad."[35]

West's soon-to-be-trademark line owed its origins more to the African-American community and the blues. Perry Bradford, the African-American songwriter, boasted that the song "He May Be Your Man but He Comes to See Me Sometimes," which he provided to West years before, was the inspiration for Lil's line. In "He May Be Your Man," a woman brags of her power and her conquests—that although she "lives six flights up," another woman's man "sure was willing to climb." Unlike Savoy's man-hungry invitation, Bradford's song more closely matched Diamond Lil's spirit and empowerment.[36]

Most certainly, the subtleties of Lil's message escaped most in the audience, but central to the tradition of signifying is its obfuscation of meaning from the dominant culture. As a result, *Diamond Lil* drew varied reactions and interpretations. One critic persisted in taking it seriously, reporting that the audience laughed inappropriately during Lil's seduction scenes and dismissing the play as a mawkish amateur melodrama. Others reveled in Lil's ribaldry and exploits. Some left the theater with feelings of disquietude. Critic Stark Young viewed *Diamond Lil* and Mae West as a riddle:

> Here is a stage figure who is not one of those players, however admirable, with whom we can feel at home, knowing that they are the same sort of human beings as we are, save for a desire to imitate or to exhibit themselves or both. You watch Miss West without this easy understanding and

also without falling asleep. Whatever ideas or conceptions she may or may not have, she is alive on the stage as nobody is in life, she shines, she astonishes—shocks, if you like—engages and puzzles you.

Young noted that West achieved her effect through contradiction—creating motion by being motionless, enacting desirability by being undesirable. He concluded that her appeal lay in the freedom it permitted spectators. "You may watch her performance and take it any way you like," he wrote. "The theater, you perceive, is a place for your pleasure."[37]

With *Diamond Lil*'s success came the first public profiles of Mae West the celebrity. In interviews, she closely wedded her star persona to Diamond Lil, later testifying, "Diamond Lil—I'm her and she's me and we're each other." This merger began backstage as she continued to entertain guests while fully costumed. Out of costume, for prying journalists, she confirmed suspicions that she was Diamond Lil with her weak attempts at separating herself from the character. In November 1928, the *New Yorker* ran one of the first biographical essays on Mae West. Written by Thyra Samter Winslow and entitled "Diamond Mae," it demonstrated how completely intertwined West's star image had become with that of Diamond Lil. In the interview, Mae claimed an unconvincingly distinguished pedigree; her father was a doctor, her sister was married to a Russian count, her brother was a car dealer, and she had grown up in her "rich grandmother's home in Greenpoint." In chronicling West's rise, Winslow detailed her years as a child performer, her successes in vaudeville, including a stint with a "strong act," and her appearances in, as Winslow put it, "Higher Things."

Winslow's skepticism dominated the article. She doubted West's biographical information, especially her claims that she was born in 1900, and noted the star's reluctance to really discuss her background. "Mae is secretive," Winslow observed. "Almost to the point of mystery, about her family, her past—a curious secretiveness." Regardless of West's claims to social standing, Winslow noted her lack of education and distinctive working-class accent and demeanor. "She does not even know the names of important theatrical figures unless she has come into direct contact with them," the writer contended. She quoted West's assessment of her popularity, "People want dirt in plays, so I give 'em dirt. See?"

As Young had detected conflicting polarities in West's portrayal of Diamond Lil, Winslow discerned them in her performance as a celebrity. The costumed West appeared gargantuan, but the star, in street clothes, was small and physically unassuming. Winslow found her perplexing, commenting that she was "self-centered, a bit greedy for the spotlight, optimistic, ea-

ger for success, frank, amusing, calm, cold and warmhearted in turn." Most
bewildering, Winslow discovered that West was "seemingly frank, with a
frankness that tells nothing." Mae had succeeded in creating a star persona
that was every bit as volatile as her stage presence. She had become a trickster both on and off the stage.[38]

With her newfound success, Mae began to challenge Timony. By now,
their relationship had become a "devoted friendship." She pursued a string of
affairs with other men that she tried to keep secret from him, but she insisted
that the ever vigilant Timony fought to control her by obligating her to new
projects. In the spring of 1928, with his encouragement, she began working
on another play, *The Pleasure Man*. She would direct it but cunningly left most
of the responsibility for the production to Timony. By summer, she was auditioning talent and recruiting vaudevillians—hoofers, double acts, acrobats,
comedians, singers, and female impersonators. Oddly, the first week of rehearsals focused solely on the first act, which West developed around the
cast's individual talents. One young actress complained, "When I signed I
thought I was going to be a gorgeous young ingenue, but Miss West could
only see me as a slavey. It's awful to think you have the personality of a slavey."
Despite grumbling from cast members, *Variety* described West as "serene."[39]

After the production completed Actors' Equity's probationary period,
which allowed players to cancel without salary forfeiture, West filled in the
rest of the script. Her delay was purely intentional. If anyone had learned of
her plans earlier, she would have found it impossible to recruit a cast. By late
August, Broadway groaned when rumors circulated that West was attempting to resurrect *The Drag*.

Only a few weeks later, on September 17, 1928, Mae's latest was ready
for tryouts in the Bronx and Queens. For two weeks, *The Pleasure Man* played
to sellout crowds. *Variety*'s Jack Conway raved, "Oh my dear, you must throw
on a shawl and run over to the Biltmore in two weeks to see Mae West's
Pleasure Man. . . . It's the queerest show you've ever seen. All the Queens are
in it." Conway, *Variety*'s maverick, branded it a surefire hit but recommended, "Go early, for some of the lines can't last."[40]

It was good advice, because *The Pleasure Man* blended *The Drag* with a sordid story of a heterosexual lothario. Rodney Terrill, the dashing heart-
breaker, is a vaudevillian who seduces and casts aside every woman he meets.
Especially crushed is the small-town girl Mary Ann. When she demands that
Terrill marry her, he knocks her cold and leaves her for dead. Bird of Paradise Dupont, leader of a drag troupe, comes to her rescue, telling onlookers, "I rushes down, seeing a sister in distress, and almost ruined my gown
stooping down and raising the poor dear's head."

While Mary Ann languishes close to death, the cast departs for a grand drag ball. But as the festivities conclude, Terrill's body is discovered. He has been murdered—the cause of death, a botched castration. In the end, Mary Ann's brother confesses to the crime, crying, "I did what I did because I wanted him to live in pain and in shame and to know that he could never again use people for his rotten pleasure."

The Pleasure Man repeated themes that had become common in West's work. As in *The Drag*, she established a kinship between women and openly gay men, both oppressed by the same patriarchal society. "She had an awful fall," Bird of Paradise reports, "like happens to all us poor girls." Even the name "Bird of Paradise" tied the production to *SEX* and its resistance to male domination. (However, "Dupont" seemed to be a reference to *The Ginger Box*'s dishonest producer.) *The Pleasure* Man was notable for the rage it expressed. Terrill is not only killed for using women, he is castrated. As *The Drag* had been a companion to *SEX*, *The Pleasure Man* functioned as *Diamond Lil*'s counterpart. The outrage that simmered beneath Lil's surface boiled over in *The Pleasure Man*.[41]

While *Diamond Lil* sailed by New York City's moral guardians, *The Pleasure Man* did not. When it premiered in Manhattan on October 1, 1928, to a sellout crowd, the authorities were ready. James Sinnott and members of the district attorney's staff sat in the audience. Outside, plainclothes policemen took up position, and at each stage door uniformed officers refused to allow anyone associated with the play to leave the building. As the play came to a close, more officers arrived and stationed themselves in front of the theater. Their presence drew a crowd that filled the streets, backing up traffic throughout the surrounding area. By midnight, over two thousand people had gathered around the theater.

When the curtain fell on *The Pleasure Man*'s final act, police took the stage and announced that everyone associated with the production was under arrest. Officers ordered the players to change into their street clothes. (When they approached Jim Timony, he avoided arrest by claiming he was just an innocent "tourist.") Slowly police escorted groups of prisoners through the mob. When the female impersonators were taken away—a few had refused to change their costumes—some in the crowd "booed and hissed" and spat on the sidewalk. Over at the Royale, just as she finished *Diamond Lil,* the police took West into custody. When she arrived at the station house, a police captain asked if she was responsible for *The Pleasure Man*. According to a reporter, she paused and "replied, 'Don't ya read ya noospapers?'" With the help of Actors' Equity, she immediately posted bail for herself as well as for the *Pleasure Man* troupe.[42]

Authorities hoped to move swiftly and prevent *The Pleasure Man* from playing again, but Mae's new attorney, Nathan Burkan, a powerful Tammany Hall leader and theatrical lawyer, applied for and immediately received a temporary injunction. The following day, tickets again sold out. Barred from interfering with the production, the police and representatives from the district attorney's office sat in the audience, several taking copious notes.

Although *The Pleasure Man* was a box office success, the reviews were bluntly negative. "A sickening excess of filth," declared the *Sun*. The *New York Times* labeled it "a coarse, vulgar and objectionable specimen," and the *New York Post* ranted that it was "smeared from the beginning to end with such filth as cannot possibly be described in print." West had touched on the taboo topics of homosexuality and castration. But her arrest, its accompanying publicity, and the reviewers' visceral condemnations simply brought more people out to see *The Pleasure Man*.[43]

By Wednesday, West's old nemesis, Assistant DA James Wallace, found a sympathetic judge to vacate Burkan's injunction. That afternoon, just as *The Pleasure Man*'s drag ball got under way, officers led by Patrick Keneally rushed down the aisles of the Biltmore, mounted the stage, and shouted that the entire company was under arrest. An Actors' Equity representative who protested was hustled out, and the curtain rang down with the crowd chanting, "Shame! Shame!" at the police. One crusading cast member, Jay Holly, pushed his way onto the stage and shouted:

"This play is going to be stopped before it has been brought to trial. . . . Do you think that is fair?"

"NO!" thundered the audience.

"The newspapers have tried to make it out a play of degeneracy. They have tried to cover the cast with filth and mire. Is that fair?"

"NO!" cried the audience.

The police yanked him off the stage as the crowd shouted, "Let him go, let him go." The authorities proceeded swiftly, taking the performers into custody before they could change their costumes. Officers told the press that this time they wanted all the female impersonators to face arraignment in full drag.[44]

The police made deliberate efforts to threaten and humiliate *The Pleasure Man*'s cast, in particular the drag queens. West's attempts to expedite their release were blocked by bureaucratic red tape. Additionally, authorities, rather than holding the men at precinct headquarters, remanded them to the Tombs, the city's roughest prison. With the NYPD's reputation for violent

treatment of gays, cast members in drag certainly had reason to fear. However, a visit from West reassured them, and *Variety* reported that as a group
they "began chanting felicitations to their colleagues and making merry."
Their demonstration became so disruptive that the guards threatened them
with additional charges. They quieted down, but it was clear that for gay cast
members, their incarceration carried a political meaning. Finally, after battling the courts into the late evening of the following day, West secured their
freedom.[45]

Mae West had always been an outsider, never fully accepted within
Broadway circles, and *The Pleasure Man* did little to enhance her reputation
among the show business elite. While industry leaders expressed sympathy
for the cast, calling for changes in the censorship law to protect actors and
actresses, some leveled hostile criticism at West. Still, many others heralded
the *Pleasure Man* controversy as an excellent opportunity to test and perhaps
force repeal of the Wales Padlock Law.

West's latest predicament was no surprise to Broadway insiders. The DA
had acted against several other productions in the weeks preceding the *Pleasure Man* raid, and rumors circulated just before its Manhattan debut that the
authorities planned to stop it. Although West had again been raided in the
mayor's absence, when he returned home Jimmy Walker pledged to see Mae
and her associates brought to trial immediately. "We shall not have disgusting
or revolting degenerate shows for exhibition in this city," he roared to reporters. But despite high-toned promises from City Hall, the case against
The Pleasure Man ground to a halt. DA Banton proceeded with a seemingly
deliberate sluggishness, and the powerful Burkan won a series of delays.
Over and over, the trial was postponed indefinitely. This time Tammany
came through.[46]

Although *The Pleasure Man* had been driven off the stage, Mae had a far
greater worry: Tillie had taken ill. Doctors had discovered a malignancy in
her left eye, and treatments had failed to prevent the cancer's spread. By the
fall of 1928, she had grown increasingly infirm. To cheer her, Mae brought
several of *The Pleasure Man*'s female impersonators out to Long Island for visits. One did her hair, and another made her extravagant hats, one of her
greatest passions. Additionally, Mae showered Tillie with gifts—gowns,
purses, and more hats. Beverly observed, "It kept both of their spirits up."[47]

Tillie continued to be involved, at some level, in her business endeavors.
The Harding was doing better than ever; its basement now housed Texas
Guinan's newest nightspot, the Intime Club, which drew Manhattan's most
notable citizens. However, in April 1929 the NYPD raided it for violating
nightclub curfew laws. The ailing Tillie found herself with Texas Guinan on

a list of co-defendants ordered to stand trial. Through her lawyer, she dis-avowed any connection to the Intime, publicly evicting it from the Harding. It was a sacrifice that had to be made to protect Tillie, her famous daughter, and the backer of both the Intime and the Harding, Owney Madden.[48]

Legal hassles and personal disappointments weighed heavily on Mae. Dur-ing the run of *Diamond Lil*, she began to experience an excruciating pain in her lower abdomen. Although it was usually brief and came infrequently, it was extremely debilitating. Doctors declared her in perfect health. West as-cribed the pain to indigestion and stress, but it is possible that she, like her Victorian predecessors, suffered the effects of daily wearing a boned and tightly laced corset.

In January 1929, Mae received good news. Burkan had convinced a judge to allow her to tour in *Diamond Lil*. Even more encouraging, the Shuberts had bought out the Linders and their associates. *Diamond Lil* went first to Pittsburgh, where it played to a full house on opening night. However, critics there panned it, and attendance fell the remainder of the week. The next stop, Chicago, was a different situation. The Shuberts had scheduled *Dia-mond Lil* to open their renovated Apollo Theater and had spent a handsome sum publicizing the production. On January 20, *Diamond Lil* made its Chicago debut to a packed theater, and for most of the next sixteen weeks it continued to draw large audiences.

While she was in Chicago, Mae's pain grew worse and more frequent, oc-casionally forcing showtime delays or longer intermissions. Another physical and some X-rays showed nothing unusual. However, the attacks grew so miserable and frequent that exploratory surgery was looming. That would have been a disaster for the profitable production, the star, and its investors. Hoping to keep Mae working, Timony arranged for treatments from Sri Deva Ram Sukul, a healer and president of the Yoga Institute of America. The Sri arrived at Mae's hotel room and, after questioning her, held her hands and prayed in Hindi. He then had her stand up and pressed his hands against her stomach for several minutes. He declared her cured and de-parted. From that moment on, Mae insisted, the pains disappeared.[49]

In early June, West hit the road again, first to Detroit. While theatergoers there gave her a hearty reception and each performance sold out, some sec-tors were less welcoming. The local drama critic declared that in *Diamond Lil* "frankness and nastiness seem to have reached their ultimate." Mayor John C. Lodge was determined to close the production; his campaign was aided when West's representatives distributed a mock-up of the *Police Gazette*, enti-tled the *Police Bulge,* that featured a scintillatingly clad West on its cover. It fell into the hands of a schoolgirl, and after two weeks of litigation, West moved on to Buffalo, New York. That city's police and newspapers received several letters demanding that the vulgar *Diamond Lil* be stopped. An enterprising official quickly discovered that the letters all bore false names and addresses. *Variety* conjectured that it was a publicity stunt perpetrated by West's own camp.[50]

While playing engagements in the Northeast, West collaborated with editor Robert Lewis Shayon to compose a defense of her work. The result was an article, "Sex in the Theatre," for Shayon's *Parade* magazine. "In my long colorful career, one thing stands out," she contended. "I have been misunderstood." She argued that her plays had "a deliberate plan and purpose" and insisted that her goals were "educational": She hoped to teach the public about moral wrongs, using the theater as a classroom. In the United States, she pointed out, discussions of sex were repressed, producing ignorance, confusion, and immorality. Young women, especially those in poverty, were forced into prostitution, men resorted to promiscuity, and homosexuals faced persecution. Her work was not a threat to society. Rather, American morality was endangered by "narrow-minded people who happen to have money or control" and who instigated campaigns to impede her attempts at uplift.[51]

"Presidents Ada L. Comstock of Radcliffe and Ella F. Pendleton of Wellesley may be surprised to learn that Mae West is an educator too," chortled one publication. For the most part, West's protestations that her work—her "art"—was serious and respectable were dismissed as nonsense. Many considered her simply a profit-driven purveyor of perversion. *Variety* snickered that Mae, the "creative genius," maintained a library that contained only "volume upon volume of treatises on white slavery and a hot collection of pictures of burlesque queens."[52]

In the fall of 1929, Mae West packed up *Diamond Lil* for a tour of the West. Although Tillie had grown thin and visibly weaker, Mae could not pass up this road trip. If successful, it promised even more profit. Additionally, she hoped to bring *Diamond Lil* to the silver screen. A Los Angeles stopover would draw the Hollywood crowd and perhaps score a movie contract.

That October, while *Diamond Lil* was on the road, the stock market crashed. West floated through relatively unscathed, although *Diamond Lil* turned only a modest profit. The Depression adversely affected attendance, and in many cities turnout was low. When she reached San Francisco just before Thanksgiving, *Lil* opened to a sellout crowd, but on subsequent nights, the audience steadily declined. Even more troubling, Mae learned that her mother's condition had worsened. Prevented from returning home by the tour, she dispatched New York's best doctors to Tillie's bedside and sent Timony to search for the Sri.

In late December, *Diamond Lil* moved on to its final stop, Los Angeles. Echoing the earlier description of Gaby Deslys almost word for word, West and *Diamond Lil* were billed as "the most talked of star and play in the world." On opening night, it drew a capacity crowd, but reviewers were disappointed, believing West had toned down to avoid police intervention. "I don't know that *Diamond Lil* has any particular purpose or value," mused the *Los Angeles Times*'s Edward Schallart while praising her performance as "sensational enough" and declaring the play an "ideal travesty." Interest in *Diamond Lil* quickly petered out; the audience shrank with each passing performance.[53]

West may have tempered *Diamond Lil* not only to appease authorities but also to court Hollywood studios, which operated under movie censor Will Hays. At first, her chances looked good. Junior Laemmle, son of the founder of Universal Studios, expressed interest in her work. But after Colonel Jason Joy, director of Hays's Studio Relations Department, attended the Los Angeles showing, he reported to his boss and the studio that *Diamond Lil*'s "vulgar dramatic situations and the highly censurable dialogue" made it thoroughly unsuitable for film. He also stridently objected to Laemmle's plan to hire West as a screenwriter. Shortly afterward, Will Hays issued an ultimatum that forever banned *Diamond Lil*, *SEX*, and *The Pleasure Man* from the screen.[54]

As *Diamond Lil*'s Los Angeles engagement came to a close, Mae received word that the cancer had spread to Tillie's liver and that she was dying. She hired a private train and on January 14, immediately after her last performance, departed with the company, racing to Brooklyn, where Tillie was being cared for in an apartment house. Mae arrived on January 17, finding her mother clinging to life. Timony's search for the Sri had failed, so she summoned more doctors. Always a trouper, she reopened *Diamond Lil* in Queens on January 20. Tillie deteriorated rapidly. On Sunday, January 26, at seven in the evening and with her devoted daughter nearby, Tillie West, the force that had nurtured an American folk icon, passed away.[55]

The Subject of the Dream

As a writer reading, I came to realize the obvious: The subject of the dream is the dreamer. The fabrication of an Africanist persona is reflexive; an extraordinary meditation on the self; a powerful exploration of the fears and desires that reside in the writerly conscious. It is an astonishing revelation of longing, of terror, of perplexity, of shame, of magnanimity. It requires hard work *not* to see this.

—Toni Morrison, *Playing in the Dark,* 1992

Tillie's passing devastated her older daughter. Mae claimed she cried out for her own life to end; it took her father and another man to subdue her. Then she, the woman who was evolving into a linguistic legend, plunged into silence. For three days, as Tillie's body lay at a local mortuary, Mae West was unable to speak. *Diamond Lil*'s Monday and Tuesday night performances were canceled. Finally, Wednesday, the West family, joined by Owney Madden, followed the funeral hearse to Cypress Hills Cemetery, where Tillie was laid to rest. She would have been proud of her daughter, for that night Mae returned to the theater and resumed *Diamond Lil*.

Finishing this run of *Diamond Lil* was painful. Each night after her performance, Mae broke down and cried in her dressing room. She was inconsolable: "I turned my face to the wall. Nothing mattered." Mae closed the Woodhaven house; she could not bear to see any of Tillie's photographs or possessions. And rather than seeking solace in spiritualism, she retreated from the mystical. Journalist Bernard Sobel, who had joined her at an earlier séance, dropped by for a visit and noted her total indifference toward the occult. Mae concluded that the afterlife was a lie; she maintained no hope of ever seeing her beloved mother again.[1]

To compound her woes, Burkan had exhausted his legal maneuvering and could no longer prevent the *Pleasure Man* matter from coming to trial. District Attorney Joab Banton, who had done little to pursue the case, had been ousted in favor of former state supreme court justice Thomas T. C. Crain. Assuming a get-tough attitude, Crain ordered *The Pleasure Man* to trial in early March 1930. Prosecutorial duties fell to James Wallace, who called for a "blue ribbon jury," men selected for their education and refined social standing. Burkan vigorously objected, contending that a "special panel" of jurors selected for their "privileged class" background would be "not democratic." "Why can't a jury of laborers and artisans decide this case rather than a jury of the intelligentsia?" Burkan demanded. "We are entitled to have this case tried by the kind of people who went to see the play, a regular panel of jurors is just as capable of trying the case as a special panel." The judge, Amedeo Bertini, overruled Burkan and ordered a call for one hundred citizens, chosen specifically for their elite backgrounds. The defense did successfully impanel three jurors who had seen *Diamond Lil*, another who patronized burlesque in his youth, and two more who conceded that they had not only seen but enjoyed performances by female impersonators.[2]

As the trial got underway, Wallace declared that he would "prove that it would take the most confirmed pervert to write such a play." Impeded by the defense's refusal to produce a script, he was forced to reconstruct *The Pleasure Man* from the arresting officers' testimony. First to the stand was Captain James J. Coy, who had led both *Pleasure Man* raids. Coy cited twelve examples of obscenity in the play, carefully replicating dialogue as well as "motions and gestures of the actors." Among these were objectionable songs like "I'm the Queen of the Bitches" (which the defense insisted was "I'm the Queen of the *Beaches*"), the performances by female impersonators dressed in women's "skanties," and a "suggestive" acrobatic routine in which one acrobat stuck his head into the pants of another.[3]

During cross-examination, it became obvious that at the *Pleasure Man* arraignment in the fall of 1928, over a year before, Coy's memory had been less clear. Under Burkan's pressure, Coy admitted he had earlier relied on sketchy notes that he had taken in a darkened section of the theater. In preparation for the trial, he had filled in gaps in his memory with the help of another arresting officer, Sergeant James T. Powers. Since the arraignment, the two officers had compiled and memorized a written synopsis of the play. Asked to produce it, the nattily attired officer testified that he had not brought it along, explaining, "I don't like to bulge myself out." One paper reported that Mae, still solemnly swathed in mourning black, studied Coy "with particular interest." It also declared that the captain was "not one to pose as a mental marvel."

Next came Sergeant Powers, whose assertions that the drag queens "talked in a high pitched voice" and walked "as I would say like a proud young woman" elicited a string of objections from Burkan. Passionately, Burkan argued that female impersonation had a long history in the theater and that there was no law against it. "That all depends on how it was done," Bertini replied. After more testimony, the prosecution concluded with its star witness, Sergeant Terence Harvey. In his particular duties, Harvey had become an expert on double meanings and street slang; he offered a translation of what the police contended were the vulgar implications of the dialogue, songs, and actions in *The Pleasure Man*.[4]

After two weeks of testimony, the prosecution rested and Burkan called his witnesses, most from the play's cast. First came Chuck Connors II. Well known to New Yorkers, he claimed to be the son of Chuck Connors I, the self-appointed mayor of Chinatown who guided wealthy slumming parties through both Chinatown and the Bowery during the 1890s. Connors II maintained that the police's account of *The Pleasure Man* was outright fabricated. He claimed that he and co-star Ed Hearn, his former vaudeville partner, simply recycled old gags that they had performed for years. Burkan then invited Connors to demonstrate how the controversial "She's the Queen of the Beaches" was delivered. With old-style dramatic flourish, Connors, "clasping his hands together, crooned the song." Even the somber Mae reacted, concealing "her laughter behind a black handkerchief."[5]

Other cast members also insisted that the prosecution had maliciously misrepresented the play. Most professed ignorance that their lines carried double meanings. The Pleasure Man himself, Alan Brooks, declared "astonishment" to learn in court—he insisted for the first time—that his character's death resulted from castration. Leo Howe, who played Bird of Paradise, was equally oblivious to the show's alleged indecencies. He insisted that his line "I get down on my knees" had nothing to do with gay sex, as claimed by expert witness Harvey, but rather that his character performed "mammy songs."

Of all the defense witnesses, none received more notice than Herman Lenzen and William Selig, who had played a vaudeville acrobatic team. For their testimony, they offered ten minutes of "handsprings, back flips, and balancing stunts." As they finished, Lenzen bounded gracefully onto "the railing of the jury box." Wallace objected, protesting that the act had been whitewashed.[6]

The outlandish trial drew hordes of onlookers and reporters to the courthouse daily. Throughout the proceedings, Mae had Jim Timony by her side.

Often her brother, John, and sister, Beverly, joined her. And while she no longer had Tillie's reassuring presence, she still had the supportive Texas Guinan, hired by the *New York American* to cover the hearing. When Guinan showed up, Mae exchanged hugs and kisses with her good friend. On April Fools' Day 1931, Burkan abruptly rested; a courtroom observer noted that Mae "flashed a tiny smile at the beaming Miss Guinan," who was seated at the press table.[7]

The next day, Judge Bertini instructed the jury to pay close attention to "innuendos and double meanings." "The greater danger lies in an appeal to the imagination," he warned, "and when the suggestion is immoral, the more that is left to the imagination, the more subtle and seductive the influence." But West's signifying style triumphed. After deliberating for ten hours, the jury announced a deadlock. They insisted that a verdict was impossible since no one could precisely determine what was said and, more important, how it was said. Shortly afterward, Crain dismissed all charges against the defendants. Many in the theater community celebrated this as the death of the Wales Padlock Law. Judge Bertini dismissed the Wales Act as ineffective; it was virtually impossible to accurately re-create portions of an allegedly obscene production in a courtroom. However, he warned Broadway to exercise more self-control or face stricter censorship.

Although some have celebrated Mae West as an advocate of free speech, at the time, most considered her purely a profiteer. Yet the trial of *The Pleasure Man* indicated she was a little of both. Judging from early box office returns, if the play had not been interrupted, West and her co-investors stood to make a considerable sum. However, the endeavor was also risky, and Mae knew it. Authorities had gone to extremes to keep *The Drag* out of Manhattan, and she was aware that police action against *The Pleasure Man* could result in a stiffer prison sentence if she were twice convicted. Furthermore, if she went to jail again, *Diamond Lil* would suffer irreversibly. When *The Pleasure Man* was raided, *Diamond Lil* was still making her very rich. Without West, it certainly would have closed. If profit was her only goal, *The Pleasure Man* was not a particularly smart move. But if she had principle in mind, it did function as an effective challenge to the Wales Act. Later, in her autobiography, she pronounced the case's dismissal as "vindication," contending that it liberated writers, producers, and actors from censorship. Certainly, Actors' Equity agreed, heralding the outcome with an article proclaiming, "*Pleasure Man* Ends Wales Act Reign of Terror."[8]

While West claimed victory—after all, a hung jury reflected disarray and confusion—she had no energy to celebrate. She still grieved deeply for her mother. Before long, Texas Guinan headed off to Chicago to open a new nightclub, and George Raft left for Hollywood with Madden, hoping to break into the movies with help from his dangerously influential pal. Jim Timony remained, the heir of Tillie's hard work, maintaining a watchful eye over his charge. But he was no substitute for Tillie, the driving force in Mae's life. He arranged for Mae to make a vaudeville comeback on the Fox Circuit, which warily offered her a contract but forbade her to shimmy or cooch. She quit after only a few appearances, her desire to perform exhausted. She later told interviewers that while the first years after her mother's death were the most difficult, she never fully recovered from the loss.

Mae had no energy for the stage, so for a time she turned to writing, something her mother had encouraged. It is interesting that for almost two entire years after Tillie's death, probably the most nightmarish period in Mae's life, the actress focused on constructions of race and ethnicity. Although she experimented with many images, a preoccupation with blackness eventually dominated her work. Through this she worked out—and eventually acted out—her "fears," "desires," "longing," "terror," "perplexity," "shame," and "magnanimity." It affirmed novelist Toni Morrison's assertion that when white Americans write about blackness, "the subject of the dream is the dreamer."[9]

At first, Mae West tinkered with a project she called *Frisco Kate*. (She had received inspiration for it while touring the old Barbary Coast with *Diamond Lil*.) A San Francisco prostitute, Kate, is shanghaied by Captain Bull Brackett, who believes she is the embodiment of his beloved white marble statue, the "Doll." He imprisons Frisco Kate in his cabin, but when he tries to force himself on her, he accidentally breaks his worshiped statue. Certain it is a bad omen, he leaves to attend to ship duties. But he soon returns, finding Kate in the arms of his first mate, Bob Stanton. He throws Stanton into the brig and then attacks Kate. She grabs a dagger and buries it in his back.

The crew, seafarers of various ethnicities and races, rush in and discover that Kate has killed the captain. She promises to give herself to every single one of them if they release Bob Stanton. They agree but insist, despite a brewing storm, on taking their liberties with her immediately. As they seize her, the ship is rocked by a clap of thunder. The portholes and the cabin door fly open. One of the sailors, a devoutly religious Scotsman named MacPherson, bursts in and rescues her. As the storm rages, the crew abandons ship. Freed from the brig, Stanton fashions a raft to carry himself, Kate, and McPherson to safety.

Frisco Kate was no masterpiece. Kate lacked Diamond Lil's forceful independence and calculated wit. Kate's attempts to manipulate men often fail, and it is a man, MacPherson, who is the story's hero, saving her from gang rape. Additionally, the play is filled with racist discourse, the crew's background signified not only by their distinctly ethnic surnames but through disparaging stereotypes. MacPherson is cheap, and Ling Foo, the ship's Chinese cook, is excessively neat and effeminate. One sailor, Spanish Joe, is obsessed with sex. The crew members exchange an endless stream of ethnic slurs. Even Frisco Kate participates, referring to one seaman as a "bohunk" and to Ling Foo as a "chink."[10]

By immersing her character in such an ethnically diverse crew and allowing her to participate in the linguistic racist degradation of "the other," West affirmed Frisco Kate's status as a white woman. The male characters constantly celebrate her white skin. Brackett gazes at her, remarking, "God, how white you are. White like marble. . . . White and pale like a sun-kissed beach." Kate's connection with Brackett's glistening white statue redoubles West's efforts to claim whiteness.[11]

However, despite its racist tone and Frisco Kate's overdetermined whiteness, the play does contain disjunctures that covertly challenge aspects of white racism. In addition to MacPherson, Ling Foo, and Spanish Joe, the crew also includes Irish, Scandinavian, German, British, and African-American members. And Frisco Kate not only knows them all but is willing to sleep with any of them regardless of race or ethnicity. Indeed, she has already shared intimacies with some, in particular the African-American crewman Jackson, who seems to know her very well.

On one hand, Kate's willingness to participate in miscegenation demonstrated, within the white mindset, her great depravity, by asserting the notion that only the most degenerate of white women crossed the color line. On the other, Kate's interracial relationships undermined white conventions that strictly separated the races. In the racist and patriarchal imagination, the bedroom of a white woman would be one of the most segregated places in the United States. Not so Kate's, for she accepted all lovers if they had something to offer in exchange. Essentially, Kate (and West) used these men of diverse backgrounds and race to rebel against both subjection as a woman and racist restrictions. Kate refused to allow the white man to imprison her and use her exclusively.

It is hard to assess West's complete intentions in *Frisco Kate*, for the play never reached the rehearsal stage, a critical step in her creative process. She sent a version of the script to the Shuberts, but like most of the theatrical community, they were feeling the Depression's pinch. By the summer of 1930, almost half of New York City's theaters had shut their doors, and the Shuberts were running deep in the red. They shelved the unproven *Frisco Kate*.[12]

In the meantime, West poured herself into another project—a novel. "The challenge of a new writing form would cloud my grief, I hoped," she wrote in her autobiography. She decided it would be about an interracial love affair between a white woman and a black man, a topic she had been pondering since the summer of 1929 while playing in *Diamond Lil*. Although she was closely tied to the African-American community, she claimed that Howard Merling, a white actor, director, and playwright, had been her catalyst. He had visited Mae in her dressing room just as Bea Jackson was on her way to see her aunt in Harlem. According to West, Jackson's presence compelled Merling to suggest a project "mixing the black and white theme together." Like Mae, he had cruised Harlem's nightspots, and he urged her to cash in on its vogue. Apparently, he later returned with a stack of indecipherable notes about Harlem. Intrigued, she gave him a small role in *Diamond Lil*'s road tour so he could "recite" his jottings to her.

During the winter of 1930, in her depths of sorrow, Mae returned to the Harlem project. Once she immersed herself in writing, she found that the story flowed. With the assistance of a Dictaphone and a secretary, she worked quickly: "I saw the story and wrote it as it came to me." She entitled it *Black and White*. Even before she finished the first draft, publishers were lining up for appointments. One of these was Lowell Brentano. A Harvard graduate, editor, and author, he headed one of the nation's most prestigious publishing houses. Brentano's list included George Bernard Shaw, Rudyard Kipling, and reprints of John Milton's poetry. Brentano, determined to add West to this distinguished list, secured a meeting with her in her hotel suite.[13]

By this point, Mae had a routine for receiving guests and interviewers—a ritual constructed to reinforce her image, a performance in itself. She selected specific attire, usually an expensive negligee. Before guests arrived, her staff arranged the room to create the proper impression, making sure her entrance was timed for the maximum impact. Mae West's home had now become a stage, designed to confirm her star persona.

Brentano got the full treatment. A "demure" Bea Jackson escorted him into an expansive living room almost devoid of furniture except for an enormous bed and a mirror emblazoned with the words "Mae West—SEX—Diamond Lil." Elevated above the rest of the room on a platform and surrounded by four small gilded chairs, the bed was adorned in lace and topped with an elaborate corniced canopy. "I was afraid to sit on the bed, afraid to sit on the chairs," Brentano anxiously reported. "So nervously I paced the room." After several suspenseful moments, West made her appearance, one hand on a hip and swaying past Brentano with a polite "How do you do?" After silently reclining on her bed, she murmured, "What can I do for you?" Then, sensing his nervousness, she "patted" the bed and cooed, "Now, Mr. Brentano, don't be bashful, come right over here and sit down."

Brentano convinced West to sign with his house, the contract specifying his right to make "limited" editorial changes. When he received the completed manuscript, he excised several passages he deemed too shocking. Although West protested the deletions, she eventually gave in. But she warned him, "Don't try to make me respectable, Mr. Brentano; my public expects me to be bad."[14]

Despite Brentano's revisions, his stodgy editorial board rejected not only the manuscript but its author as well. Members expressed disbelief that he even dared to consider anything written by Mae West. The board's vigorous opposition forced him to sell West's contract to another publisher, Macaulay. An eclectic house, it published popular writers including Dashiell Hammett, serious authors like John Dos Passos and William Carlos Williams, and the Harlem Renaissance novelist Wallace Thurman. Macaulay dispensed with West's title, *Black and White* and renamed the book *Babe Gordon*, after its central character.

The beautiful Babe Gordon is a white prostitute who operates in contemporary Harlem pursuing two things—sex and money. Her philosophy is straightforward: "If any man can have as many women as he wants, there is no reason why a woman should not do the same thing." As the novel opens, Babe works a Harlem prizefight, where she hopes to entice victorious boxers out of their winnings, and successfully attracts the middleweight championship contender, a white boxer named Bearcat Delaney. Impressed by his power, strength, and earning potential, she tricks him into believing that she is an innocent, sheltered from society's underside. Masking her true identity, she quits hustling to become a fashion model. Delaney, deeply in love, showers her with money, presents, and a surprise marriage proposal. Even though she disdains matrimony, Babe accepts, anticipating that as middleweight champion he will have a handsome income. However, under her influence, Delaney neglects his training and ultimately loses his shot at the title. Determined to support his wife, he buys a taxi, but Babe, deciding that he has exhausted his usefulness, leaves him.[15]

She returns to Harlem and supports her lavish tastes by peddling illegal drugs from the cosmetics counter of Baldwin's Five and Dime. She takes a new lover, Money Johnson, an African-American pimp, bootlegger, and gambling kingpin, described as an "Apollo" with "self-assurance," "hot burning eyes," and "magnetism." Together they make a stunningly beautiful pair, throwing extravagant parties in Johnson's elaborately furnished Strivers Row home and frequenting Harlem's nightspots.[16]

At one of these after-hours cabarets, the Harlem Breakfast Club, Wayne Baldwin, a Manhattan blue blood and owner of Baldwin's Five and Dime, spots Babe and Johnson. Repulsed but beguiled by the interracial couple, he is seized by an unquenchable desire for Babe. Later, after police imprison Johnson for his criminal activities, Baldwin discovers that Babe works in his store. Wanting her for his lover, he offers her an uptown apartment with a maid and a large monthly allowance. Babe eagerly accepts, leaving the Harlem nightlife behind for Baldwin's high-society circles.

When Johnson is released from prison, he immediately summons Babe to a Harlem apartment where he has resumed his illegal operations. She arrives intending to end their affair, but when his robe falls open, she "hesitated a moment; her eyes traveled over his symmetrical body. Finally her eyes met his . . . Babe thought: 'Oh, what the hell. A couple of hours won't hurt.' " A couple of hours dissolves quickly into a night of sensual pleasures.[17]

Both Baldwin and Delaney learn of Babe's tryst and race over to Johnson's hideout. Baldwin arrives first, bolts into the apartment, attacks the Harlem crime boss, and shoots him dead. At Babe's urging, the dime store mogul escapes out a back window. Next Delaney bursts in and discovers Babe sobbing in apparent despair over Money Johnson's lifeless body. She convinces him that Johnson assaulted her and, while defending herself, she killed him. She professes her love to her husband, and to protect her he volunteers to take the blame for the crime.

Delaney stands trial for Johnson's murder, defended by Baldwin's high-priced lawyer, who argues that the boxer acted in a just defense "of his most cherished possession, a good and beautiful wife." He praises Delaney for preserving what he calls "the best traditions of the white race, the honor of its womanhood," and declares Johnson's behavior an "affront to the whole white world." As a result, the all-white jury acquits Bearcat. Shortly afterward, Babe runs away with Baldwin to Paris. As the story closes, Baldwin puzzles over the interracial nature of Parisian society, which serves as a constant reminder of Babe with Johnson, a memory that is for Baldwin a "thrill" as well as an abhorrence.[18]

West's dizzying venture into race relations functioned as a very personal statement. Only a few months before she began the project, she told a journalist that she was planning to write her autobiography, and in many ways *Babe Gordon* became just that. The major players in her life appear in the novel's pages. Babe was clearly a composite of Mae's perceptions of herself and her mother. Bearcat, the clueless and hapless has-been boxer, the target of Babe's most deceptive acts, called up the image of Jack West. His manager, Charlie Yates, obsessed by profit and maintaining a suffocating grip on

Bearcat, drew from Timony and his dictatorial control over her life. "Charlie's a jailer, I tell ya," remarks another boxer. "Yer under lock and key alla time yer scrappin' for him. He don't let you have no life." Money Johnson offered a composite of her black and white lovers and male friends, including white racketeer Owney Madden and black nightclub proprietor Johnny Carey. In the novel, Mae revisited old stomping grounds; the Harlem Breakfast Club bore striking similarities to Carey's Nest Club, popular for its breakfast dance.[19]

In many ways, through *Babe Gordon* West enacted revenge against those who had abused, dominated, or impeded her. Although her attack on Timony through Charlie Yates, who only values Bearcat as a commodity, is particularly pointed, most of the novel's animus is directed at Battling Jack West. Babe lashes out against all male authority, but none of her lovers is more duped than Bearcat. He shows an occasional flare of temper, but overall he is helpless against her. Physically strong, he is emotionally and intellectually weak. Bearcat is so gullible that he actually believes Babe goes to church each Sunday.

West's deepest autobiographical confessions occurred through her manipulation of both the racial other and her racial self, expressing various psychic and societal tensions over white identity. Using African-American characters, West created a space where she probed the construction of her stage, real, and star identities. Black characters, like Money Johnson, permitted an exploration of power and self through a manipulation of the ideology of racism.

Throughout *Babe Gordon*, scenes, characterizations, and dialogue reinforce racism. West freely employs racist epithets and degrading black stereotypes. Almost all black characters adhere to traditional racist images; they are either ridiculously foolish or dangerously hypersexual. Their dialect is contrived to display childlike ignorance or savage drives. Furthermore, West animalizes her African-American characters. Money Johnson has "lynx eyes" and is described as a "lordly lion," a "magnificent animal," and even a "gorilla." West repeatedly refers to Harlem as a "jungle."[20]

Additionally, West portrays blacks as exotic. The men are physically strong and sensual; the women possess "soft brown eyes and fertile bodies filled with primitive fire." She depicts Harlem as consumed with carnality, calling it "a museum of occult sex" where the "old story of civilization's lusts was being retold." Her description of a Harlem cabaret's dance floor reinforces this: "The bodies of almost naked colored women, wriggling and squirming, moved about. . . . The music excited, irritated, inflamed the animal instincts. . . . A society group had its eyes riveted on a black hula dancer, weaving sensuously up and down near the corner of their table." From West's perspective, Harlem's nightlife was an "orgy."[21]

West also upholds racism using what seems to be an attack on miscegenation. With his high-society pedigree, Wayne Baldwin appears as the novel's most respectable character. He is wealthy, educated, and powerful, one of society's leaders. West prominently features his revulsion to interracial relations. Driven by what she describes as his "instinctive antagonism" when he first encounters Babe and Johnson, he "wanted to do something to shame the woman and put that burly dinge back in his place." Baldwin's outrage springs from his belief that Johnson had violated white society's most sacred taboo by "intruding into the forbidden circle of white caste." Ultimately, Johnson pays with his life for his affair with a white woman, and Bearcat Delaney is exonerated of murder because he has protected "the honor and virtue" of his white wife. Racist ideology dictated that Johnson pay for defying its codes and granted white men immunity from prosecution for crimes against black men. But it also permitted white women, like Babe Gordon, to hypocritically sacrifice their black lovers to protect their own reputations.[22]

Still, *Babe Gordon* offered a myriad of subtextual, intertextual, and signified meanings. Statements against interracial relations are countered by assertions supporting them that West then reverses and reverses again, her narrative imparting signfying's sensation of being in a "hall of mirrors." Among the many layers of her novel, a rebellion against racism also emerges, primarily through the signifying character, Babe Gordon.

For Babe Gordon, men are men; race is unimportant, and only money (or Money) matters. Living and working in Harlem, she establishes friendships with black residents and is integrated into the community's underclass. Of her nonsexual relationships, her closest is with her African-American maid, Pearl. A clear demarcation exists between the two, but they share a friendship, and Babe accepts Pearl's counsel. Babe has no relationships with white women— all portrayed, as in West's Welfare Island article, as repulsive and asexual— and vehemently despises them for their weaknesses and helplessness.

In one sense, West's novel is not about Babe Gordon's steamy romances but is a tale of African-American and European-American intermixing that challenged racial segregation. Beginning with the book's opening passages, in which Babe solicits in a racially integrated crowd during a boxing match, West presents a society that differs dramatically from the white dominant culture's fantasy of a strictly racially separated America. Rather, in West's story, African Americans and European Americans come together on a daily basis. Their lives constantly intersect—while shopping, in Harlem's nightclubs, at work, and even in the bedroom, where the races mix with consensual intimacy. "Harlem is the pool of sex, where all colors are blended, all bloods are mingled," she writes. When Baldwin first realizes that Babe has an African-American lover, he is shocked and infuriated, but the novel's narrative voice comments, "Why not? Other white women had them." Wayne Baldwin may represent the sentiments of many whites, but he is out of touch with reality.[23]

What motivates the two races to come together? According to Baldwin's friend Jack Rathburne, a patron of Harlem nightspots, curiosity and "sexual preference" drive interracial relationships. At this juncture West intersects her notions of race with her views on sex. From her standpoint, repressive Victorian attitudes about sex, which she labeled "Puritanism," severely damaged society. With *Babe Gordon*, she continued a call for sexual liberation, promoting her conviction that if Americans approached sex more honestly and viewed it as a positive, not negative, force, then society would be freed of many of its problems. Although her personal experiences were more complicated, she argued for the acceptance of sex as normal and healthy, not to mention fun.[24]

West uses interracial sex to signify, reflecting but revising racist stereotypes. She uncritically accepts the racist assertion that African Americans are more passionate and sensual than whites but rejects the assumption that these qualities are inferior. Her work contends that African Americans possess healthier attitudes toward sex and therefore are superior to whites. She brands Harlem as "a sensual oasis in the sterile desert of white civilization," insisting that white Americans are drawn to it because there "the lusts that ancient Rome and Athens could not purge from their proud and disciplined cultures—the flesh cry that has persisted through all time—found expression and release." In Harlem, European Americans engaged in interracial relationships and, under the influence of what West depicts as black culture, were emancipated from white society's constraints. She concludes, therefore, that miscegenation is natural and beneficial, not to mention satisfying. In later years, when discussing racial discrimination, West stated, "I've always been against repression of any kind." The linguistic parallels between her description of racism and classical Freudian terminology for sexual prudishness indicate that in her mind the two were linked.[25]

West chose to articulate her key messages through an elderly African-American woman, Old Liza. In a passage that serves no other purpose than to expose the reader to a discussion of miscegenation, Liza resolves the text's internal debate over racial intermixing. When one of Johnson's spurned black lovers, Big Ida, fumes about his relationship with "dat dirty white trash" Babe Gordon, Liza calms her. "Yes, ol' Liza sho' knows life," she states. "Had a heap o' experience." And she observes:

Ah seed duh white and duh black mixin' jus' lak now. Duh colored gals
and duh white men and duh white gals and duh colored men. Duh mixin'
o' duh black an' white been goin' on fo' ages an' ages. Yo' read 'bout dat
whay back in duh Bible. Yes, chile, it's right dere in duh Good Book.

Liza proclaims the inevitability of racial mixing: Interracial relations have
and will occur. By invoking the Bible, she legitimizes them, declaring them
unstoppable. In West's view, despite the dominant culture's attempt to prevent miscegenation, it had already begun. Its impact, she insisted, "will color
the mind and body of countless thousand generations to come." It is possible,
given her own ambiguous paternal heritage, that this signified a glimpse
through one of her "secret doors." Regardless, it was an ominous wake-up
call to racist Americans, alerting them that their efforts to claim and preserve racial purity were futile.[26]

Additionally, Bearcat Delaney's trial could be viewed as another statement against racism, a satire on the justice system. It signifies on the incom-
petence of and inequalities in the legal system, resulting from the corrupt
partnership between racism and Puritanical repressiveness. Money Johnson's murderer cannot be brought to justice in white courts. In a trial involving what essentially is a lynching of an African-American man, whites can
manipulate the proceedings into a not-guilty decision. While Johnson's
crimes are numerous, he is innocent of attacking Babe Gordon. However,
the wealthy Baldwin, who is never even implicated, is guilty of murdering a
man out of racist, jealous rage. Nonetheless, the accused, Bearcat Delaney,
goes free, not because of his innocence but as the result of his lawyer's appeal
to oppressive sexual and racial attitudes and to what West identifies as the
"unwritten law" that exonerates white males in crimes against the African-
American people.

As West's work veered between embracing and undermining white
racism, it continually functioned as a personal cathartic. She had crossed the
color line herself and, no doubt, grappled with what that meant in society's
broader context. *Babe Gordon* allowed her to explore her internal conflicts,
including her personal crisis over the issue of race. Much of West's identity
was grounded in a racist ideology that defined whiteness in juxtaposition to
the imagined inferior and negative qualities of African Americans. However,
as an actress since childhood, onstage West had internalized oppositional
and conflicting identities, eventually rejecting hegemonic societal forces by
embracing African-American culture. Despite its racist overtones, *Babe Gordon* reveals West's deep connection to the black community. Wayne Baldwin's snobbish sister, learning of Babe's background, exclaims with horror,
"Do you mean that her associations all her life have been with prizefighters

and negroes?" It reflected some of West's autobiographical reality, one of her "secret doors," and indicated that she believed that she shared a marginalized status similar to that of African Americans.[27]

West's identification with what she perceived as "blackness" went to the core of her real self, star image, and stage persona. While it is true, as several scholars have argued, that West used black characters to highlight her whiteness, their presence served also to destabilize her racial identity. She created racial confusion primarily by embracing primitivism, an ideology that exoticizes black people, contending they are more emotional, sexual, and instinctual than whites. Rather than denigrating primitivism, as racist thought did, she celebrated it as a superior way of life, invoking the image of the happy and fulfilled noble savage freed of Western restraints. West contended that a suppressed primitivist drive beats within everyone; Babe refuses to deny her primitive impulses. Although she is lured to Bearcat's physical roughness and Baldwin's "sophistication," neither man is any match for the supercharged, irresistible Money Johnson, a passionate and powerful lover. But Babe rescues these white men; her primitivism is infectious. Bearcat discovers "the compelling force of his inner passion," and the austere Wayne Baldwin is transformed "from the polished society man to a primitive male hungry and thirsty for her body."[28]

Although primitivism was ultimately another manifestation of racist ideology, West heralded it as preferable to what she discerned as European-American frigidity. She was not alone, for other writers of the era also experimented with primitivism. Many white authors, scholars, and playwrights, confronting Western society's problems and anxieties, were entranced by the so-called primitive, using it throughout their works. Historian Nathan Huggins contends that primitivism became so pervasive during the 1920s that even the Harlem Renaissance's African-American writers and artists subscribed to it, celebrating its superiority and liberating energy.

While West's work had long leaned toward primitivism, her affinity may have been augmented by a direct link to the Harlem Renaissance. It is likely that her manuscript passed through the hands of Wallace Thurman, who worked for Macaulay as a reader, editor, and ghostwriter and eventually became its editor in chief. Macaulay was small, and Thurman would have been the most logical editor for West's book. He was thoroughly familiar with all aspects of Harlem life; he lived there and wrote extensively about the community. A satirist and cunning critic, he borrowed from primitivism and, like West, hailed its emancipating effects. And he was familiar with Mae West: He had paid a passing tribute to her by having one of his African-American male characters in a novel run off with the "Diamond Lil of whore row."[29]

No matter how much control Thurman had over West's manuscript, *Babe Gordon* was an outgrowth of the Harlem Renaissance. West had immersed herself in Harlem's creative energy through her relationships with African-American musicians and performers as well as her presence on the nightclub scene. She even linked her novel to the movement, conceiving of it as a response to the work of white author Carl Van Vechten. Characterized by Huggins as the "midwife to the Harlem Renaissance," Van Vechten promoted many African-American writers, including James Weldon Johnson, Countee Cullen, and Langston Hughes. He often entertained Renaissance participants at mixed-race parties in his uptown apartment and was a familiar figure in Harlem, haunting its cabarets and acting as a tour guide for whites desiring a glimpse into the community and its nightlife.

In 1926, Van Vechten produced his most famous novel, *Nigger Heaven*, which explored the effects of racism on Harlem's population. Many credited, or blamed, it for attracting droves of white thrill seekers to Harlem. It received mixed reviews from the African-American community: Some applauded its portrayal of the black struggle; many condemned it as racist. Either way, Van Vechten's use of the pejorative title offended most African Americans. Yet it became a bestseller and, in the white public's eyes, established its author as an authority on Harlem. West criticized Van Vechten's work, which she insisted was directed only at "intellectuals" and "long haired village types." Contending her work was more important because she addressed the masses, West dismissed Van Vechten as "blond, chi-chi, and bored" and "a hunter of sinister sensations to be found in odd parts of New York." In her view—and many African Americans agreed—Van Vechten exploited Harlem for his own profit and amusement.[30]

West saw herself and her work in an entirely different category from Van Vechten. Class divisions separated these two authors. Although both were active in Harlem at the same time, they met only once, when Van Vechten showed up with other oglers backstage at *Diamond Lil*. For him, Mae West, like the Harlem he roved, was another "sinister sensation," and she knew it. It is not surprising that West decided to use *Babe Gordon* to dialogue with, or signify on, the acclaimed, upper-crust, white Harlem expert. Scholar Henry Louis Gates Jr. contends that texts signify on other texts, that books talk to other books, reflecting and revising previous works. Although West's plot differs significantly from Van Vechten's, she plays on and with his images and themes, mirroring some and altering others.

As a signifying text, West's work diverges from Van Vechten's, differing over the nature of primitivism. Van Vechten implies that it has biological underpinnings absent in European Americans. His light-skinned character, Mary

Love, blames her lack of passion on her predominantly European heredity. However, West maintains that primitivism is environmental, and from her perspective everyone has primitivist potential. Babe proves it. In fact, West not only rejects the essentialist argument but links it to class affiliation rather than racial differences. Wayne Baldwin is much further from his primitive drives than Babe's working-class prizefighter husband, aptly named Bearcat.

In contrast to Van Vechten, West never directly addresses the African-American struggle against racism. Van Vechten examines racism and its impact by placing his characters in situations where they encounter white racial hostility. While West acknowledges the presence of black rage in a prizefight scene where the black crowd roars with pride when an African-American boxer triumphs against his white opponent, she never directly links it to its white sources: segregation and bigotry.

Despite this shortcoming, West successfully signifies on Van Vechten's approach to race relations. While he praises the African-American underclass for "primitive virtues," underclass characters appear only briefly in his tale. Van Vechten concentrates on the African-American elite, basing his central characters on African-American writers, intellectuals, and artists he had befriended. It was their fight for equality that captivated him. In contrast, the African-American bourgeoisie is absent from West's work; she concentrates entirely on the black working-class underworld. Her work implies that Harlem's real story does not lie with the black or white elite; rather, it can be found in the underclass, where the races merge. In Van Vechten's novel, blacks and whites rarely mix. But in West's work they are in constant contact; it is the classes that are segregated. Although Van Vechten's characters intellectualize about various liberation strategies, they never pursue any effective action against racism, leaving the race problem in an abyss. West, however, offers a solution—miscegenation. Her vision of a racially fused population renders racism obsolete in the future; the underclass seizes the lead in reconstructing race relations and healing America's racial divisions.

In a sense, *Babe Gordon* (as well as Babe Gordon) was a product of interracial mixing, projecting West's conceptions of both whiteness and blackness. Mae herself appeared not only in Babe but also in the black characters in her book. She materializes within a shimmy dancer and a blues singer at the Harlem Breakfast Club. She is also reflected in an African-American female comedian who discloses West's fundamental secret—the power of illusion. "Just give me a pair of eyes what Ah can prestidigitate wit'," she brags, "an' Ah make any man think I got the rest." But she is also Money Johnson; no other character even approximates her self-professed extreme eroticism and passion. Her identification with him runs deep. West decorates Johnson's home as she later did her own—with mirrors that doubled and redoubled its resident's image. Babe, Mae, and Money Johnson play in the "hall of mirrors," befuddling spectators who see them everywhere but cannot discern which of their images is real. And despite the confusion created by the infinite reflections, only one truly exists—the trickster, Mae.[31]

The troubling ambiguities of West's novel exist because it is a trickster tale that uses racism to sabotage racism. The central character, Babe Gordon, is a trickster, a signifier who creates and revels in chaos. Babe revises all the rules that prescribe white women's conduct. By defying society's strictest codes, especially those that forbid miscegenation, Babe signifies not only on male authority but also on white Americans and their racism. As the trickster, she empowers herself by pitting man against man, man against woman, rich against poor, and white against black. But most important, West's narrative signifies on the reader. Filled with conflicting messages about race, *Babe Gordon* dupes its audience into believing that it reaffirms their attitudes, no matter what those are, while at the same time opposing their firmly held assumptions. Mae West's work had evolved to a dangerous stage; her unsettling vagaries now compelled her audience to decode whatever meaning they desired and/or feared.

So the question remains: Was Mae West promoting racism or fighting racism? The answer is yes—not only because as a signifier she had two voices but also because she, like many other Americans, was in turmoil over the subject of race. Racism continued to shape her worldview, but her close ties to the African-American community constantly challenged racist hegemony. *Babe Gordon* reveals that the race question, like issues of class and gender, remained unresolved in Mae West's mind. West was conscious that her ambivalence surfaced in her work, stating, "I wrote in innuendos, I write the way I feel. It just comes out that way."[32]

Babe Gordon was an important step for Mae West. She had reached a milestone in the development of her subversive presence. When she completed her novel, she claimed the experience had renewed her. Although she still mourned her mother, she was, she asserted, "alive and living again. I felt my old drive, my familiar urges." In the summer of 1930, Macaulay sent the book to press and began planning an elaborate promotional campaign.[33]

In the meantime, West had convinced the Shuberts to back a road tour of the controversial *SEX*. At the end of August, *SEX* departed for its first stop—Chicago. The Shuberts mounted a cheap but attention-getting publicity campaign with playbills cautioning theatergoers, "WARNING—if you cannot stand excitement—see your doctor before visiting Mae West in *SEX*." Chicago turned out in droves for most of *SEX*'s eleven-week engagement. A journalist noted the loyalty of female fans, who filled matinees to capacity almost until the end of the show's run. In early November, the show left to tour the Midwest for an uneventful eight weeks. According to *Variety*, first-night audiences were enormously large, but in each city attendance declined quickly.[34]

In November, while West was on the road, Macaulay issued *Babe Gordon* with press releases promising that it possessed "those qualities which made her plays *SEX* and *Diamond Lil* appeal to all ranges of the public." Readers snapped it up. Within a few weeks, the press issued a second run, and by spring it had already gone into a fourth printing. As a promotional gimmick, Macaulay sponsored a contest that allowed readers to give the book a new title. In March, after receiving over 4,000 suggestions, the publisher selected *The Constant Sinner* and issued the rest of the printings under that title. While book reviewers bypassed West's novel—it was pulp fiction—a few newspapers congratulated her for authenticity and "racy dialogue." By West's estimation *The Constant Sinner* was Macaulay's bestselling book in five seasons. Later, Brentano, pointing to the profits it raked in, confessed that he felt satisfactorily vindicated.[35]

In early January 1931, West returned home and, eyeing the success of her novel, decided *The Constant Sinner* could be transformed into a money-making play. By July, she had opened negotiations with the Shuberts. Wary of the play's controversial topic, they cloaked their dealings with the notorious Mae West behind a third party, their general manager, Joseph M. Gaites, who organized an independent production company called Constant Productions Incorporated. Soon, West secured a contract promising her generous royalties for the play, paying her 50 percent of the box office, and covering Bea Jackson's thirty-dollar-a-week salary. West secured the Royale and began searching for her cast.

While West recruited mostly inexperienced and inexpensive white cast members, she secured several highly acclaimed African-American performers for the play. She signed up Trixie Smith, one of the era's most popular blues singers, as Liza. For the Harlem nightclub scene, West enlisted Connie's Inn dancing sensation Paul Meers, who had performed with the celebrated Josephine Baker. From the successful all-black production *Green Pastures* came Harry Owens, Henry Matthews, Allen Cohen, and Florence Lee. As Clara, the revamped Big Ida, West selected Olive Burgoyne, a veteran of numerous Broadway productions who, along with several others in the cast, had appeared in *Show Boat*. Rudolph Toombs, who played a new character, a Harlem resident named Mister Gay, had won critical praise in vaudeville as a tap dancer. In all, West signed up fourteen African-American actors and actresses; most had impressive credentials, and several had broken down the barriers in the white entertainment world.[36]

But a major casting problem loomed: finding the appropriate actor to play Money Johnson. In West's mind, there was only one choice, the man known to African-American audiences as "the black Valentino," the handsome and debonair Lorenzo Tucker. He had a long list of credits and had starred in several movies for African-American filmmaker Oscar Micheaux. Additionally, he had appeared in small parts on Broadway, most recently in Wallace Thurman's play *Harlem*, and often served as master of ceremonies at several Harlem nightclubs. He was dashing and suave, a heartthrob in the African-American community. His audition convinced West he was perfect for the role.

Even though it was a black part, when the Shuberts and Jim Timony discovered that West intended to cast an African-American man as her lover, they stridently objected. The topic of interracial love could potentially ignite another court case and a general outcry from white New Yorkers. Intimacy between black men and white women had been a taboo subject in New York theater. In 1924, Eugene O'Neill's *All God's Chillun Got Wings* had induced an uproar with its depiction of an interracial marriage. West's conception of interracial relations was far bolder than O'Neill's portrayal of an unbalanced white woman and her anguished African-American husband. Babe was a perfectly sane white woman, and her affair with Money Johnson, a man she was not even married to, smouldered with passion.

According to Lorenzo Tucker, the Shuberts demanded that Money Johnson be portrayed by a white man in blackface. West capitulated and hired white actor and vaudevillian George Givot for the part, but only under the condition that Tucker replace Givot for the road tour. She retained Tucker, casting him as the Harlem Breakfast Club's headwaiter and as an extra who gives Babe an inviting glance. The Shuberts mandated that Givot remove his wig at the end of each performance to assure audiences that a white man, not a black man, was romancing Mae West onstage.

The Shuberts were not through with Tucker. Rumors abounded that Mae West was, in reality, having an affair with the charming actor. Although Tucker later denied they were involved, the two shared a close relationship. When the Shuberts attempted to fire him for drinking on the job, West interceded. She then called Tucker to her dressing room and warned him to stay strictly sober at the theater. Tucker claimed, "I kissed her and she said, 'Don't worry.'" The Shuberts hassled him for several more weeks, but West prevailed.[37]

At the end of August, *The Constant Sinner* headed to Atlantic City for a break-in performance. So many locals and out-of-towners clamored for tickets that the theater filled aisles with folding chairs and packed two rows of standees into the back. The press was favorable, declaring that *The Constant Sinner* was "underworld material from start to finish and Miss West handles her role with surety and a sufficiency of wise-cracks that provide laughter with frequency." The next week in New Brighton, critics were less kind. One decried the dialogue as "vile and foul," although he conceded that West achieved a unique genuineness: "She seems to have a sense of pace, of something like dramatic rhythm that makes her plays take on a semblance of something like life."[38]

On September 14, 1931, *The Constant Sinner* opened in Manhattan to a capacity crowd of firstnighters, Mae West fans, and thrill seekers. And, critics noted, all West had to do was make an entrance and the audience applauded exuberantly. While the plot deviated little from the novel, the play lacked the book's more serious tone, relying more heavily on Westian double entendres and witticisms. Cutting a deal with two small-time white hoodlums, Babe attests, "I never turn down anything but the bedcovers." When a detective warns Babe she is in a "hot spot," she retorts, "I can always handle hot spots." Later she complains, "I opened my door the other morning and five racketeers fell in. I wouldn't mind so much but two of them was dead." And of course, she issued her trademark invitation: "Come up sometime, boys," she beckons to a group of male admirers. "I'll tell your fortune." It sent her fans into convulsions of laughter. One journalist wrote, "They greet every suggestive line with giggles, gurgles, shrieks and other strange noises not usually heard in civilized society."[39]

Not surprisingly, some of the most celebrated scenes occurred in Babe's boudoir, adorned with paintings of famous women including Cleopatra, Madame Du Barry, and Catherine the Great. "She kept the biggest standing army in the world," Babe remarks, admiring the Russian empress. "She kept them standing outside her bedroom door." Her gallery also includes a portrait of Othello and Desdemona. When a guest calls Othello a "dinge," Babe vehemently objects. She insists, "He's not a dinge, he's a Moor." With West's trademark murmur, it sounded less like a nationality and more like the French word for love—*amour*.[40]

In many ways, West's play was even more rebellious than her novel. While Money Johnson's scenes are few, he is far more powerful and respected in the play. Onstage, Johnson has not only built a gambling and bootlegging empire but owns most of Harlem's nightclubs. Both blacks and whites respect his power and authority. Although some whites disparage him, they also clamor to do business with him, for Money and money transcend race. In his dealings, he is forceful and straightforward; he does not hesitate to speak his mind and give orders to whites. When two white gang-sters approach him to back a scheme, he forcefully warns them to keep Babe away from drug dealing: "Now git dat into yo' head an' keep it dere. Ah ain't tellin' you twice." The novel's Johnson is mute during his struggle for his life with Wayne Baldwin; in the play he verbally strikes out, calling the murder-ous blue blood a "Goddam Ofay." It was bold: "Ofay" was the black commu-nity's in-group term for a foe. But Johnson is not the only character who comments on white society. Mister Gay, when cornered by Charlie Yates about Babe's previous trysts with black men, protests, "Dis ain't Harlem—dis is downtown an' mixin' up wid white folks yo' gotta be a little careful." It reflected a very real situation, for African-American people could not trust whites and had to be cautious in all their dealings with white society. It also demonstrated that West at least recognized this reality.[41]

Although West's play perpetuated racism, for the time it proved ex-tremely controversial. On opening night, West received several ovations and curtain calls; still, most reviewers blasted *The Constant Sinner*. The *New York Herald Tribune* complained, "She is an atrocious playwright and appearing in her own dramas is her only failing as an actress." Several insisted that *The Constant Sinner* was dull, probably in hopes of undermining West's sensation-alized box office potential. Almost all denounced it for what one declared its "depravity and degradation." The *New York Journal* snorted that it moved from "the gutter to the sewer," and others decried it for its "filth." "Seldom, come to think of it," wrote the *New York Times* reviewer, "has fouler talk been heard on the Broadway stage."[42]

While *The Constant Sinner* committed some of the sins found in *SEX*, its dialogue was, in general, more frank. But it was not so much the language and salacious double entendres, which one critic claimed the audience heard even when they were clearly not there, that upset the reviewers. It was the theme of miscegenation that brought the harshest condemnation. It was such a forbidden subject that the conservative dailies declined to even mention it, one stiffly noting that "the idea is generally considered a shocking one, not generally bandied about on the stage." More outspoken reviewers virulently attacked the theme of racial intermixing. The *Standard Union* maintained that the Harlem Breakfast Club scenes featuring interracial couples "turn the stomach." Hearst's *American* declared the play a "tawdry slumming party" that focused on the "nauseous theme of miscegenation." It was more than just the "filth" that *SEX* had been; *The Constant Sinner*'s radical interracial love affair induced feelings of physical illness in these white reviewers.[43]

Some in the African-American community publicly acknowledged *The Constant Sinner*'s volatile message. While Harlem's local papers did not review it, the *New York Amsterdam News*, the community's most popular paper, did hail the appearances made by several of the African-American players in Mae's production. Floyd Snelson of the *Pittsburgh Courier*, one of the nation's leading African-American dailies, pronounced *The Constant Sinner* "the cleverest piece of artistry to be expected from a woman of the Caucasian race." He praised West as a "constant admirer of the negro" and for providing roles for so many African-American performers. In his opinion, the play explored the most important problems facing American society: race relations and inequality. He pronounced the Harlem Breakfast Club scene, which had offended many white reviewers, to be the play's high point. He urged the *Courier*'s readers to patronize *The Constant Sinner*: "I glory in the spunk of the 'world's greatest lioness of human hearts'; that she has demonstrated her mettle to govern." In his later years, Lorenzo Tucker agreed that by upsetting racial conventions West had made an extremely rebellious statement. He praised her support of African Americans, insisting that "we have to look at folks like her with raised eyes and give them credit for their contributions."[44]

Inevitably, West's exploration of interracial mixing reinvigorated the city's self-appointed custodians of morality. Ever vigilant, John Sumner had been monitoring her activities. In November 1930, when *Babe Gordon* first rolled off the presses, he received several complaints about the book and immediately secured his own copy. When the play version made its way onto the stage, he diligently attended a performance; he reported that it was "disgusting throughout." The newly formed Conference Board of Theater, Broadway's self-regulatory body, attempted to respond to the mounting concerns over *The Constant Sinner*. Playwrights' representatives charged censorship and walked out, bringing the board to collapse. At Sumner's urging, authorities dispatched officers to the Royale. After they viewed a showing, they mandated deletion of only two lines. Probably fearing that police action would only result in publicity for *The Constant Sinner*, the NYPD informed Sumner that they believed a raid would be unwise.[45]

For a time, the production rode on West's enormous and growing popularity. She had finally achieved star status. New York theatergoers culled lines from her performances and made them a part of the city's speech. According to newspaper reports, mobs gathered whenever she appeared in public. Her bodyguards fought off admirers, and even a few detractors determined to reform the lady of the stage's streets.

West had been transformed into not only a celebrity but also a symbol. Since the controversy over *SEX*, several New York performers had mimicked her in their acts. She had also become a favorite among both white and black female impersonators; many a Mae West took first place at the city's drag balls. African-American film actress and performer Nina Mae McKinney incorporated a Mae West characterization into her act, and black audiences loved it. McKinney added another layer of subversion to Westian image. In her routine, McKinney became a black woman enacting a white woman enacting a black woman enacting a white woman. It was a house of mirrors, a parody of a parody, and it made the mythical Mae West even more subversive.

As West's popularity increased, fans demanded more information about the star. In classic fashion, she obliged with a trail of confusing and contradictory statements. To one tabloid reporter, she insisted that the characters in *The Constant Sinner* were real; she confided that one often visited her in her dressing room. Although she refused to confirm or deny her links to Babe Gordon's lifestyle, she did admit, "I have to feel what I portray on stage." Conversely, in the *New York Times*, she lashed out at those who insisted that her work drew on her own experiences. She adamantly denied that she had any firsthand knowledge of the world of Babe Gordon. "I do not drink, I do not smoke," West insisted. "I have my books, my writing, my friends—that is my private life." In a short speech at each curtain call, she renounced any relationship to Babe, contending that she preferred to stay home rather than partake of New York's wild nightlife. The *New York Times* quipped, "She did not, however, confirm reports that she would act next year for the Children's Theater in *Snow White and the Seven Dwarfs*."[46]

West's contradictory statements had become characteristic of her star persona, forcing both her fans and her adversaries into endless circles of speculation on her alleged wickedness. They also served to generate publicity, and by October, the production needed a boost. Despite a strong early showing, audiences soon dwindled. Several factors combined to hurt the show. Foremost was the deepening Depression; in 1931 the unemployment rate had reached almost 16 percent. Fewer people could afford to attend the theater, and even though it was early in the season, several Broadway shows had already closed. Theaters, not only in New York but also in other parts of the country, went dark. A number of show business impresarios, including the Great Ziegfeld and Arthur Hammerstein, lost their fortunes. The Shuberts ended up in receivership, their stock practically worthless. Babe's advice to a luckless hustler, Cokey Jenny, came in handy: "It's the depression, why don't you cut your prices?" Soon, most of Broadway did just that in hopes of saving shows that had survived into late fall.[47]

The Constant Sinner was also affected by a shift in American attitudes. The mood of the city, as well as of the nation, had changed. For many, the party of the 1920s was over. The economic crisis hit Manhattan especially hard.

Jobless men stood on corners selling apples. Streets were filled with home-less and desperate people begging for food or jobs. The after-hours spirit was dying, and many nightclubs closed their doors. For many, slumming was no longer a taste of the unknown; poverty threatened to become a reality. West could no longer count on the limousine crowd's unlimited support.

Additionally, many New Yorkers, no matter how jaded and worldly, prob-ably shared the critics' objection to the show's interracial nature. Miscegena-tion was a touchy subject bound to make even some of West's diehard fans, most of them white, uncomfortable and perhaps even angry. And while *The Constant Sinner*'s message was obscured, both challenging and conveying racist notions, any rejection of rigid racial norms was considered unaccept-able by many whites. *The Constant Sinner* never really caught fire, and on No-vember 4, after only sixty-four performances, its New York run ended.

But West was not finished. She secured a one-week stint at Washington, D.C.'s, Belasco Theater. As promised, Lorenzo Tucker assumed the role of Money Johnson. To head off advance opposition, she used Givot's name in her publicity. As residents of the nation's capital eagerly prepared to wel-come Mae West and her show, the *Pittsburgh Courier*'s Floyd Snelson wrote, "Hope that Herbert Hoover gets a chance to see the devilish blonde."[48]

On November 23, when *The Constant Sinner* made its Washington debut, the Belasco was packed with "one of the largest first night audiences of the sea-son." This time the miscegenation that existed only as fiction in the pages of *Babe Gordon* became a reality when Mae West and Lorenzo Tucker embraced and kissed onstage. Through theater, West had actualized contact between the races forbidden in society. Unanimously, reviewers gave the production an icy reception, condemning its salaciousness, with one commenting that "the inter-mixture of race in this play is not a pleasant quality." But they also noted that the audience roared with laughter, offering up "catcalls" and "lusty grunts." Tickets for the rest of the week had been almost sold out.[49]

The next day, the theater's management, sensing problems, ordered West to cut some of the play. The situation looked grim as complaints about the show poured into the district attorney's office. That evening, Assistant Dis-trict Attorney Michael F. Keogh and three police officers attended the per-formance. Reportedly, Keogh was so outraged at the play's "lewd and lascivious" nature and what he claimed was an "objectionable intermingling of race" that he considered closing the show even before its final curtain call. Fearing such action would incite a disturbance among appreciative fans, he simply confiscated the script and departed.

The next morning, Keogh's boss, District Attorney Leo A. Rover, or-dered the play closed and threatened the theater's manager, the cast, and the crew with prosecution if they attempted another performance. While Rover's official report skirted the interracial issue, reporters, both black and white, believed it was the impetus behind his actions. Some Washingtonians were not only opposed to seeing racial intermixing onstage but also horrified that such fraternizing occurred backstage among the play's cast. Integration was intolerable to most southerners—and Washington, D.C., remained, after all, a southern city. Authorities there would not permit such a rebellious defiance of strictly defined racial segregation. One local newspaper columnist denounced the city's race-conscious moralists as hypocrites, charging that, when securely distant from their Washingtonian homes, they "make up the slumming parties that seek out precisely what Miss West in her latest play accommodatingly brings to their very doorsteps."[50]

While enjoying the races at a track just outside the city, West received word that the DA had shut down her play. She also learned more disturbing news: A lynch mob was searching for Tucker. Her defiance of the color barrier had occurred during a period of heightened racial violence. In the preceding year, the number of lynchings had reached a thirty-year high; the area around Washington had been the site of several violent murders of African-American men. Additionally, newspapers chronicled the trial of the Scottsboro Nine, a group of African-American teenagers falsely accused of raping two white women. West called the cast together, paid them for two shows, and arranged for them to return immediately to New York. She took Tucker aside, warned him about the threats against his life, and gave him an extra two weeks' salary. Tucker checked into a black Washington hotel under an assumed name and stayed there until he could safely get out of town.[51]

The Constant Sinner had been a disappointment. Its New York run was mediocre, and the short tour had been a dangerous fiasco. While still trying to obtain out-of-town engagements for the play, West signed a contract with Macaulay to turn Diamond Lil into a novel. But in early June, just as she had secured a Chicago booking for The Constant Sinner, West was happily sidetracked by a call from Paramount Studios. George Raft, starring as a young gangster in Scarface, had become Tinsel Town's latest matinee idol. He was busily preparing for his next film, Night After Night, and had convinced the studio that Mae West was a perfect fit for one of the film's roles. But the question remained: Could Paramount afford Diamond Lil? [52]

Good Night to
the Dichotomies

There is more to the rapid growth of Miss Mae West's public than meets the first glance, and it is more than hips, hips, hurray. . . . Diamond Lil is Victorian on the other side of the fence and the fence is up, but the spirit of the ladies may also be up. They may refuse to stay on their side. In that case it is again good night to the dichotomies.

—*Chicago Daily Tribune*, December 7, 1933

George Raft had been cast as *Night After Night*'s Joe Anton, an exboxer with underworld connections who runs a speakeasy. Hoping to capitalize on the handsome actor's reputation as a New York tough guy, Paramount sought an actress who could bring authenticity to the role of Anton's ex-flame, the colorful Maudie Triplett. While West seemed a natural, Adolph Zukor, Paramount's founder, was apprehensive, later explaining, "No one believed that the Mae West of stage could be transferred almost intact to the screen." The studio had considered Texas Guinan for the part, but she was fifty and in failing health. Raft, probably with Owney Madden's help, continued to lobby for Mae West. For West, it was a chance to enter Hollywood through the back door, slipping past Will Hays, who had banned her from moviedom.[1]

In early June 1932, Paramount began pressuring West to sign immediately. Determined to make them pay well, she engaged the William Morris Agency, which negotiated a generous contract. Paramount provided transportation to Los Angeles and a salary of $4,000 a week while filming with $20,000 guaranteed up-front money. Although she was billed fourth, her take was the highest among the cast; the star, George Raft, earned only $191.69 a week. West canceled *The Constant Sinner*'s Chicago dates and on

June 16, 1932, departed with Timony, a secretary, and a maid on a train bound for California.

The final leg of her trip across the western deserts was hot and tiresome. Not once did she emerge from her private car; she claimed she spent most of the time under a fan with an ice bag pressed to her forehead. When she arrived, after traveling for four long days, she was greeted by a William Morris agent, Murray Feil, Paramount representatives, and several reporters. Although she was miffed at the absence of photographers, she provided journalists with some choice comments. When asked about Broadway's recent slump, she attributed it to "bum shows." And she put Tinsel Town on notice: "I'm not a little girl from a little town making good in a big town," she boasted. "I'm a big girl from a big town making good in a little town."[2]

West stopped briefly at Paramount, where she was reunited with *A La Broadway*'s William Le Baron, who had become one of the studio's most successful producers. At first, Le Baron did not recognize her, but he soon recalled her as the "peppy vivacious 'tomboy' " who had rewritten her part in his play almost twenty years before. After looking over the lot, she retired to a two-bedroom apartment at the Ravenswood. Only a mile from the studio, the Ravenswood was reminiscent of New York City's residential hotels. A highrise topped with a large neon sign, it had an elegant lobby, desk clerk, doorman, and switchboard. According to one legend, William Morris first attempted to book a suite at the swankier El Royale, where George Raft lived, but, learning it was for the notorious Mae West, the management refused.[3]

With Timony in the spare bedroom, West settled comfortably into her new apartment. Although it was decorated with simple furnishings, she was delighted. The apartment's number, 611, when added up equaled eight, which she believed was her lucky number. The studio had not completed *Night After Night*'s script, so she worked on her *Diamond Lil* novel, went sightseeing with Timony, and patronized prizefights. Almost immediately, journalists noted her peculiar detachment, observing that as the boxers pummeled each other, she sat, staring, completely emotionless. "If she is enjoying the punches, the world never knows it," *Movie Classic* reported. It was an effective performance by Mae West, celebrity—a public demeanor that demonstrated reserve and rock-solid control.[4]

Tinsel Town received Mae West stiffly. She was never spotted at celebrity functions and, by most accounts, was ignored by Hollywood's elite, who were embarrassed by her rowdy reputation. The *Los Angeles Times*'s Muriel Babcock informed readers that New York critics disparaged West's acting and that one had characterized her fans as "the lowest form of animal life." Although Babcock conceded that in person West was much less "menacing" than she had expected, she wagered that Broadway's bad girl was not cut out for films. Other Hollywood insiders felt the same. *Movie Classic* remarked, "Hollywood wonders if she will be a sensation in Hollywood where sex is a trademark not a novelty."[5]

As in the past, West remained behind a buffer of close confidants. She made a few acquaintances in the boxing community but remained aloof from show business types. Her isolation from familiar New York surroundings gave Timony, who now served as her personal and financial manager, more opportunities to dominate her. He shadowed her everywhere; one journalist characterized him as a "devoted police dog." While West maintained that their relationship was purely platonic, Hollywood whispered that they were husband and wife.

Sometime that summer, West added a new member to her inner circle, an old acquaintance from Chicago named Harry Voiler. He had been Texas Guinan's lover, her manager, and co-owner of her Windy City nightclub. But his fame there derived from his underworld ties; he had been a member of Detroit's notorious Purple Gang, had served time for armed robbery, and maintained ties to Al Capone. Somehow he had made his way to California. No doubt, West knew exactly who she was dealing with and probably hoped to benefit from Voiler's underworld connections. Among other services, he could provide her with protection. He quickly became a trusted confidant, acting as West's driver and often escorting her to and from the studio.[6]

As West waited, Paramount wrestled with *Night After Night*. In July, the studio replaced the first director, David Burton, with a second, Archie Mayo. Dissatisfied with the script, Paramount assigned twelve different writers to rework it. Le Baron continually revised the cast list. The studio's sluggishness astonished West, and she grew impatient. She had already pocketed $20,000, but Paramount's deal was less lucrative as she remained idle. She feared she had made a mistake.

Her worries were confirmed in August when she finally received her first look at a script. According to West, she "hit the overhead lights." The writers had conceived of Maudie Triplett as a pathetic working-class lush, a former "looker" gone to seed. For years, West had carefully crafted her stage presence and was determined not to compromise in any way. Just as shooting began, she informed studio heads that regardless of her contract, she would not play such a demeaning role. Her actions brought another halt to *Night After Night*.

According to Adolph Zukor, the entire studio brass attempted to convince her to accept the role as it was. Yet she remained steadfast. The longer she held out, the more desperate Paramount became, particularly studio executive Al Kaufman, who believed that West, while risky, could be a huge success. In an effort to persuade West to stick with the film, on August 17, her thirty-ninth birthday, he treated her and Timony to a meal at a tony restaurant. At the evening's end, after listening to Kaufman's pitch, West reached into her handbag and fished out a check for $20,000. Handing it to him, she announced plans to depart for New York the next day.

According to West, Kaufman refused the check and declared his intention to hold her to her contract. That night, she claimed, William Le Baron telephoned, offering her the opportunity to rewrite her part. Zukor recalled testing a scene the next day. First they shot it from the original script. Next they tried West's changes. Zukor recalled that "she directed herself according to her own script and ideas. Plainly her own characterization was much better." West's reconception of Maudie was a go, and Paramount sweetened her deal with an extra $16,000.[7]

West's first clash with the studio was just a hint of what was to come. Mae West would find herself repeatedly pitted against the men who dominated filmmaking. In August 1932, West was a Hollywood newcomer who marveled at the differences between cinema and stage. She was flabbergasted by the studio's wastefulness, amazed at the expensive multiple takes that it seemed to her would be needless with proper rehearsals. Regardless of studio practices, she would not allow herself to give a substandard performance. A tireless worker since childhood, she was a perfectionist with definite ideas about technique and delivery. Over the years, she had wrestled control from others, primarily male directors and writers, to assert complete ownership of her fictionalized self. The male-dominated studio system presented a new challenge. Traditionally, directors shape their films, their control being so absolute that many cinema theorists contend they are films' "auteurs." As Zukor rapidly discerned, however, West had been accustomed to directing herself and was not willing to surrender that control to anyone.

Of course, Archie Mayo had different ideas. A director since 1916, he knew what he wanted in his films and what he expected from actors and actresses. George Raft recalled Mayo as domineering and ill-tempered, and West's relationship with Mayo was definitely strained. The two clashed over her first scene. An experienced comedian, West was determined to squeeze as many laughs out of her lines as possible. Concerned with timing, she demanded that Mayo change the scene's ending and have the camera follow her up a long flight of stairs to maximize the effect of her last line. Mayo refused.

West remained defiant of Mayo. After her first day on the set, she decided that the film's pace was too slow and her languid style would further weigh it down. For the next shoot, she deliberately picked up her tempo, playing Maudie fast and loud. If Mayo resisted, it went unrecorded. But newspapers did report that Alison Skipworth, who was a veteran actress of the legitimate stage and played prim schoolmarm Miss Mabel Jellyman, protested, lecturing West, "You forget—I'm an actress." Mae shot back, "I'll keep your secret."[8]

Shooting and feuding wrapped up in late September, and on October 14, 1932, *Night After Night* was ready to make its debut. The film's ad campaign invited fans to meet "dangerous shady people who live on the outside on the naked edge of the law." One of these was Joe Anton, a "third rate pug" who has made a fortune as owner of a luxurious Manhattan nightclub. But Anton finds his wealth empty and aspires to better himself and win the heart of a society woman, Jerry Healy. Anxious to acquire refinement, he takes language and deportment lessons from Miss Jellyman. While Anton attempts to erase his past, his old sweetheart, the gregarious Maudie Triplett, blows into town.[9]

Maudie first shows up outside of Anton's speakeasy, surrounded by a group of admiring men. She pounds her fist on the door, and when a voice inside booms, "Who is it?" she tosses her head and laughs, "The fairy princess, you mug." Then she strolls, hand on hip, into the club. Parading over to the hatcheck, she greets the African-American woman who takes her fur familiarly. "Hello, honey. How's business?" Maudie asks. "Been insulted lately?" As she hands over her wrap, the hatcheck exclaims, "Goodness what diamonds!" Maudie confides, "Goodness had nothing to do with it, dearie."

Maudie then surprises Joe, who is dining with Jerry Healy and Miss Jellyman. She proceeds, innocently, to betray his working-class roots. Slapping Miss Jellyman on the back, she shouts to Anton, "Kiss me, you dog." Embarrassed, he shuttles Jerry off, leaving Maudie and Miss Jellyman to share a bottle of champagne. They immediately bond, and the next morning finds them recovering from hangovers in the doorman's bed. While Maudie is spry and ready for another round, Miss Jellyman languishes with an ice pack. Maudie urges the prim teacher to go into business with her. Taken aback, Miss Jellyman, thinking Maudie is a prostitute, praises her for having "protected our good women." Maudie retorts, "Listen dearie, you got me all wrong," and reveals that she owns a chain of beauty salons. As the film closes, Miss Jellyman agrees to sign on as a hostess in Maudie's "Institute du Beaut," and Anton has won Jerry Healy's heart.

In her first brief moments on the screen, West introduced the nation's filmgoers to the major themes that had long dominated her work: critiques of the dominant culture's assumptions about class, gender, and race. For one of the first times, an American film actress dared to use an authentic working-class accent rather than the unconvincing blue-collar dialects or upper-crust stage affectations common in early talking films. West's proud working-class consciousness fit the Depression-weary audience's mood, and her proletarian Brooklynese revealed Maudie's class affiliation without shame or embarrassment. While Joe struggles to transcend his background, Maudie accepts hers, even revels in it. She warns him against denying his class, congratulating him for canceling his sessions with Miss Jellyman and for sensibly discovering that he was "all right in the first place." Maudie has keen insight into life. She both knows and enjoys herself. As the film's hero, she rescues Miss Jellyman from her dull existence and proves that wisdom really lies with "regular folks," not the elite.

Maudie's class identity is interwoven with messages about gender. Her class affiliation allows her to defy norms for respectable middle- and upper-class women. She is rough and unrefined, refusing to bow to male authority. Jerry Healy immediately admires her, and Miss Jellyman is quickly won over. West's revisions transformed Maudie from a dumpy, cast-off lover pining for an old beau into a bold and independent woman who has plenty of male attention. "Do you believe in love at first sight?" asks Miss Jellyman. "I don't know, but it sure saves time," Maudie replies.[10]

In each scene, Maudie bucked gender expectations. Her skintight gowns proudly displayed West's ample proportions, an aberration from the still popular stick-thin flapper figure. Cigarette in hand, swaggering through her scenes, West undermined assumptions about delicate femininity with her heavy-handed mannerisms. Many have interpreted this as a masculine layer in her performance. West certainly was influenced by male performers and had impersonated men since her earliest years. Her retort to the doorman, that she is "the fairy princess," suggests, in gay slang, that Maudie may be a man in drag. Some contemporary viewers clearly saw it that way: Vanity Fair's George Davis declared, "I love you, Miss West, because YOU are the greatest female impersonator of all time."[11]

While West's style challenged gender assumptions, reactions to it also revealed that a patriarchal society could only interpret a forceful and strong woman in terms of masculinity. Such explanations denied and resisted the liberating female image that West had created. Maudie's boldness and brazen sexuality could also be viewed as thoroughly womanish, an outgrowth of West's blues consciousness. Although West did not perform any songs in this film, her role as the blues singer was signified. When Maudie first appears, the soundtrack switches from a light, orchestral ballad to the distinctive wail of the blues, cementing Maudie (and Mae) to an undercurrent of blackness reinforced by her interactions with the African-American hatcheck woman. With "Been insulted lately?" Maudie signifies their shared experiences as exploited working-class women who not only suffered rudeness but sexual "insult," another term for rape. On another level, Maudie's remark is a reference to the verbal and sometimes physical violence of racism that black women often endured when dealing with whites. Furthermore, Maudie and the hatcheck are bonded in a conversation that somewhat clouds racial lines. When the hatcheck admires her diamonds, Maudie shares her secret, engaging in a distinctly black verbal exchange. As Maudie testifies that "Goodness had nothing to do with it," and swaggers off, someone utters, "Um-hum." It is unclear whether it is Maudie or the hatcheck. Regardless, using this common African-American response of affirmation is a subversive technique that undermines Maudie's whiteness.

George Raft claimed that when he first saw the hatcheck scene, he knew West would be a hit, and all indicators pointed to the potential success of *Night After Night*. Even so, the studio encountered several challenges in promoting the film. With a production bearing such a cosmopolitan tone, Paramount publicity had to find a way to court small-town and rural audiences. While they encouraged exhibitors to play up the film's underworld angle and Raft's genuineness, they also devised contests that encouraged fans to correct the bad grammar and poor manners of working-class characters.

West's well-tarnished reputation and her unusual persona presented yet another dilemma. Paramount needed to exploit the film's risqué nature within the bounds of respectability, and West's record lent itself to the former much better than the latter. Following a strategy that she had originated to promote her stage career, they distanced the character from the star. Press releases described Maudie as "low born, brutal," while emphasizing that the real Mae West differed greatly from her character. Publicists insisted that West had come from a respectable theatrical family and was not only an accomplished actress but a producer, playwright, and novelist as well.[12]

Additionally, Paramount tried to push West as a standard Hollywood ingenue. West was almost forty, but for fans she became vaguely thirty. Obscuring her age was one thing; dealing with her unfashionable curves was another. To persuade cinemagoers that the real Mae West was remarkably typical, press releases documented studio bosses' surprise when they discovered that beneath all her padding, Diamond Lil was remarkably petite. According to one report, as studio heads looked on, West stepped onto a scale and weighed in at a mere 119 pounds. It was important that filmgoers, especially those in America's heartland, distinguish between Mae West and her larger-than-life characters. It would be far too threatening to both the box office and Will Hays if the public mistook Mae for Maudie.

When reminiscing about *Night After Night*, George Raft was fond of saying that Mae West "stole everything but the cameras." Indeed, audiences howled at West's every line. At the premiere, it was obvious that despite her limited screen time, she dominated the entire film. Although the film's debut was a star-studded event, West, dissatisfied with *Night After Night*'s quality, skipped it. Her concern was somewhat quelled when Murray Feil, who had attended the premiere, reported that even the jaded Hollywood crowd had laughed long and hard at her performance.[13]

While *Night After Night* received lukewarm reviews and several reviewers chided the other performers for their lethargic performances, almost all critics raved about Mae West. The conservative *New York Times* rated her "quite amusing." *Motion Picture Herald* heartily praised her contribution, contending that she "came near stealing the show" and noting that her "peculiar personality stands out vividly on the screen." *Variety* congratulated West for her "auspicious start" and declared that her lines were "unmistakably her own. It is doubtful if anyone else could write it just that way." The trade sheet counseled the film industry that "it wouldn't be taking a chance to shoot the works on her from now on."[14]

Paramount was already convinced. On October 6, before the film's release, they signed West to a lucrative contract. It permitted her almost total creative control, allowing her to either write, revise, or select her scripts, unusual since contract players normally played whatever parts the studio assigned them. West was also guaranteed two films a year and, according to some reports, $100,000 annually in addition to generous royalties for all scripts that she authored. Paramount assigned her to bungalow number one on "Peacock Alley," the area housing the studio's biggest stars, including Claudette Colbert, Carole Lombard, and—West's new next door neighbor—Marlene Dietrich.

It is possible, as *Variety* intimated, that Paramount had all along intended to ease Mae West into films despite Will Hays's edict. The studio was desperate for new blood. By the fall of 1932, the entire film industry had fallen into the Depression's grip. In October, when West first hit movie screens, almost every major studio was in debt, Paramount sustaining its greatest losses ever and running $21 million in the red. West seemed like a good bet, but it remained uncertain whether she could help the floundering studio.[15]

Paramount immediately organized a promotional campaign for their latest acquisition, and early on, they got some free press. On October 13, the day before *Night After Night* was released, local newspapers reported that West had been a victim of a holdup. Reportedly, on the evening of September 28, while West and Voiler sat in her car outside the Ravenswood, a man approached, stuck a revolver through her open window, and commanded, "Toss out that poke and those rocks." West handed over her purse with

$3,400 in cash and a diamond bracelet, necklace, and ring worth over $16,000. The gunman then muttered, "Forget what I look like," crossed the street, and disappeared into a getaway car.

West immediately alerted the Los Angeles police, who began a secret investigation. Two days later, an anonymous tip led them to a vacant lot where they recovered West's purse sans her cash and jewels. By mid-October, with no leads, detectives encouraged West to go public. She pleaded for the return of her diamonds, all gifts from admirers, and offered to "make a deal" with the robbers. Harry Voiler, using his connections, negotiated for the robbers to surrender her jewels in exchange for a $5,000 ransom. West refused. She even rejected their offer to lower it to $3,000. In the meantime, while authorities continued their unsuccessful probe, the unsolved robbery enveloped the star in underworld mystique. Later, some charged that the jewel heist had been a studio publicity stunt. West vehemently denied it.[16]

Jewel thieves were not West's only problem. Learning of Paramount's long-term contract with Mae West, Hays deluged Adolph Zukor with memorandums reminding him that Diamond Lil remained banned and warning that any attempt to produce it would result in drastic action. Zukor repeatedly assured Hays of his intention to cooperate. Meanwhile, Paramount's publicity department announced that West was composing a new piece, Ruby Red. The Hays office remained suspicious that West was recycling Diamond Lil under another name. They had good reason to be leery. Sometime in 1931, long before West had signed up for Night After Night, Paramount had purchased the film rights to Diamond Lil, and Paramount's production staff was indeed proceeding with it.

By early November, West, assisted by Paramount screenwriters, began script revisions. The studio had already assigned director Lowell Sherman to the project. A member of an old theatrical family, Sherman had worked as an actor with film pioneer D. W. Griffith before turning to directing. With William Le Baron as producer, Paramount was clearly serious about bringing Diamond Lil to the screen.

By November 10, James Wingate, who now headed Hays's Studio Relations Department, secured a copy of Ruby Red. The former director of the New York Department of Education's Film Censorship Division, Wingate was known for his indulgence of the studios. After reading West's script, he telegrammed Hays confirming that it was Diamond Lil but, in his estimation, could be acceptably revised. The chief censor remained unconvinced, instructing underlings to meet confidentially with the studio and demand that Paramount drop the project.[17]

Paramount continued to ignore Hays and released more assurances to the press that West was not working on Diamond Lil. The studio's tactics were not unusual. Although Hollywood had been under Will Hays's watch for almost twelve years, he had been fairly powerless over filmmakers. During a series of Hollywood scandals in the 1920s, studio heads had appointed him to assure the public they were committed to clean entertainment and self-regulation. They paid his salary and, in turn, often ignored his dictates. Throughout his tenure, Hays had been the target of criticism, particularly from moralists who decried what they contended was the increasing salaciousness of Hollywood film. In 1930, after pressure from the Catholic Church, other religious denominations, and several social agencies, the Hays Office adopted strict standards known as the Production Code. Authored by Father Daniel Lord and Martin Quigley, a devout Catholic and owner of the influential *Motion Picture Daily*, the Production Code of 1930 banned most depictions of sex, violence, interracial relationships, drugs, alcohol, and numerous other topics. But Hays still had little power—outside of persuasion—to enforce the Code. Studios habitually disregarded it. Such was the case with *Diamond Lil*; Paramount was determined to proceed with the project regardless of Hays's opposition.

Hays remained equally determined and, at the end of November, held a face-to-face meeting with Zukor and several other studio chiefs. Unable to convince Zukor to abandon *Diamond Lil*, Hays finally elicited several concessions from Paramount's founder. Zukor agreed to make no reference to *Diamond Lil* in the film's publicity, excise all references to white slavery, and cut the lyrics of "Easy Rider" and "A Guy What Takes His Time," another blues song West had added. In a weak attempt to distance the film further from *Diamond Lil*, West renamed her character Lady Lou and eventually retitled the film *She Done Him Wrong*.[18]

By the time Paramount reached an agreement with Hays, *She Done Him Wrong* was in its second week of filming. Anxious to forge ahead and probably to undermine any other action Hays might pursue, the studio had moved expeditiously. Paramount's fortunes were rapidly dissolving; they needed to get West's film into the theaters. Mae claimed that she devised a cost-cutting strategy, insisting that the cast rehearse one week before shooting and promising the studio that filming would be completed in three weeks. Despite West's boasts, abbreviated production schedules were common during these bleak economic times; by mid-December, Warner Bros. had mandated that all films be shot in no more than eighteen days. *She Done Him Wrong*'s hurry-up mode may have been as much Paramount's idea as West's.

For her supporting cast, West had a mixture of old friends, seasoned picture players, and a few newcomers. As Rita, transformed into a Russian by studio bosses eyeing the Latin American market, West recruited Rafaela Ottiano, who had played the part onstage. In the role of Chick Clark, the studio cast Owen Moore, a silent film star and Mary Pickford's ex-husband. Veteran actor Noah Berry Sr. played Gus Jordan, and film heartthrob Gilbert Roland was recruited for Serge Stanieff, the film's equivalent to Pablo Juarez. For this version, West added a new character, Pearl, a black maid played by Louise Beavers, a former singer who had already appeared in several films.

Finding the right actor to play Captain Cummings proved difficult. West rejected all those suggested by the studio. She claimed that one day, leaving a meeting with studio heads, she spotted a strikingly handsome man walking across the lot and remarked, "If he can talk, I'll take him." It was Cary Grant, and he not only possessed an elegant English accent but was also an experienced actor. Even though he had appeared in more than half a dozen films, West would always claim she had discovered him.[19]

West oversaw each detail of the production, even the wardrobe. She had revised the script so the story took place over a short span of time and in few locations, saving money on sets and on supporting characters' costumes. But West was determined that her gowns be elaborate and eye-catching. Paramount's head costumer, Travis Banton (coincidentally DA Joab Banton's nephew) was working abroad, and the studio assigned his assistant, a young designer named Edith Head, to design West's wardrobe. Arriving at the Ravenswood for her first appointment, Head found West clad in "a long, tight, white dress cut down to her navel, her bosom thrust out seductively. . . . Before I could even introduce myself, she said, 'This *is* the Mae West look.'" The two women hit it off immediately and became lifelong friends. Head was willing to work with West and understood that the actress needed to be an equal partner in the conceptualization of her image. Additionally, Head appreciated West's fashion sense. Mae West understood that wearing a gown was an event. Head, who later won Academy Awards for her designs, credited West with teaching her "all I know about sex, clotheswise."[20]

Head had a glimpse into the creation of the Mae West illusion. Much of the character was signified through the body and its adornments. Mae wanted her gowns tight and long, exposing the neck and arms but nothing else so the spectators' imaginations did the rest of the work. Head indulged her and designed extravagant, skintight 1890s revival gowns with boned bodices so that no undergarments spoiled their lines. West's dresses were so tight that she could not sit or even recline, forcing the studio to devise a tilting board with armrests for her to lean on between scenes. For seated shots, Head made a duplicate set of slightly looser gowns. As a whole, West's wardrobe created an illusion of a healthy and well-formed figure. Augmented with five-inch heels that exaggerated her shimmying strut, Mae as Lou appeared larger than life, almost like a superhero.

Edith Head may have understood Mae West, but Lowell Sherman did not. To his surprise, she insisted on discussing every aspect of the film, demanded Sherman justify his directions, and constantly made suggestions. Sherman was appalled: In the studio system no one challenged the director, especially an actress. One journalist observed that "a director of a Mae West picture not only directs the picture, he has to spare the time to explain why she is wrong in thinking as she does or else simply agree and change matters to her current approval." Sherman's dislike for West grew. He harassed her for being tardy to the set, and behind her back he called her the "bitch-goddess." When he complained about her attempts to control the film, he found Le Baron unsympathetic and totally supportive of West. Actress Ann Sheridan, then a novice contract player, remembered proudly, "The directors had very little to do with her films, you know. Miss West said exactly what she wanted done. She got exactly what she wanted." But Cary Grant was also alienated by her domineering presence both on and off the screen. "She did her own thing to the detriment of everyone around her," he contended.[21]

Despite the tension, She Done Him Wrong clocked in, according to West, at only eighteen days, three days short of its projected finish date. Additionally, the film cost only $200,000 to shoot, a remarkably lean budget for a major feature. Although the film's future looked bright, Paramount's did not. By January, the studio had declared bankruptcy and was in receivership.

On January 9, Paramount invited the public, film critics, and Hays Office representatives to a preview of She Done Him Wrong. Variety's West Coast correspondent declared it a smashing achievement certain to make Mae West a matinee idol and turn her studio a big profit. He celebrated "Diamond Lil's" appearance on the screen, noting that she had been "slightly chastened for the film house." But he predicted that it had just enough sex to sell the film, declaring that "the entire production depends on the personality of the SEX star who gets across each jibe and point with a delivery that will soon be imitated in every home that has a sixteen-year-old daughter." According to Hays's staff, the audience responded with "hearty, if somewhat rowdy amusement." At another early showing, Harrison Reports, a trade paper for film exhibitors, found West's film "entertaining" but warned that it was "not suitable for children or for Sunday showing." The formerly optimistic James Wingate was concerned. He felt certain that while Southern California preview audiences had enjoyed She Done Him Wrong, fans in other regions would find it offensive. He feared that it might add fuel to forces pressing for stricter censorship through governmental legislation.[22]

As film censors fretted over West's potential impact, the studio was preparing to exploit her wanton reputation. During filming, the studio arranged for West to appear with popular evangelist Billy Sunday in news-reel footage and publicity photographs; one shot showed him with a chair raised in defense against the actress, the caption reading, "Still fighting devil's rum." Publicists built up *She Done Him Wrong*'s authenticity, offering theaters an article purportedly penned by West in which she attested, "I have known the great and near great of the Bowery and believe you me they tell stories that sound like the fabulous imaginings of a dope fiend." At the same time, Paramount continued to distance the real person from the Bowery queen, depicting West as a serious, professional artist. Borrowing from Paramount press releases, several articles repeated claims that "not the faintest breath of scandal has ever brushed the damask cheek of Mae."[23]

Firmly aware of the hurdles they faced selling Mae West to the public, Paramount bypassed Los Angeles for an elaborate New York City premiere. With West's hometown ties and the film's metropolitan setting, success seemed most likely there. The studio went all out, hiring a gay nineties horse-drawn carriage to meet West at Grand Central Station and carry her down Broadway. Paramount's publicity department planted articles in the local newspapers recounting her life and achievements. Advertisements an-nouncing the film promised a personal midnight appearance by the star in a live stage show called *Knights of Love*.

The strategy worked. On February 9, Manhattanites lined up in droves for *She Done Him Wrong*. At midnight, sporting a tight black gown, La West made her entrance supported by a chorus line of male dancers dressed in po-lice uniforms. After a song, "some hot chatter," and then a change of set, she appeared in a bedroom where she received male admirers and bantered with her black maid, played by actress Libby Taylor. While *Variety* rated it over-done, the audience loved it. They packed the Paramount Theater, which had recently seen dismal times, to capacity. At the end of the first week, *She Done Him Wrong* had broken box office records, and Paramount decided to hold it over for a second week. Surprisingly, it drew even bigger crowds.

After two record-breaking weeks in Manhattan, West and her film moved on to Brooklyn, where it also scored an astonishing take. After she finished a week there, Paramount brought her back to Manhattan. It was the first time the studio had ever rebooked a picture in a first-run house. After another successful seven days, West bounced back to Brooklyn. Although times were bleak—the government had declared a bank holiday, and cash was scarce—the film made another impressive showing. Exploiting the moment, Paramount plastered Mae West's image on broadsides declaring, "You can bank on me."[24]

Across the country, it was the same. Film lovers packed theaters for *She Done Him Wrong*. By February 18, only a few days after its general release, newspapers reported that it had broken box office records in more than thirty cities. One Texan film exhibitor reported that its gross exceeded that of any other movie he had played in seven years. Around the nation, exhibitors rebooked the film before the finish of its first run. "The whole country is going West," Paramount publicity proclaimed. Only a few short weeks after the film's release, Mae West had become a national icon. Many filmgoers saw the movie several times. Ushers had to chase out fans who insisted on staying for two and three showings in a row. Although to many it seemed an abrupt rise to fame, West's ascendance had come after a lifetime of commitment and hard work. Her only regret was that her mother had not lived to see her, and Diamond Lil, reach superstardom.[25]

The movie public went wild over what one fan magazine called West's "red hot momma personality." The assessment of professional film critics was not as glowing. Unlike his Hollywood counterpart, *Variety*'s New York correspondent found the film lacking. He complained about West's roughness, insisting that despite attempts to clean her up, "Mae couldn't sing a lullaby without making it sexy." While several others decried the film's vulgarities, some reviewers applauded West's effort. The *New York Herald Tribune* praised West's "comic honesty" and recommended the film as "a hearty, hilarious and handsomely rowdy motion picture." John Mason Brown declared that West belonged in the category of mythological heroes and legends, noting that "as authoress and actress, she continues the Paul Bunyan tradition." He congratulated Mae not only for her humor but also for her frankness: "To her sex is sex, and that is all there is to it, or for that matter to life."[26]

The Hays Office, noting her popularity, was alarmed at the number of reviewers who persisted in identifying the production as *Diamond Lil*. Indeed, the *New York Times* entitled its review "Diamond Lil," and *Variety* commented that "nothing much has changed except the title. But don't tell that to Will Hays." Despite all Hays's efforts, *She Done Him Wrong* differed little from *Diamond Lil*, and everyone knew it. In fact, his meddling had produced an even more volatile version. As ineffectual as Will Hays was, his efforts to mediate Mae West drove her to rely more heavily on signification. The result was a more nuanced but, in some ways, more powerful rebellion.[27]

The plot of *She Done Him Wrong* differed only slightly from *Diamond Lil*. Lady Lou is the Queen of the Bowery, pursued by all men but desiring only one—Captain Cummings. At Hays's insistence, Gus Jordon became a counterfeiter, Rita procured young women to become "classy dips and burglars," and Captain Cummings was forbidden to wear a Salvation Army uniform.

Allusions to Dan Flynn's homosexuality were thoroughly expunged. And, of course, West's dialogue was toned down.[28]

Still, *She Done Him Wrong* was subversive. Hays's exclusion of religious themes effectively deleted Lil's/Lou's turmoil over faith. Although Lou appears big-hearted—she tenderly nurses Sally after a suicide attempt—the Bowery queen emerges as more unregenerate than Diamond Lil. Like Lil, she maintains that she has "got no soul." But unlike her predecessor, Lou never seeks deeper spiritual awareness. Rather, she resorts to a string of wisecracks. After luring Cummings up to her bedroom, Lou boasts, "You know it was a toss up whether I went in for diamonds or sing in the choir." She pauses, "The choir lost." In fact, Lou is far more blatantly scarlet than Lil. A female acquaintance praises her, "Ah Lady Lou, you're a fine gal, a fine woman." Lou responds, "One of the finest that ever walked the streets."

Like *Diamond Lil*, *She Done Him Wrong* was rooted in West's appropriation of a blues womanist consciousness and her rejection of WASPish notions of white womanhood. Lou is kind to children, patting a tyke on the head, but she rejects motherhood. Frankly libidinous, she enjoys sex and celebrates her sensuality. She refuses to yield to any man. In the eyes of contemporary viewers, Lou was dangerous. One writer characterized her as the "hardest, wickedest, and most vicious destroyer of men you can imagine."[29]

The boudoir scene between Lou and Cummings carried a far greater punch than it did in the play. In the film, as Cummings opens the door to leave, Lou slams it shut with one hand. To block his exit, she slowly maneuvers her body against his, with head held high but eyes fixed downward. Her invasion of his space and her refusal to meet his eyes makes Cummings nervous. After an uncomfortable pause, he embraces her, but before he kisses her, she pushes him back. Lou opens the door and bids him, "Come up again, anytime." After he leaves, she announces, "Well, it won't be long now." In the play, Lil settles for a kiss on the forehead and then plots her next move. On the screen, Lou claims victory over the most unattainable man she has ever encountered.

The film's conclusion came from *Diamond Lil*'s earlier and more rebellious drafts. When Cummings places her under arrest, Lou demands he fetch her fur wrap and then hand her its train. As they ride off together, he attempts to hold her hand. She pulls it back: "It ain't heavy. I can hold it myself." He persists, removing the diamonds from her fingers and presenting her with a new ring. "You're my prisoner," he tells her, "and I'm going to be your jailer." He playfully scolds her, "You bad girl," but she warns him, "Oh, you'll find out." As they kissed, the film faded out. Although it concluded one of the era's most popular comedies, West's ending offered a serious indictment of marriage and gender expectations.

The American public went wild over this untamed woman and her crafty witticisms. "You can be had" became a popular retort among young and old alike. While being evicted from her residence, Mrs. America Grant told reporters, "They done me wrong." Of all the Westianisms, none became more famous than "Come up and see me sometime." Actually, Lou never uttered those exact words; her invitation was "Come up sometime and see me." In the public imagination, the line was altered, and it quickly became one of the era's most popular sayings. In turn, West, always scouting for the best material, reclaimed it and made it her trademark. She even had a doormat emblazoned with "Come Up and See Me Sometime" made for her dressing room's front step. Significantly, since West's original version was rooted in an African-American blues song, "Come up and see me sometime" not only maintained her ties to African-American culture but furthered the subversive black presence within American culture. Few, except Perry Bradford and his circle, recognized West's prank on the white moviegoers who were elevating her to the status of a white female sex symbol.[30]

Like *Diamond Lil*, *She Done Him Wrong* displayed the strong influence that African-American culture had on Mae West and her performance. In fact, Hays's tampering, which compelled West to rename the film *She Done Him Wrong*, only underscored her links to "Frankie and Johnny" and African-American culture. By inverting the song's refrain "He done me wrong," West made Lou even more audacious, highlighting Frankie's revenge against her man. Like Lil's, Lou's resistance rested in her infidelity, her rejection of the double standard for men and women. "Haven't you ever met a man who makes you happy?" Cummings asks. "Sure," she replies. "Lots of times." *She Done Him Wrong*, which reached a larger audience than the play, inverted expectations and put society's dichotomies on a collision course. Lou, the woman, is strong and powerful; the men she conquers are weak and submissive. She is the trickster hero who defies her subordinate position in society and seizes control by pitting men against each other. She is also an enigma, exposing contradictions and creating chaos wherever she goes. Lou the blues singer, a contradiction in herself, takes center stage and croons to the men fixated on her larger-than-life image, telling them, "I'm a fast moving woman who likes to take it slow."

As with the play, many critics heralded West's cinematic "Frankie and Johnny" as a classic. When she appeared on the Rudy Vallee radio show to plug her film, she performed a live version of the song, complete with male backup singers, a honky-tonk pianist, and jazz orchestra. Essentially, she directly assumed the role of Frankie, becoming the mixed-race prostitute and enacting her retaliation against her lover. With the male chorus intoning,

"She shot her man because he done her wrong," Frankie gets the electric chair, and Mae West, the blues singer, trickster, and interpreter, sings:

> This moral has no story,
> This story has no end.
> Story only goes to show,
> There ain't no good in men.[31]

The confusing, almost nonsensical conclusion furthered West's trickster-ism. On one level, the moral appears to be that a woman who avenges her lover's disloyalty and defies gender roles will pay with her life. But that is the fiction of a patriarchal society, not Frankie's story. Her story shows that a fatal consequence awaits an angry woman's unfaithful lover; its moral, for all women, is that "There ain't no good in men." This was one of West's most pointed critiques of male privilege and authority.

While West's screen version of "Frankie and Johnny" was truncated by Cummings's raid on Gus Jordon's saloon, it not only challenged gender roles but, as the plot's driving force, also contested racism. Like Lil's, Lou's white-ness is established and then interrogated. In addition to calling on the blues, West also destablizes Lou's racial identity using Pearl, the black maid. On one hand, Pearl offers testimony to Lou's whiteness. As film scholar Donald Bogle points out, the rotund Pearl, a recycled stereotype of the black mammy, helped transform Lou into a spectacle of shapely Victorian WASPish beauty. Additionally, while Pearl appears in the traditional black dress and apron, Lou's whiteness is often highlighted by her contrasting light gowns and sparkling diamonds. Furthermore, racist discourse also estab-lishes Lou's position as a white woman. Lou disparages Pearl, accusing her of laziness, even calling her "eightball," while Pearl gushes, "I just loves to work for you." Beyond this, Pearl serves as Lou's foil. When the Bowery queen complains about uncomfortable petticoats, Pearl remarks, "I wouldn't want no policeman to catch me with no petticoats on." Lou inquires, "No police-man? What about a fireman?"[32]

Yet, at the same time, Pearl represented a departure in the cinematic por-trayal of black maids. As on the stage, filmmakers used these characters as props; they served as backdrops and markers of both class and race for white characters. But Pearl conversed freely with her employer and, as some schol-ars have pointed out, enjoyed an existence outside of her job. She even man-ifested a boldness and was not afraid to challenge a white woman. When Lou accuses her of sleeping on the job, Pearl retorts, "I ain't been sleepin' so much that I don't know what's goin' on around here." She then forces Lou to confront her attraction to Cummings. Pearl evidences West's continuing use of primitivism; she imagined her black characters as being more in touch with their feelings than even her white fictional self.

Pearl's defiance and her superior insight were cautiously crafted. Louise Beavers speaks her lines—and her mind—while on her knees fussing with the hem of Lou's dress. The overall effect again was mixed: Pearl's assertive dialogue was countered by her passive body language. It was consistent with West's double vision, which produced a fiction both safe and dangerous. First drafts of She Done Him Wrong indicate that West's initial conceptions of Pearl were even more complicated. Originally, West named Lou's maid Maizie. In a scene that was never filmed, Lou complains about a male suitor's attempts to control her, remarking to Maizie, "I thought Lincoln put an end to slavery." Maizie responds, "Ah ain't heard tell of it."

On one level, the scene emphasized Lou as the white mistress and Maizie as the black servant, reaffirming the disparaging image of the ignorant and submissive black maid. But it also coyly reversed its racist underpinnings. Maizie's response, "Ah ain't heard tell of it," was sarcastic commentary on her treatment by both Lou and white society. Lou reacts with a laugh, and quips, "Well, that guy never heard of it either," returning their exchange to a critique of male domination and linking the status of women to that of slaves.[33]

Equally symbolic was West's choice of names. Her original conception, Maizie, revealed her deep identification with her black characters, for Maizie was a common nickname for Mae. It indicated that, at some level, West acknowledged that her black characters were reflections of herself and her struggles with identity. Her decision to change the maid's name to Pearl, which she had also used in The Constant Sinner, also carried a double-voicedness. Pearl was a name commonly used for fictive black maids, the whiteness of pearls providing a supposedly comedic contrast to the character's blackness. While West's use of Pearl reinforced such racist humor, it also contained a rebellious message. For West, pearls carried a deep significance. As Edith Head quickly learned, Mae adamantly refused to wear pearls or anything with pearls on it because she believed they symbolized endless sorrow. West was too in tune with the multiple meanings encoded in language for Pearl's name to be an accident. Linking her maid's name with endless sorrow suggests that West was far more aware of the oppressive past suffered by African Americans than it appeared on the surface.[34]

West's dualistic qualities, as Stark Young had earlier observed, permitted spectators to enjoy West's performance as they wished. Her malleability allowed her to reach a variety of audiences, and as a result, by the late winter of 1933, she achieved unprecedented popularity. Fan mail poured in, according to William Morris's estimate, at fifteen hundred letters a week. Movie magazines and the national media regularly featured her; several fought for the rights to her life story. In September 1933, she appeared on *Life* magazine's cover as the queen of diamonds above a caption reading, "C'mon up sometime." She was accorded numerous honors; she became an honorary Kentucky Colonel and was selected "dream girl" by Columbia University's freshman class. References to her made their way into fiction and films. Mae West dolls became a popular carnival prize; George Raft, enjoying a day at the Venice Beach boardwalk, actually won one.

Before long, more Mae West imitators, both amateur and professional, sprang up. One of the 1920s' greatest African-American blues artists, Ida Cox, began a successful tour billed as "the Sepia Mae West." Ironically, African-American singers, like Cox struggled during the Depression while stars like West achieved success with material that they had appropriated from the black community. Cox reported that Bessie Smith "saw me at rehearsal all dressed up like Mae West, and she just laughed her head off." Other notable Mae West impersonators also appeared. One precocious child actress, who appeared in Baby Burlesque shorts, was instructed by the director to mimic the increasingly popular Mae West. Her name was Shirley Temple. In *Polly Tix in Washington*, Shirley struts in, hand on hip, and seduces a baby senator in diapers with "Oh come now, you can be had."[35]

As West rapidly became ingrained in the American consciousness, observers began speculating about her seemingly overnight success. Curiously, West, the Brooklyn bombshell, differed dramatically from almost all previous movie queens. She lacked the sophistication of Garbo and Dietrich; she was not delicate like Norma Shearer; and she was not at all vulnerable like the "It Girl," Clara Bow, nor as brassy as Jean Harlow. Most contended that West's popularity derived from a single source—the Depression. By 1933, the American economy had collapsed, the unemployment rate had risen to almost 25 percent, and breadlines and soup kitchens sprouted in cities and towns across the country. People forced from their homes lived in their cars or in shantytowns. Those less desperate saw their salaries and their standard of living decline. After enduring more than three years of hardship and despair, and a seemingly uncaring and ineffectual President Herbert Hoover, Americans were in the mood for change.

Significantly, West's starring debut coincided with the buoyant, optimistic, and confident Franklin Delano Roosevelt's election to the presidency. The promise of his new leadership discernibly boosted the national mood. Previously, pessimistic gangster pictures and the Marx Brothers' nihilistic comedies had been favorites among movie audiences. But with Roo-

sevelt's election in the fall of 1932, fans gravitated toward movies that reflected more hope and cheer. West's studied humor signaled the beginning
of this trend. The *New York Daily News* observed, "Mae, right or wrong, has
started something new in the movies." *Motion Picture Magazine* concluded that
West and Roosevelt shared similarities:

> Mae . . . fits the temper of the times, say the experts. This, they aver, is the
> day of directness, honesty, 'facing things.' It is the day of Roosevelt in the
> White House—warm, human, and earthy, a forthright person doing un-
> derstandable things to comfort us. It is the day of Mae West in films—
> warm, human, and earthy, doing equally understandable things to cheer us.

Americans wanted to reclaim pride and confidence, and nobody seemed
more proud or confident than Mae West.[36]

Through Lou, West rose as a working-class heroine for the era,
unashamed of her proletarian origins and, no matter how rich or successful,
never surrendering her strong Brooklynese accent or her linguistic working-
class ties. Furthermore, audiences knew that Lou had come from the poorest of the poor; as a woman of the underclass, she started at the lowest rungs
of the societal ladder but, through perseverance and living by her wits, had
climbed high. West's trickster tale, where the seemingly weak triumphs over
the powerful, had strong appeal for Depression-era audiences. West believed
she had won over Americans because they "admire cleverness, resourceful-
ness, and they applaud honesty. They despise a quitter or a crook."[37]

Like most of West's earlier characterizations, Lou rejected the rich and
their affluence. While affirming the American belief in independence and
self-reliance, Lou, like Lil, discovers that her diamonds are meaningless—
that they have no soul. As she begins to liberate herself from her worldly
possessions, she finds herself nearing her goal. While the message was subtle, it still stood as a reminder that happiness and fulfillment did not always
lie in the material and that "goodness had nothing to do with" wealth. West
gave a much needed boost to a people who had lost so much and struggled
on with so little.

Even West's star persona provided Americans a working-class role
model. Paramount now sought to exploit her working-class background, revealing that her father had been a prizefighter and that she had been raised in
Brooklyn's blue-collar neighborhoods. According to the media, fans liked
West because she seemed "real," "regular," and "on the level." Press releases
and fan magazines emphasized her solid work ethic—that she had plied her
trade since childhood. One writer declared that "nothing has been given to

her on a silver platter. She's indignant at the very thought of those who expect something for nothing." Such qualities no doubt resonated with Depression-era resentment for the rich as well as with the American faith in individualism and hard work. West was fast becoming a star for the people. [38]

Publicity also stressed that while West had enjoyed success, she had not forgotten her roots. She helped friends in need—neighbors in Woodhaven, women from Welfare Island, and old show business pals who had fallen on hard times. While journalists noted her penchant for expensive perfumes and gowns, they also reported that her tastes, for the most part, remained working-class. One revealed that West preferred thick steaks, corned beef and cabbage, and potatoes over the more exotic fare consumed by most female film luminaries. Of course, they also publicized her devotion to prizefighting. Every Friday night, she was in the front row at the Olympic Auditorium, and she often awarded the trophy to the evening's top winner. When one writer divulged that some in Hollywood looked askance at her enthusiasm for such a rough and masculine sport, West responded that boxing could, and should, be enjoyed by everyone regardless of gender. Before long, a few film colony celebrities, including Lupe Velez, Johnny Weismuller, and even gossip columnist Hedda Hopper, joined West and her entourage at ringside.

On the whole, West remained isolated from the film colony, which, in turn, only increased her popularity among movie fans. Her status as a Hollywood outsider served to confirm, in the American mind, her links to common folk. Tinsel Town had evolved its own group of aristocrats—wealthy and adored but strictly untouchable. It was well known that Hollywood's elite had snubbed Mae. Years later, Miriam Hopkins, a Paramount starlet in the early 1930s, scolded writer John Kobal for daring to even mention one of her films in connection with Mae West. "They don't belong in the same conversation or category," she ranted. Paramount's publicists made the most of West's outcast status, reporting her disdain for Hollywood and its social whirl. "I'm always too busy to go in for a lot of front, and besides, I know too many people who are down and out," she told *Motion Picture Magazine*. [39]

The studio eagerly tapped into fan reaction to promote the Westian star persona. In addition to touting her working-class ties, the publicity campaign played up West's defiance of gender roles. At a time when women had little influence in the studios, West had amassed a remarkable amount of power. Rather than ignoring or hiding this anomaly, publicists used it, indicating that she was as bold offscreen as she was on. West told one interviewer, "I never enter a room—either on social or business duties—without letting the man across from me know that he is talking to a woman. And I have had to do my share of outsmarting men through necessity." Publicists reported that West wrote her own material and directed herself in her films. Press releases depicted her as constantly engaged in writing but also revealed that she did "her best work in bed."[40]

Paramount concentrated on courting Mae West's female fans. Women comprised a large portion of movie patrons, and their support had been critical to Mae's rise. While West's detractors predicted that she would only appeal to men, *She Done Him Wrong*'s massive success proved that many women also found her compelling. Fan mail came from both men and women, and women sent not only letters of appreciation but also ones that asked for advice. One fan having marital difficulties complained that after she tried out some Westian mannerisms and sayings on her husband, he promptly gave her a black eye. West's response, printed in a fan magazine, mediated her message. Rather than speak out against physical abuse, she confessed that her style was uniquely her own and might not work for others.

Indeed, women, young and old, were imitating West's bold walk, talk, and mannerisms. At one high school dress-up day, the most popular costume among teenage girls was that of Mae West. In Chicago, a four-year-old competing in a children's pageant took first prize for her impersonation of Mae West. Writer Janet Frame recalled that as a child in New Zealand, "everyone was talking about Mae West and Mae West stories" and making up double entendres. The Los Angeles Jewish Women's Council, like other women's groups, sponsored a gay nineties benefit costume party, and members turned out in full turn-of-the-century regalia. One writer noted that West owed much of her popularity to support from women, who "particularly approve of her. This is easy to understand for Mae makes fools of the men."[41]

Beyond influencing women's self-perceptions, behavior, and speech, West also was in the process of transforming notions about the female body. Her full figure and turn-of-the-century fashions became the latest craze. The studio's insistence that West was typically svelte diminished (although never completely) as it tapped into the rising popularity of the Mae West look. One female journalist, who disapproved of *She Done Him Wrong*, nonetheless hailed West for breaking down the notion that women had to starve themselves into beauty. "To see anyone so spontaneously vulgar and exaggeratedly alluring after years and years of flat chested, hipless ladies is by no means displeasing," she wrote. *Motion Picture Magazine*'s Elza Schallert trumpeted West as "healthy and Amazonian." "The movie audiences have become curve conscious again—and Mae is leading the way," Schallert wrote. "She spells doom to the hollow-eyed, sunken-cheeked, flat-chested, hipless exponents of the neurotic." Others documented West's hearty stamina. The studio also emphasized her love of exercise, reportedly inherited from her prizefighting father. Her image became one of physical prowess and strength. In one interview, Jim Timony bragged that she could lift five men at once and possessed "the most beautiful and strongest feminine body in the world." Publicists promoted West's measurements as being similar to those of the Venus de Milo. "Only I got arms," Mae added.[42]

Repeatedly, West made plain her intention to exalt the female form. Celebrating the end of Prohibition with a studio-concocted beer-drinking contest against Gary Cooper, she declared, "Now that beer is really back and we are all drinking it, why not wage a campaign for the return of the woman's natural figure?" In her opinion, women no longer looked like women. She blamed the 1920s flapper look on French designers, who, reacting first to World War I and later to the Depression, pushed the lean and straight lines that forced women into an endless cycle of dieting. The pressure to lose weight seemed completely out of step in a society that suffered from economic deprivation. "Millions of women are undernourished and lack the vitality to wear the flapper fashion," she stated. Rather, women should be encouraged to eat and be healthy. She boldly advised women that there was "no need to diet anymore" and interpreted the popularity of her figure as "a return to normal, the ladies' way of saying that the depression is over." One female movie critic noted that "the ladies, God bless them, are now luxuriously ordering whipped cream with their chocolate and dressing up à la Mae West because even Mrs. Grundy's jolly well fed up with being 'prohibited.' "[43]

Some have criticized West's revival of 1890s styles as a return to an oppressive image for women. Most assessments of women's fashions celebrate the flapper as a rebellion against restrictive Victorian dress. Victorian corsets were not only unhealthy, causing damage to internal organs and breaking ribs (something that West probably knew firsthand), but also molded women's bodies into unreal shapes. However, West argued that the newer, supposedly more liberated image of the 1920s was equally, if not more, unreal. She contended that she did not replicate nineties dress but rather revised it for modern women. Revealing that her corset was refashioned, she—falsely of course—insisted to *Vogue* magazine that it did not in any way bind her figure. *Vogue* concluded that the Westian image was "an illusion, but a healthier one for women." West understood how to use her body to fight convention and reverse notions of beauty and desirability. If she could convince society that the bigger the woman the better, then she had upset one of the era's most powerful restrictions on women's bodies.[44]

It did not take long for the fashion world to jump on the Mae West bandwagon. That summer, as the film began to make its way around the world,

Lady Lou parties became the latest craze in Paris. Designers in both Europe
and the United States incorporated elements of Edith Head's costumes into
their fall lineups. Ornate gowns emphasizing hips and busts and accented
with sequins, boas, picture hats, feathers, and, of course, diamond jewelry
became the rage. Soon, Head's distinctive nineties revival look had its impact
on Hollywood. Female stars appeared in updated versions of 1890s gowns.
Collier's noted the rising popularity of the Mae West look, especially in hats:
"Even less dressy people will wear a feather in their caps this season—not
just a modest tip but one worthy of the name of plume." Margy Lamont and
her Bird of Paradise had come a long way.[45]

The West revolt against the popular feminine body and fashions was subversively empowering, but the context definitely was not even proto-feminist.
The studio and West promoted her look by plugging its appeal to men:
Women should develop their bodies not only to improve their health but
also to attract men. "Why is it you never see men turn around and look at a
girl as she passes them on the streets the way they used to when women
were women?" West asked a *Vogue* interviewer, concluding, "Because there's
nothing for them to look at anymore." Although she denounced binding undergarments, she also advised women to accent their curves with "a little
squeeze of the waist" that was sure to catch a man's "roving eye." Again, West
had submerged her resistance within a message acceptable to the dominant
culture. Her fictionalized illusionary body itself exemplified this double-
voicedness, constrained at the waist and liberated at the hips and bust.

West's pronouncements about fashion and the body were linked to her
belief that the genders were in a constant struggle. *Vogue* commented, "She
believes in the Battle of the Sexes—and in being well equipped for the fray."
For West, a sensual physique that excited men's passions was a woman's
greatest weapon. Women could exert an extraordinary amount of power by
appealing to what West believed was men's fatal flaw: their sex drive.[46]

Of course, some were appalled by West's attitudes. One editorialist expressed fears that West heralded "the dawn of a pagan age in America." But
many found her refreshing, applauding her open approach to a topic deemed
unmentionable in American society. A few congratulated West for bucking society's hypocritical attitudes, for bringing sex "right out into the open" and celebrating it as "beautiful." *Photoplay* praised West's message: "Sex is no tragedy.
Nor should there be any sense of guilt attached to it. Sex is something to enjoy,
something to laugh about. Certainly not a harmful, sinful thing." Ironically,
West, decked out in Victorian finery, confronted Victorian taboos head on.
She not only made sex a public matter but provided a female role model who
delighted in it. West's approach was even more subversive than that of pre-

sumably liberated flappers: They may have enjoyed sex; the Westian character not only enjoyed it but enjoyed it very much and very often.[47]

Interestingly, many contended that West only got away with such blatant sensuality by submerging it within humor. Several contemporaries pointed out that if West had been serious, her work would have been too dangerous to ever appear on the screen. Even West's own assessment—"I kid sex"— indicates the complexities in her approach. On the one hand, she seemed to supply an honest and serious appraisal of sex. On the other, it appeared as one big joke. By signifying, she caricatured, parodied, and satirized sex, both undermining and underscoring the carnality she exuded. One writer argued that her "sense of humor is her crowning attribute."[48]

But in the unreal real world of Mae West's work, sex is almost completely absent. In *She Done Him Wrong*, with the exception of a rare, stiff embrace and one kiss as the film concludes, sex never happens. West never portrayed sex; she signified it. In her films, as in her plays, sex occurred through linguistic play, verbal competitions, and double entendres. When Lou resists Cummings's attempts to handcuff her, telling him she was not "born with 'em," he states, "A lot of men would have been safer it you had." Lou grumbles, "Oh, I don't know, hands ain't everything." Ironically, the woman whom many would celebrate as filmdom's sexiest star achieved her honors with almost no love scenes.

It was this trickster that people came to admire—the character who created action through inaction, who seemed both real and imagined at the same time. Lou's wit and guile provided much of the foundation of West's appeal. She was worshiped not just for her hourglass figure but for her shrewdness and cunning, communicated through language. *Motion Picture Magazine* praised West and her character for "a wit and quick mind that are as broad as the world and as encompassing." Lou was boldly intelligent, smarter than everyone else in her fictional world. Interviewers claimed West possessed a similar verve, sharp mind, and quick tongue. West knew that her characters existed in a verbal realm, describing herself as "an articulate image" that "mocked and delighted" both men and women.

West reacted to her growing fame with detachment. "I became suddenly a star seen in the third person, even by myself," she wrote in her autobiography. As the celebrity and the fictional characters she portrayed became more intertwined, West's real self was increasingly submerged within these elements. She lamented her growing isolation, both internal and external; "I soon saw that I was a prisoner of my publicity and success." Since childhood her life had revolved around acting, passing for someone she was not. As an adult, she had merged her autobiographical struggles with her fantasized presence, blurring her fictionalized and real selves. The efficient Hollywood machine would continue fusing these elements—the real person, the star, and the characters—into one successful blockbuster image. For West, it became a proud accomplishment but also a frustrating confinement.[49]

As West became increasingly entrapped by her particular star presence, she became more dependent on her small trustworthy entourage. Harry Voiler, who had failed to help West secure her stolen jewels, soon vanished. After her New York premiere, she added three others. First was her brother, John West. He had never settled into a career, and Mae convinced Paramount to hire him. He took her spare bedroom at the Ravenswood, and Jim Timony moved to an apartment down the hall, which he shared with another addition to the Westian inner circle, Russian emigré Boris Petroff. A ballet master and former vaudevillian, Petroff had produced Mae's *Knights of Love* stage show. Impressed with his work, she talked the studio into bringing him to California, where he assumed duties as her "adviser." Along with Timony, he appeared constantly by her side.[50]

The third new member of West's entourage was Libby Taylor. According to Lorenzo Tucker, West had known her since the 1920s when they met at Harlem's Black and Gold, a barbecue spot. Although Taylor worked there as a cook, she was also a comedic actress, who like many other African-Americans had found show business almost impermeable. Unable to use her in *The Constant Sinner*, West made sure Taylor got the role in *She Done Him Wrong*'s stage show. Hoping to break into the motion pictures, Taylor returned with West to Hollywood and served as her personal maid. Many of the era's African-American actresses worked behind the scenes as domestics while waiting for their film careers to take off; what made Taylor different was that she became a very visible presence. She attended West at home and the studio, answered the telephone, received and introduced guests, spoke with reporters, posed for photographs with the star, and also cooked and cleaned.[51]

Despite her astonishing success, only one of Paramount's featured stars forged a friendship with Mae West, and that was Marlene Dietrich. The German-born actress was an outsider considered standoffish by Hollywood insiders. Dietrich's daughter, Maria Riva, remembered her mother's genuine admiration for the brash but thoroughly lovable Mae West. West barged into Dietrich's dressing room unannounced (the only one on the lot who could get away with it), swiped her flowers, gossiped and kidded with her, and always offered blunt opinions. When Dietrich anguished over the studio's exploitation of her legs, West motioning to her bosom, joked, "You give 'em the bottom and I'll give 'em the top." But she also cautioned, "Ducks—we have to go for the women too. Not just the men. Remember that."

Even with Dietrich, West maintained her distance. Riva claimed the two never socialized outside of the studio. Furthermore, she also remembered

West's repeated attempts to shock her mother. Emphasizing that female filmgoers were just as important as male fans, West told Dietrich, "If it were just the men, all I'd have to do is take 'em out," and with that proclamation, she exposed one breast. She then tucked it away, "patted the inside of Dietrich's naked thigh, and sashayed out." Dietrich laughed uproariously. Riva described it as "a perfect performance." Calculating her actions for maximum effect, West remained a performer both on and off the stage. Dietrich probably never penetrated beyond West's star persona, but she still regarded Mae with special esteem. They did share an important link: They were both strong women battling a patriarchal studio and profession. Dietrich proclaimed West a "very good friend." She was one of the few who ever made such a statement about Mae, and later in life she wrote of her regret that she had never expressed her gratitude or affection for her old friend.[52]

Some have alleged that Dietrich and West were romantically involved. However, Riva, who knew her mother's female lovers well, claimed that West was one of Dietrich's few nonsexual relationships. Riva did remember knocking on West's dressing room door and finding her father alone with Mae, who was quickly slipping on a dressing gown. For the most part, West's life seemed to focus on work. Tinsel Town wags linked her with Paramount's Gary Cooper as well as numerous boxers and wrestlers, both black and white, but she insisted she had no time for lovers. Columnist Sidney Skolsky did report that when Jim Timony was identified as Mae's boyfriend, someone on the set exclaimed, "My, what a job." Generally, publicists portrayed West as hardworking, dedicated to her craft, and so devoted to her family that she had never married out of respect for her departed mother.[53]

Although the studio built a life story for West that blurred reality and fantasy, it was true that her success had come after years of commitment and sacrifice. By the summer of 1933, *She Done Him Wrong* had made over $2 million in profit with proceeds still pouring in. West's film had become one of the industry's biggest draws ever. In the history of film, only D. W. Griffith's *Birth of a Nation* had enjoyed so many repeat showings. *She Done Him Wrong*'s success also drove up demand for *Night After Night*. This time, West's name appeared above Raft's on the marquee.

While West's success reinvigorated Paramount's sagging fortunes, it seemed hardly enough to make up for the studio's massive deficit. Yet in July 1933, the Hays Office noted that Paramount had paid off its debts. Although the studio remained in receivership for two more years, many, including Adolph Zukor, credited West with rescuing Paramount. Hoping to ride on her amazing popularity, Paramount rushed to get her next film into production. They had discouraged West from adapting *SEX* for the screen, but Will Hays could not rest easy. West's next feature would be entitled *I'm No Angel*.[54]

If You Can't Go Straight,
You've Got to Go Around

Who's afraid of the big bad censors? Not Mae West. "If you can't go straight; then you've got to go around," she says. And bingo, how double meanings flash from that.
——*Los Angeles Times*, September 23, 1934

I n late April 1933, while *She Done Him Wrong* was still fresh in the theaters, Paramount purchased, at West's insistence, a circus-themed script by Lowell Brentano. Since childhood, West had maintained a general curiosity about exotic animals; several interviewers noted she was now always accompanied by an impish pet monkey, Boogey. Over the next few months, with the assistance of studio writers, West developed *I'm No Angel,* a story about the rise of Tira from sideshow cooch dancer to celebrity lion tamer. Eyeing West's profitability, Paramount hoped to begin shooting before the end of June, but there was one big problem: This time, Will Hays intended to monitor Mae West most carefully.

While her fan following was still growing, there were those who did not love Mae. Daily reports, culled from the national press for Hays by his assistant Kirk Russell, revealed a growing split between average filmgoers, who strongly supported Mae West, and self-appointed movie reformers, who found her work distasteful and dangerous. Several censorship advocates cited her rise as evidence of Hays's powerlessness. Hays countered that the public would reject "vulgarity" at the ticket office. One editorialist, noting West's success, huffed, "Vulgarity doesn't pay? Well we don't split hairs over a definition of vulgarity but if it [*She Done Him Wrong*] is not vulgarity, it is the most pointed suggestion you ever heard that comes from the talking screen today."[1]

Of more concern were charges leveled by Catholic leaders who actively pressed for stricter film regulation. In February 1933, Father Daniel Lord, the co-author of the 1930 Production Code, sent Hays a stinging letter, branding *She Done Him Wrong* as "the filthy *Diamond Lil* slipping by under a new name." He warned that Catholics, tiring of Hays's permissiveness, would demand either political or ecclesiastical oversight of Hollywood films. While by some estimates an average of 60,000 Americans filled theaters weekly for *She Done Him Wrong*, several states excised portions of the film, more evidence to Catholic leaders and other censorship advocates of the indecent nature of West's work.[2]

West's role in the evolution of movie censorship was and continues to be widely debated. Many have attributed film censorship directly to Mae West and her movies. In many ways, it appeared a logical extension of her bawdy stage career, and a direct correlation did appear to exist between the advent of the cinematic Mae West and the tightening of film censorship. Others have pointed out that she arrived on the silver screen just as calls for movie "purity" escalated. Certainly, the attempt to regulate films long predated West's arrival in Hollywood. Both before and after her debut, the Hays Office scrutinized numerous films deemed offensive and dangerous. At the same time, West's overwhelming popularity made her a visible target. But she was more than symbolic; her controversial screen presence became a major impetus that accelerated a process already set into motion.

Just as *I'm No Angel* was coming together, the Hays Office and the film industry confronted a major threat. In spring 1933, Franklin Delano Roosevelt proposed the National Recovery Administration (NRA), a New Deal program designed to establish price and wage controls and fair codes of industrial competition. Hays and studio bosses feared that the NRA, accompanied by an inevitable congressional investigation into the studio's finances, would not only hurt profits and expose some shaky financial practices but also open the door for federal censorship. Hays concluded that the only way to head off the NRA and a congressional probe was stricter adherence to the Motion Picture Code of 1930. He believed that if the Code were publicly enforced, filmmakers could argue that they had, in part, already complied with the NRA.

In April 1933, Hays assumed a "get-tough" attitude for the benefit of the press. Holding a series of meetings with producers in Hollywood, he laid out the fearful consequences of government intervention. *Variety* reported that Hays announced, no doubt with West's film in mind, that "he was getting tired of squaring 'dirt' and prostie pictures." He threatened to report all questionable productions to the New York–based studio executives who controlled the studios' finances. If they did not act, he promised, he would file complaints with the lending institutions that held the industry's purse strings.[3]

Hays's efforts were thwarted by deep and long-standing divisions between the highly competitive studio heads. Interestingly, one of the earliest complaints regarding *She Done Him Wrong* actually came from within the film colony. Fox executive and former Paramount boss Sidney Kent complained to Hays that West's film was "far more suggestive in word and what is not said is suggested in action . . . I cannot understand how your people on the coast could let this get by." Squabbling extended beyond studio executives. For years, film exhibitors and independent theater owners had protested block booking, the studios' practice of marketing films in clusters. Commonly, studios lumped weaker films in with blockbusters, forcing exhibitors to pay for and show movies guaranteed to lose money. By 1933, exhibitors started to resist the practice more aggressively. Alleging that block booking required them to run morally offensive films, many exhibitors adopted the rhetoric of movie reformers and called for censorship. But Kirk Russell assured Hays that Mae West enjoyed great popularity, even among exhibitors and independent houses, who had offered some of the strongest praise for her film. When confronted with the contradiction between exhibitors' demand for *She Done Him Wrong* and their push for censorship, one of their representatives exclaimed, "Why there was nothing wrong with *She Done Him Wrong*. It is a classic."[4]

Despite West's growing popularity and her contributions to reviving the film industry, Hays had to appease people like the vocal Martin Quigley, whose *Motion Picture Herald* catered to exhibitors. In the summer of 1932, Quigley had privately begun pressuring Hays to pursue "some conspicuous case far enough to convince all concerned, and all observers, that you mean business." A year later, Quigley had a target in mind. His *Herald* documented Mary Pickford's shock when she discovered her teenage niece "singing bits from that song from *Diamond Lil*." The sweetheart of silent screen explained, "I say 'that song' just because I'd blush to quote the title line here." Paramount countered with its own interview with Pickford, in which Little Mary professed admiration for Mae: "I like her because she is so low down. So real and natural."[5]

Reeling in Mae West just as she was bringing Paramount unprecedented profits, gaining more fans daily, and influencing everything from the nation's fashions to its language was going to be difficult. Determined to hold West to the Code, Hays and his underlings maintained a vigilant watch over *I'm No Angel*. Previewing drafts of the script and song lyrics, they bombarded the studio with mandated cuts and revisions. At the end of June, after weeks of correspondence, James Wingate informed Paramount that "as to theme, the story seems to present no difficulties but of course, it will depend very largely on the way in which many of the scenes are treated." He stressed that the censors would withhold their "final opinion" until they viewed the finished product. The censors faced a challenging situation: They were attempting to rein in West's signifying. Due to its subversive essence, it was extremely difficult to harness.[6]

As in the past, Paramount attempted to dodge the censor, submitting incomplete material—scripts with missing scenes and dialogue. But the Hays Office held its ground. Receiving only the title to a song called "No One Does It Like That Dallas Man," it immediately declared the number unacceptable. The studio appealed and sent lyrics. Discovering such lines as "He's a wild horse trainer, with a special whip; gals, you'll go insaner," the censors refused to reconsider. Studio executives persisted, claiming that all "the Dallas man does is kiss, hug the ladies, and ride a horse." The wrangling ended only after "loves me" replaced "does it" and the rest of the lyrics were sanitized. In the film, West resorted to humming through parts of the song, which, in the end, allowed the audience to imagine their own bawdy rhymes.[7]

The Hays Office was particularly alarmed about a scene where Tira, still a sideshow performer, appears on a runway. As she parades past a group of gawking men, a carnival barker shouts out that she is "the only girl who has satisfied more patrons than Chesterfields." The line had to go, the censors insisted. They also cautioned that Tira's midway song and dance had to be "handled carefully." Anticipating trouble, the costume department created two versions of her dress, one so outrageously daring that it guaranteed they would pass the other, a sheer bodysuit with key parts of her anatomy disguised only by beadwork.

Into July, the Hays office continued with numerous deletions and alterations. They prohibited West from singing "I Want You, I Need You" as a blues song, insisting it be delivered as a ballad. They put the studio on notice that her line "From now on I don't want no part of you" had to be carefully spoken "in order to avoid giving it any suggestive inference." Their extreme caution revealed the power of Westian signification—that any line could be made to mean almost anything. She chortled about how the censors had even axed material that was perfectly innocent, reading their own double meanings into it.[8]

In July, as the Hays Office issued another round of missives, *I'm No Angel* began shooting. Paramount selected an experienced director, Wesley Ruggles, to guide the controversial production. This time Travis Banton designed her gowns, assured that she had no hard feelings over her clash with his uncle Joab Banton. Producer William Le Baron assigned Cary Grant to play Jack Clayton, Tira's major love interest. Gregory Ratoff, a Broadway actor, played Tira's attorney, and Edward Arnold, a veteran of many films, was cast as Big Bill Barton, a circus owner. Paramount recruited four African-American women to play Tira's maids. One went uncredited, but Gertrude

Howard, in films since 1914, and Hattie McDaniel, who later won an Academy Award for her performance in *Gone With the Wind*, were experienced actresses. The fourth slot went to Libby Taylor, who continued as West's real-life maid. West secured small roles for two other friends: Edward Hearn, who had appeared in *The Drag* and *The Pleasure Man,* and Morrie Cohen, a prizefight promoter. When Sidney Skolsky dropped by the set, she used him as an extra. Even Boogey got a scene.

Despite her early professed abhorrence of Hollywood's wastefulness, West insisted that this time filming proceed carefully and deliberately. Skolsky noted the total control she exerted; she revised the script repeatedly, demanding that many scenes be reshot. She spent hours grilling Ruggles and reviewing daily rushes. She was absolutely meticulous. Reportedly, she insisted on redoing one song eighteen times before she was satisfied. Ruggles had been happy after the sixth take.

While she was pleasant to other performers and traded wisecracks with the crew, she generally maintained her distance on the lot. She refused to dine in the studio commissary and had lunch delivered to her dressing room. During breaks, she retreated to her bungalow to go over production details, surrounded by Libby Taylor, Boris Petroff, and Jim Timony. Although his power was declining, Timony still attempted to control Mae. During the filming, he announced, without her consent, that she was not giving interviews. When she found out, she was furious and overrode his order. Jokingly, some studio workers tacked a sign reading "Timony Hall" to her dressing room door.[9]

Finally, after numerous delays, on September 16, Paramount previewed *I'm No Angel* for James Wingate. Afterward, Wingate telegrammed the Hays Office that with some deletions it would meet the Code, noting that it was "on the whole much better than we expected." Paramount made the changes and rescreened the film for Vincent Hart, the censors' legal counsel. In a letter to the Hays Office, he raved that it would "be box office to the nth degree" and predicted that West's newest lines would be on everyone's lips. While he anticipated some criticism, he announced, "I'm for it irrespective!"[10]

On October 12, 1933, *I'm No Angel* made its Hollywood debut at Sid Grauman's Chinese Theater. Grauman personally oversaw the evening's program, called *Under the Big Top,* which featured clowns, a dog act, trained seals, a tightrope walker, and other circus performers. Streets around the theater were packed. As traffic backed up for blocks, "thirty thousand citizens howled in [sic] Hollywood Boulevard." Police were called in to control the mob. According to the *Los Angeles Times*, when West arrived, resplendent in furs, diamonds, and lace gown, "she got one of the biggest hands from the street crowd ever." She took the microphone and announced that she was happy to be where "the stars leave their fingerprints . . . I mean footprints." The crowd "roared."[11]

I'm No Angel was one of Hollywood's biggest premieres of the early Depression era. All of Paramount's executives and all of the film's stars were present—even Libby Taylor, described as "gloriously bedecked in yellow velvet and gardenias" but forced, because of de facto Hollywood segregation, to remain backstage. Yet newspapers noted most of Tinsel Town was visibly absent; the *Los Angeles Times* interpreted the meager star turnout as evidence of "cold shouldering" from Hollywood's elite. Later, Sidney Skolsky lamented when an announcer at another Hollywood function purposefully ignored West's presence. Many attributed it to jealousy; others contended that she was ostracized because she counted gays, boxers, wrestlers, and African Americans as close friends. Some viewed it as a protest against the woman who was bringing the censors' wrath down on Hollywood. Marlene Dietrich commented, "I like Mae, but it is all her fault that we have the Hays Office and this childish censorship. So American—to see sex everywhere and then try to hide it."

Publicly, West fired back. Citing the presence of socialites at the premiere, she remarked, "Personally, I don't care whether people in pictures come to see me or not, but I sure would feel bad if the society people weren't there. . . . I always try to play to the best." She later dismissed the Hollywood crowd as "sodden, gilded people." Regardless of the snubs, she could take heart in the response of the opening night audience, which one journalist described as rolling "with hilarity and enthusiasm."[12]

I'm No Angel gave the public what it wanted—more laughs, more of Mae West, and even more of her playful sayings. It moved West out of the gay nineties into a modern setting where Diamond Lil reappeared as Tira, the "marvel of the age." The carnival barker declares, "With the right kind of encouragement, she'll throw discretion to the wind and her hips to the north, east, south and west," as Tira slinks down the runway into a tent with hordes of men eagerly following her. Once inside West resurrected one of the oldest elements of her act, the cooch. As Tira grinds away, singing "They Call Me Sister Honkey Tonk," she asks the male audience, "Am I making myself clear, boys?" They whistle; they cheer. Under her breath she mutters, "Suckers."[13]

After the show, she rendezvous with a member of the audience, Ernest Brown, a Dallas man who sports an impressively large diamond ring. As she croons to him, her jealous boyfriend, a pickpocket named Slick Wiley, bursts in and knocks Brown out cold. Believing Brown is dead, they try to flee, but the police nab Slick. To get money for a lawyer, Tira agrees to take over a lion-taming act in exchange for a loan from Big Bill Barton. The act is a sensation, and before long she becomes a big-time circus star, entertaining crowds with her total command of the lions. When she daringly puts her head in a lion's mouth, a sailor in the audience remarks, "If those lions don't show some sense, I'm goin' down there and bite her myself."

Tira's act becomes a favorite diversion for slumming blue bloods. In particular, the wealthy Kirk Lawrence is completely captivated by her. But outside her dressing room, where the high-society crowd gathers, his jealous fiancée, Alicia Hatton, denounces Tira as "crude and ill-bred." She contends, "She would impress the men; they all have low minds and she's certainly low enough to appeal to them." Hearing this, Tira sips some water, opens her door, and spits on the unsuspecting Hatton.

With her success under the big top and generous gifts from her new beau, Lawrence, Tira secures a luxurious apartment and four black maids. Hatton, determined to win back Lawrence, arrives, attempting to buy Tira off. "I'll trouble you to scram," Tira says, pushing her out the door as two maids look on approvingly. Then, crossing the room, nonchalantly she commands, "Oh Beulah, peel me a grape."[14]

Lawrence's cousin, Jack Clayton, also pays her a visit, attempting to convince the circus queen to end the relationship. But he becomes entranced by her. The feeling is mutual, and Tira quickly abandons Lawrence for his even richer cousin. "I could be your slave," Clayton tells her. "Well," she muses, "I guess that could be arranged." She immediately accepts Clayton's marriage proposal. Barton, who fears matrimony will end Tira's lucrative career, plots to break up the affair. While Tira is out, he plants the recently released Slick Wiley in her apartment. Clayton discovers the ex-convict there in silk pajamas and calls the wedding off.

Heartbroken, Tira sues Clayton for breach of promise. At the trial, Clayton's attorney calls a number of men who testify that Tira had defrauded them. She insists on cross-examining each one, devastating them on the witness stand. When Beulah testifies, Clayton realizes his mistake and agrees to an immediate settlement. As the courtroom clears out, a female reporter asks Tira, "Why did you admit to knowing so many men?" The circus star replies, "It's not the men in my life, but the life in my men." Shortly afterward, Clayton turns up at her apartment, professing his love. He kisses Tira, and as the screen fades to black, she sings, "I can make it heaven when the shades are down; I'm no angel, believe me."

For all of Hays's attempts to control Mae West, she had succeeded in creating one of the most popular as well as subversive films of her cinematic career. In the end, West slipped in dialogue and action that made this film far more suggestive than *She Done Him Wrong*. When dancing with Ernest Brown, she pushes him back, looks below his waist, and remarks, "You put your heart and soul into your dancing, don't you, honey?" Resisting Barton's attempts to force her into lion taming, she exclaims, "Who's sticking whose head in whose mouth?" As predicted, movie fans borrowed liberally from the film's dialogue. "When I'm good, I'm very good, but when I'm bad, I'm better," a line that the censors had tried to delete, became a famous Westianism. "Peel me a grape" quickly made its way into American slang. While many have speculated that this Westianism carried a covertly sexual message, Mae laughed. It was inspired, she revealed, by Boogey, who only ate peeled grapes.[15]

Although *I'm No Angel* was rowdy and bawdy, it also furthered West's serious exploration of class, gender, and race. Tira's rise to fame and fortune as she "climbed the ladder of success wrong by wrong" was conveyed through a twisting tale that reinforced and challenged American values. In many ways, she affirmed the American Dream. Tira's success and wealth result from her hard work and ingenuity. Even her gifts are hard earned. She is an independent and self-supporting woman, her income mostly derived from her career. If anything, Tira is ambitious, and that pays off.

But other aspects of *I'm No Angel* counter this celebration of the American myth of success. Like other Westian characters, Tira finds that while money is nice, it does not bring happiness, and like the star Mae West, she refuses to sell out and join the elite. She retains her working-class drawl throughout; she stays "regular." Depression-era audiences were probably a little shocked and a little gleeful to see Tira spit on Alicia Hatton. It was a stunning moment of proletarian rage.

Some have discerned the autobiographical nature of Tira's climb, replicating West's ascent from cooch dancer to Hollywood star. The manipulative Big Bill Barton, in many ways, paralleled Timony. Additionally, West's ostracism from the Hollywood aristocracy paralleled Tira's marginalization. And certainly, Tira's success in the circus was a metaphor for West's achievements in filmdom. Tira works with dangerous predators, all male; her stepping into a cage of lions named Big Boy, Romeo, and Gussie it echoed West's battles in an industry controlled by male studio bosses and male censors.

West understood her role as a lion tamer in terms of resistance to patriarchy. She viewed her preoccupation with lion taming as a manifestation of her own "animal instincts"—her connectedness to primitivism. West was immersed in astrology and rationalized that her birth sign, Leo the Lion, shaped her personal qualities. Additionally, she remained transfixed by the relationship between power and violence played out in the lion tamer's ring. In her mind, it reflected the struggle between the genders and linked sex with violence. In the ring, Tira cracks her whip and shoots her gun, intimidating the cats into submission. It reinforced Tira's—and West's—image as a strong woman who feared nothing and conquered not only lions but also men.[16]

Although focused on the conventional theme of a woman pursuing a man for fulfillment, much of the film attempted to empower women. At many levels, West constructed Tira for the female spectator. When a female so-cialite praises her as "perfectly wonderful," Tira replies, "Coming from a woman that's a compliment." While West's character is superior to every-one, she does embrace a notion of sisterhood through women's shared expe-riences. "Find 'em, fool 'em, and forget 'em," Tira advises a lovelorn female friend. Women continued to project themselves into this cinematic heroine. The *New York Herald Tribune* observed that at least two-thirds of *I'm No Angel*'s audience was women. The *Kansas City Star* summed up the source of her fe-male appeal as "woman triumphant, ruthless and unscrupulously tri-umphant, over poor, blundering, simpleminded men."[17]

I'm No Angel also revealed West's continuing preoccupation with race. Again, the message pivoted around the acceptance and rejection of racist as-sumptions. As before, the black maid affirmed the Westian character's whiteness as well as signifying her wealth. On her ascent, Tira first secures the services of Beulah. Once she reaches the top, she adds more maids, sym-bolizing her immense material success. Attired in dark uniforms, in contrast to Tira's light-colored sequined gowns, the maids highlight her link to a glit-tering fantasy of white womanhood.

Equally instrumental in establishing Westian whiteness were publicity re-leases that reinforced Libby Taylor's role as both Tira's and West's maid. Ob-scuring the two women's previous friendship, the studio claimed that West had approached Actors' Equity looking for an unemployed actress to serve as her real-life maid in New York in winter of 1933. Another story claimed that Taylor happily surrendered her acting career to serve La West. This racist fic-tion both on and off the screen redoubled West's claims to whiteness.[18]

Furthermore, the roles created for Taylor, Howard, and McDaniel, all pro-ficient actresses, reentrenched racist notions. They appeared simpleminded, jolly, and overjoyed to work for Tira. Specifically, Howard's portrayal of Beu-lah, with rolling eyes and exaggerated smile, evoked the most derogatory of black stereotypes. Tira disparages Beulah, whom she calls "shadow," using her for the most mundane and difficult tasks—like peeling grapes.

But *I'm No Angel* is more complex than a straightforward reiteration of racism. While seemingly simple, Beulah actually possesses more refinement and knowledge than Tira. Tira orders Beulah to bring her "beads." Beulah, realizing she is asking for one of her strings or priceless diamonds, corrects

Tira, asking, "You mean that pretty necklace?" Tira self-consciously mutters, "I will say beads." Furthermore, Beulah is no fool. She possesses, like West's other black female characters, innate wisdom. She has insights into Tira's inner self, perceptively anticipating her employer's reactions and emotions. At the trial, it is clear, no one understands Tira better than Beulah. And while referring to Beulah as "shadow" reinforced racism, it also signaled a link between Tira and her black maid, between the black and white characters emerging from and blending together in West's racist imagination. Beulah is not an African-American maid; she is Tira's shadow, an extension and reflection of the circus queen's (and West's) white self that clearly demonstrated how white fictional blackness functioned as a reflection of the white psyche.

West's connections to fantasized blackness are also apparent in other aspects of *I'm No Angel*. The Hays Office attempted to curtail her blues style, but it remained in her rendition of the film's songs, especially prevalent as Tira prepares for an evening on the town. Tira appears in a black gown that contrasts with her maids' now-white uniforms. They pamper, coif, and bedizen Tira, sharing in her discussion about men and romance. When Tira breaks into a bluesy song, "I Found a New Way to Go to Town," she beckons Howard and Taylor to join in. Together the three strut in line across the apartment, singing as a trio and borrowing from the African-American tradition of call and response. To Tira's "It takes a good man to break me," Taylor replies, "Sure does." And when the circus star sings, "No man can shake me," Howard observes, "I knows it." As they finish, the three women collapse together in hearty laughter. In this shared moment, these imaginary black and white women become musically fused. Later, as she attempts to seduce Jack Clayton, Tira looks over her shoulder and asks Howard and Taylor, "How am I doin'?" "Just fine, just fine," affirms Howard. As the maids exit, Tira remarks to Clayton, "Great gals aren't they?"

West even sneaked in one of the filmdom's most taboo topics—miscegenation. Early in the film, Tira admires a collage of her former lovers' photos lining the top of her trunk. Among the snapshots of sailors, acrobats, boxers, athletes, and men in business suits is a portrait of an African-American man. In profile, Tira's muscular black lover sits on a block, clad only in dark shorts, his head down. Certainly, West chose the photo for its artistic composition—it stands out from the rest—and its sensuality dramatizes her notion that the African-American male was more physical and erotic than European-American men, reasserting her belief in primitivism and its superiority. However, Tira's black lover also remains exiled to a far corner of her montage.

While the African-American lover's photograph enhanced Tira's sinfulness and exoticism, it also served as a covert rebellion against white society's abhorrence of miscegenation. Interracial love between black men and white women was strictly excluded from Hollywood films, and West's use of this photo was a defiant act against this racist restriction. While it clearly by-passed Hays, studio officials, movie reviewers, and probably most film fans—in most scenes only an edge is visible—it stood as a quiet revolt against racist ideology. It functioned as yet another of the trickster's pranks, a rejection of society's racial divisions that never quite escaped racism.

I'm No Angel, the pinnacle of West's film career, represented some of her most efficient deployment of the African-American tradition of significa-tion. Language play ran rampant in the film. Although many probably missed the multiple meanings, almost everyone knew something was up. One re-viewer decided that West did not create sayings but rather "epigrams," puz-zles to be deciphered for their satirical messages and double meanings. The film's promotional campaign tutored viewers in the art of West's significa-tion with contests encouraging fans to write witticisms for Mae. "It's easy to do, so do it every way you can think of. The more ways, the more fun," it ad-vised. This compelled fans to engage in their own subversive language play.[19]

I'm No Angel proved an instant hit. Around the country it broke box office records. In Boston, one journalist reported that the lines outside the theater extending down several blocks looked like a "run on the neighboring bank." In Chicago, where the film ran twenty hours a day, patrolmen had to call out reserve officers to help them control the crowds. New York's Paramount Theater also added extra showings and held the film over for several weeks. Some patrons attended several times; the audience laughed so uproariously that diehard fans returned again and again to catch all the lines. West was as popular as ever; she had become one of Hollywood's biggest stars.[20]

Critics were less enthusiastic. Many declared *I'm No Angel* inferior to *She Done Him Wrong*. Several decried the modern setting, contending that West was better suited and less dangerous as a denizen of the gay nineties. Others complained that she hogged the screen and some charged that the film bor-dered on bad taste. But the *New York Times*'s Mordaunt Hall gave it a ringing en-dorsement. "It is rapid fire entertainment," he wrote, "with shameless but thoroughly contagious humor and one in which Tira is always mistress of the situation, whether it be in the cage of wild beasts, in her boudoir with admir-ers or in a court of law." Despite Hays's efforts, West retained, as one reviewer cheerfully celebrated, "her crudeness, vulgarity, and irrepressible gusto."[21]

I'm No Angel outraged the reform minded. Martin Quigley condemned it as "morally objectionable" and declared that there was "no more pretense here of romance than a stud-farm." One film patron wrote *New Movie Maga-zine* complaining, "Her talks and lyrics are in many cases an affront and insult

to good morals. . . . Why go backward just to attract those that have not advanced with civilization?" The *Tampa Tribune* branded the film a "bad picture
for youth." They were offended that Tira, for all her lascivious behavior,
"does not come to grief—far from it. . . . The picture parades pleasure and
plenty as the perquisites of prostitution—and, as such is vile and evil in its
impairment to the young."[22]

West retorted that her unpunished wantonness was her biggest drawing
card. "The movies, in picturing erring women as doomed to suffer heartbreak and misery, have been only half right," she told a reporter. "Maybe
years ago that situation prevailed. But not today. People are more broad-
minded." This was a new age for women. According to West, they could enjoy themselves—they no longer had to "pay and pay."[23]

West still had plenty of support. The *New York Herald Tribune* rated her "as
much one of the major phenomena of 1933 as the NRA, *The Three Little Pigs*,
or Senator Huey Long." Kirk Russell still maintained that she had more supporters than detractors. He acknowledged the growing protest against her
films but also noted that she enjoyed unprecedented popularity with movie
fans. He reported that her film helped reopen a bankrupt theater in Pittsburgh, giving employment to over twenty people. He cited those who hailed
the rise of the Mae West film as coinciding with the fall of the gangster
genre, which many censorship advocates had considered one of the most
pernicious influences on modern society. In one daily report, entitled
"Who's Afraid of Big Bad Mae," Russell highlighted one newspaper's claim
that "breadlines were giving way to theater lines" thanks to Mae West. Despite the block-booking controversy, he pointed out that exhibitors were
scurrying to rebook *I'm No Angel*. Furthermore, the medical community declared that "Mae's ideas are good for women's health." In Russell's view, *I'm
No Angel*, while controversial, was doing more good than harm.[24]

By late 1933, *She Done Him Wrong* ranked as one of the year's top-grossing
films, and *I'm No Angel* was not far behind. Named one of Hollywood's top
ten box office draws, West renegotiated her salary to, reportedly, $300,000
with a percentage of the box office proceeds and continued screenplay royalties. Her new contract promised her two films annually for four years. It was
probably one of the most generous contracts offered to any star of the era
and testified to both West's popularity among filmgoers and her power
within the studio.

West used her good fortune to help family and friends. With Mae's assistance, Beverly first starred in a New York City radio show and then later
toured the country in vaudeville as a Mae West impersonator. Mae also cam-
paigned for the release of Owney Madden, who had been returned to Sing

Sing for parole violations. In another instance, she called on California governor Jim Rolph to block extradition of film projectionist and union leader C. D. Cooper, who turned out to be an escaped convict from South Carolina. In a letter to Rolph she cited Cooper's good behavior and wrote, "Now Jim, you know I know men." It served as free publicity and underscored the underworld ties that were components of both her real and imagined selves.[25]

This image was further strengthened when on November 27, 1933, the LAPD arrested Edward "Happy" Friedman, a Chicago gangster and longtime associate of Harry Voiler. After thirty-six hours of interrogation, the mobster confessed to the Mae West jewel heist, implicating Voiler as the mastermind and another Detroit gang member, Morris Cohen (no relation to Mae's boxing friend Morrie Cohen), as his accomplice. The police then took Friedman to the Ravenswood, where West identified him as the thief.

The news of Friedman's arrest broke on December 5. For those following West's career, the gangster's confession was not a complete surprise. As early as September, Los Angeles newspapers hinted that Voiler had been involved in the West robbery. (The reports coincided with the mysterious death of West's beloved Boogey, who had been poisoned, possibly a message from the underworld.) When Texas Guinan passed through town that fall, West would not see her; most likely she blamed Texas for the Voiler predicament. (It was a breach that never healed, since Guinan died that November.) In December, West publicly revealed she had been suspicious of Voiler, who by that time had fled to Chicago. "I guess you might as well say," she remarked, "he has been a friend in the grass."[26]

Voiler fought extradition, and Cohen remained on the lam. Shortly after testifying before a grand jury, Friedman hired Voiler's attorney, W. V. Clark, to represent him. He recanted his confession, charging that the LAPD had subjected him to brutal beatings, and announced his refusal to testify against Voiler. West pushed on with the case. After she received anonymous threats, the police provided her with two armed bodyguards. When reporters pressed her about the risks of taking on the underworld, she replied, "Afraid? Not a bit. . . . I owe this duty to my public, they believe in me. I'm just another citizen doing my duty. If I get my jewels back all the better because I'll give them to charity."[27]

When Friedman's trial began on January 15, 1934, all eyes were on the nation's most famous star. During her first day in court, she appeared in a black silk gown and sable furs. A photographer asked her to pose giving a famous roll of her eyes; she, the ever-savvy self-promoter, replied, "Sure, I'm no angel." Once on the stand, she furthered the blending of the star and fic-

Resting place of Copley family, including Martin Copley (1805–1875), great-grandfather of Mae West, Holy Cross Catholic Cemetery, Brooklyn, New York.

Photo: Jillian Martin.

Delker family burial site, including Christiana (1838–1901) and Jacob (1835–1902) Delker, maternal grandparents of Mae West, Lutheran Cemetery, Middle Village, New York.

Photo: Jillian Martin.

Mae West (far right) and Frank Wallace (center), c. 1910. Possibly with sister, Beverly (far left, second row) and mother, Tillie (far left, top row). African-American woman at top and the rest unidentified.

Wisconsin Center for Film and Theater Research.

In vaudeville, October 1912.

Wisconsin Center for Film and Theater Research.

Bert Williams in non-blackface publicity pose.

Courtesy of the Academy of Motion Picture Arts and Sciences.

Eva Tanguay.

Courtesy of the Academy of Motion Picture Arts and Sciences.

The inscription reads: "The Golf Hounds: May West, Orpheum, Denny Wiley, Oakland Right Fielder, Harvey Harper, Pitcher, Mable Thomas, Pat Conners." 1918, Los Angeles.

Gift of Stephen Deyo.

In 1927, on release from Welfare Island, with prison warden Harry O. Schleth.

Courtesy of the Academy of Motion Picture Arts and Sciences.

Mae West with attorney and
Tammany leader Nathan Burkan
on her right during the *Pleasure
Man* trial, 1930.

Courtesy of the Academy of Motion
Picture Arts and Sciences.

With Texas Guinan during the
Pleasure Man trial, 1930.

Courtesy of the Academy of Motion
Picture Arts and Sciences.

With hatcheck (unidentified actress) in *Night After Night*, 1932.

Courtesy of the Academy of Motion Picture Arts and Sciences.

In the early 1930s.

Courtesy of the Academy of
Motion Picture Arts and Sciences

With Lowell Sherman on set
of *She Done Him Wrong*, 1933.

Courtesy of the Academy of Motion
Picture Arts and Sciences.

As Lady Lou (Diamond Lil) with Cary Grant as Captain Cummings, *She Done Him Wrong*, 1933.

Courtesy of the Academy of Motion Picture Arts and Sciences.

In Ravenswood bedroom, 1930s.

Courtesy of the Academy of Motion Pictures Arts and Sciences.

I'm No Angel, 1933. Tira shows Thelma (Dorothy Peterson) a collage of her lovers, including portrait of African American on far left.

Courtesy of the Academy of Motion Pictures Arts and Sciences.

With Libby Taylor, 1934.

Courtesy of the Academy of Motion Pictures Arts and Sciences.

With Duke Ellington and his orchestra. *Belle of the Nineties*, 1934.

Courtesy of the Academy of Motion Pictures Arts and Sciences.

Chalky Wright, police detective Harry Dean disguised as Mae West, and police bodyguard Jack Southern in 1935 attempt to trap extortionist.

Courtesy of the Academy of Motion Pictures Arts and Sciences.

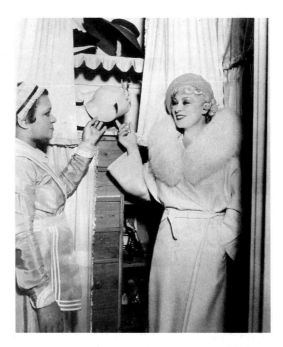

With Daisy Jones, c. 1934.

Courtesy of the Academy of Motion
Pictures Arts and Sciences.

As Frisco Doll with Chan Lo (Harold Huber) in *Klondike Annie*, 1935.

Courtesy of the Academy of Motion Pictures Arts and Sciences

John (brother) and Jack (father) West at a prizefight in Los Angeles, 1934.

Los Angeles Times Photograph Collection, UCLA Department of Special Collections.

With Jim Timony, 1942.

Los Angeles Times Photograph Collection, UCLA Department of Special Collections.

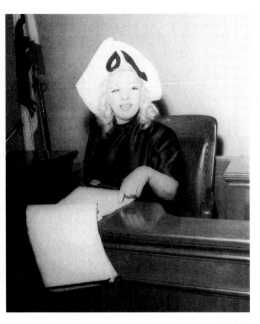

Reading from playscript during *Catherine Was Great* plagiarism trial, 1948.

Diamond Lil revival, 1949.

Las Vegas muscleman act, 1954.

Courtesy of the Academy of
Motion Pictures Arts and Sciences.

In Santa Monica
beach house
bedroom, 1960s.

Courtesy of
the Academy of
Motion Pictures
Arts and Sciences.

With Paul Novak, 1978.

Accepting UCLA's Woman of the Century Award, 1971.

Los Angeles Times Photograph Collection, UCLA Department of Special Collections.

tional character, calmly recounting the stickup. When Clark alleged that the robbery was a publicity stunt and that the missing diamond ring was itself stolen, she maintained her cool, appearing straightforward, intelligent, and, of course, alluring. Newspaper headlines read, "Lawyer Baffled by Miss West" and "Actress' Wiggle Creates Courtroom Sensation." To prove police coerced Friedman's confession, Clark questioned her on his client's condition when she identified him. Shown a picture of Friedman shirtless and bruised, Mae West replied, "You know, Mr. Clark, that I have never seen anything but this defendant's face." Laughter filled the courtroom.[28]

The trial played out like a Mae West movie. Reporters and fans crowded the courthouse hoping to get a seat or just a glimpse of the celebrity, now under heavy police guard. Newspapers reported that a delegation of menacing Chicago gangsters had arrived in town. Officers discovered Harry Voiler's cousin lurking in the courthouse halls. Death threats proliferated— not only against West but also against Friedman, who was now hustled around under tight security. When he finally took the stand, he steadfastly proclaimed his innocence. He also insisted Jim Timony had paid him ten dollars for his grand jury testimony against Voiler.

On February 2, after only three hours of deliberation, the jury found Friedman guilty. He was sentenced to two years in San Quentin. Cohen was never arrested, and Voiler attempted to escape to Havana to elude prosecution. Rumors circulated that Chicago's crimeland had threatened to throw acid in West's face. District Attorney Buron Fitts assigned two detectives, Jack Southern and Jack Criss, to provide her with ongoing protection. Newspapers praised her bravery and willingness to "fight in the open" against criminals who preyed on Hollywood celebrities. Boldly West declared, "It is time someone called their bluff—and it looks like it will have to be me."[29]

Of course, West was not new to underworld dealings. It is likely that whatever transpired publicly was just a hint of a power struggle between Chicagoans, the Detroit mob, and the New York crime syndicate, still under Owney Madden. Friedman's attorney claimed that Timony had a deep "grudge" against Voiler, intimating that the former barrister set up the Detroit gangster. Regardless, it allowed West to continue to build herself into, as she described it, a "super woman" who was smarter than even the most skilled trial attorneys and unafraid of even the most violent criminals.[30]

West insisted the trial had provided her with inspiration for a new script. In reality, she had already begun it in October 1933, well before Friedman's arrest. The new film was to be called *It Ain't No Sin*. While its plot did contain a jewel heist, it was really a veiled adaptation of *Babe Gordon* with all overt references to miscegenation banished.

In West's first drafts, her central character, Ruby Carter, is a former lady of the evening who has beaten murder and theft charges in 1890s St. Louis. Soon she leaves crime behind to become the city's most worshiped burlesque queen. Ruby falls for an up-and-coming prizefighter, an ex-con named Tiger Kid, but their affair is broken up by his ambitious manager. She accepts an engagement in New Orleans, at Ace Lamont's Sensation House. Lamont falls in love with her and competes for her heart and more with another local, the wealthy socialite Brooks Claybourne. In the end, she is reunited with Tiger, who kills the unscrupulous Lamont. To cover the murder, Ruby and Tiger set the Sensation House on fire and flee as an African-American spiritual plays behind them. As they sail off on a Mississippi riverboat, Tiger asks, "Where do we go from here?" Ruby replies, "Didn't your mother tell you anything?"[31]

In spring 1934, just as West's latest film was getting off the ground, pressure on the chief censor escalated. Growing impatient with what they considered escalating cinematic licentiousness and the studios' evasions of the Production Code, Catholic leaders mobilized. In November, the Conference of Catholic Bishops in Washington, D.C., organized the Legion of Decency, dedicated to combating indecency in films. The Legion threatened to boycott movies deemed immoral by the church and required parishioners to pledge to patronize only wholesome films. Soon Protestant and Jewish leaders joined the cause. Hays was alarmed. The growing push for censorship threatened the film industry's tradition of self-regulation as well as the profits that the recent movies had generated. It became apparent that for Hays to survive and for the industry to retain some measure of independence, the censor's office would have to be drastically reorganized.

The first step consisted of demoting Wingate, whom Catholic leaders and other reformers viewed as thoroughly ineffective. In Wingate's place, Hays appointed Joseph Breen, a devout Catholic and former journalist with strong connections to the church's leadership. Breen was allotted broad oversight of all Hollywood productions, fortified by a new system that permitted distribution of only those films bearing the censors' official certificate of approval. On the one hand, Hays hoped Breen would appease the Catholic Church. On the other hand, since the studios paid Breen's salary, they felt certain that they could court him as they had previous Hays Office representatives. But it became clear that Breen felt no allegiance to Hollywood. In fact, he despised and distrusted studio bosses. Virulently anti-Semitic, he privately referred to the Jewish studio heads, who led the industry, as a "dirty, filthy lot," contending that they were "crazed with sex." Although press releases identified West as of Irish, German, and French background, rumors that she possessed Jewish heritage circulated widely and could not have helped in her dealings with Breen.[32]

As Breen took office, many speculated that it marked a new era for film-makers. Although numerous other film projects sat on his desk, Breen deter-mined that La West was not going to slip anything past him and made *It Ain't No Sin* a top priority. Many speculated that Breen's heavy hand would be her ruin. One newspaper ran a cartoon picturing West teetering fearfully on a cliff, the caption reading, "With censorship, what now, Mae?" The answer was clear. Breen's office immediately began ordering cuts and deletions.[33]

West fought back with attempts to muddle the censorship issue. Publicly, she announced her support of censorship. "If I am told to take out a line," she attested, "I take it out without argument." But she also affirmed her intention to resist the censors. She warned that increased censorship would only com-pel her to imply—to signify—her meanings even more covertly. "I can re-ally accomplish a lot with a scene today with the little innuendoes, and depending not so much on what I may actually say and do, but on the reac-tion of the other characters," she confided to a reporter. Privately, she was angered by the attempts to alter her work. When censors asked her to inter-pret ambiguous dialogue, in signifying fashion she scoffed, "I can't tell you because it isn't something you can explain by numbers. You take it or leave it." Breen was determined to take it.[34]

To combat Breen's campaign, she peppered the script with outlandish vio-lations of the Code. She calculated that censors would focus on these blatantly scandalous components and miss her work's subtleties. In a scene Breen im-mediately deleted, a bellhop peeks under Ruby's skirt, remarking, "I always wondered just how far up you wore your garters." She even offered up an in-terracial love song entitled "Creole Man" about a "hotter than hot" paramour with "warm high brown skin." Of course, it never made it into the film.[35]

At the same time, Paramount, to assure Breen that they were following the Code, brought out New York studio executive John Hammell to act as the film's personal censor. When filming commenced in March, despite Breen's rejection of its story as a "vulgar and highly offensive yarn which is quite patently a glorification of prostitution and violent crime without any compensating moral values," Hammell was on the set each day, reportedly supervising each scene. Several publications noted his presence; Skolsky re-ported that the studio was "trying to keep this one as clean as possible."[36]

Paramount also tried to counter censorship's rising tide with a campaign designed to rally public sentiment. Certainly not every moviegoer embraced Mae West, but she entered 1934 as one of Hollywood's biggest stars. That year *She Done Him Wrong* earned an Academy Award nomination for best picture; it lost but remained a picture-house favorite. If Paramount could convince the public that Mae West was a victim in the censorship battles, it would give the studio the upper hand.

In part, this strategy worked. While some fan magazines ran letters supporting censorship, others exploded with indignation over Breen's tampering. One publication cried, "Are they trying to make a Puritan out of Mae West? . . . If they are, isn't it a crime?" *Motion Picture Magazine*'s Gladys Hall lashed out with seemingly sincere resentment: "They're trying to make a lady out of Diamond Lil. They are trying to pose Lady Lou in a kitchen to put an 'apron around her man spanned waist.' " She joined others who decried censors' attempts to turn West into a traditional woman, sapping her empowering energy. Since the movie magazines usually shared a close relationship with the studios, often operating as Hollywood's publicity arm, Hall and others were not simply reflecting public sentiment but assisting Paramount in its struggle against Breen. "Don't let them ruin you Mae," Hall pleaded. "Don't let them make a first rate sinner into a second rate blond."[37]

Hays, Breen, and their assistants continually warned Paramount that West's film would probably be rejected, urging the project's termination. But filming on *It Ain't No Sin* continued. The movie's set remained restricted to only those directly involved with the film; guards were stationed at the soundstage's entrance. When journalists, angered at being shut out, began to allege West had "gone high hat," she granted several interviews and explained that the Voiler affair forced the studio to tighten security. Of course the closed set not only protected West from unsavory gangsters but also kept the Hays people in the dark regarding the film's progress.

Despite the censorship pressures, relations on the set were warm, and West showered the cast and crew with generous gifts. She was pleased by the film's director, Leo McCarey, a genial fellow who had worked with the Marx Brothers and who allowed his comedic stars free rein. Additionally, cameraman Karl Struss's cinematography delighted her. As a young photographer in the 1890s, Struss had specialized in women's portraits, and he understood precisely the gay nineties look West wanted. An innovator, he artistically used shadows, light, superimposed images, and unique camera angles. Most important, he appreciated West's visual sense and was willing to work with her suggestions.

West's cast included three leading men—Roger Pryor, John Mack Brown, and John Miljan—old friends Edward Hearn and Morrie Cohen, and new acquaintances from the sporting world, among them her new bodyguard, wrestler Mike Mazurki. She created a much larger role for Libby Taylor as Ruby's maid, Jasmine. West also demanded that Paramount hire Duke

Ellington and his orchestra to supply the film's soundtrack and play Ruby Carter's band. Initially, Paramount refused, claiming that Ellington was too expensive (although the studio had already used the band several times before). West recalled that they first assigned a white jazz band to the film and, after her continued complaints, later offered her black extras to sit in and mimic music played by white musicians. She held fast, insisting that "you can't take white people and play black music." Later, both West and Ellington attributed the studio's opposition more to racism than to finances. Despite Paramount's resistance, West won out, and not only did Ellington play a visible role in the film, his orchestra provided all the music. Although white songwriters Sam Coslow and Arthur Johnson were credited with the film's score, Ellington substantially reworked the film's two central numbers, "My Old Flame" and "Troubled Waters."[38]

While West was filming It Ain't No Sin, her personal life passed through a difficult period. Early in 1934, Beverly arrived in Los Angeles with her new husband, Vladimir Baikoff, who was her vaudeville partner and Gregory Ratoff's cousin. Although Mae's relationship with her sister remained strained, she supported the newlyweds and rented a Ravenswood apartment for them. Mae was bankrolling most of her inner circle, including Jim Timony, whose duties continually shrank as she grew more powerful and famous. Significantly, by the end of April, both Timony and Petroff had been barred from the set, and West assumed complete control over her negotiations on the lot.

Both West and Timony publicly denied a split, but his sudden absence was conspicuous evidence of a rift. West insisted that he remained her investment manager while William Morris had taken on more responsibility for her career. Still, she admitted to quarreling with Timony over business matters. One journalist speculated that Timony's aggressive manner—he had barged in on a meeting between two high-powered studio executives at Paramount's commissary—may have compelled the studio to banish him. Regardless, West, for the first time in her life, was in such secure circumstances that she could afford her own rebellion, asserting herself in private life as she had in the public eye. Timony left the Ravenswood for a small house behind the Hollytown Theater, where he and Petroff began producing plays. He continued to advise West on investments, helping her secure a large San Fernando Valley ranch.

Her liberation from Timony also allowed West to assume more control over her personal life. Mike Mazurki, who claimed to have pursued a clandestine affair with West, maintained that Timony threatened every man who came anywhere near her. With Timony's exit, West's love life picked up. She had a fling with the world heavyweight wrestling champion, Vincent Lopez, and was also seen about town with the dashing young actor Jack Durant. Mazurki also remembered West's other lovers, mostly boxers and wrestlers of all races.

To complicate matters, Jack West, who had been living in Florida, turned up in March. Mae refused to take time off while filming and dispatched John Junior to meet their father at the depot. For a time, Jack had an apartment at the Ravenswood, but soon Mae shuttled Jack and John, who had lost his studio job, out to her ranch. It was an impressive property with orange groves, a large main house, two guest houses, stables, and racehorses. She purchased the adjoining property for Beverly and her husband. Sometimes Jack joined her at the studio, wandering the lot and chatting with employees and executives. Reportedly, he helped with *It Ain't No Sin*'s fight scenes. Press releases noted his colorful past as a prizefighter and described him as a "stocky, well-built man, bearing none of the usual physiological mementos of the ring."[39]

West spent little time at her San Fernando Valley ranch, preferring her tiny two-bedroom at the Ravenswood, now equipped with a steel door to protect her from thieves and gangsters. Settling in permanently, she completely redecorated the apartment. Journalists who visited could not help but remark on its uniqueness. A stunning shrine to the Westian character and star image, the entire apartment was done in white and gold. Her canopied bed was redone in gold with an upholstered pink headboard, its cornice now trimmed in mirrors. Stark white polar bear rugs covered the floor. In one corner stood a white baby grand piano. Columnist Hedda Hopper noted that even the fresh flowers accenting the decor were white.

Throughout the apartment, West's image was doubled and redoubled. Photographs of the star abounded. A painting on one wall and a marble statue in a corner displayed the nude La West. (Both were done by women because Timony refused to commission male artists for the task.) Even more impressive were the numerous gold-backed mirrors—on the walls, on the tables, above the bed—reflecting a multitude of gilded Mae Wests. She was, in trickster fashion, everywhere but nowhere at all.

While to many the apartment appeared a narcissistic celebration, it functioned, like everything else Westian, as a double message. Small and modest, it was full of expensive, albeit nouveau riche, furnishings and decor, replicating but parodying a Hollywood celebrity palace. It also reinforced West's obsession with whiteness. She continued to play with contrasts; for a photo shoot in her newly redecorated abode, she donned a black gown. The apartment, which she insisted was just like one of her movie sets, became still another stage upon which West played with and in between extremes. Meeting with author and screenwriter Anita Loos, West pulled up in a "chocolate-colored Rolls Royce," her African-American driver and footman dressed in dark brown uniforms. Inside the automobile, Loos found West engulfed in a sea of white ostrich feathers.[40]

At the end of May, Paramount screened *It Ain't No Sin* for Breen. He instantaneously rejected it, declaring it a flagrant violation of the Production Code. At a meeting a few days later, Cohen pleaded with Breen not to put his decision in writing and offered to make cuts in the film. In the past, censors, to protect studios' public image, had rarely documented their objections, but Breen, believing Cohen had conspired to conceal his activities from Paramount's New York bosses, fired off a letter rejecting *It Ain't No Sin* with carbon copies to all Paramount heads. Breen's action put filmmakers on notice that the days of gentility were over and that he was willing to take drastic action to enforce the Code.

Cohen, with McCarey and no doubt West, quickly reworked *It Ain't No Sin*. On June 6, he rescreened it for Breen. In this version, Paramount deleted all references to Ruby as an ex-prostitute and Tiger as an ex-con, as well as a series of dissolves implying that the couple had not left her apartment for five days—and five nights, of course. Satisfied, Breen approved the film and informed Will Hays the picture was ready for release.

But when *It Ain't No Sin* was previewed in New York, the state censorship board rejected the film outright. It caught Breen and Hays off guard, although they should have known something was awry. When Catholic leaders saw Paramount's Broadway billboards announcing *It Ain't No Sin*, they responded with their own signs proclaiming, "IT IS." Across the country, moral guardians had garnered more power, increasing their pressure on state censor boards. Like New York, Chicago condemned the film before it was even released. Pennsylvania joined in, banning the film there. The furor compelled Paramount to rework it once more. As a public testament to their serious determination to clean up films, Breen and Hays ordered even more cuts.[41]

In early July, Paramount began revisions. Since New Yorkers had taken such offense to the "it" in the original title, they renamed the film *Belle of the Nineties*. McCarey refilmed several love scenes and edited other passages, and, at Breen's insistence, they dropped the first ending and filmed a new one with Ruby marrying Tiger. "It is Mae West's shotgun wedding by the censors," sighed Skolsky. With all these retakes, the production's budget ballooned to $800,000, four times the amount it took to make *She Done Him Wrong*.[42]

On August 3, Breen reported to Hays that he had seen the latest version of West's film. He was satisfied that the "sex angle" had been expunged and claimed only a few more cuts would "wash out the crime angle." Several days later, he issued a certificate of approval pending further deletions. In his daily column, Skolsky gleefully proclaimed that the film was "still good entertainment" and that the censors had missed several choice lines.[43]

On August 17, West's forty-first birthday, *Belle of the Nineties* debuted. This time, Hollywood turned out in force for the premiere; good friend Marlene Dietrich was highly visible, signing autographs for fans. West arrived with a police escort and accompanied by bodyguards, the exiled Jim Timony, and Boris Petroff. The entire West family showed up—Beverly with her husband, John Junior, and Jack. The crowd outside the theater was so large that the LAPD called for backup.[44]

In *Belle of the Nineties*'s final version, Ruby Carter becomes a hard-working St. Louis burlesque queen. Her act, a throwback to nineteenth-century artist model shows, consists of posing in skintight gowns in front of a series of screens that transform her from a rose to a spider, then to a bat, and after several suspenseful moments to the Statue of Liberty. (Reportedly, a similar pose in *Vanity Fair* induced George Jean Nathan to remark that Mae looked more like "the Statue of Libido.") As originally planned, Ruby's romance with Tiger Kid, a champion prizefighter, is broken up by his manager. She moves on to New Orleans where, singing the blues, she becomes the toast of the Sensation House and is pursued by Brooks Claybourne and Ace Lamont. Ruby's life becomes even more complicated when Tiger Kid arrives in town. Lamont sets up the unwitting boxer to steal Ruby's diamonds while she is out for a carriage ride with the Sensation House's dishonest owner.[45]

Ruby quickly figures out that Lamont and Tiger have lifted her jewels and plots revenge. She also decides to return her gems to Claybourne; she confesses to Jasmine that she feels guilty for accepting them from a man she does not love. As they talk, a crowd of African-American worshipers gathers for a prayer meeting in the street below. "That's Brother Eben and his flock," reports Jasmine. "He preaches bad sass to the devil." As Jasmine departs to join in, Ruby requests that she "say a little prayer for me," handing her a donation for the collection plate. Then she watches the throng from her balcony above the street.

Ruby proceeds with her retribution. She makes sure Tiger Kid loses a championship bout. Lamont, who has wagered heavily on Tiger's victory, cannot cover his debts and decides to flee to Havana. Tricked by Ruby into believing that Lamont is responsible for his loss, Tiger attacks and unintentionally kills the Sensation House's owner. As Ruby ponders their predicament, she sets the Sensation House on fire with an accidental flick of her cigarette. In the end, Tiger turns himself in for Lamont's murder, and a series of newspaper headlines—a sequence mandated by Breen—reveals that a jury exonerates the boxer. The film concludes with Tiger and Ruby, their love renewed, saying their wedding vows.

While Breen believed he had excised all salaciousness from *Belle of the Nineties*, West successfully signified Ruby's wantonness. When Tiger's manager warns him that "all she thinks about is having a good time," Ruby shoots back, "I don't only think about it." After arriving in New Orleans, a group of handsome men at the Sensation House gathers around her, one asking, "Are you in town for good?" "I expect to be here," she replies, "but not for good." She also successfully communicated her scarlet past, observing that "a man in the house is worth two on the street."

The critics gave *Belle of the Nineties* a supportive reception. *Variety*, although insisting that it was "not up to par," maintained that it contained a healthy share of humorous Westianisms despite the censors' tampering. The *New York Times* rated it "among the best screen comedies of the year." The *Motion Picture Daily* predicted it would be profitable but warned, like several other critics, that it was purely an adult film. Several critics felt *She Done Him Wrong* was a much better film but contended that *Belle of the Nineties* had surpassed *I'm No Angel*. One reviewer predicted that the censorship battle over *Belle of the Nineties* would sell even more tickets.

Several critics hailed Duke Ellington and Brother Eben's prayer meeting as, next to West's performance, the film's most compelling features. *Variety* rated Ellington and his band as "nifty," and *Motion Picture Daily* praised the prayer meeting as "particularly effective to the eye and ear." According to Paramount, West's inspiration for the Brother Eben scene came as she listened to a revival meeting broadcast over the radio. A collaborative effort involving West, McCarey, Struss, Ellington, and ninety-two African-American men, women, and children recruited to play worshipers, the prayer meeting was a unique cinematic passage embedded with complex messages.[46]

Brother Eben's revival takes place just beneath Ruby's window, where he sings, "Pray, children, pray and you'll be saved," as a crowd grows. From the throng, Jasmine shouts, "Bow down, bow down," and Ruby strolls on her balcony surveying the scene below. The entire flock breaks into song, declaring, "If the Good Book say so, it's so." Ruby then begins to sing along, but a different tune. In blues style, she laments, "I'm going to drown, down in those troubled waters, they're creeping around my soul." (The song borrowed from several African-American spirituals.) The camera begins to switch between the balcony and the street below, where the worshipers are seized by the holy spirit, finally superimposing their images on Ruby's as they join with her in song.

This passage, clearly intended as a statement about sin and redemption, also demonstrated West's reliance on primitivism, for in her view its emotionalism was not confined to erotic passion but included its apparent opposite, religious fervor. In this configuration, the black characters are closer not only to nature but to God as well. Ruby asks Jasmine to pray for her, as if her black maid were an intercessor or saint. Thus Jasmine becomes the spiritual superior who calls Ruby to worship, commanding her to "bow down." Racial separation prevents Ruby from attending Brother Eben's revival; she can only participate from afar as she looks on longingly. But together Ruby and the throng deliver songs of suffering and redemption. When Ruby sings about drowning, worshipers below wave their arms and sway, appearing to drown along with her. As she declares that the "troubled waters" will "wash away my sins before morning," the crowd's jubilation climaxes. Baptized together, Ruby and the throng find redemption as their images become fused, the camera superimposing them in a visual symbol of racial intermixing. What West could not accomplish on film with sex, she did with religion.

Belle of the Nineties carried a pointed critique of the American racial climate. Behind the sermonizing Brother Eben, African-American men stack heavy sacks of grain at the waterfront. The workers are ill clad; their skin glistens with perspiration; their expressions convey dejection as well as discontent. As they work, Brother Eben leads the congregation:

> Brother Eben: Who's the cause of all sickness?
> Crowd: The devil.
> Brother Eben: Who's the cause of all the poor crops?
> Crowd: The devil.
> Brother Eben: Who's the cause of all evil?
> Crowd: The devil.
> Brother Eben: What did the devil ever do for us?
> Crowd: Nothing.

He then pledges, as the throng gives freely, to use the collection to "fight the devil."

Immersed in black culture and attuned to the multiple possibilities of language, West certainly knew that the devil was a common African-American metaphor for whites and white society. Framed by the image of exploited black workers laboring away, Brother Eben's message implies a critique of white society that abuses and grows rich off African-American labor. It also underscores a fighting determination to throw off white oppression.[47]

Ruby stands on the divide between privileged white society and the African-American community that suffers discrimination and exploitation. When she sings, "They say that I'm one of the devil's daughters; they look at me with scorn," West does not simply impart Ruby's (and her own) scandalous reputation. She signifies the racial ambiguity of her character. As a "devil's daughter," she is a white woman, who participates fully in the racist oppression of African-American people. But she also imparts uncertainty about her racial identity. "They say" implies that her whiteness, although publicly assumed, may be debatable. As her character struggles to assert her whiteness, she finds she cannot, much like American culture in general, escape her black roots.

While the "Troubled Waters" sequence bore Struss's distinctive style, West was its primary auteur. She was equally engaged in directing this film, and she carefully rehearsed each song with a pianist in her dressing room. As with all aspects of her work, West fiercely controlled her performance; it was her presence, and the black presence, that gave these cinematic moments meaning.

West also offered other challenges to racist ideology. Ruby's occupation, in addition to posing, is that of blues singer. Her point of origin, St. Louis, subtly resurrects the biracial prostitute Frankie Baker. Reaching New Orleans, Ruby performs several old blues standards, including "St. Louis Blues," "Memphis Blues," and, most important, a heavily edited version of "He Comes to See Me Sometimes," an echo of her trademark invitation. Ellington backed her for each number; his music and orchestra were integral components of the film. However, Ruby and the band, adhering to segregation, were separated by space. While Ruby is onstage, Ellington and company are placed at a distance in an orchestra pit, and when she delivers a song in the Sensation House bar, several white men are positioned between her and her black accompanists. But as she sings, she signifies her connection with them, making eye contact with the bandleader and his musicians and introducing each band member to the audience. While emphasizing West's debt to African-American culture, it also introduces Ruby as a mediator. She is the white woman who delivers black music. She exists in the space between the creators of that music and the white spectator.

The white public continued, as in the past, to link her performance with a black presence. *Vanity Fair* borrowed African-American bandleader Cab Calloway's "hi-de-hi" to hail West's raucous characterizations. *Variety* suggested that Ellington and his orchestra were "a natural for Mae West." A cartoon depicted West surrounded by her admiring male co-stars, including, although relegated to a far corner, Duke Ellington. (Ellington clipped it and kept it in his scrapbook.) Gilbert Seldes, who had panned *Diamond Lil*, became a convert. He heralded West as "good news" for films, contending that she outdistanced all other Hollywood actresses with the exception of comedic legend

Marie Dressler and "that superb, almost anonymous negress whose great mahogany smiling face and divine smile are among the major pleasures of dozens of films through which she passes." In a sense, Seldes's odd tribute posited West somewhere between the cinematic extremes of comedic whiteness and blackness.[48]

In interviews, West now encouraged the public to associate her with black performance. She repeatedly acknowledged her debt to African-American culture, recounting her appropriation of the shimmy, ragtime, and blues from the black community. These assertions were repeated in studio biographies and press materials that declared her "the first white shimmy dancer," told of her early Bert Williams impersonations, and identified her as a former "coon shouter." As with the screen character, these details served to reentrench West's "badness," linking her with hypersexuality and the forbidden crossing of racial lines, but they also functioned covertly to undermine Depression-era America's racial divide.[49]

However, *Belle of the Nineties* carefully backtracks to cover its rebelliousness. Libby Taylor, who was light-skinned, wore dark makeup, essentially appearing in blackface that exaggerated Ruby's whiteness. Taylor's character remains intellectually simple, unable to understand and carry out Ruby's more complex requests. Her distorted dialect, along with that of other black characters, reentrenches a buffoonishness. Additionally, Brother Eben's followers appear ignorant and childlike, carried away by emotions and perhaps even tricked out of their meager earnings by a con-artist preacher. As the scene concludes, distorted shots of the black worshipers' faces fill the screen, their shouting, screaming, and crying producing a nightmarish effect. Some viewers did not know what to make of it; several concluded it was a distasteful satire of religion.

Gauging African-American response to Mae West and her films is difficult. Always confident, West believed that she had a large African-American following, especially after *Belle of the Nineties*, since she had successfully compelled the studio to feature Ellington and employ a large number of African-American performers for the film. She seemed to have the support of African-American colleagues. When later asked about West, Ellington commented, "That lady is one of a kind. But besides being unusual and fascinating, she's concerned with other people, which is rare for a woman or man in that position." Other African-American entertainers praised her for opening doors for blacks in show business and helping black performers who struggled against the racism of the studio system. After *Belle of the Nineties*, Libby Taylor became so sought-after that she left West to pursue her own career full-time. West jokingly told the *New York Times*, "When she started wanting me to wake her up in the morning, I told her she better stop being a maid and give all her time to her public." Over the next fifteen years, Taylor appeared in thirty-three films, most often playing servant roles; ironically, like many black actresses, she quit being a maid to play a maid.[50]

It is likely that West's guess was right: A number of African Americans were probably among those who snatched up tickets for *Belle of the Nineties*. After its official release in September, the film proved that West retained her box office magic. As crowds filled theaters throughout the country, movie houses geared up for big business. In Chicago, the film made $60,000 in its first week. Indianapolis immediately rebooked the picture for a second week, and Boston reported that hordes of fans clamored for tickets. In Atlantic City, one theater offered twelve showings daily to accommodate the demand. *Belle of the Nineties* ultimately fell short of West's previous films, but it still made a sizable profit.

Although some insisted that West had cleaned up nicely, others remained unconvinced. Women's Club leader Alice Ames Winter immediately charged censors with laxity. "I can't see how you can put the seal of the association approval on the Mae West picture," she complained to Will Hays, asserting that it manifested "a low level from a sex point of view." She feared for the moral well-being of the population, especially the children. "They don't need Mae West as a teacher," she scolded. Despite the Production Code seal of approval, several state censor boards cut dialogue as well as some of West's songs out of their copies. Internationally, a few countries banned the film outright. Father J. A. Smith of Sayville, Long Island, commenced a one-man protest, picketing the local theater showing *Belle of the Nineties* and noting down everyone who went in. He proudly reported that after only a few days, the audience declined, forcing the theater to cancel the rest of the showings. Hollywood took note and shifted more and more blame for stricter censorship onto the reckless Mae West. "She was the straw that broke the poor old camel's back," ventured *Motion Picture Magazine*.[51]

West still had plenty of defenders. At the end of September 1934, the *New York Times*'s Andre Sennwald insisted that censors had misinterpreted West and that her work was no danger to American morals because it was a satire and a "sly burlesque" of sex. She was, he asserted, no longer the Mae West of *SEX* and Welfare Island; her style had matured since those randy years. "She is so sane, so frank, so vigorous," he argued, "and, withal, so uproariously funny that she composes the healthiest influence which has reached Hollywood in years." The *Boston Herald*'s Elinor Hughes dismissed the criticisms of the popular star. "We do not think she is doing any real harm," she wrote, "because she is never serious about what she puts across."

Gilbert Seldes celebrated West as a "phenomenal woman" and compared her to the innocent Shirley Temple, asserting both were "rude and rowdy" with "an air of command." After seeing *Belle of the Nineties*, one Mae West fan wrote Breen, "You certainly ruined that picture—didn't you? . . . We the people don't know the names and addresses of these prudes who are suddenly trying to rob us of our human rights by telling us . . . what we shall look at and what we shall listen to."[52]

To be on the safe side, the studio began to tip publicity in a more conservative direction, assuring the public that West was no moral hazard. One press release revealed an astrologer's prediction that she would marry in 1938; another emphasized that West believed that good wives gave up their careers. Combating the speculation that West was through in Hollywood, Paramount publicity also claimed that she was so versatile that alterations in her work would never impede her appeal. An article written by director Leo McCarey declared that West could play any role ranging from Peg o' My Heart to Catherine the Great. The studio also highlighted *Belle of the Nineties* censorship to show that West had voluntarily "gone good." Now more than ever, publicists emphasized that she led an absolutely morally upright life offscreen, contending that she attended church every Sunday. One fan magazine, observing her popularity among children, asserted that they loved her because she represented a mother figure, in particular, a "mammy."[53]

West's comments indicated a growing frustration with censorship. She alleged it was never clear what the censors really wanted. But she also assured fans she had finally figured out "that things the censors think are bad I think are alright and I've learned that there are a number of things that I shy at that they see nothing wrong in." That statement probably caused a double-take in the Hays Office, whose representatives believed they had purged all suggestiveness from her work. In one interview she feigned innocence, complaining, "I can't say the things that other actresses say. When they say 'em, they're funny; when I say 'em I'm vulgar. People seem to read double meanings into every word I speak." She affirmed her intention to defy the censors and continue to implant explosive messages in her films. "If you can't go straight," she told the *Los Angeles Times*, "then you've got to go around."[54]

After *Belle of the Nineties*, West answered critics wagering that censorship would finish her off with a song called "That's All Brother." Borrowing the title from an African-American jazz chant, she recorded an ode to signification, both a serious and comedic statement of her determination to fight censorship:

It's not what I say, it's the way that I say it.
That's all, brother, that's all.

It's not what I play, but the way that I play it.
That's all, brother, that's all.

Imaging herself as Red Riding Hood, Cinderella, and Snow White ("with seven dwarfs to entertain, I should do alright"), she sent the Hays Office a message:

Now please don't misunderstand me.
I take much of what they hand me,
Though it cramps my style
I'll never be defeated.[55]

Mae West was resolute. No censor could rest easy.

Naturally I Disagree

Sometimes I grow weary of fighting to keep faith with the
public. They liked me as Diamond Lil. I know they want me
to continue in that type of characterization. But certain well-
meaning executives believe I should do something different.
Naturally I disagree. Then I get a reputation for being obstinate, hard to handle. Well, I've always had to battle for my
rights.

—Mae West to writer Lew Garvey, 1936

S ince the spring of 1934, Mae West had been telling reporters that
she had a follow-up project to *Belle of the Nineties* in mind; she
planned to play the Queen of Sheba. She assured the media her treatment of this biblical character would primarily be dramatic: "I might
kid around with Solomon a little, but I won't go too far." It seemed an odd
choice to some. "The Queen of Sheba was Ethiopian," protested Michael
Kane, a writer Timony engaged to assist with the script. "I thought the
blonde coloring of Miss West should be taken into consideration." The contradiction did not disturb West; most likely it made the role even more attractive. Additionally, the Queen of Sheba, who perplexed King Solomon
with a series of riddles, presented a beguiling trickster image—a perfect
match for Mae West. Of course, West's idea was nixed; journalists speculated the Hays Office had a big hand in killing the project.[1]

Instead, in August 1934, the studio rushed West into her next film. Paramount had already purchased a script, *Now I'm a Lady*. Its central character,
Cleo Bordon, was no Queen of Sheba, but their efforts to join the elite resonated with *The Hussy*. Mae decided the screenplay should be set, in part, in
the Wild West. Proudly, she announced a national talent search for a Native
American to co-star as one of her paramours.

After reviewing West's first draft, Breen declared that *Now I'm a Lady* was "basically in compliance" and required only a few changes. He deleted some suggestive lines and references to prostitution; he also excised several Latin American characters and a gay interior decorator. On December 19, 1934, the day Paramount received Breen's okay, they began shooting. Everything went so well that a few weeks later Breen informed Hays that "a sincere effort has been made to get away from any basically questionable elements" and that Hammell was diligently monitoring this production.[2]

But West's honeymoon with censors did not last long. Shortly after Breen's report, new material and songs filtered in, including a love song containing the lyrics "Now I'm a lady, I get my sugar refined." Breen promptly ordered deletions. Next to dialogue reading, "I only break one each night" and "my hips would do a jelly roll," lines drawn from blues songs, he penciled in a large "NO!" He also excised a scene with a Latin American suitor asking Cleo, "Do you like Spanish men?" She responds, "Why should they be an exception?" Somewhere in the process, Cleo's Native American lover also disappeared, and eventually the film was renamed *Goin' to Town*.[3]

Censorship was only a minor problem compared to the other setbacks that plagued *Goin' to Town*. On January 5, 1935, Battling Jack West died in Oakland, California, of a stroke. It was not entirely unexpected. He had suffered a severe heart attack in November and had been under the treatment of a Bay Area cardiologist since then. West's reaction to his passing was markedly detached. She canceled only one afternoon of filming to attend a funeral held for her father in Hollywood and remained in Los Angeles while Timony, Beverly, and John Junior followed Jack's body to Brooklyn for burial in the family crypt. The next day, she was again at work, telling reporters that despite her grief, she could not bear seeing the cast and crew suffer without pay if filming was delayed.[4]

Although Paramount was certainly anxious to get West's film out, her concern over delays was belied by her habitual tardiness in getting to the set. Everyone knew West was chronically late, but her lateness became extreme and costly to the studio, sometimes forcing the cast and crew to wait for over four hours for her to show up. Filming was also delayed by her meticulous demands. On at least two occasions, she forced Banton to redesign her gowns after they had been finished. Several times, dissatisfied with daily rushes, she insisted on reshooting not only scenes but entire sequences, sometimes on location. The film's expenditures soared. West also insisted the studio supply a personal vocal coach for a planned opera scene. After filming commenced, she demanded a role for her brother-in-law, Vladimir Baikoff. She compelled the studio to pay Timony as her associate producer.

Later, she insisted that Paramount ship a car belonging to Tito Coral, one of her male co-stars, to Detroit. A studio staff member indignantly scribbled next to West's request, "What is this?"[5]

During her years in vaudeville, West, parodying Gaby Deslys, had cultivated a temperamental reputation. Indeed, she had a willful side to her personality and, when provoked, a stormy temper. Although Paramount had promoted her as down-to-earth, by 1935 rumors of her extreme behavior trickled out to the public. Co-workers seemed more willing to testify that she was demanding, high-strung, and capricious. Stories of Lowell Sherman's impatience and unnamed insiders' frustrations circulated widely. A year before, the public read that necessity had forced West to reluctantly get a new car. "The other one just could not get me places without my worrying whether it would hold together," she explained. In 1935, they learned it was a customized limousine with her name printed on its cushions. It appeared to some that Mae West had "gone Hollywood"; she was no longer the people's star. "She has become aware of her fame," alleged the New York Times. This signaled the beginning of a transformation of her star image that would affect her career, films, and relationship with the press and her fans.[6]

The shifts in the Westian star image coincided with changes at Paramount. Her co-workers' public intolerance of her demands increased in direct proportion to the growth of her power within the studio. Studio workers, in particular directors and lower-level executives, had become resentful of this mighty female force and began airing their grievances. But they were taking advantage of an upheaval at the studio that allowed more public condemnation of La West. In February, just as filming on Goin' to Town was wrapping up, production chief Emanuel Cohen, one of West's strongest supporters at Paramount, was driven out. Rumors regarding reasons for his abrupt departure abounded. Some speculated that it was his overindulgence of demanding stars like Mae West; others believed that Paramount executives blamed Cohen, who pushed risqué productions, for the escalating censorship controversy. Later a few claimed that the studio fired Cohen after discovering that he had independently signed exclusive agreements with Paramount's biggest names, including Bing Crosby, Gary Cooper, and, of course, Mae West. These agreements forced Paramount to negotiate with him to renew their own stars' contracts.

While many at Paramount despised Cohen, West had lost a sympathetic ally. His replacement, director Ernst Lubitsch, proved to be much less tolerant. Lubitsch was a highly regarded artist; his films carried what industry insiders identified as the "Lubitsch touch," a distinctive and sophisticated wittiness. Despite his cinematic brilliance, he was a clumsy executive who micromanaged every picture on the lot, often insisting on personally direct-ing critical scenes in films under production. His heavy-handedness would definitely clash with Mae West's style.

It is not clear whether Lubitsch exerted directorial control over *Goin' to Town*, but it is certain that, in his position, he played a role in ordering the film back into production in March. A preview audience's tepid response in-dicated the film needed punching up. After adding a scene of Mae in western gear on horseback, reshooting scenes on location, and redoing the opera se-quence, Paramount screened the film for censors and received approval in early April. When the film was finished, many weeks behind schedule, the budget had soared to almost $925,500.[7]

Although *Goin' to Town* was ready by mid-April, Paramount held back its release, hoping to drum up public support for West's latest offering. After two years of constant attention, media coverage of the star was on the wane. Now, when West did receive press, it was alarmingly polarized. There were those who lamented the reformed Mae and longed for the Diamond Lil of yore. Others complained about her sameness; one newspaper reported that an exhibitor compared her to the "state fair" and contended that "when you've seen her once, you've seen everything." As a result, *Goin' to Town*'s promotional campaign took on a schizophrenic form. Although press re-leases emphasized a "streamlined" West in a contemporary setting, they also relied heavily on the Diamond Lil mystique. Paramount urged theaters to run clips from *She Done Him Wrong* and *I'm No Angel*. It was an ingenious move, for in early 1935 Hays had banned both films from further exhibition, warning Zukor that there was "no possibility of such pictures ever being shown again." The studio's tactic kept the legend of Diamond Lil alive.[8]

Paramount aimed for a big release on May 1, advising exhibitors to de-clare it "Mae Day" in their communities. Curiously, however, the studio post-poned the premiere until May 10. They were waiting for a storm to pass, for at the end of April, West suddenly received a barrage of free but troubling publicity. Journalists had dug up the only secret that could damage Mae West's reputation—she was married.

It turned out that Myrtle Sands, a Milwaukee WPA worker assigned to refile old vital records, had stumbled across a marriage certificate that bore the name of a Mae West of Brooklyn, New York, who in April 1911 had married a Frank Wallace. Sands notified the local press, and they immedi-ately located an old review of *A Florida Enchantment* praising the dancing team of Wallace and West. By April 22, Associated Press newswires carried the story across the country. Fans read headlines proclaiming, "Mae West in 1911 Wed in Milwaukee," and scrutinized a hazy facsimile of the marriage certificate. West issued a denial. "I never heard of the guy," she told reporters. Beverly assured reporters that it was a mistake. Eva Tanguay, living in retirement in Los Angeles, insisted that Mae was too young to have married in 1911 and speculated that the certificate belonged to another Mae West, a tall, brunette old-time burlesque queen. "I've had a lot of things come my way on Easter," West told reporters. "But this is the first time I ever got a husband for a present."[9]

Despite the wisecracks, the alleged marriage severely threatened West's star persona. She grew terse with reporters hounding her about the story, which only further confirmed her transformation into a Hollywood diva. For journalists, the news was a boon, and the hunt for evidence was on. One Manhattan reporter dug up a photo of a Frank Wallace who played a singing waiter in *Diamond Lil*. Even though Mark Linder confirmed that this Wallace spent quite a bit of time in West's dressing room, the media determined he was the wrong man. Another journalist discovered the Burmeister wedding license application. When confronted, Burmeister blustered that it was just some cheap publicity stunt.

Soon reporters were hot on the trail of another Frank Wallace, a down-on-his-luck vaudevillian living in a cheap New York theatrical hotel. Gaunt, balding, and middle-aged, he was hardly "the tall, dark, and handsome" suitor that seemed to be West's standard fare. On April 24, national newspapers quoted Wallace exclaiming, "What a girl — what a girl! If I had the money I would still be sending her flowers every week. . . . I suppose she has long forgotten her old partner and husband." Wallace insisted they had kept the marriage secret, parting so West could get ahead in show business. Initially, he also claimed they had divorced. Reporters, failing to locate divorce papers, did discover Wallace had been married to another woman since 1916. Wallace blamed Timony for mishandling the matter but his second wife divorced him anyway. He soon picked up a partner named Trixie La Mae for his new vaudeville act — called "Mr. Mae West."

West continued to deny the marriage. She declared the marriage certificate a fake and Wallace an opportunist. "I'm glad if some New York hoofer has been able to get a job out of all this publicity," she stated. "But personally, I've had enough of it." On the eve of *Goin' to Town*'s debut, West was in a precarious position. The press's persistence in contrasting Wallace's impoverishment with her opulent lifestyle threatened her populist appeal. Furthermore, she had evaded the question of her birth date, shaving a few years off her age, but the Milwaukee marriage certificate made it difficult to conceal that she was over forty.[10]

Even more harmful was the notion that Mae West, America's most inviting sex symbol, was a married woman. Studios had traditionally covered up stars' marriages, especially those of actresses, fearing that matrimony would undermine their public appeal. Such revelations were especially harmful to Mae West. In part, her image rested on her rejection of the cult of domesticity and its most fundamental institution, marriage. The appearance of a husband jeopardized this rebellion. No matter what the censors mandated, for West to be married was unthinkable, a contradiction to her image as an independent woman resisting male domination.

West's seemingly unwedded state had permitted her characters to straddle a line between acceptable and unacceptable behavior. As a single woman, she had more freedom to challenge the double standard she so detested; she could enjoy the company of as many men as she liked. "Essential to the Westian tradition of cozy hospitality," observed *Time*, "is the point that she has never married." For West to be both married and of easy virtue was too much of a jolt to conventional morality. Verification of her marriage threatened to convert West, along with her inseparable fictional character, from a freewheeling celebrant of Eros into one of the era's most shameful of female figures, an adulteress. Maybe Mae West was not really, as fans had seen her, "on the level" and "regular." The impression was reinforced by a suit Wallace filed in mid-May in New York alleging that West's denials had resulted in "humiliation [and] unpleasantness and caused the public and my friends to assume I am an imposter."[11]

Wallace's suit hit the newspapers just as *Goin' to Town* debuted in theaters nationally. Despite his claims, fans were eager to see how West was faring under Breen's increasing control. With the help of loyal moviegoers, *Goin' to Town* opened big in cities throughout the country, generating solid box office its first week out.[12]

In *Goin' to Town*, Cleo Bordon inherits a western ranch from her deceased cattle-rustler fiancé. The property comes complete with racehorses, oil wells, and a handsome, well-bred oil engineer, Edward Barrington, who rebuffs her advances. "She's rather crude oil," he snickers. Cleo's financial adviser, Winslow, warns her that Barrington is only interested in women of his own social class. This makes him even more of a challenge, and Cleo resolves to make him love her.

She follows Barrington to Buenos Aires, where she enters one of her horses in a championship race. All of European and American high society has ventured to the city for the races, and Winslow tutors Cleo on social graces. But his attempts are futile, and the blue bloods, especially the female set, look upon her with disdain, one remarking that she needs a "lesson in keeping her place." Nonetheless, Cleo is indefatigable. Her horse comes in first, beating one backed by the snobbish Mrs. Crane Brittany. Unable to win over Barrington, Cleo buys her way into a marriage with Brittany's nephew,

Fletcher Colton. It is purely a business venture; she promises to pay his gambling debts, and he offers her a sterling family name.

Settling with Colton in the upscale Long Island community of Southampton, she redecorates his mansion with exotic animals and imposing nude male statues. She throws a high-society ball and finds that one of her guests, the Earl of Stranton, is really Barrington. He confesses that he has fallen for her. In the meantime, Cleo's faithful Indian servant discovers Colton has been murdered. The police determine that his killer is Ivan Valdov, a Russian gigolo hired by Brittany to expose Cleo's scandalous reputation. The film ends with Cleo betrothed to Barrington, warning the earl, "Take it easy, you'll last longer."[13]

Shortly before the picture's release, Breen declared to Hays that Paramount had "conscientiously avoided the more serious difficulties that have attended some of this star's previous pictures." But when theater lights went up, *Goin' to Town*'s audiences discerned that West had successfully slipped much past the censors. In the end, this film was lustier than *Belle of the Nineties*. Although Breen cut all references to prostitution, West successfully signified it anyway. For moviegoers, Mae was Diamond Lil, and advance publicity, drawing on clips from her now banned films, served as mementos of her scarlet past. West also planted subtle reminders in the dialogue. When a character exclaims, "I didn't know you speak Spanish," Cleo replies, "Don't think I worked in Tijuana for nothing." Furthermore, in lines Breen attempted to delete, Cleo confesses, "For a long time I was ashamed of the way I lived." Another character asks, "You mean to say you've reformed?" "No," answers Cleo. "I got over being ashamed." While playing craps, she tells her male opponent she does not mind losing—"I'll roll you whether I do or I don't." In an even bawdier exchange with Ivan, she refuses his marriage proposal, telling him, "As a husband, you'd get in my hair."[14]

After *Goin' to Town*'s release, both critics and reformers burst forth with complaints. *Motion Picture Daily* pounced: "The Decency League and those in charge of the Production Code must have taken a vacation while this picture went into circulation." The *New York Times* condemned it as "gutter vulgarity." E. Robb Zaring of Indiana's Methodist Episcopal Church fired off a letter to Breen. "Several of my friends report that it is the same old May [*sic*] with no effort at cleaning up," he protested. "But what I cannot understand is how this particular actor who stands for a particular phase of morals should have been permitted to put another over on the American youth."[15]

Others simply branded it a bad film. "Writing is shoddy," huffed the *Hollywood Reporter*. "Mae West's poorest," declared *Variety*. The *New York Times*'s Andre Sennwald, earlier a defender, charged that "Joe Breen and his censorial shears have not killed Mae West. Mae West has committed artistic harakiri." In his opinion, this film lacked West's "splendid earthiness." He decreed *Goin' to Town* West's "swan song," noting that her attempts to create a new character revealed both the enduring popularity of the original and her inability to move beyond a role censors now refused to allow her to play. "She seems doomed regardless what road she chooses," he concluded.[16]

Although it produced above-average box office returns, *Goin' to Town* fell well below West's earlier films. As Sennwald observed, much of this resulted from attempts to move West's character in a new direction. For all Cleo shared with her Westian sisters, she was, as many detected, a departure. Based on *The Hussy*'s Nona Ramsey, Cleo resurrected an earlier formation of West's stage persona, an immature version of Diamond Lil. Like Nona, Cleo lacks the self-reflective and transcendent qualities that made the Mae West character so popular. Lil, Tira, and Ruby did not need a Winslow to explain Barrington's class prejudices; they would have quickly discerned and rejected them. In *Goin' to Town*, however, West's trademark rejection of high society was missing. Like Nona, Cleo is a climber, willing to deny her class background to attract a man of the elite. "You have the uncomfortable feeling," Sennwald wrote, "that she has developed a slight feeling of inferiority toward the socially elect whom she is presumably lampooning." Lil, Tira, and Ruby did not really aspire to join the upper class; they just wanted its money and its men.[17]

West may have known that the absence of substantive class critique threatened the film's appeal. Initially, the opera scene, where West performed an aria from *Samson and Delilah*, functioned to give not only Cleo but also West some "class." When it was first filmed, she presented it seriously to demonstrate that she could stretch beyond popular ballads and blues, but after previews, the scene was completely reshot with West burlesquing it. Still, *Variety* complained that the final version seemed lacking, just a little too serious. In May 1935, the country still lingered in depression, and seeing the Westian character of the working-class heroine throw in, even just a little, with silk hats did not sit well, especially when the star herself seemed to be selling out.

Cleo also presented a less emboldening image for women. She embarrasses, disparages, and even literally lassos the snobbish Edward Barrington, yet Cleo has to work far harder than the mature Westian character to get her man. While Lil, Tira, and even Ruby find that their male suitors often deceive them, they remain supremely manipulative. Men fall left and right for Cleo, but her relentless and often futile pursuit of Barrington lacks Westian boldness. Barrington's uncontested elitism and conceit prevents West's trickster from shining triumphant. Cleo seems just a little too desperate, traveling the world and giving in to upper-crust affectations for just one man. Sennwald bellowed, "Whoever heard of Mae West chasing a man?"[18]

Still, *Goin' to Town* reaped a profit, and Paramount reportedly boosted her salary to assure that she would not bolt for a better offer. Newspapers calculated that West was one of the richest women in the United States; she earned almost $340,000 in 1934 and was well on her way to earning over $480,000 for 1935. By 1936, only one other American made as much as Mae West: the powerful newspaper publisher and old Tammany nemesis William Randolph Hearst.

Throughout the summer of 1935, Mae West remained the subject of media glare as Frank Wallace continued to push his claims. More evidence of the marriage surfaced. West's police record listed her as married, and newswires flashed a photo of a spry, brunette Mae posed in a crescent moon with a straw-hatted, cigar-chomping Frank Wallace. Anyone who looked carefully at it could see that she proudly displayed a small wedding band on her left hand. Reporters tracked down the judge and the county clerk present for the marriage ceremony, but neither recalled the couple. An interview with Anna Szatkus, Frank Wallace's mother, was no help. She remembered her son's wife Mamie but could not tell whether Mamie was the infamous Mae West because she never went to the movies. However, one movie magazine writer, Robert Eichberg, revealed that when he approached Wallace, the hoofer promised to give "any sort of story we wanted on Mae—if we hired him." Eichberg concluded the marriage was a scam.[19]

West had other supporters. In July, the nation's leading fan magazine, *Photoplay*, featured an article in which she denied Wallace's claims. "I am not married. Not to Frank Wallace. Not to Jim Timony, my manager," she declared. "Shall I draw a diagram? I'm a single gal with a single-track mind." *Motion Picture Magazine* also came to her aid. In his regular feature, J. Eugene Chrisman, who had befriended West, ignored the Wallace scandal. Rather, he focused on West's reputation for extreme generosity, reporting on friends and strangers alike whom West had helped. Keeping the legend alive, Sidney Skolsky, in his nationally syndicated newspaper column, reassured fans that West was unchanged by fame and fortune. "She doesn't pretend," he wrote. "She talks the same language to all men, whether they are congressmen or prizefighters."[20]

During the Wallace scandal, Jim Timony began to emerge from exile. He assumed an active role in fighting off Wallace's claims and the negative publicity that accompanied them. Wallace claimed the former barrister threatened him with ruin if he did not retract his allegations. Furthermore,

Timony continued to handle West's business affairs, advising her as she purchased more real estate in the Los Angeles area. In addition to expanding her holdings in the San Fernando Valley, some of which she eventually sold to Mary Pickford, West acquired a restaurant for Beverly to run. She also purchased the Ravenswood and its adjoining property.

West bought the Ravenswood for personal reasons. She remained securely entrenched in her apartment, well protected by a team of bodyguards that now included former prizefighter Johnny Indrisano. But she ran into resistance from the Ravenswood's owner when she began entertaining the African-American middleweight boxing champion William "Gorilla" Jones in her apartment. In the past, African Americans who called at the Ravenswood for West were either employees or there on the pretense of business. Jones's visits were clearly social. Finally, one day the management refused to allow her to bring him up. Rather than protest against such racism, West purchased the building. She also hired his parents, Henry and Daisy, to supervise her two-bedroom apartment's household staff and to deal with reporters.

West had met their son in 1934 and was acting as his sponsor and manager. Jones was a good-looking, powerful boxer who wore expensive clothes, drove fancy cars, and shared West's love of jewels and exotic animals. (He had a pet lion that sported a diamond-encrusted collar.) West provided him with financial advisers and urged him to invest his winnings in real estate and a trust fund. Jones was fiercely loyal to West; he claimed that she forbade the use of racial slurs in her presence. Reportedly, he throttled a man he overheard making an unflattering comment about her. Both West and Jones publicly denied that they had an affair, but privately she admitted it was true. They would remain friends until her death.

Knowing Mae West, a permanent fixture at local fights, was advantageous for any boxer. West was more than just a celebrity; she had money and, even more important, connections. Owney Madden was a powerful figure in prizefighting, capable of arranging critical bouts for fighters. West insisted that her influence with Madden helped set up the match between Joe Louis and James Braddock in 1937. Louis, the victor, become the first African American since Jack Johnson to claim the world's heavyweight championship title. While West's boast was probably exaggerated, it may have contained some truth. Racial barriers had prevented Louis from his shot at the crown, and his management often relied on underworld ties to arrange bouts.

West seemed particularly predisposed toward supporting African-American boxers. She had hired another, featherweight Chalky Wright, as her chauffeur. (She eventually replaced him with his brother Lee to prepare Chalky to

return to the ring.) As with Jones, Tinsel Town gossips maintained that
Wright and West were intimate. Both parties denied the rumors.[21]

Wright figured prominently in West's life in the fall of 1935 as she faced a
series of extortion threats. In early September, she received a letter demanding $1,000 and warning that acid would be thrown in her face. The district
attorney assigned special investigator Blayney Matthews to the case. Over the
next few weeks, several more notes arrived, now threatening death. Finally, a
letter arrived instructing West to place $1,000 in a tin can in some bushes in
front of a Sunset Boulevard studio. A police detective, Harry Dean, in a white
fur-trimmed coat and makeup, posed as Mae West and accompanied Chalky
Wright to make the drop. Police surrounded the area; Wright showed up and
deposited the money. The extortionist never materialized.

A follow-up note directed West to leave the money in a purse in a vacant
lot near the Warner Bros. studio. This time West went in person. Wright,
who carried a pistol to protect her, pulled up with her in the back. He
climbed out of her enormous limousine, deposited the purse, and then
whisked her away. After several minutes, police observed a man approach
the lot, examine the purse, replace it, and walk away. He later returned,
grabbed the purse, and fled. Police descended on the suspect and wrestled
him to the ground. He was a Greek immigrant named George Janios, and he
worked as a studio cafeteria busboy. At the same time, officers did a sweep of
the area, rounding up several more men and booking them all on suspicion
of extortion.

The FBI learned of the extortion letters on October 8, when they read the
reports of Janios's arrest in the newspapers. FBI Director J. Edgar Hoover
sent an angry letter to Los Angeles bureau head Joseph E. P. Dunn, pointing
out that mail threats were the agency's responsibility. Dunn reported that the
Los Angeles DA had bypassed the local office and that police had been carrying out an investigation for almost a month without his knowledge. Dunn
telephoned West, who refused to talk to him. When he showed up at the
Ravenswood at two A.M., he was informed that she was not home. He then
contacted Blayney Matthews, who abruptly informed the agent that "he
would not turn these extortion letters over even to President Roosevelt." Another agent, E. A. Tamm, confided to Hoover that the DA had provided West
with free police protection for over a year. He also reported that agents had
ascertained that "the District Attorney's office out there and the newspapers
run a sort of a racket relative to information about the 'stars' and 'they simply
won't let go until the information is on the streets.'"

When Agent Dunn threatened to call the DA and West before a grand
jury, they both had a quick change of heart. The studio arranged for West to

meet with the agent, and the DA relinquished the investigation to the feds. Solving the case, however, was another matter. Of those arrested, only George Janios remained in jail, and he obviously could not read or write English. A judge, determining that Janios was simply an innocent passerby, set him free. For several months, federal agents collected evidence, even taking handwriting samples from Paramount employees, but it all proved inconclusive. Newspapers soon reported that West had requested the case be "deferred."[22]

While the FBI remained stumped, West's police bodyguard, Jack Chriss, offered to solve the case for one hundred dollars a day. West agreed, and, in turn, Chriss hired two high school students, one of them James Robert Parrish, who later became a Hollywood director, to carry out surveillance for ten dollars a night. For several weeks, the teens tailed Wright and Indrisano, reporting to Chriss that neither man was a likely suspect. Although the FBI failed to make any arrests, Parrish believed that Chriss was behind the extortion plot. Reportedly, the detective was eventually kicked off the force and ended up in prison.[23]

The extortion scandal occurred several weeks into filming on West's next project. The studio had presented her with a story entitled *Hallelujah, I'm a Saint* that chronicled the metamorphosis of a scarlet woman into a devout missionary. West believed it could be nicely merged with Frisco Kate and, with help, produced a screenplay that eventually was entitled *Klondike Annie*. It chronicled the adventures of the Frisco Doll as she traveled from Shanghai to San Francisco to the Klondike.

For the film, West demanded and got acclaimed director Raoul Walsh, who had worked on *Sadie Thompson*, a screen adaptation of *Rain*. Although early in filming the two had a blowup (West had covered only four pages of script in eleven days, angered because the studio had failed to assign Struss as her cameraman), they quickly patched up their differences. Walsh actually appreciated her careful attention to detail and often went along with her suggestions. West liked Walsh's willingness to coach rather than direct her. Skolsky reported that "no matter who is on a Mae West set and who is directing the flicker, you can tell what Mae West says, goes."[24]

West was equally satisfied with her cast. For her leading man, the studio supplied the talented Victor McLaughlin. West found parts for old friends and colleagues as well as her brother-in-law. While Doll's Chinese employer, Chan Lo, was played by a white actor, West insisted on Chinese-American actors for other roles and on Chinese-American musicians to accompany her onscreen.[25]

From the moment the project reached Will Hays in late June 1935, it was clear—West was going to be embroiled in one of the hardest-fought censorship battles of her career. *Klondike Annie* was born amidst escalating criticism of the Hays Office. On the studio's side, John Hammell was again on duty to assure censors and the public that West would not get out of hand. But it was evident that Hammell functioned more as a public relations tool than a quality control expert. His first act was to circumvent Breen by working directly with Hays over the telephone. Breen eventually interceded, resolute that the studio would conform to his demands. *Klondike Annie* was a critical test of his power and effectiveness. This time Breen was determined to rein in Paramount and Mae West; he not only ordered cuts but personally rewrote unacceptable scenes and dialogue.[26]

Klondike Annie's original drafts told a tale of spiritual regeneration during the gay nineties. Frisco Doll is a Shanghai gambling palace "hostess," who accidentally kills Chan Lo while fighting off his advances. Fearing retribution and arrest, Doll escapes to San Francisco, where she secures passage to the Klondike on a frigate. On board she meets an evangelist named Soul Savin' Annie. They establish a warm friendship, and when Annie falls ill, Doll remains faithfully by her side. Despite Doll's efforts, Annie dies before they reach Nome.

To elude capture in Nome, Doll assumes Annie's identity. She soon "becomes a changed woman," embracing Annie's cause and leading a religious revival that brings salvation to the rowdy settlement. In the end, her deception revealed, she resolves to stand trial for Chan Lo's murder, believing that her faith will sustain her and that she will be exonerated because she killed him in self-defense.[27]

While the original plot showed the redemption of Frisco Doll, censors refused to permit the moral regeneration of West's imagined self. The proposed story flagrantly violated the Production Code by depicting prostitution, miscegenation, murder, and, in Breen's estimation, a burlesque of religion. He went to work cutting the script. Among numerous deletions, he excluded any hint of sexual intimacies, especially between the races. In the end, his alterations prevented West from being either too bad or too good; he would not allow her to portray either a prostitute or a missionary. Breen warned the studio to take care "that Doll is *not* in any sense masquerading as a preacher or any other character known and accepted as a minister of religion ordained or otherwise. Rather her assumed character should be that of a social service worker." He prohibited West from wearing "religious garb," quoting or even handling the Bible, singing hymns, and preaching. Demanding that the mission become a settlement house, Breen devised what he considered to be acceptable and entertaining substitutions:

Shots of Doll playing games with the rough miners, teaching them Mother Goose rhymes, etc. Settlement workers make it a practice to gather children around the settlement house to cut out paper dolls or play charades. Why not have Doll giving the rough miners a bit of the same instruction?

Additionally, he mandated the inclusion of a temperance message, transforming Doll into a "sort of Carrie Nation, cleaning up the saloon."[28]

Breen had underestimated West's ingenuity, the studio's tenacity, and the power that Diamond Lil had over the public's imagination. Combining these forces, West presented, or signified, her original story. Regardless of the censors' dogged interference, the film retained most of its original content.

In the final version, Doll is a blues singer in a San Francisco casino owned by wealthy Chinese prince Chan Lo. Captivated by Doll's beauty, he keeps her virtually a prisoner, but she grows restless under his obsessive attentiveness and schemes to run away. When Chan Lo tries to punish her with torture, she stabs him to death. She flees San Francisco on a freighter bound for the Klondike's gold fields and captures the heart of its captain, Bull Brackett.

At a stopover in Vancouver, the frail and aged Sister Annie Alden boards. Bound for a settlement house in Nome, she tells Doll of her determination to "provide material and spiritual guidance" to the unruly frontier folk. Annie learns of Doll's sordid past and sweetly urges her to repent. "It takes courage to be good, but I know you have the courage," Annie says. "If you'd try you could resist every temptation." Doll puffs a cigarette and drawls, "What's the good of resisting temptation? There'll always be more."

Annie continues her efforts to "save" Doll, offering her a book entitled *Settlement Maxims*. Over the course of the long voyage, Doll develops affection and respect for the fragile settlement house worker. But the trip is hard and Annie declines, eventually suffering a heart attack. Doll nurses the failing reformer, feeding her spoonfuls of soup. As their ship pulls into Nome's harbor, Doll returns Annie's book, admitting, "I've begun to see things different now. . . . You know I actually enjoyed readin' it." With her last breath Annie gasps, "I won't need it anymore. May it keep you in the path of righteousness all the days of your life."

Doll mourns only briefly, for Nome's handsome police inspector, Jack Forrest, has boarded the vessel with a warrant for her arrest. Desperate, she switches places with Annie. Slipping on Annie's bonnet and modest black dress, she convinces Forrest that the Frisco Doll died en route to Nome.

Debarking, Doll unhappily discovers that she must continue her masquerade until Bull's ship receives clearance to depart. But after she dupes Nome's settlement house workers into believing she is Sister Annie, guilt overcomes her. She realizes Annie's death has benefited her and decides to repay her fallen friend by revitalizing the struggling settlement house. She organizes a town meeting, invites the entire community, and solicits support from the suggestively clad and tightly corseted saloon proprietress, Fanny Radler. When Radler balks, Doll warns her, "Listen you, I speak your language too. . . . Anytime you take religion for a joke, the laugh's on you and if you know what's good for you, you'll be there."

The following Sunday night the settlement house overflows with happy celebrants. Doll enters to cheers and delivers a rousing temperance song. The auditorium grows quiet as she speaks:

> I once made the mistake of thinking that religion was only for certain kinds of people. But I found out different. I came to realize that you don't have to go around lookin' sad and wearing a long face to be good. I want to show you that you can think right and do right every day of your lives and still have a good time in this world.

Overcome, a member of the audience rises and offers a confession, and Doll miraculously reunites him with his wife. At the meeting's conclusion, congregants eagerly fill the collection plate and happily recess for refreshments served by Fanny Radler and her dance hall girls.

The town marvels at Doll's talents, one settlement worker exclaiming "Sister Annie has accomplished the impossible! They're shutting down the town on Sundays and promise law and order will be restored!" Singlehandedly, Doll has saved Nome and uplifted its residents. Furthermore, her love life improves. Bull waits in port hoping she will join him on the high seas, but she has also attracted the affections of Jack Forrest, who, after discovering her true identity, offers to resign his post and help her escape.

What will Doll do? Choose Brackett or Forrest? Remain a saint or a sinner? "Caught between two evils," she muses, "I generally like to pick the one I've never tried before." But after reflection, Doll sheds Annie's dowdy attire and emerges in full Diamond Lil regalia. She instructs the flock to construct a new building and a large sign reading "Sister Annie Alden's Settlement House" and swaggers offscreen and out of town.

The film ends with Doll aboard Bull Brackett's ship determined to return to San Francisco and turn herself in. She tells Bull of a dream in which "Annie spoke to me. I heard her say 'Go back and do the right thing.'" Certain the jury will find her innocent of Chan Lo's murder, Doll explains, "I've got to make up for my past." Bull objects to her reformation, and as she reclines on a couch, she takes him in her arms. "You're no oil paintin'," she purrs, "but you sure are a fascinatin' monster." The scene fades out with a passionate kiss.[29]

Much hoopla surrounded the making of *Klondike Annie*. Rumors circulated about the film's scandalous material; Skolsky reported that West could not "even sit close to McLaughlin without alarming the censors." When the studio screened it for the censors on New Year's Eve 1935, however, Breen immediately granted it the seal of approval. Soon he discovered he had been tricked. Reading newspaper reports of *Klondike Annie*'s Los Angeles preview, he discovered that the studio had issued a different version of the film. Enraged, Breen demanded, after viewing this print, that the studio delete the unapproved dialogue and the scenes depicting torture, Chan Lo's murder, and Doll making up the deceased Sister Annie, complete with cigarette, to look like a prostitute. Privately, Breen wrote, "Just so long as we have Mae West on our hands with this particular kind of story which she goes in for, we are going to have trouble. . . . Lines and pieces of business, which in the script seem to be thoroughly innocuous, turn out when shown on the screen to be questionable at best, when they are not definitely offensive." As a result, *Klondike Annie* was not ready for release until late February 1936.[30]

The studio began a promotional campaign to undermine the censors' efforts to eliminate both religion and sex from the production. Studio publicity identified Sister Annie as "going to Alaska to join a band of missionaries" and Doll's Nome activities as "prayer meetings." Advertising highlighted the film's sexual undertones; publicists created slogans out of traditional Westian innuendos. "Come up and see me again, fellows. Thar's more gold in them thar hills," exclaimed one lobby poster. Another read, "Out where the whiskers grow just a little bigger, out where the he-men are faster on the trigger, out where the gold's awaiting the digger, that's where the West begins." More contests encouraging fans to submit Westian double entendres continued to instruct the public to recognize when and what West signified.[31]

As a result, most, if not all, of the audience left *Klondike Annie* thinking they had just seen a film about sex and religion. Diamond Lil was back. West affirmed this, declaring, "The character I created in *She Done Him Wrong* is the one I'm still using and it seems to be doin' alright." Several reviewers interpreted Doll to be what one labeled a "prostie." Many also perceived Doll and Chan Lo as lovers, signified by West's performance of a song entitled "I'm an Occidental Woman in an Oriental Mood for Love." Kindled by visual signification, viewers immediately recognized Doll's frock as that of a Salvationist; critics identified Sister Annie as a missionary, hearing West singing hymns and delivering sermons. Soon censors realized that they had been duped; Will Hays lamented, "My worst worry is not the alleged salaciousness, but the producer's failure to avoid the impression that it is a mission house picture and the Doll is masquerading as a missionary." Despite Breen's efforts, Diamond Lil had been saved.[32]

Of all her films, West was proudest of *Klondike Annie*. This project represented the most complex and articulate vision of her cinematic presence, a climax to Diamond Lil's saga. In *Klondike Annie*, West successfully intertwined sex and religion with sin and redemption in a tale that explored the primary components of American identity: race, class, and gender. Her work became a creative space that provided entertainment and also functioned as a social critique through an exploration of the self as well as the other. It revived the blues voice that had empowered her earlier work, following Doll on a journey, both physical and spiritual, where she faced junctures and commented about experiencing that experience. This film addressed the central questions that had driven West's work since she was a child doing imitations in her parents' living room. Identity became the pivotal issue at all levels of *Klondike Annie*. When Doll (alias Diamond Lil alias Mae West) switched places with Sister Annie, the masquerader assumed yet another masquerade. *Klondike Annie*'s power rested in its construction as the trickster's trickster tale. Journalist Eleanor Barnes compared West with enduring images of tricksterism: "There is no Mae West in reality today," she wrote. "She is as complete a creature of fancy and fantasy as Puck or the three witches in Macbeth."[33]

West had long comprehended that her character's appeal and power lay in its suspension between opposites. What made Diamond Lil and her sisters compelling was their existence somewhere between the good, represented by the stalwart Captain Cummings, and the bad, conveyed by the brutality of Gus, Chick, and Rita. But the Production Code's banishment of cinematic evil robbed West's characters of their sinfulness as well as undermining the contrasting pure wickedness that they struggled against both internally and externally. In *Klondike Annie*, West overcame this impediment through her artful implementation of signification, resurrecting the double voice lost in *Goin' to Town*. The blues-singing trickster had come home. Humorist James Thurber recognized West's dualistic essence and her role as mediator. In an illustration accompanying his hearty endorsement of *Klondike Annie*, he depicted Mae West with wings and halo, soaring in the heavens "invisibly above the bad boys and girls she goes to Alaska to join but remains to save or darn near."[34]

West as Doll had unleashed her trickster heroine to mediate between the sacred and the profane. *Klondike Annie* was so fluid and so powerfully covert that through it West played the ultimate prank. Censorship czars Breen and Hays diverged in their interpretation of the film, quarreling over its true nature and intent. Responding to Hays's allegations that *Klondike Annie* lampooned religion, Breen defensively denied that the film "even remotely hinted at . . . a travesty of religion." Both on and off the screen, the trickster had created chaos.[35]

What Breen and Hays both missed was that *Klondike Annie* functioned simultaneously as a "travesty of religion" and an exploration of the pathos of faith. As the Doll, or a doll, West becomes the ultimate signifier, a toy that is only representational and is never what it really is. Continually she pivots, mocking both the religious and irreligious. West even successfully incorporates a showdown between her selves, forcing Doll (posing as Sister Annie) into a confrontation with the symbolic prostitute Fanny Radler (signifying Diamond Lil). Doll speaks in both sacred and secular tongues, reminding Radler, the viewer, and even herself that "when you take religion for a joke, the laugh's on you."

By reversal and revision, *Klondike Annie* transforms a ridicule of religion into a morality play. Essentially the film assumes the motif of a conversion tale, following Doll as she passes from a state of sin to a state of grace, along the way challenging the contours of those stages.

In the beginning, Doll appears as a sinner. Playing on racist assumptions, she exists in what white society of the 1930s considered a degraded state; she is a white woman living among the Chinese in San Francisco's Chinatown, a community disparaged by whites as pagan. But immediately, Doll, the trickster, commences signification through inversion and reversal. Manipulating a series of polarities, Doll rebels by exploiting and inverting the racist stereotypes of the Chinese and Chinese Americans. In *Klondike Annie*, Chinese characters appear as either docile, subservient, and ingratiating or inscrutable, devious, and violent. While this reifies white racism, at the same time, West challenges some of its components. Her rendering of the blues-tinged "I'm an Occidental Woman in an Oriental Mood for Love" implies not only her desire for Asian men but that she has acted on it. As she sings, backed by Chinese musicians, the camera pans the crowd, showing a sellout audience composed almost exclusively of Chinese men who gaze yearningly upon her. But the stereotype of the predatory Chinese male is countered by shots of Doll gazing back with reciprocal passion. It constitutes a revolt against the cinematic male gaze, for West not only uses it to establish herself as an object of male desire but also to signify a filmic miscegenation. This is reasserted as she thanks the handsome Lon Fang, who aids her escape from Chan Lo. Glancing below Fang's waist, she murmurs, "I wish I could reward you somehow."

These Chinese characters serve as substitutes for black images prevalent in West's early films. Similarly, they highlight Doll's whiteness: She is the

"Occidental woman" and "a white doll," who, enslaved to Chan Lo, is the "pearl of pearls," sorrowful at her captivity. Yet her racial identity is contested. Her contacts remain confined to the Chinese. Doll speaks fluent Mandarin, appears in Asian dress, and shares the same status as the rest of Chan Lo's employees, all Chinese and also totally under his control. Like Doll, they remain virtual slaves to his whims. While Chan Lo reentrenches racism, he is counterbalanced by the other Chinese characters and their kindness. In a sense, his cruelty derives also from his class position; he is a prince, a capitalist, a composite of Western fiendishness and stereotyped Eastern brutality. It is those who serve him, Doll and his Chinese employees, who possess a humanness denied to Chan Lo by his aristocratic background.

Doll's escape with her Chinese maid, Fah Wong, on Bull Brackett's ship symbolizes the next stage in her conversion. Significantly, her repentance commences during an ocean voyage, a setting replete with Christian symbolism. As Doll crosses over to freedom, liberated from Chan Lo's enslavement, she is reborn into a new life (and identity) through a baptism of sorts on the high seas. But the ideology of racism lingers in this construction. Doll does not begin her spiritual renewal until freed from all Chinese ties, signaled when Fah Wong disembarks just before Sister Annie boards.

For the most part, Doll's conversion occurs through a linguistic match with Annie. And as Annie declines, Doll blossoms, growing in both allure and spiritual strength. By the time the ship reaches Nome, Doll has, in syncretic fashion, absorbed some of Annie's faith. Yet Doll emerges even more powerful than the evangelist, for she possesses the best of both the spirit and the flesh.

In the final stage of the conversion tale, the convert spreads the word. Doll's particular spirituality, a combination of the sacred and the profane, revises normal expectations regarding faith and provides her with an electric presence that furthers her evangelical efforts. Nome's settlement house workers are a weak, joyless, and lackluster bunch; they preach tiresome sermons and sing off key. But in her masquerade, Doll injects a renewed energy into their faith. With her raucous and demonstrative revival, she rejects dreary conventionality and religious formalism. This disruption of tradition creates a sacred space of empowerment. Doll seizes the pulpit, unseating ecclesiastical patriarchy, leading the entire town and its most hardened sinner, herself, to salvation.

Doll's reformulation of faith signifies on American society's relegation of sex and religion to polar extremes of the moral spectrum. Essentially, Doll resolves Diamond Lil's greatest dilemma, proving that sex and salvation need not be mutually exclusive, that the sexually experienced woman is not necessarily an evil woman. In West's re-vision of spirituality, the strongest believer is both righteous and sexual. "I didn't feel anywhere near as damned at this movie as I did, when I was a young man, at *Rain*," James Thurber confessed. "For in *Rain* a religious man goes sexual, and that disturbed me, but in *Klondike Annie* a sexual woman goes religious, and that gave me a sense of peace."[36]

Yet, in trickster fashion, West could leave no tale closed. In the final scenes, Doll calls into question not only her own conversion but even her success in wresting power from the male-dominated society. Coming full circle, Doll reemerges as Diamond Lil, corseted, gowned, and beplumed, seemingly ready to return to the scarlet life. Doll capitulates to Brackett, a pairing, like that in *SEX,* more suited to her station in life. However, even as she succumbs to the appropriate match, she signifies on gender restrictions. In the final scene, as Bull hungrily sizes her up, she calls him a "monster," revealing her passion but also latent resentment.

With *Klondike Annie*, West proved she still had box office pull. Record crowds turned out for this effort. New York City's Paramount Theater quickly scheduled extra shows starting at 8:30 A.M. and continuing until two in the morning. New York observers noted that fans were "storming" theaters despite horrific weather conditions. Although the film generally received negative reviews—*Variety* complained about its "rough, if unpalatable humor," and the *New York Times* declared it "excessively stupid"—fans remained loyal. Quigley's *Motion Picture Herald* reported that across the country the picture was raking in $2,500 to $8,500 over the average box office proceeds.[37]

Many speculated that West had been helped along by newspaper magnate William Randolph Hearst, an old foe from her censorship battles in New York. *Klondike Annie* had reawakened his ire. In an internal memorandum to his editors, he declared it "a filthy picture" and "an affront to the decency of the public." Banning advertisements for the film, he instructed, "After you have had a couple of good editorials regarding the indecency of this picture, then DO NOT mention Mae West in our papers again while she is on screen." Criticism of West, Paramount, and the censors appeared in Hearst publications nationwide; some called on Congress to take action against the star. Several editorials attacked the miscegenationist theme. "Mae West's Klondike Annie is a disgrace to everyone connected with it," declared one publication. "Paramount and Will Hays should be ashamed."[38]

Speculation on Hearst's motivations came from various sectors. Some theorized that the interracial love affair between Doll and Chan Lo outraged the conservative editor. Several contended that his ire stemmed from West's reported criticism of Hearst's mistress, actress Marion Davies. Still others cited West's refusal to appear gratis on *Hollywood Hotel,* a radio show hosted by Hearst columnist Louella Parsons. The *Motion Picture Herald* wagered that it had nothing to do with West but rather was aimed at Will Hays, who had tampered with a Hearst-backed film called *Ceiling Zero*. West ascribed it to sexism, jealously, and elitism—that Hearst "hated to see a woman in his own class."[39]

Paramount circumvented Hearst's attacks by running ads in his papers urging moviegoers to call theaters for information regarding an "important feature," which, of course, was *Klondike Annie*. Non-Hearst publications, citing the crowds filling theaters for the film, chuckled at the ineffectiveness of his campaign against Mae West. "Hearst papers have not stopped or even delayed her climb to fame," remarked Hollywood's *Citizen-News*. "This year she was rated well up in the list of the 10 biggest box office stars."[40]

Although *Klondike Annie* had allies, many joined the Hearst attack. While the Legion of Decency had rated the film suitable for adults, several individual parishes condemned it. Father Joseph B. Buckley of Washington, D.C., praised the Hearst editorials and urged fellow Catholics to boycott *Klondike Annie*. In a letter to Paramount, the San Francisco Motion Picture Council, representing religious and community organizations, complained that "any picture that represents its heroine as a mistress to an Oriental, even as murderess, then a cheap imitator of a missionary jazzing religion is not in harmony with the other educational forces." A postcard arrived at Paramount, addressed to both Will Hays and Mae West, bearing a scrawled message, "Shame on you."[41]

West also emerged in the center of another crisis. Just as *Klondike Annie* hit the silver screen, a Senate subcommittee proceeded with hearings on block booking. Quigley's *Motion Picture Herald* proclaimed that "the block booking controversy" had "narrowed down to the heaving bosom and bustles of Mae West." Noting that West "symbolized" the arguments against the practice, the publication reported that exhibitors now used her censurable reputation as ammunition in their fight against the studios. Movie moguls responded that box office evidence bore out that exhibitors not only profited from her films but had demanded them, canceling films of the "quality type that have good moral standing but questionable commercial appeal." In the end, the studios won this round; block booking was not outlawed until 1948. But West's image as the anti–block booking poster girl lingered on.[42]

As West confronted censors, negative reviews, Hearst, opposition from movie reformers, and the block-booking controversy, she also encountered big problems with Ernst Lubitsch. He had proven to be an almost universally despised studio boss. His domineering style alienated many at Paramount, especially West, whose contract had accorded her creative control. She resisted his directives regarding casting and claimed she fought off his attempts at taking over a critical scene in *Klondike Annie*. After he criticized the thinness of McLaughlin's part, she expanded it but warned him, "Shakespeare had his style and I have mine." One morning Lubitsch appeared in West's onset dressing room to reprimand her for chronic tardiness. West turned to her dressing table, grabbed a hand mirror, and began hitting him with it. He bolted from the set as a group of extras burst into applause.

After Cohen's departure, Paramount was a much less accommodating place for Mae West. "Paramount didn't seem like home to me any longer," she remembered. She was not the only one who felt that way; Lubitsch's reign had produced many disgruntled studio workers. To make matters worse, in January 1936, West was warned that she must strictly follow orders and that Paramount's production chief would not tolerate any challenges or deviations; several directors found similar missives in their mailboxes.[43]

Lubitsch's actions placed the studio in a precarious position. As the film industry bounced back, several producers, including Cohen, established independent film companies and began competing for stars who were in the market for better deals. In West's case, the studio had failed to get *Klondike Annie* out before the end of 1935, a violation of her two-picture-a-year contract. In January, she notified Paramount that she considered her contract null and void and intended to sign with another studio. Paramount insisted that the contract stood and that *she* had violated it by refusing to prepare another picture in time.

In February, angered by Paramount's response, West, disguised in a black wig, boarded a Chicago-bound train. Meeting Cohen in the Windy City, she attended a hit play, a Broadway touring show called *Personal Appearance*. The Hollywood gossip mill reported that West had decided to exercise her option with Cohen and make a picture for him.

While there were those on the lot—among them, most likely, Lubitsch, who were ready to let her go, it appears others wanted desperately to hang on to Mae West. She calculated that by 1936 she had made the studio almost $15 million. While she was in Chicago, one of her strongest supporters, William Le Baron, was elevated to production chief, and he informed West that Lubitsch had been excused to return to directing. Timony trumpeted victory, telling the press that Lubitsch had mistakenly "thought in his Hitler way, he could push Miss West around." Yet Timony cautioned that West was still scouting for a better deal. For West's part, when she returned to Los Angeles, she refused to comment. But upon her arrival, she coined one of her most famous lines; she greeted an LAPD officer assigned to escort her home with "Is that a gun in your pocket or are you happy to see me?"[44]

Lubitsch may have significantly hurt Paramount's efforts to retain Mae West. When confronted by reporters as he departed for a European vacation, he claimed that most of the friction between himself and the star originated over her weak screenplay. He criticized West for pairing herself with actors that he thought were too young and claimed she had reduced McLaughlin to a "mere stooge." When pressed about Timony's comments, he responded, "Try to push her around did I? She's much too heavy."[45]

Within a week, West announced she would make pictures for Cohen but under Paramount's name. Some have argued that this was a clean break with the studio, that Paramount executives were anxious to get rid of her and distance the studio from her rowdy reputation. But Paramount supplied her with their directors, cameramen, cast, and crew, as well as handling her publicity and putting their name all over her films. In early March, a moving van arrived at the Paramount lot with West following in her limousine. In true Westian fashion, she personally supervised the movers who loaded the truck with her belongings. Her bungalow went to Mary Boland, a comedic actress popular for playing wives and mothers. Skolsky lamented in his column, "It isn't the same."[46]

Cohen had a project in mind for West when she arrived on his Major Motion Pictures lot—a cinematic version of *Personal Appearance*. For several years, Hollywood studios had considered filming the play. A lampoon of the film industry, it centered on the adventures of an egotistical star, Mavis Arden, who is stranded in rural Pennsylvania. Although the play had not been officially banned, Hays had blocked earlier attempts to film it, contending that it constituted "a libel on the industry and its employees." It was the perfect vehicle for West to vent her disgust with moviedom.[47]

In February, even before West made her move, Cohen began maneuvering to secure the Hays Office's approval of *Personal Appearance*. Initially he sent drafts of the script, asking for Breen's confidential and unofficial feedback. Breen rejected it. Nonetheless, Cohen assured Breen that all revisions would conform to Production Code guidelines. In May, West sent her version. Again, Breen declared it unacceptable, citing a negative depiction of a Jewish producer, Mavis Arden's promiscuity, the dialogue's double entendres, and "all the business of the hay in the barn" as Code violations. Into the summer, Cohen inundated Breen with new drafts of *Personal Appearance*. Breen began to offer suggestions for revisions. By August, the script had been renamed *Go West Young Man*, and with the exception of a few plugs for Paramount performers, direct mention of Hollywood personalities had been almost entirely deleted, including several references to Mae West herself. (Mavis Arden, to her intense frustration, is constantly being mistaken for La

West.) Additionally, it was a presidential election year, and censors excised the movie's political content. Mavis's observation that "a politician is usually a guy that promises the working man a full dinner pail—and then after the election, he steals the dinner pail" disappeared, as did her anti–New Deal contention that the government spent "millions" on "silly old dams"—about which "nobody gives a damn."[48]

Filming finally began in late summer 1936. One of the most attractive features of West's deal with Cohen was his apparent willingness to allow her artistic freedom. For the most part, he met all her demands. For her leading man, Cohen recruited cinema heartthrob Randolph Scott. Struss was brought on board, Baikoff received a role, Johnny Indrisano was cast as her chauffeur, and Jack La Rue, who had played Pablo Juarez in the original *Diamond Lil*, got a part. West also insisted on the inclusion of Nicodemus Stewart, an African-American singer and dancer who appeared with the Cab Calloway Orchestra, which had taken over as the Cotton Club's house band.[49]

In *Go West Young Man*, Mavis Arden, one of Hollywood's biggest stars, is selfish, temperamental, and ill educated—a limited actress with a melodramatic delivery. She constantly misuses words. "A. K. [her producer] was right when he said we was makin' pictures for maroons," she tells her press agent Morgan, hired to make sure she upholds her contract, which forbids her from marrying for five years. Morgan's task is not easy, for Mavis is constantly on the prowl for male companionship.

On the road during a personal appearance tour, Mavis's limousine breaks down outside a small Pennsylvania town. Waiting for her car to be repaired, she endures several days at a local boardinghouse that is home to a teenage female movie fan, a stodgy old aunt, a disapproving professor, and, fortunately, a handsome young mechanic, Bud Norton. An aspiring inventor, Bud tells Mavis of his improvements in motion picture technology. "I'd just love to see your model," she remarks. Offering to take him to Hollywood, Mavis tells Bud, "I can't tell you the number of men I've helped to realize themselves." But Morgan intervenes, deceiving Mavis into believing that Bud would be leaving a local woman who is carrying his child. Mavis eventually discovers Morgan has lied and forces him to confess—he did it because *he* loves her. As the movie ends, Morgan and Mavis ride off together and she murmurs, "Men are my life."[50]

It seemed fitting that West would poke fun at her own star persona. Starting with her early appropriation of Gaby Deslys's star image, the Westian celebrity had been a parody. Mavis seemed to either confirm or challenge what everyone alleged West had become. With Mavis, West exposed the phoniness of stardom and Hollywood. Mavis is a complete fake, pretending to adore her fans but disparaging them behind their backs. Like her fans, who live for and through her pictures, she has no existence outside of the screen, interpreting life's crises by relating them to her movies' plots and relying on film dialogue to get her out of tight spots. Like the Mae West star image, Mavis seemed indistinguishable from her screen character. And the film revealed that Mavis was every bit the vamp that she played on the screen, leaving audiences doubting West's continued protestations that she and her characters were nothing alike. Significantly, the stage version's central character was a married woman who schemes to seduce men. But the image of a sexually promiscuous married woman was too bold, and too real, for censors, who mandated that Mavis be single. Still, society's rejection of the adulteress was exactly what West confronted as she battled to maintain her star persona. This blur of fantasy and reality created a dizzy array of mirrored images replicated over and over again, until it became a parody (Mavis) of a parody (Mae West). In this film, West, the trickster, rejected celebrity, the cult of celebrity, and the studios that manufactured celebrities. For some, it suggested that West was nothing like Mavis. For others, as the *New York Times* put it, Mae was "what casting directors call a natural."[51]

Mae also used *Go West* to criticize other aspects of the movie industry. Mavis denounces her producer because he "only cares about money." As Morgan recites press materials about Mavis's "heart of gold," an image also affixed to West, he looks dubious. West also took a jab at critics and censors. Teen movie fan Gladys relates a Mavis Arden plot to Aunt Kate, who dismisses the actress's pictures as all the same. Flustered, Gladys confesses confusion regarding the story, sighing, "You know how they cut pictures these days."

The censors had significantly altered *Go West Young Man*. As well as excluding sexual overtones and movie colony references, Breen excised elements of blackness. Initially, West had created four parts for African-American performers: a maid, a chauffeur, a cook, and a buffoonish mechanic for actor Nicodemus Stewart. Breen restricted West to white servants, stripping the script of all black characters with the exception of Stewart's mechanic.

Stewart played a lazy and dopey car mechanic in the style popularized by African-American actor Stepin Fetchit, slurring his words and moving with contorted and slow mannerisms. In early versions of the script, West contrasted him with a black female cook who speaks in dialect but is hardworking, sharp, and witty. Breen's deletion of this character as well as of the maid and chauffeur left only the most degrading of racial stereotypes to stand unanswered by any other black presence. Breen may have been responding to African-American protests over the almost uniform depiction of blacks in films as servants. More likely, since he made no alterations in Stewart's role, he was preventing West from signifying her affiliation with her black characters and her more rebellious messages. He also eliminated references to Mavis as a former Chicago blues singer. Ultimately, Breen's deletions created the most forceful affirmation of racist ideology in any Mae West film. At least one reviewer cited Stewart's character as the film's weakest part.[52]

However, most critics applauded *Go West Young Man*. The *New York Times* deemed the film "engagingly robustious." *Variety* congratulated West for successfully working within the Production Code but also noted, "No Mae West picture has been more Westful or zestful." Hearst ended his Mae West boycott, and his *New York Evening Journal*, joining with several others, proclaimed *Go West Young Man* to be her best film since *She Done Him Wrong*. Several reviewers praised her satire on filmdom. The *Indianapolis Star* declared it "a gorgeous lampoon at the expense of 'the beautiful and the dumb' of Hollywood." Mae's latest Westianism, "A thrill a day keeps the chill away," was added to her growing list of famous sayings.

Fans were equally satisfied. Paramount had scheduled *Go West Young Man* as the feature celebrating their Manhattan theater's tenth anniversary. Moviegoers packed the theater, and the *New York American* declared, " 'It's always sex o'clock at the Paramount,' as Joe Miller used to say. And Paramount is crowded." In December, after it had been out for almost a month, *Variety* announced that the film was "on the way to snug profits."[53]

Despite the enthusiasm of fans and critics, plenty disparaged this effort. Leading the pack was Quigley's *Motion Picture Herald*, which declared *Go West Young Man* "a new low mark in entertainment." Complaining that censors had again allowed her to run afoul of the Production Code, it labeled West's film as "a collection of coarseness and vulgarity." Women's clubs denounced the movie, and a California educators' group declared it "destructive of ethical standards, somewhat demoralizing, and totally lacking in charm." Author Graham Greene characterized West as "an overfed python" and claimed the film was "tedious, as slow and wobbling in its pace as Miss West's famous walk."[54]

In November 1936, just as *Go West Young Man* hit the theaters, *Photoplay* ran an article by a "Madame Sylvia" entitled "Is Mae West Skidding on the Curves?" It was a devastatingly negative assessment of West's career. Reviewing West's achievements since 1933, Sylvia observed, "She was one of the Big Ten at the box office that year. Now, she's number . . . well, I can't tell. I haven't got my specs." She blamed West's decline, in part, on censorship, "which removed nice, clean dirt from her pictures," but also complained that the star's famous full figure was her undoing. West had indeed gained weight since *I'm No Angel*, but she prided herself on her buxom proportions. With

Goin' to Town, however, a backlash against the Westian figure commenced. Criticism of West's curves paralleled the press's (and Paramount's) mounting disaffection with the actress. By rejecting the ample West, the media not only attacked her influence and success but also undermined one of her most empowering contributions to women, reentrenching traditional and oppressive notions regarding the female body and deglamorizing the Westian persona overall. "Plumpness is an insidious thing," wrote Madame Sylvia. "It sneaks up on you and becomes just plain fat."[55]

West battled back. In interviews, she reasserted her dedication to the people, attributing her negative publicity to her struggle with the powerful studios and censors. "I've had to fight for things all my life," she said. "Ever since I entered show business I've had to battle to give the people the sort of entertainment that they enjoy. As long as the public supports my pictures, I'll fight to provide what the people want." She understood keenly that her temperamental reputation resulted, at least in part, from her position as a strong woman defying the male-dominated film world. "Sometimes I grow weary of fighting to keep faith with the public," she told one fan magazine. "They liked me as Diamond Lil . . . but certain well-meaning executives believe I should do something different. Naturally I disagree. Then I get a reputation for being obstinate, hard to handle." The movie industry, initially so eager to celebrate the superwoman, was willing to undercut that image now that she had garnered so much real power.[56]

West's star image suffered even greater blows as Frank Wallace continued to file suits against her and disseminate stories of their early, giddy courtship. In November, coinciding with the release of *Goin' to Town*, Wallace filed an affidavit claiming he possessed letters addressed "My Dear Husband" and signed "Your little Mae." The *Los Angeles Daily News*, describing West as a "middle-aged screen siren," quoted her snapping, "I don't write letters."[57]

Yet Wallace persisted. In 1937, *Look* magazine reported that West was a millionaire. If Wallace could prove she was his wife, her assets would become his under California community property laws. In May 1937, his attempts to force her to admit to the marriage in court failed, but that summer, a judge ordered West to testify or face contempt charges. On July 7, West filed a statement in California Superior Court confirming that she was Mrs. Frank Wallace. But she maintained that his claim to her fortune was abrogated by two factors: They had never lived together as man and wife, and he had married another woman without obtaining a divorce.

It was a stunning admission that would forever change West's image in the public's mind. It confirmed that the woman that America had worshiped as a superwoman—powerful, funny, and sexy—was not only married but was also forty-three years old. Of all the attempts by the censors to desex Mae West, nothing came near the revelation that she was some man's middle-aged wife. Even worse, it further corroded her genuineness, a quality celebrated by her Depression-era fans. The press was especially unforgiving. One publication blasted West as "an overstuffed idol with feet of clay." " 'Mrs. Mamie Szatkus' was scarcely box-office for glamorous Mae West," snorted *Time*. Sidney Skolsky, one of her greatest supporters, was infuriated. "The villain of the week is Mae West," he huffed. "It will be difficult . . . for the Hollywood reporters to believe statements made by Mae West for she insisted that she was leveling with the press when she told them that she had never been married to Frank Wallace." For the rest of her career, West would struggle to reassert her credibility and desirability.[58]

Bring Me Rabelais

Varvara: Whom does your majesty wish in bed with her
  tonight—Rabelais or Voltaire?
Catherine: Bring me Rabelais, that's more to my mood.
            —Mae West, *Catherine Was Great*, 1943

A fter *Go West Young Man*, Mae West had a definite plan for her next project, a film on the life of the Russian empress Catherine the Great. Actually, West's interest in Catherine was an outgrowth of her aborted Queen of Sheba project. Realizing that the Queen of Sheba would never make it to the screen, she substituted Catherine. Mae identified with the German-born empress; she was impressed by Catherine's vast array of lovers and reputed proletarian sympathies. Beyond that, the empress was a woman who successfully confronted a patriarchal society and assumed a role normally restricted to men. "After years of surviving studio politics and handling vice-presidents," she wrote, "I saw Catherine was really a portrait of myself."[1]

Cohen firmly opposed the idea of Mae West playing Catherine the Great. In 1934, Dietrich's portrayal of Catherine in *The Scarlet Empress* had flopped. If Dietrich had failed as the regal empress, obviously the bawdy Mae West could hardly succeed. Cohen urged West to abandon the idea, revealing he had already decided on her next project, a film that would propel her back to the 1890s, the era that had made her famous.

West reviewed Cohen's script and immediately rejected it, insisting that she would only appear as Catherine. Cohen ignored her. In fact, he had already constructed a gay nineties set, recruited a director, hired a crew, and signed on cameraman Karl Struss. Additionally, he had arranged for gowns by acclaimed French designer Schiaparelli. West protested; she had prepared a script for Catherine. Cohen stubbornly countered that any film on early Russia was too expensive.

Eventually Cohen convinced West to preview a few songs composed for his film. After a listening session in her dressing room, she chose the tune that Cohen disliked the most, "Mademoiselle Fifi." She then announced she had an inspiration. Over the next ninety minutes, she dictated a new story-line, merging the original script with the song. Her version followed the exploits of a beautiful blond Bowery con artist, Peaches O'Day, who, to escape incarceration, dons a black wig and poses as a French entertainer. The film would be called *Every Day's a Holiday*.[2]

In early August 1937, Cohen delivered the first draft of *Every Day's a Holiday* to Joseph Breen. In a letter, the producer stated that Mae West had "bent over backward" to produce a clean script, to the extent "that it marred the entertainment value." "It is our belief," he wrote, "that there is not a single line or situation which can be considered objectionable from a censorship standpoint or from a public standpoint." Of course, Breen immediately rejected the script, branding it "enormously dangerous" and a blatant violation of the Production Code. He listed numerous lines and scenes carrying what he identified as "double meaning" that required revision or deletion before he could tender approval.

Curiously, Cohen did not protest Breen's decision but rather asked him to resend his letter with even more deletions. In his personal files, Breen noted that Cohen requested that he eradicate several more scenes and pleaded for an even more strident letter, hoping that it would "have some force or effect with his associates at the studio." It marked a turning point in Mae West's career. Rather than standing firm for her artistic freedom, the producer whom she trusted so implicitly secretly collaborated with Breen to redirect her work. Without her studio's support, she would find it nearly impossible to fight the Hays Office.[3]

Breen combed *Every Day's a Holiday* and, with Cohen's cooperation, excised a heavy portion of Westianisms. Mae contended that two of her most famous lines, "I wouldn't let him touch me with a ten-foot pole" and "I wouldn't even lift my veil for that guy," fell under his axe. While Cohen continually assured censors that West's character had been transformed into a con artist, freeing the production of all sexual situations, Breen remained skeptical. Even after the film went into production, he gave it only tentative approval. All script changes were carefully reviewed, and a Hays Office representative hovered on the set.[4]

For the cast, Cohen recruited four leading men and, in addition to standard players, hired an assortment of West's friends. At her insistence, he signed up African-American musician Louis Armstrong. "Miss Mae went to the head of Paramount and told them they'd better hire me or else," remembered Armstrong, who had been a featured artist in Harlem clubs since the 1920s. Still, his presence led to controversy. Mae and the musician forged a strong bond; she created a stir on the lot when she lunched alone with him in her dressing room. "That was unheard of in those days," he remarked, "for a white star to mix with any black."[5]

West included Armstrong in giving final approval to the film's score, which was completed by Hoagy Carmichael. Summoned to her dressing room, Carmichael found West waiting with Armstrong. Together they rejected every song he had written. After a sleepless night, Carmichael returned the next day with a new song. West was gracious but still dissatisfied. "No, darling," she remarked as he finished the tune. Exhausted, he offered an old composition, "Jubilee." Mae and Armstrong were both pleased. "Yes, yes, darling," she affirmed.[6]

Every Day's a Holiday opens on New Year's Eve 1899 with Peaches O'Day selling the Brooklyn Bridge to an unwitting mark. A stalwart police detective, Jim McCarey, curtails her activities. Dispatched by the corrupt police commissioner and mayoral candidate John Quade to arrest Peaches, McCarey is beguiled by her and allows her to flee the city. Peaches returns disguised as the talented but temperamental Mademoiselle Fifi. As Fifi, she takes Manhattan by storm. When he discovers her true identity, Quade becomes enraged and vows to get her. However, in the end, it is Peaches who triumphs. She convinces the honest McCarey, who is now even more infatuated with her, to run against Quade. On election eve, she leads a big parade, under the banner "Laugh, Sing, and Vote." McCarey exposes Quade's wrongdoing to the crowd in a speech and then rides off with Peaches, certain he will win the election.[7]

In *Every Day's a Holiday*, Breen successfully cooled off Mae West. The Hays Office had realized that harnessing her rested less on suppressing her films' content and more on expunging her style—taming the signifying West. In the margins of correspondence with Cohen, Breen scrawled "look out when shot" and "wait till we see," constraining Peaches from any hint of a sexual self. Between Cohen and Breen, she was reduced to a petty criminal, a sham artist with a purse full of brass knuckles, safecracking tools, and loaded dice. She remained more powerful than the men who surrounded her, but Breen's constraints, finally effective with Cohen's help, cut back West's social criticism and bold womanish style that had made her popular.[8]

West's original vision of Peaches was much more powerful than the final product. In an early script, Peaches is a vocal suffragette who runs for mayor herself. Breen's alterations reduced Mae to uttering, "I don't know a lot about politics but I know a good party man when I see one," and even that line was eventually cut. When one character observes that Peaches has been arrested twenty-five times, she responds with the film's most defiant statement: "No woman is perfect."[9]

West's initial script contained a sequence featuring an African-American spiritual. With *Belle of the Nineties* in mind, Breen struck it out, claiming the censorship boards—sensitive to anything dealing with religion—would delete it anyway. The result was another nullification of the black presence in West's imaginary world. Armstrong was relegated to a brief appearance in the parade. Yet her debt to African-American culture remained present. Fighting the censors, she reverted to a Bert Williams technique, talking through her only song, "Mademoiselle Fifi." Using a mock French accent, she signified a sensual presence despite lyrics that had been thoroughly scoured by Breen.

Still, West clearly had intended to offer a critique of American politics. In this film, she revived *Diamond Lil*'s exploration of dishonesty among politicians and the police. While her recent experiences with law enforcement may have provided her with renewed inspiration, since the twenties her work had conveyed a suspicion of elected officials and the police. From its earliest drafts, the script incorporated these themes, and Quade, completely unscrupulous, embodied the worst of both politicians and the police.

Breen reacted with alarm to the script's first version, heavily laden with allegations of political corruption and characters who were closely based on real public officials. He warned Cohen to eliminate politics, because the depiction of police and governmental officials as dishonest could lead to lawsuits. The producer made concessions but held firm to some political content. And West was able to slip at least one jab through: Calling upon an old device she had used in the 1920s to taunt the authorities, she played on homophobia by quipping that Quade and a crime boss were so close that "they sleep together."

In early November, Cohen screened the final cut for Breen. Later in the month, the censor sent Cohen a certificate of approval, but with a stern warning. Breen cautioned him that they would be watching to make sure that his studio distributed only the approved version. Breen was determined not to be outsmarted, tackling head-on the studio's tactics of releasing, as with *Klondike Annie*, an unapproved version.[10]

Paramount and Cohen geared up to open *Every Day's a Holiday* during the holiday season. Press materials distributed to theaters and exhibitors promised, "Mae West means *Every Day's a Holiday* at the box office." To further promote the film, West was booked on one of the nation's most popular radio programs, NBC's *Chase and Sanborn Hour* starring Edgar Bergen and Charlie

McCarthy. What Paramount and Emanuel Cohen did not know was the incredible amount of publicity Mae's appearance would generate; it became one of the most notable, if not most notorious, moments in radio history.[11]

According to some reports, West proposed to do scenes from *Every Day's a Holiday* for the show, standard practice for stars plugging their films. But the show's producer thought he had a better, and probably cheaper, idea. He pulled out an old Garden of Eden skit that they had already used three times. West would play Eve opposite series regulars Don Ameche as Adam and Bergen as the snake. Less than twenty-four hours before the broadcast, Chase and Sanborn contracted with writer Arch Oboler to revise the script, leaving little time to rehearse West's much publicized appearance. On Sunday, December 12, newspapers across the country advised listeners to tune in at eight o'clock, Eastern Standard Time, to hear Hollywood's most famous siren trade quips with America's favorite dummy. Bergen believed that on that evening the show scored its highest ratings ever; he estimated that it drew an 84 percent share of the listening audience.[12]

After the usual musical introductions, a short appearance by Bergen with McCarthy, and a plug for Chase and Sanborn coffee, Don Ameche introduced Mae West in the role of the "most fascinatin' woman of them all— Eve." Mae's Eve is a disgruntled resident of Eden, impeded in her quest to "develop her personality" by her lazy husband, Adam. Preferring the easy life, where he can nap in the sun, Adam refuses to allow Eve to leave, contending that their "lease" prohibits it. But Eve longs for excitement. When Adam warns her that leaving would only bring them trouble, she proclaims, "If trouble means something that makes your blood run through your veins like seltzer water—Adam, my man, give me trouble."

All of Eve's attempts to spur passion in Adam fail; he just wants to hold hands. So when he sets out to go fishing, she decides to get them evicted by eating apples from the forbidden tree. She cons the snake into fetching a few from its branches. "Now get me a big one," she instructs. "I feel like doin' a big apple." Disguising the forbidden fruit as applesauce, she offers it to Adam. "Here," she murmurs, "have a bite of this." He swallows and experiences an overwhelming attraction to Eve. A smack accompanied by a clap of thunder sends him reeling. "Eve," he cries, "what was that?" "That," she breathes, "was the original kiss."[13]

Before many even heard West's next sketch, where she invited Charlie McCarthy to "come up and see me. . . . I'll let you play in my woodpile," switchboards at NBC stations across the country were ablaze with calls. Outraged listeners jammed phone lines with complaints about West's indecent rendition of Eve, which the network had unwisely presented on a Sunday evening. It was just the beginning. Catholic leaders, journalists, women's clubs, and congressmen denounced NBC, Chase and Sanborn, Edgar Bergen, Don Ameche, Arch Oboler, and, of course, Mae West. Her appearance was described as "profane," "filthy," "obscene," "horrible blasphemy," and "vomitous." The Legion of Decency began agitating for a production code for radio. New York congressman Donald O'Toole, who referred to West as a "certain so-called actress who has served, in the past, a jail sentence for giving an indecent theatrical performance," declared on the floor of the House of Representatives that the Adam and Eve skit was an "all time low in this particular field." Some sectors called on the Federal Communications Commission to suspend the licenses of stations that had broadcast the show. The *New York Sun* commented, "Miss West had her day in court, her day in the film, and now her night on the air."

A flurry of explanations, denials, and apologies was forthcoming. Don Ameche claimed that he was so offended by the script that he wanted to walk out but his contract prohibited it. Neither Charlie McCarthy nor his partner had much to say; Bergen retreated to Palm Springs without comment. West was also unavailable to reporters, but her representatives insisted that she had also expressed reservations regarding the script before airtime. The J. Walter Thompson Company, the advertising agency that coordinated the show for Chase and Sanborn, took credit for the script, apologized to NBC, and assured all parties that "the same mistake will not be made again."[14]

At first, NBC was defensive. One network boss, Don Gilman, maintained that Oboler had toned down a script they had used several times before with no complaint. He denied reports that West had ad-libbed and contended that it was her "inflection" that created the controversy. (Indeed, she had delivered her lines as written.) "The whole situation is regrettable," he told reporters, "but I am certain the objectionable features were solely a matter of interpretation." Again, West had succeeded. It was not what she had said, it was how she said it. Breen might have shut down her cinematic channels for signification; she now rebelled through a new medium. Martin Quigley ranted against her latest indiscretion, roaring that she was "a symbolism of attainable sex, garnished with ostrich plumes of the red plush parlor period." It was up to the audience to hear whatever message they pleased, or feared. Later Bergen contended that the controversy was inevitable: "If she says 'I've got appendicitis,' it sounds like sex."[15]

West's victory was short-lived. While for a moment she had found another platform for signification, it did not last long. With the outcry for radio's regulation and the criticism of the FCC, something had to be done. The following Sunday, an announcer read over the air an apology on behalf of NBC, Chase and Sanborn, and the J. Walter Thompson Company. Radio executives then agreed to exile Mae West from the airwaves; NBC even banned the mention of her name on all of its affiliates. However, the network still received an official reprimand from the FCC. One of West's studio bosses was unconcerned: "You don't hear any shooting from the boys in the street do you? West's public likes that stuff."[16]

Nonetheless, many speculated the studio was holding back *Every Day's a Holiday*'s release to allow the furor to die. Some predicted that her latest transgression would draw bigger audiences. When the film finally hit the screens in mid-January, critics registered divided reactions. Several heralded it as revealing a pleasingly new Mae West. *Motion Picture Daily* declared it "louder and funnier" as well as cleaner than any of her other films. The *Indianapolis Star* praised West for going decent without becoming a "sissy." Yet many mourned the loss of the old ribald Westian persona. "Clean and dull" was the *New York Herald Tribune*'s opinion. The *New York Times* lamented, "Sex ain't what it used to be or maybe Miss West isn't." Ironically, one exhibitor complained that "the cleanest of the Wests is so clean that it is disappointing."[17]

Indeed, *Every Day's a Holiday* proved disappointing. After an initial welcome at the box office, ticket sales dropped rapidly. One New Hampshire theater owner reported that "the Mae West fans—if there are any left—were on their holiday. We didn't see them at our theater." Some Hollywood circles wagered that Mae West was really finished, that the novelty had finally worn off. For the first time, after four years of profit, a Mae West movie lost money.[18]

Breen's attack on Mae's signifying style had succeeded. French critic Colette mourned the loss of the original West. She noted that West had slimmed down but bemoaned the sacrifice of Mae's ample figure, which she viewed as the actress's most powerful asset. Denouncing the film, she maintained that Mae's "essential signification of sensuality and animality abandons the shrunken body." Then Colette offered a eulogy:

> She alone, out of an enormous and dull catalogue of heroines, does not get married at the end of the film, does not die, does not take the road to exile, does not gaze sadly at her declining youth in a silver-framed mirror. . . . She alone has no parents, no children, no husband. This impudent woman is, in her style, as solitary as Chaplin used to be.[19]

Aside from Breen's triumphant tampering with West's work, *Every Day's a Holiday* suffered numerous other impediments. Although the economy had improved, the nation experienced another downturn in 1937. For people who had endured more than eight years of depression, it was disheartening. The resurgence of financial uncertainty forced many to tighten their belts and hurt ticket sales for many films, including *Every Day's a Holiday*. It was one thing to sacrifice a little to see the working-class heroine when she was at her best, baddest, and bawdiest, but it was another to shell out money for a clean Mae West picture.

Another force that was inducing changes in the film industry also had an impact on West's career. The economic slump of 1937–1938 reignited the block-booking controversy. Exhibitors exploited the dip in attendance to renew their protest campaign. They cited fans' complaints, not so much about the salaciousness of the movies but rather about their blandness. In the spring of 1938, just as exhibitors entered into their annual negotiations with the studios, their representatives ran a large announcement in the *Hollywood Reporter* declaring some of Hollywood's major stars "box office poison." West joined Dietrich, Greta Garbo, Katharine Hepburn, and Joan Crawford on a list that contained a number of actresses famous for their portrayals of strong women. Breen's victorious enforcement of the Production Code had come at a high cost to the studios; the result forced some of the era's most commanding actresses into diluted roles, unsuited for their talents. While savvy observers immediately linked the exhibitors' actions to their continued agitation against block booking, the label of "box office poison" badly damaged these actresses' careers. It became a no-win situation: Breen manipulated scripts, poor scripts produced poor films, poor films produced poor box office receipts. In turn, the stars shouldered the blame. Paramount scratched Dietrich's pending film and canceled her contract. Hepburn found herself in a similar situation. West fought to hang on.

These forces shifted the cinematic portrayal of women in a safer, more traditional direction. The biggest success of the 1937–1938 season was Walt Disney's first animated feature, the fairy tale *Snow White and the Seven Dwarfs*. West's reaction was flip: She retorted, "I used to be Snow White but I drifted." The other top films of the season, *A Star Is Born*, starring Janet Gaynor, and *Marie Antoinette* with Norma Shearer, showed ambitious women paying a heavy price for their public ambitions. It was hardly a fertile atmosphere for Mae West or Diamond Lil. When confronted by *Every Day's a Holiday*'s disappointing showing, she confidently proclaimed, "The only picture to make money recently was *Snow White and the Seven Dwarfs* and that would have made twice as much if they had let me play Snow White."[20]

West's situation became even more precarious with a downturn in Emanuel Cohen's fortunes. In January, after tensions had escalated between the exiled producer and Adolph Zukor, Paramount severed connections with Cohen. This effectively terminated Paramount's relations with all of Cohen's stars, including Mae West. Reports circulated that Cohen intended to jettison her, tired of her continued insistence on starring as Catherine the Great. But for the time being, he scheduled her for a ten-week nationwide personal appearance tour to promote *Every Day's a Holiday*.

For these personal appearances, West resurrected, on a grand scale, her old vaudeville act. She assembled a large troupe that included a leading man, Milton Watson, a male chorus in evening dress dubbed the "Sextet," a black maid, and an orchestra. A member of the troupe remembered West as a hard-driving perfectionist, constantly rehearsing and showing little patience for unprofessionalism. Watson told Sidney Skolsky that West prohibited him from pursuing love affairs during the tour. "Miss West," Skolsky reported, "said that the trouble with most of the Hollywood leading men is that they are all kissed out when they get on the screen."[21]

The tour opened in Los Angeles, continued on across the Midwest, and finally ended up in New York City in April. While her detractors back in Hollywood toasted her final demise, the tour proved they were wrong. Across the country, crowds greeted and cheered Mae West at depots. When she arrived in New York, Penn Station was mobbed. The *New York Times* noted that she was welcomed by "porters, commuters, arriving or departing Southerners, and an indiscriminate mob of hoydens, street urchins and public school pupils with autograph albums who tugged at the iron gates and hooted 'Hey Mae.'" The depot and surrounding streets were so packed that West had to sneak through the baggage department to a car waiting to whisk her away. Fans filled theaters to see her live show. In most locations, West and her troupe played long after *Every Day's a Holiday* had come and gone, breaking box office records. Regardless of those who pronounced West a "freak attraction" whose career was over, fans stood loyally by.[22]

Mae enjoyed performing before live audiences again but found the tour's pace exhausting. She worked herself and the cast hard, on occasion insisting on an extra rehearsal between shows. The six, sometimes seven, appearances a day left her weary. She frequently refused to see old friends or entertain guests, remaining surrounded by bodyguards, Jim Timony, Daisy Jones, and often local police. But in Newark she generously received fifteen of her father's old boxing buddies, furnishing each a generous wad of cash and a new suit.

The tour served several purposes. First and foremost, it liberated the Westian persona, to some degree, from the clutches of censorship. With no Joe Breen in the audience, West got away with much more in person than she did on the screen. In turn, the promise of the original and unadulterated West drew out the fans. And Mae West's admirers—especially the women— were not disappointed. Discussing her male chorus line with a reporter, she remarked, "They always put pretty dames on the stage for the men, but how about the women? Don't the women like to look at somebody handsome sometimes?" She victoriously reasserted her female heroine, her "articulate image," totally dominating the male pseudo-*Florodora* sextet. It was a character that women could project themselves into and one that could never be completely possessed by the male spectator.[23]

West claimed that when she returned from her tour in the spring of 1938, Cohen bombarded her with scripts, all of which she rejected. She continued to insist on playing Catherine the Great. In September, she formally presented her Catherine the Great screenplay to Cohen. He turned her down flat, and they finally parted ways. Many in Hollywood were now satisfied that West had reached her end. When studio underlings at MGM suggested her for the role of *Gone With the Wind*'s brothel madam, Belle Watling, producer David O. Selznick scoffed; she was "out of the question of course."[24]

In the meantime, West returned to the stage and early in 1939 took the personal appearance troupe out for another tour. As before, devoted fans packed theaters. At a New York stop, she unveiled plans to begin filming *Catherine the Great* that spring with her own production company. When a reporter expressed reservations that her trademark "nasal Brooklyn drawl" would blemish her portrayal of a Russian empress, she retorted, "Why shouldn't I play Catherine? The part fits my personality fine. She changed her men like she changed her clothes." For Mae, Catherine the Great's life represented an ultimate triumph in the struggle between the genders.[25]

Still, coverage of Mae West's career in fan magazines and gossip columns plummeted. She was a married woman, unattainable and not a real contender in the fantasy of romance. No longer did fan magazines seek her advice for the lovelorn: She had fallen for a seedy vaudevillian and a teenage marriage. No more could she discuss Hollywood's sexiest men: It was bad taste for a married woman, not to mention for a woman of her age, to be ogling young actors.

West realized that she needed to revamp her image to retain her position in the American imagination. When discussing the Catherine project, she began to appropriate the Russian empress's reputation. By borrowing such an image she absorbed Catherine's appeal as the people's empress who enjoyed young lovers throughout her lifetime. With Catherine, West could grow old gracefully. She would reinvent herself in an attempt to compel the youth-obsessed public to accept a forty-five-year-old sexual woman. It was critical for Mae West to continue to claim her desirability, for within her philosophy of gender relations, a woman's most powerful weapon was sex. To the *New York Post*, West boasted of Catherine's accomplishments in the realm of *l'amour*. "When she was sixty-eight," Mae declared, "she still had a lover of twenty-two. And not because she was the empress, either. She still had plenty of sex appeal."[26]

By the end of May 1939, when West returned from touring, she had entered into negotiations with Universal Studios to co-star with another major cinematic comedian, W. C. Fields, in a new film. She entered the project with reservations. While she recognized Fields's genius, she was uncomfortable with his reputation as a drinker. Universal, anxious to move ahead, offered her a generous contract of $300,000 for the film, compensation for a screenplay, and a promise that if Fields showed up inebriated, he would be dismissed for the day. It happened only once. The first time Fields came staggering in, West commanded, "Pour him out of here." Fields bowed and tipped his hat to her as he was rushed off the set.

Bringing two stars of such distinctive talents together proved to be a challenge for studio executives. Both West and Fields were legendarily difficult and insisted on meticulous control over their performances. Universal had to produce a vehicle acceptable to both stars, as well as to the censors and public. In early May, Fields submitted a story called *December and Mae*, in which the two, married in name only, appeared as co-owners of an 1880s western saloon. That summer, the studio assigned screenwriter Grover Jones to the project. At the end of July, Fields reviewed Jones's script and immediately fired off a letter to the studio protesting its weaknesses. In another to West, urging that they collaborate, he effused, "I have great admiration for you as a writer and actress and for you yourself." West never replied.

At the end of August, Fields received a final draft of the script, which infuriated him even further. He sent a thundering condemnation of the screenplay along with detailed criticism to Universal. Charging that his part was more suitable to "Shirley Temple" than W. C. Fields, he found West's role was equally inappropriate. "Here's Mae West," he wrote sarcastically. "Oh boy—will she hand them a line. Look, she's sewing something—a 'Sampler'—What the Hell's a sampler?" After an attempt to back out of the project failed, Fields was reduced to inserting his material into drafts of the screenplay, even after shooting began.[27]

It may be no coincidence that in the midst of the script dispute, an anonymous source tipped off Breen that Universal was planning a film with the two stars, contending that writers had been ordered "to make it plenty dirty." Signed "a listening post in Hollywood," the letter warned that the "smut gags" were so subtle that they would slip by the censors to be deci-phered by more worldly filmgoers.[28]

It is likely that the script that Fields found so abominable was conceived by West and Jones. The original contained telltale Westian imprints—a shake dance, a love affair with a handsome Indian warrior, and a rendition of "Frankie and Johnny" in a Native American language. After Fields's death, West—whom Fields described as "a plumber's idea of Cleopatra"—insisted that he had very little to do with the writing and that she had been the script's true author.[29]

When Breen received the script, eventually called *My Little Chickadee*, in late September, he declared the story acceptable but cited several scenes, many with West, as Code violations. He deleted West's fling with the Indian warrior and, fearing she intended to slip in a shimmy, eliminated all of her dance scenes. Throughout the fall, even after the film went into production, Breen rejected dialogue and scenes, warning Universal that West's character could not offer any "indication of sex" or "undue exposure."[30]

That December, after months of wrangling among the studio, stars, and censors, shooting wrapped up. In this film, West created the character of Flower Belle Lee, who is banished from her hometown for her shameful re-lationship with the notorious Masked Bandit. On the train bound for the next town, Greasewood City, she meets the inept snake oil salesman Cuth-bert J. Twillie, played by Fields. Thinking he is wealthy, she marries him, only to discover once they reach Greasewood City that his money is counter-feit, an advertising gimmick. There the local saloon proprietor and the newspaper editor are smitten with Flower Belle, who also continues her af-fair with the Masked Bandit. She briefly substitutes at the local schoolhouse, reciting the day's lesson, "I am a good boy. I am a good man. I am a good woman." She slaps her pointer down. "What is this? Propaganda?"

Although she rejects him, Twillie continues to pursue Flower Belle, disguis-ing himself as the Masked Bandit. She sees through his masquerade, but the townsfolk, believing he is the real bandit, drag him into the town square to lynch him. Flower Belle, who has discovered that the saloonkeeper is really the Masked Bandit, compels him to return all his stolen booty, in full view of Greasewood City's residents. Twillie's life is saved, and in the end Flower Belle returns her wedding ring to him, confessing that their nuptials were faked by an impostor posing as a minister. As they part, Twillie tells her, "Anytime you're near the Gampain Hills, you must come up and see me sometime." Flower Belle smiles, "Oh yeah, yeah, I'll do that, my little chickadee."[31]

Universal put considerable effort into promoting *My Little Chickadee*. Press releases celebrated the pairing of the era's most famous comedic performers. On her part, West worked to silence rumors that the two super-stars were feuding. She insisted to the *New York Times* that she enjoyed a per-fectly harmonious relationship with Fields. She also maintained that they shared a common commitment to the picture's success and that their charac-ters, despite their differences, were complementary. Certainly, the West and Fields partnership appeared thoroughly mismatched as well as volatile. Fields's character was hardly a typical Westian leading man: He was luckless, not handsome, misogynistic, and a buffoon.

Yet West professed, "Our styles don't conflict." In part West's sunny as-sessment derived from a vigilant studio public relations campaign. But in many ways she was correct—Fields and West were kindred spirits. Both were nurtured in vaudeville, carefully attuned to the importance of timing and delivery. And both were known for their adept manipulation of lan-guage. Among Fields's most prized possessions was his dictionary; he was constantly searching for word combinations that carried subtle meanings just by sound alone. His style differed from Mae's; one writer characterized Westian dialogue as "sparse" and Fields's handiwork as "rococo." However, their approach to language was similar; both appreciated the multiplicity of messages that could be imparted with adept verbal games.[32]

For these two language artists, their screen encounter was a playful war of words. A scene ad-libbed by Fields blurred the fantasy of the conflict be-tween Flower Belle and Twillie with the reality of two master wordsmiths squaring off to do battle. "You are the epitome of erudition," Twillie fawn-ingly praises Flower Belle. Then he remarks out of the side of his mouth, "Double superlative, can you handle it?" The camera cuts to West, who in her classic drawl responds, "Yeah, and I can kick it around too." Appropriat-ing this line from Sophie Tucker, who was famous for saying, "Gentlemen don't love, they just like to kick it around," Mae matched Fields's challenge and upended gender expectations. Throughout the production as well as the film, a contest over the use of language raged between Fields and West. And at the film's end, when the two reverse lines, they parody each other, almost signifying a draw in this linguistic match.[33]

The West and Fields pairing also teamed up two trickster figures. While Fields's tricksterism diverges from West's—he plays the fool, oblivious to the chaos he creates—nonetheless, like Mae he disrupts accepted order. Both characters stand apart from the narrative while propelling the action along. They are weaker figures, Mae as a woman and W. C. as a silly eccen-tric. Regardless, they both emerge as victors. Flower Belle has the Masked Bandit and the handsome newspaper editor showering her with affection, and while Fields, the comedic tragedian, fails to win the woman he loves, he

is free to totter off and create more mayhem. Their presence restores order
in Greasewood City; no longer will the residents be plagued by the Masked
Bandit's crime spree.

The much anticipated West and Fields collaboration finally debuted at the
beginning of February 1940. Most critics immediately disparaged the film.
The *Hollywood Reporter* observed that "the story doesn't amount to much,"
and the *New York Times* blasted it for "the generally bad odor it exudes." *Variety*
was kinder; labeling the humor as "slim," it predicted success through the
loyal support of West's and Fields's fans.[34]

Variety guessed right. Moviegoers lined up at ticket offices for *My Little
Chickadee*. The film still fell short of Mae's halcyon days of 1933–1934 but
outdistanced Fields's more recent efforts. It brought the studio a tidy profit,
and it was clean, or obtuse, enough to remain in circulation for years. After
her two-year absence, West's return to the screen was a success.

Much of *My Little Chickadee*'s popularity may have resulted from the turbulence of the times operating in tandem with the reemergence of the old
West. Mae and W. C. were familiar faces and a welcome diversion from the
escalation of international antagonisms. In September 1939, just as the film
went into production, Hitler invaded Poland and France. Together, France
and England declared war on Germany. In the Pacific, tensions grew with
Japanese aggression. In 1940, FDR ran for an unprecedented third term,
promising to keep America off the battlefield. Although Americans clung to
isolationism, many feared it would be impossible to remain aloof from inten-
sifying international conflicts.

In the middle of growing global disarray, *My Little Chickadee* hit theater
screens. One journalist, Delight Evans, celebrated West's comeback. Noting
that "the world has changed" since Mae's heyday of the mid-thirties, Evans
averred that she was "welcome as a breath of springtime or maybe I should
say a whiff of rich ripe summer." This time Breen had failed to completely
impede the return of the old West; Mae successfully evoked the spirit of Diamond Lil, signifying the comforting presence of the trickster in a world
again gone awry. Flower Belle, whose name resonated with Diamond Lil's,
mirrored some of her old sauciness. Although Breen excised the interracial
relationship between Flower Belle and her Native American paramour, with
Universal on her side, Mae refused to allow her character to be completely
sanitized. She evoked, through a variety of means, memories of her former
transgressiveness, reminding audiences of Flower Belle's legacy by recycling
situations and dialogue verbatim from her earlier films and plays. Furthermore, the blues voice whispered through with Flower Belle's repeated invitation to come up and see her as well as in the film's one song, a bluesy

lament about a mining accident. West also signified restlessness with the censorship. One suitor ponders, "I wonder what kind of woman you really are?" Flower Belle agonizes, "Too bad I can't give out samples."[35]

Despite *My Little Chickadee*'s popularity, West's film career stagnated during the early years of World War II. To a great degree, it was her own doing. She clung to her hopes of bringing *Catherine the Great* to the screen and had decided it should be in Technicolor, a pricey proposition that no studio would back. But unlike the period between *Every Day's a Holiday* and *My Little Chickadee*, when the studios backed away, between 1940 and 1943 she received several offers. Universal attempted unsuccessfully to woo her back for another film. MGM courted her to play opposite Wallace Beery, and later the press reported that she would appear in a spy picture with John Barrymore. Both projects fell through. According to West, she was too hard to please. "Every script presented to me, no matter how imaginative a story, was built around a woman and man," she remembered. "Mae West pictures, as written by me, were built around a woman and *men*, the more the better." She refused to succumb to the Hollywood love story genre; Mae had forged her own formula—a female heroine, not only pursued by men but in constant battle with them. Studio executives, despite years of dealing with Mae West, failed to understand her. Central in all her work were issues of power and gender conflict; anything that minimized such themes was not only unacceptable but unthinkable for the Mae West character.[36]

In part, Mae still suffered from the repercussions of the Frank Wallace scandal. Now that she was identified as an older and married woman, society perceived her differently. Her desirability and allure became no longer contesting but contested. Reviewers rejected the notion of a middle-aged sex siren. The *New York Times* scolded her, "It's one thing to burlesque sex and quite another to be burlesqued by it." Her Ravenswood apartment stood no longer as a den of pleasurable iniquity but rather as a symbol of eccentric decline. When a *Time* magazine reporter came up in 1943, the year she turned fifty, his depiction sounded more like that of a grandmother's dusty attic than a Hollywood starlet's retreat. He described the air as reeking with the "husky odor" of perfume and the furniture as "white satin brocade, slowly aging."[37]

West fought back, continuing to revise her public image. A *Life* magazine layout showed her in a skintight silk negligee, posed with one hand on her hip, admiring herself in one of her numerous mirrors. Another revealed her lounging in her Ravenswood bed, eyes rolled skyward. One story ran with a photo of her writing her latest novel in bed, the article's title blaring, "Never Grows Old!" West's faith in mind power rang through. "Too many women make the mistake of waking up some morning and saying, 'I am no longer attractive to men,'" she told the reporter. "That does it, brother, from then on they're not!" Key to allure and sensuality was self-perception. "There are others," West pontificated, "who keep right on thinking they can be something special to a certain man—and they are." This piece assured fans that Mae West was still "a torrid creature" and contended that the marriage scandal had induced her into "retirement until she felt the nation was ready to appreciate her once more."[38]

West, in her battle against social conventions that desexed older and married women, relied increasingly on her status as an icon. However, until the disclosure of her marriage and true age, observers had been divided. Was Mae real or an illusion? Was she serious or was she kidding? While she was literally both, the reality that Mae West was married compelled many to view her as pure fiction, a symbol that represented but did not possess sexuality. More and more, she appeared as an illusion. Many concluded that if she was serious, she was self-deceived. In 1943, the *Time* assessment signaled a turning point in the general perception of Mae West's star image. In fact, the reporter observed that she entered the room and greeted him "like a parody of herself."

Many have contended that West was clinging to an image of youthful desirability that had long passed her by. However, their assessment rested in the assumption that Mae West, the star, had reached an age where she was no longer entitled to play the role of Mae West, the star. Yet she remained determined to defy gender norms that denied women over forty their claim to their sexuality and embraced her status as a signifier of sex and bold womanhood. She had always burlesqued her star persona, itself grounded in a burlesque of celebrity. Increasingly, she moved away from proclaiming her private life as the opposite of her stage persona; she began to assert that Lil's badness was real. More than ever, her performance as the star Mae West seemed to confirm her linkage to her characters. When an Annapolis plebe and his date visited her backstage at an appearance in 1943, she pulled him aside and whispered, "You should have come alone, sonny." When she interviewed the young Kirk Douglas in her apartment for a possible role, she received him in a sheer negligee. Informed that the British Royal Air Force had nicknamed their life vests "Mae Wests," she slyly remarked, "Sort of makes me feel like I started a second front of my own."[39]

As the public Mae West struggled to revamp her image, the private Mae West continued to confront a series of challenges. She fought off Mark Linder's attempts to lay claim to *She Done Him Wrong*. New York state courts demanded she pay back taxes on income earned between 1931 and 1933. She faced another extortion attempt, this time by a teenager who told police he just wanted to meet movie stars. But most annoying were Frank Wallace's persistent attempts at pushing his claims to her fortune. Finally, in the summer of 1943, he granted West a divorce in exchange for a generous undisclosed out-of-court settlement. Wallace retired with Trixie La Mae to her hometown of Henderson, Kentucky.[40]

In the early 1940s, West was one of Hollywood's wealthiest women. Her wise land investments earned tremendous returns. Years of backing Chalky Wright paid off when he became the world featherweight champion in 1941. (West compelled Morrie Cohen to override the racism against black boxers and arrange the match.) Although her career was at a standstill, she enjoyed continued national and international fame. Yet, she claimed, she felt a void in her life. She told of a suitor, an unnamed notoriously violent gangster, who had compelled her into a phase of introspection—to weigh good against evil, much as Lil had done. Between fall 1941 and spring 1942, she decided to devote her energies to investigating spirituality and the possibility of life after death.

Since her mother's death, West had remained skeptical about faith. She claimed she rejected the concept of eternal life and had spurned séances as chicanery. However, despite these statements, she clearly maintained some curiosity regarding spiritual matters. Soon after her father's passing, she hosted a séance at the celebrity desert resort La Quinta. She claimed it was conducted by aviatrix Amelia Earhart, whose husband, George Putnam, worked for Paramount and had overseen Go West Young Man's premiere. Mae believed that she had made contact with her father using spirit tapping, in which the deceased supposedly tap out messages for the living. Her interest in the supernatural, was also piqued when, in the late thirties, Sri Deva Ram Sukul showed up at Jim Timony's Hollytown Theater. Mae was delighted, and the Sri joined her inner circle, always close at hand to give her advice.

West's work indicates that the sacred was never too far from her mind. She wrote of her continued interest in the "closeness of goodness and evil embedded" in the human soul. Since Diamond Lil, Mae had explored the juxtaposition of purity and wickedness, reaching a climax with Klondike Annie, a film that clearly indicated her ongoing preoccupation with religion. Mae also dabbled in astrology, numerology, and fortune telling and always adhered to a rigid set of superstitions. Despite her condemnation by the Legion of Decency, she also claimed she attended mass with Jim Timony, which she described as "restful and inspirational." Mae's mind was not always on sin; she did a fair amount of contemplation of salvation as well. Her frustration with mainstream religions came from the lack of tangible, definite proof of the hereafter. Unlike sin, salvation did not appear to manifest itself as experiential. "It was not that I was jaded," she wrote. "It was only that I had no answers to serious things."[41]

Mae's spiritual journey took her toward religious alternatives. In the fall of 1941, she discovered an advertisement in a Los Angeles newspaper for a spiritualist convention where a Universalist minister, the Reverend Jack Kelly, was lecturing on extrasensory perception. She dispatched Jim Timony to investigate, and he returned with glowing reports of Kelly's remarkable abilities. After meeting Kelly and testing his ESP, she began studying his teachings and techniques. He became Mae's frequent guest when in Los Angeles, and she supported his ministry with generous contributions.

Still seeking assurance of eternal life, West became determined to develop her own psychic abilities. She solicited assistance from the Reverend Mae M. Taylor of the Spiritualist Science Church of Hollywood, who instructed her on communicating directly with the spirit world. Taylor taught a meditative technique that encouraged practitioners to banish all conscious thoughts so that "the inner voice" could be clearly discerned. West worked diligently to achieve a meditative state; for three weeks she sequestered herself each day in a darkened room, striving to cleanse her mind and seeking a connection with the spiritual realm.

Finally, in the third week, she claimed to have a breakthrough. She began to hear psychic voices, and before long their images became clear. In later years, she told of her first visit from a small female child named Juliet, who greeted her with "Good morning, good morning, good morning, dear." Next came a deep masculine voice, emanating, she asserted, from her solar plexus; his speech, peppered with "thees" and "thous," was completely incomprehensible to her. She received a visitation from her mother, dressed in black, telling her, "There's so much to do . . . there are so many to bring over." According to her recollections, the visions became so frequent that she could hardly sleep at night. Finally, one night a ring of spirits, mostly men attired in Victorian dress, floated above her bed, continuing to chatter. She told one interviewer that, exhausted, she pleaded, "I have to get my sleep. I'm a working girl! Could we cut down on the visits?" While they appeared less regularly, she claimed to have visions for the rest of her life.[42]

It is possible that West manufactured such stories, either as jokes on prying journalists or as a challenge to conventional religious thought. However, she took her spiritualism seriously. While some would classify Mae's visions as signs of instability, her interest in unconventional religious beliefs and spiritualism was not entirely out of the ordinary. Los Angeles, and in particular Hollywood, boasted a variety of nontraditional sects and cults, many focusing on mind power, positive thinking, and spiritualism. Traditionally, religious alternatives like spiritualism drew many women. Such belief systems provided channels by which female believers could not only explain the unexplainable but also rebel against the mainstream male-dominated religious hierarchy. Women were able to assert more power in nontraditional faiths, and, no doubt, such options were enticing to someone like Mae West, who had made a career out of resisting patriarchy. Significantly, it was not Kelly but a female psychic who assisted Mae in finding the spiritual forces within her. And her first voices were polar opposites, male and female, that emanated from her body—a metaphor for the double-voicedness that had long graced her work.

It is also not surprising that West grew frustrated with mediums and decided to contact the spirit world herself. Characteristically, she needed to be in control not only of her material but also of her sacred affairs. She was not going to surrender ecclesiastical authority to anyone, especially to the men who dominated conventional religious institutions. She cited I Corinthians 12:7 as her inspiration: "But the manifestation of the Spirit is given to every man to profit withal." In this configuration, everyone, regardless of gender, race, or class, had access to God's inner-dwelling spirit. In all realms, Mae had made a claim to parity and authority. Finally, after years of struggling with faith, she found a satisfactory route to spiritual equality.

Satisfied that she had found evidence for faith, Mae emerged with renewed energy. Not surprisingly, her quest involved issues of identity. She embraced the notion of reincarnation, revising it to conclude that Catherine the Great was a "pre-incarnation" of herself. She decided that she was destined to play the Russian empress. Reinvigorated, she plunged into the project, this time determined to stage it as a play. In early 1943, the Shuberts appeared interested, but a search for other investors failed. Yet Mae was confident. The year 1943, according to her numerological computations, equaled eight, her lucky number.[43]

In early 1943, as West worked on Catherine, Gregory Ratoff approached her with an idea for a new film for Columbia Pictures to be called *Heat's On*. Additionally, he expressed interest in producing *Catherine the Great* for the stage. Ratoff was an old friend and a relative by marriage. After hearing his pitch, Mae signed on and announced her return to the screen.

But she soon grew impatient. Delayed by a commitment to another film, Ratoff disappeared for several weeks. Once free, he began shooting extravagant musical numbers without a completed script. The Breen office immediately excised West's song "Can't Be Bothered," objecting to the lyric "I'm giving it to somebody new." According to West, after the musical numbers were finished, a script materialized. While Breen approved it with a few changes, West was outraged. She found herself playing the role of an aging and jealous actress, Fay Lawrence, scheming to prevent an ingenue from taking her place in a Broadway show. She immediately informed Ratoff that the project was off.[44]

After some tense sessions, Ratoff prevailed and convinced her to stay on. Losing his star attraction would have not only plunged him into bankruptcy but, according to West, also angered some of his backers, who had ties to organized crime. She agreed to rewrite her scenes and insert them into Ratoff's script.

While allowing West to rework her part seemed like a reasonable solution, her revisions significantly altered the plotline, forcing Ratoff to revise the film as he was shooting it. One of the screenwriters brought in to patch up the script remembered filming as chaotic. Scenes and dialogue were rewritten only hours before shooting; West and Ratoff constantly battled each other over almost every aspect of the production.

The result was a jumbled, cut-rate movie, far from the carefully crafted earlier Mae West films. For the first time since *Night After Night*, West had not exerted complete creative control over her work. Working with Ratoff left her with a vehicle that was not a Mae West film but a film with Mae West. She did manage to slip in a few Westianisms, and, briefly, a little of the bold sensuality still smoldered. When a suitor asks, "Doesn't your conscience bother you?" Fay calmly replies, "No, it annoys me."[45]

Despite the friction between West and Ratoff over *Heat's On*, the filming proved that Hollywood had become a somewhat different place. Ratoff recruited African-American performer Hazel Scott for two musical numbers. Scott compelled him to treat her sequences with dignity; instead of Ratoff's planned mammy costume she appeared in evening dress and in a military uniform. When correspondents from two African-American newspapers, the *Chicago Defender* and the *Pittsburgh Courier*, arrived at the studio to interview Scott, it became clear that on this set, race relations had changed. They found Scott dining with white colleagues; that kind of interracial mixing had been scandalous when Mae had lunched with Louis Armstrong only six years before. While the journalists complained that Scott snubbed them, they informed their readers that they received a warm welcome from *Heat's On*'s star attraction, Mae West.

"The title is a misnomer," the *New York Times* declared in its review of West's latest, "for the heat is off, but definitely." Overwhelmingly, this film received negative reviews. Most decried it as a letdown. Although *Variety* predicted it would see average ticket sales, fans stayed away. The *New York Times*, while citing her trademark signifying swagger as "more articulate than words," declared that she no longer possessed the fire of her earlier years. *Time* found the film "weary" but insisted that its weaknesses resulted from Mae's diminutive role. "West is not on-screen half enough," the reporter wrote. "But she is still one of the most entertaining and original personalities in pictures."[46]

West acknowledged the film's failure. She declared it a "dismal experience" and announced that she would never return to the screen again unless she was guaranteed total control. Her deep dissatisfaction may have been most poignantly expressed within the film itself. Borrowing a line from Shakespeare's *Macbeth*, Fay Lawrence detachedly observes that another character's ravings are "a tale told by an idiot, full of sound and fury, signifying nothing."[47]

In the summer of 1943, even before *Heat's On* was in production, the *New York Times* received an unusual telegram. The message read, "Unless unforeseen developments occur, I will appear for Michael Todd in my play 'Catherine Was Great.' She ruled Russia with one hand and her men with another." It was signed, "Imperially yours, Catherine the Great; sincerely yours, Mae West." After finishing *Heat's On,* West at last launched into the final phases of bringing her script, now called *Catherine Was Great,* to the New York stage. She invested some of her own money and, with the Shuberts' help, secured backing from the energetic and extravagant producer Michael Todd. If the play was a success, she would reap fifty percent of the box office receipts.[48]

Todd, as was his reputation, went all out for the production, spending $150,000 on the set and props. His idea was to stage the most opulent and outrageous of plays. West's gowns were expensive and elaborate. One bore a train that weighed over seventy-five pounds, and her crowns towered almost two feet above her head. At a casting call in New York City in May 1944, she hired an army of tall—all over six feet—and handsome actors to play Catherine's guardsmen and filled out the rest of the cast, which was almost entirely male, with equally striking young men.

Early that summer, West launched into rehearsals. Surrounded by her entourage, including Jim Timony and the Sri, she began preparing for a tryout run in early July. Thoroughly dedicated to her vision of Catherine, West attempted to dominate the production. As she had with her previous plays and films, she assumed the role of director, driving the cast, insisting on precision and hard work. The play's real director quickly faded into the background. (He literally fell off the stage when she lectured him at one rehearsal.) Dick Ellis, later famous as fashion critic Mr. Blackwell, had a role as a court page and remembered West as temperamental and cold. She grew impatient quickly and berated cast members who made mistakes. For Ellis, it became "a nightmare of hostility." During the entire time he was in the show, he met her only once. He sent her a bouquet of white roses, and after he begged for weeks for an appointment with the star, she granted him one in her dressing room. Upon his arrival, West glared at the young actor. "I just wanted to know if you received the flowers I sent," he said. The star turned and, staring at her reflection in the mirror, replied, "Yes, she did." Blackwell was then ushered out.

West's response left him spinning. Was this really Mae West? Was it "a slip of the tongue?" Did she view herself as two distinct people?[49]

West's moodiness may have resulted from many factors. Certainly, she maintained a deep identification with Catherine as her telegram to the *New York Times* indicated. A member of the crew observed that in scenes requiring Catherine to sign public documents, West inscribed her own name. Indeed, she had long viewed her star persona "in the third person," as an entity detached from her true self. Yet her outbursts and aloofness functioned as a power play. West's return to the New York stage had proven a challenge. While she may have succeeded in cowing the director, Michael Todd had a much stronger personality and was dissatisfied with her depiction of the empress. West countered with royal-size temper tantrums. Her outbursts not only kept Todd under her thumb but also compelled male cast members to keep a respectful distance both offstage and onstage. It was an atmosphere befitting an empress. This time her character was not just another Bowery maiden but rather a royal ruler whose authority was total and without question.

But West was hardly antagonistic toward the entire troupe. She remembered enjoying a clandestine affair with one cast member. Another player was the son of an old friend, a tailor who had given her a wardrobe when she was still a struggling New York actress. Actor Gene Barry, her leading man, remembered West fondly. During rehearsals, she told him not to call her "Miss West." Barry asked, "What should I call you?" Mae replied, "Mmmm. Just call me honey."[50]

Regardless of her varied relationships with the cast members, West's disagreements with Todd became legendary. In later years, she insisted that Lee Shubert described the flamboyant producer as "not too smart but he'll run the legs off you." Before long, West banished him from rehearsals for cigar smoking; later, she even quit speaking to him. Many contended that Todd and West clashed over the nature of the production. Todd was said to object to her conception of *Catherine* as a drama, demanding she play it as a comedy. Reportedly, after the play's trial run and abysmal early reviews, he angrily confronted her, cursing her in front of a cast member. He was forced by the Shuberts to apologize. Nonetheless, many credited him with compelling West to work a generous share of humor into the play.[51]

In reality, West had originally envisioned *Catherine* within her unique genre of comedy-drama. As early as 1939, when she first discussed the project publicly, she told a reporter that she would "play it on a high plane" but assured him that it would "have plenty of laughs." Mae was conscious of her talents as a comedian, aware her strength rested in humor, surmising, "I don't think my public would care for me straight."[52]

By April 1944, even before the play was cast, West had drafted *Catherine Was Great*. It contained her classic mixture of humorous language play and serious interludes. While she punched up the dialogue and gags after tryouts, the final script ran close to the original. From the beginning, this play was a paradox, both a historical drama and a rollicking burlesque. Todd, like many others West had encountered in her long career, could not accept this hybridity: Plays were either comedies or dramas, and fusing such dichotomies appeared nonsensical. Yet the root of Westian rebellion existed in the rupture between extremes. Her Catherine would not only rule Russia but also create total mayhem both on and off the stage. West used almost every tool of signification, including parody, satire, and pastiche, to empower her empress. Todd was so sure it would flop that he returned money to a co-investor.[53]

When the curtain rose on the first act, the audience found itself sitting before Catherine's court, filled entirely with men moving about restlessly. A group of senators and noblemen smugly speculate that Catherine, as a woman, will be just a figurehead. Finally, amid much fanfare, Catherine regally enters. As the court stands at attention, she skims legislation awaiting her signature. She denounces it as "the ruthless robbery of our peasants by oppressive taxes" and refuses to sign. As the senators and noblemen fume, she proceeds to more important business. Prince Potemkin, recently returned from battle, informs the empress that her forces are triumphing against the Turks, but he can only reveal details on the war in private. Catherine is enthusiastic. "The Turkish situation interests me," she declares. "Come to the Royal Suite and we shall talk Turkey." Potemkin meets the empress in her boudoir, telling her "I am yours to command." Catherine sizes him up and responds, "I command you to attack." The lights darken, and a flurry of boots and male clothing flies from her bed.[54]

Later, the scheming and power-hungry Count Mirovich informs Catherine of a plot to install a pretender, Ivan VI, on the throne. When Catherine realizes that Ivan, who has been locked away in a prison for his entire life, has never seen a woman, she muses, "What a tragedy for a man, what an opportunity for a woman." She orders him brought to her castle and hidden in a secret room adjacent to her royal bedchamber.[55]

She also faces a peasant uprising led by the rough but handsome and charismatic Pugacheff. A case of boils has left him with hair on his chest shaped like a cross, which peasants interpret as God's sign that Pugacheff is destined to lead Russia. While Catherine announces her dedication to the people, vowing to end "oppression and misrule," she remains determined not to surrender authority. She disguises herself as a peasant woman, locates the rebel leader, and seduces him with a song, "Strong, Solid, and Sensational." She then lures Pugacheff to the Double Eagle Inn, where her royal guardsmen capture him. Discovering that someone within her circle of advisers has supplied weapons to his ragtag army, she executes his soldiers and grills him on the traitor's name. Pugacheff refuses, but she spares him, sending the burly revolutionary to the dungeon "to give him time to think of what he will miss by being dead."[56]

While Catherine later reclines in bed, reading French author François Rabelais, Potemkin climbs through her window dodging gunshots from below. He tells her that Mirovich has ordered her guards to fire on him in an attempt to stop their relationship. Catherine also learns that the count and his aide, Dronsky, have located Ivan. Plotting to kill him, they intend to implicate her in the murder. Catherine tricks Dronsky into drinking sedative-laced wine, removes Ivan from his hiding place, and has the slumbering conspirator placed in his bed. Mirovich steals in and, thinking his collaborator is Ivan, stabs him to death.

Then Catherine has her hair done. As she preens, in preparation for a palace reception in her honor, her guards arrive with Mirovich. She admonishes him for using his talents for evil rather than good. The count explains that his disloyalty resulted from his belief that she "disliked" him. Catherine assures him, "The man I don't like doesn't exist." She sends him off to be beheaded and exits on the arm of Prince Potemkin, promising, "With my great men, I shall do *more* and *more* and *more*."[57]

When *Catherine Was Great* arrived on Broadway in early August 1944, theater critics were merciless. "Bawdy, distasteful, and repetitious," cried one. "Forgettable," sniffed *Life* magazine. The *New Yorker* condemned her performance as "baffling and rather pathetic," and the *New York Times* pleaded for "more leer and less history." The *Nation*'s Joseph Wood Krutch raged that he had always found West confusing, uncertain whether she viewed her sexual allure in jest. In his opinion, *Catherine* settled it. She was not joking. "Its bawdiness is as deadly serious in intention as it is deadly dull in effect," he concluded. Many predicted *Catherine Was Great* would bomb. The *Daily News*'s John Chapman remarked, "I'm afraid it will be a bust, which will give Miss West one more than she needs."[58]

The critics were wrong. Manhattanites flocked to *Catherine Was Great*. Well into its Broadway run, fans continued to pack the theater. Each time West made an entrance, the audience broke into "show stopping ovations." At the play's end, she made repeated curtain calls. After each performance she thanked the audience and repeated, "Catherine was a great empress. She also had three hundred lovers. I did the best I could in a couple of hours." It brought the audience to its feet, and applause rang out long after the house lights went up. "The West admirers are legion," observed one journalist. Fans committed her lines to memory, and many imitated West's distinctive royal command, shouting in a regal but sultry Brooklynese, "Entah!" In November, stage manager Robert Downing wrote a friend in Boston, "We have now given 120 New York performances of 'Catherine'—to everyone's astonishment but the author's."[59]

Catherine Was Great provided fans with an opportunity to enjoy a little of the old West, freer than she had been in years. Part of Catherine's popularity with the public rested in her kinship to her successful prototype, Diamond Lil. Critics immediately connected the two characters, one even asserting that "Miss West's interpretation of the empress differs only in costuming from Diamond Lil." West's vision of Catherine as a royal Lil rang through. Mae claimed Catherine was, like the Bowery queen, "low in vivid sexuality," only exerting power "on a higher plane of authority." It became the most effective inversion of "Frankie and Johnny" since *Diamond Lil*. Catherine not only could do men wrong, moving through a multitude of lovers, she could execute any or all of them at will. *Catherine Was Great* went beyond a tale of a woman's reign of a country; it was a story of a woman's reign of terror.

Although West's more overt debts to black culture were less visible in this piece, it remained tied to African-American signification. Rife with paradoxes, *Catherine Was Great* offered a twoness, a double-voicedness, and an array of mixed and conflicting messages. It was a comedy-drama montage that fans cheered and critics sneered. Even the germination of *Catherine*, rooted in West's desire to play the Queen of Sheba, indicated that West's empress was biracial in origin. Her delineation of Catherine served to swing the audience between extremes, never resting in one place. In constant motion, the play oscillated between high drama and a parody of serious theatrics, with Mae West delivering royal dialogue in her seemingly ill-suited working-class Brooklynese. For one writer, the most "cherished" line of the play came when Empress Catherine drawled, "I remember the incident puffeckly." With West's Catherine on the throne, the trickster ruled again.[60]

Indeed, *Catherine Was Great* revived West's dazzling tricksterism. The play was timeless. Fraught with anachronisms, it undermined all potential for any narrative certainty. *Catherine Was Great* blended past with present; the dialogue sounded stiffly courtly as well as loosely modern. When Mirovich offers flowery praise for the empress's leadership skills, one guardsman observes, "She turns the trick as neatly as you please." Characters bow, speak formally, and click their heels. But it then turns bawdy and lewd. Posing as a peasant and admiring Pugacheff's dagger, Catherine rests her hand on its sheath and remarks, "It is such a big knife."

Catherine, the consummate trickster, is a purely paradoxical being. She is the people's empress, yet she represses their leaders. She finds Potemkin's worldliness alluring but is also drawn to the ethereal Ivan. She fights wars to extend her kingdom and spends hours inspecting her troops. Marching down a line of soldiers, she stops, examines one, looks down below his belt, and observes, "You're new here." Without hesitation, she orders executions and a new coif at the same time. At one point in the play, she confuses the seven deadly sins with the ten commandments. When her dresser corrects her, Catherine thunders, "Are you suggesting I don't know the difference between right and wrong?" He apologizes profusely; she muses, "Well, sometimes I wonder myself."[61]

Some reviewers attributed *Catherine*'s topsy-turvy nature to West's amateurish writing, one commenting, "It doesn't seem that anyone over 21 would admit to having written such a play." However, others applauded the raucous and contradictory essence of the piece. Her longtime admirer Stark Young proclaimed her performance both "presentational" and "representational," evoking simultaneously the real and unreal. The dualistic nature of *Catherine Was Great* was so apparent that a reviewer from the *Christian Science Monitor* noted it as the most outstanding feature of the piece. He observed that the production's specially crafted curtain, bearing the double-eagle crest of the Russian royal family, functioned as a metaphor for the play itself. "It might well stand for other things besides the pageantry of Imperial Russia," this critic asserted. "It could, for instance, stand for double entendre." But he also insisted that "the heraldic fowl could just as well represent, though, the strange double effect of the whole affair."[62]

These writers had stumbled into the trickster's hall of mirrors and doubled images. Exaggerated and erased, real and reflected, these images imparted a multitude of possibilities. Was *Catherine* an exposé of the frightening consequences of dictatorial rule so prevalent in the minds of wartime Americans? Or was it a plea for firm leadership over the masses who could be so easily deceived? *Catherine* provides no right or wrong answer but reveals that all positions are absurd. Both the leaders and the masses are misguided; neither can be trusted. This chaotic world is made even crazier by Catherine, the trickster, who lives in lavish comfort, plotting her conquests of foreign lands, seducing young officers, and then sending her men off to slaughter. "What do you think I have an army for?" she asks a member of her court. "Don't answer that."[63]

It is not surprising that West's Catherine, who also reads Voltaire, chooses Rabelais to take to bed. The spirit of the sixteenth-century French writer captured the essence of West's play. While it is doubtful that she actually read much Rabelais, she certainly was familiar with the French author, famous for his bawdy satire. In the past, several reviewers had described her as "Rabelaisian." West always carefully checked out such references. And in Rabelais, she found someone who resonated with both her experiences and style. Rabelais's work was controversial; he too not only generated debate but also suffered censorship. His lusty political and social farces, centering on the saga of two giant kings, Gargantua and Pantagruel, also paralleled her work. Rabelais laced his novels with every possible comedic device ranging from simple puns to lengthy parodies. As literary theorist Mikhail Bakhtin argues, Rabelais's humor was intrinsically subversive: "No dogma, no authoritarianism, no narrow-minded seriousness can co-exist with Rabelaisian images. These images are opposed to all that is finished and polished, to all pomposity, to every ready-made solution in the sphere of thought and world outlook." Bakhtin's appraisal of Rabelais could have applied to Mae West.[64]

West's work had long contained similarities to Rabelais's rowdy style, and with *Catherine Was Great*—the giant queen—the resemblance became even sharper. Her kinship with African-American signification made Rabelais a natural bedfellow for Catherine. One of the many devices employed by West and Rabelais is parody, a double-voicedness, used not only to mock but also to wrest control from those in power. Catherine speechifies on the horrors of war and deplores the waste of young Russian men as she continues to dispatch them to the front. At the same time, she leeringly announces, "Russia needs her men. I need them. I cannot spare a single one more than is necessary."[65]

Yet another Rabelaisian quality spins within *Catherine Was Great*. Bakhtin links Rabelais's novels to the tradition of carnival, contending that such public festivals serve as a forum for ordinary people to resist those who control them. Through inversion of convention and by defying social norms, these interludes function not only as safety valves but also as rowdy challenges to authority. Similarly, African-American signification often harbors an element of carnival, its rejection of white dominance operating within similar societal ruptures. Not surprisingly, West's creation, laden with signification, assumed a parallel function. In *Catherine*, she created a carnival of nonsense and rowdy fun, featuring a house of mirrors. Spectators at Mae West plays, who often stomped, cheered, and applauded, reveled in a moment of rebellion, as the trickster seized power by exposing the madness of those in control.

With *Catherine*, Mae resuscitated the genuine and untainted Mae West, the modern-day trickster hero. Masked, she puts down an eighteenth-century peasant revolt with modern song; she dupes Mirovich, her most dangerous enemy, into murdering Dronsky, his most faithful ally. From the first moment she appeared on the stage, West declared victory in the battle between genders. As the curtain rose, senators, royal counselors, soldiers, aristocrats, and ambassadors bustled about preparing for Catherine's arrival. When a page announced her entrance, a hush fell over this mob of men. One journalist described the scene:

> The tension is terrific, the suspense unbearable; you can't wait another second, it seems. And then, in somber majesty, not to mention fourteen yards of brocade, appears the Great Catherine. . . . She approaches the center of the stage (amid thunderous applause). She stops and surveys the flunkies, guards, councillors, etc. with a special survey of the audience. And then she smirks. It is a sensation.[66]

Truly, *Catherine* was a sensation. After thirty-four weeks in New York City, West took *Catherine Was Great* on the road. In several cities throughout the East and Midwest, it received overwhelming audience support. Yet despite *Catherine*'s positive reception, in May 1945 she closed the show. The hot summer would make the heavy costumes unbearable. While she may have intended to take *Catherine* out again in the fall, the world was already in flux. That spring the Allies defeated Germany, and in August Japan surrendered. The ensuing Cold War, the standoff between the United States and the Soviet Union, made it clear: *Catherine* was great, but with its sympathetic treatment of a Russian leader and her devotion to the masses, it would never be seen onstage again.[67]

A Glittering Facsimile

She gives her public what it wants: a glittering facsimile of
what it craves and, through laughter, a means of keeping itself
free of what it fears. She horses around with sex so that we
can have our cake and not eat it.

—*New Republic*, February 21, 1949

E ven though the Cold War had dethroned *Catherine Was Great*, it was
not long before Mae West was drawn back to the stage. In January
1946, Jim Timony negotiated for the Shuberts to back West's
newest play, a spy story called *Come On Up*. It was a simple, low-
budget piece, confined to a single set. The action took place over a span of a
few hours and required no costume changes for supporting characters, although West's wardrobe would, of course, be extravagant. For the cast, she
looked to unknown actors and actresses, paying them, on average, eighty
dollars a week. It was not a huge salary, but working with Mae West was a
great opportunity for a young player trying to break into the big time.[1]

Come On Up centered on Carliss Dale, an undercover FBI agent who poses
as an entertainer to gain entrance into international circles. At the play's beginning, Carliss flees Mexico City after being implicated in the murder of a
Nazi sympathizer. She arrives in Washington, D.C., and seeks refuge in an
apartment owned by her fiancé, the wealthy Jeff Bentley, who, like everyone
else, is ignorant of Carliss's true vocation. Carliss remains secluded in his
high-rise suite while he works to clear her name.

Accustomed to excitement, Carliss quickly grows restless. Bentley's maid
decides to alleviate Carliss's boredom by releasing balloons bearing the message "Come on up and see Carliss." Over the next few hours, Carliss receives
surprise visits from two sailors, a cab driver, an astronomy professor, a gangster, a senator, a general, and a South American former beau. When Krafft, a

Nazi spy, shows up, she adeptly fells him with one blow. Bentley discovers Krafft tied up in a closet, and Carliss reveals she is an undercover FBI operative. "Some time I'll show you my badge," she promises. Postponing her wedding, she departs with her South American friend to take care of "a little unfinished business."[2]

West declared *Come On Up* a departure from her preferred genre of comedy-drama, claiming she played it purely for laughs. At first glance, the play lacked the characteristic depth of her mature work. With its assortment of suitors, all immediately smitten by Carliss, it clearly drew from *The Ruby Ring*. Additionally, Mae used it to recycle a variety of her most popular Westianisms, borrowing lines from work spanning *Diamond Lil* to *My Little Chickadee*, with her trademark "come up" echoing throughout the play.

It is likely that West, responding to the times, backed away from her subversive critiques of American society. While Carliss betrays and fools men, her motivation is less the desire to avenge the woman wronged and more a sense of duty to her country. *Come On Up* was unembarrassedly patriotic, an affirmation of West's allegiance to the red, white, and blue. Carliss hunts down Nazis and their allies, protecting her country from threats to democracy and freedom. She even entertains two sailors, remarking, "At least you can't say I'm not patriotic."[3]

West was riding on the wave of nationalism that had swept the country during and just after World War II. But other forces, no doubt, inspired her sudden surge of nationalistic pride. With the war's end and the decay of the U.S.–U.S.S.R. alliance into a hostile standoff, anti-Soviet and anti-Communist sentiments flourished in the United States. The postwar years led Americans into a period of conservatism and conformity. Communism and socialism, long suspect, were branded eminent threats; deviant or rebellious behavior was considered un-American. Several politicians targeted Hollywood; Congressman John Rankin, the vocal leader of the House Committee on Un-American Activities (HUAC), declared the film colony potentially "the greatest hotbed of subversive activities in the United States." Such shifts in the national mood certainly affected West's performance; she had always been a little deviant, subversive, and very class-conscious.[4]

West composed *Come On Up* in this climate of growing fear and apprehension. Although initially Congress's investigation of Hollywood proceeded slowly, conservative politicians continued to cast aspersions on the loyalty of Tinsel Town. *Catherine Was Great,* which had benefited from the United States' wartime alliance with the Soviets, became a potential liability to West during peacetime. The decline in her film career made West less of a concern to politicians gunning for Hollywood notables, yet West—who had uncompromisingly faced down the New York City Police Department, the legal system of her home state, society's moral guardians, and even film censors—took special care to ensure she would not be red-baited.

No doubt, West worried she could be targeted as a fellow traveler as the atmosphere of fear gripped the nation. Later, comedian Milton Berle remembered that in the 1920s West had sent President Warren G. Harding a letter of congratulations for freeing socialist Eugene Debs from jail. Additionally, she had been one of the founding members of the Screen Actors Guild, a union heavily scrutinized by Communist-hunting politicians. Heralded in lean times as a proletarian heroine, during the war she had chosen to depict herself as the people's empress of Russia. Although she had obscured her political opinions, her work carried on a dialogue over class divisions and conflict. Suspicious and conformist Cold War America interpreted cultural products more rigidly than ever before. As a good trickster, West realized that she had to shift her work. In this hostile climate, she needed to play with the conservative attitudes of the era.[5]

In *Come On Up*'s early drafts, West revealed her preoccupation with the Cold War mood. When Russian revolutionary Stanislaus Kovacs comes up to see her, Carliss denounces his ravings as "an infection known as communism—a very virulent disease that is affecting the minds of even some intelligent people nowadays." "I expect you to sneer at the philosophy of collectivism," the revolutionary announces. "For you it is not the Brotherhood of Man." Carliss entangles him in his own words. "I can go along with the idea of Brotherhood of Man very nicely—even with enthusiasm," responds Carliss, "but not your way, brother."[6]

Yet, as in the past, West's work contained subtextual meanings that challenged some of the play's overriding themes. On the one hand, she distances her character from her working-class roots; Carliss is a member of the elite. The *Los Angeles Times* noted West's transformation, observing, "She's fending off the boys with fancy words loaded with laughs." Yet she did not pass up the chance for at least one shot at wealth and privilege. Reverting to an earlier strategy, she deflected class commentary into other characters, particularly using the role of Irish-American cabbie Mike Harrigan, whom she had initially intended to call "Red." Described as "Brooklynese," a male counterpart to Mae's popular image, he is tough-talking and openly disparages the rich. He mistakes Carliss for a prostitute, and when she rebuffs his advances, he retorts, "I can see you're just after the big stuff. I'm just 'little people.'" While Harrigan's response is far from revolutionary, he stands as Carliss's alter ego, interrogating her position as one of the elite.

West even slipped in a challenge to her whiteness. When the astronomy professor reports that the constellation Hercules has bypassed the planet

Venus for the star cluster Cassiopeia, Carliss asks, "What's Cassie got that Venus hasn't?" The professor, gazing at Carliss, responds, "Cassiopeia is unusually attractive this time of year." Clearly, West was attempting to link Cassiopeia, named for an Ethiopian queen, with her character—yet another subtle attempt to connect with fictional blackness.[7]

Come On Up even further challenged the notion of a fixed identity. A trickster, Carliss appears both mutable and immutable. As with Carliss's prototypes in *The Ruby Ring* and *The Hussy*, each man views her differently. Harrigan thinks she is a lady of the evening, Bentley sees her as a society woman, and the gangster believes she is a sharpie. Carliss could be all of these things; she is a spy, and her occupation rests on duping those who surround her into misreading her identity. At the same time, however, and unlike her predecessors in *The Ruby Ring* and *The Hussy*, Carliss does nothing to assume a new persona but remains the same throughout, functioning as a mirror that permits men to see what they desire. She leaves the work to the male imagination and allows their mind power to create her many masks.

Come On Up premiered on May 16, 1946, for a short engagement in Long Beach, California, then, for nine months, played stands around the country that ran as short as one night and as long as two weeks. It was a grueling tour, especially for the cast and crew. It meant long train rides through the night, a seemingly endless stream of small towns, tiny theaters, and second-rate hotels. Several members of the troupe, including the company manager, did not make it through the entire tour. West, who turned fifty-three that summer, quickly replaced dropouts and continued on the road.

Those cast members who traveled with *Come On Up* were divided in their opinions about Mae West. Some looked upon her with admiration; others resented her overbearing work ethic. To almost all, she appeared an enigma; everyone maintained a respectful distance from her. The Sri accompanied her on the tour and led her in a series of chants and meditations before performances. One cast member, Harry Gibson, who played a sailor, interpreted her relationship with the Sri as more sexual than spiritual. Given the paradoxical nature of Mae's views, it was probably both. For her, sex and religion were not necessarily mutually exclusive.

Gibson also claimed to have enjoyed a brief affair with West. (While many third parties testified that she was as libertine as rumored, few of her lovers came forward publicly.) He maintained he was only admitted to her hotel room late at night when no one was around. Interestingly, his impressions of the intimate Mae West were similar to Harry Richman's: Sex with West was distinctly impersonal; she was curiously detached. Gibson remarked that when it came to lovemaking, "Mae West didn't need anybody"; men were only incidental to her pleasure. She demanded that he replicate the scripted moves of her cinematic lovers. Odd as it was, it revealed West's obsession with sex and power. Every interaction was a public performance, and each performance of sex was a battle between the genders. There was also sport in conquering men. Her affair with Gibson was calculated to have an unsettling effect on him. It also revealed that even in the most intimate moments, West always remained in control, independent, and very much alone.

It was this independence, drilled into her during her formative years by Tillie, that drove West to trek on. Come On Up took her throughout the country, as Gibson observed, to "every one-horse whistle-stop in the middle of no place." While the tour was much easier on her than it was for the rest of the company—she had first-rate accommodations—it was still a long, hard road. Not since her vaudeville days had West played so many short stints throughout the American heartland. For some it was puzzling. Why would a performer of her wealth and stature undertake such a demanding tour on the small-time theater circuit? Gibson believed that West longed for "the old days, the glamour," that she was desperately clinging to her heyday.[8]

While West optimistically believed that Come On Up would boost her sagging career, she had never sold herself cheaply, and in 1946 she was hardly a failure. Catherine Was Great had proved that she still had a following. Come On Up helped to keep her career alive, but it also fulfilled a very fundamental need in the Westian psyche. Since childhood, she had needed to perform, and she had spent most of her fifty-three years onstage; it was, by her own admission, the place where she was most alive. It was safe and secure, always scripted and with no need for spiritualists or mediums to forewarn of pitfalls and surprises. "This was live theater show business as I liked it," she wrote. "And it liked me."[9]

Beyond the certainty of performing, Come On Up allowed West to affirm her allegiance not only to America but also to Americans. Despite the shifts in her image, Mae still saw herself as the people's star. While other film celebrities sat snugly in their Hollywood mansions enjoying the life of cinematic aristocrats, Mae went to the fans, in person. In small towns across America, she shook hands with local leaders who greeted her at depots; she accepted keys to their burgs as they showered her with bouquets of flowers. Fans packed theaters for her show. After taking her bows, she reemerged from behind the curtains, graciously meeting the audience and forever obliging the fans with autographs. For many in Middle America, it not only offered them a glimpse of a celebrity but also allowed them to meet a real star.

In early February 1947, Come On Up returned to Los Angeles and opened at the Biltmore Theater. West had high hopes. The first night was a sellout, and for two consecutive weeks she filled the theater. But the reviews, as they had been on the road, were mixed. The *Los Angeles Times*'s Edwin Shallert, while conceding that *Come On Up* was "packed with laughs," rated the play overall as not "too good." A *Variety* reviewer who had caught the show in Oakland, California, declared that West had reverted "to the style of drama that once sent her to the workhouse" and predicted that *Come On Up* would never make it to Broadway.[10]

He was right. *Come On Up* never did see the lights of the Great White Way. While it had done respectable business, its nine months of short hops suggested that it could not sustain a Broadway run. One source claimed that J. J. Shubert, after sitting through one of the play's final performances, immediately canceled its scheduled New York City dates; a trade publication said that the Shuberts had "decided discretion was the better part of valor."[11]

Another opportunity soon presented itself. In May, Jim Timony announced that West would take *Diamond Lil* on tour in Great Britain. That summer, she hired two leading men and decided to cast the rest of the play in London to cut costs. In September, she journeyed by train to New York City and, fearful of flying, boarded the *Queen Mary* with Jim Timony, her two leading men, and seven large steamer trunks filled with costumes, clothes, and jewels.

She left just in time. Only a few weeks after she departed the country, the HUAC commenced a public investigation of purported Communist infiltration of Hollywood. It divided the film colony; some supported HUAC's probe, and others openly opposed its oppressive tactics and the threat to First Amendment rights. Some of Hollywood's biggest stars, including Lucille Ball, Gary Cooper, and Ronald Reagan, and many screenwriters, directors, and studio executives were called to testify. The committee failed to uncover any movieland Communist conspiracy, but those who were suspected of leftist sympathies or who refused to testify found themselves blacklisted, leaving their careers in shambles. Although West's status in Hollywood was marginal, by being out of the country, coincidentally and perhaps conveniently, she avoided entanglement in this deeply divisive controversy.

On the other side of the Atlantic, West received a hearty welcome; although British authorities had heavily censored her films, she was popular among movie fans there. When her ship docked at two o'clock in the morning, the press was on hand to greet her. She did not disappoint them, telling reporters, "I want every man in England to come up and see me." A crowd of customs agents, longshoremen, ship stewards, and cab drivers surrounded her, and she patiently signed autographs before departing for her London hotel.[12]

West assembled and rehearsed the *Diamond Lil* cast quickly, then set out on tour. She opened in Manchester and played cities and towns throughout

England and Scotland, where she was warmly received. Millionaire Eli Pearson threw her an extravagant party, rumored to be one of the most expensive affairs ever staged in British society. The Dunlop company, manufacturer of the Royal Air Force's "Mae West" life preservers, honored her with a ceremony at their factory. Examining one of the life vests, she commented to onlookers, "Yes, I see the resemblance." At the ceremony's end, she circulated one of the evening's programs for each factory worker to sign as a souvenir for her to take home.[13]

In January 1948, she returned to London and opened at the Prince of Wales Theatre. She was an immediate hit. Fans mobbed the theater and treated her to standing ovations. *Diamond Lil*'s appeal cut across the rigid class structure of British society, drawing royals, including queen-to-be Elizabeth (reportedly a fan), celebrities, and performers, as well as everyday people. While some British critics praised *Diamond Lil*, several condemned it, labeling it "vulgar," "crude," "tawdry," and "shoddy." One even denounced it as a "fifteen-minute vaudeville act padded out to two hours." Their disapproval did little to impede West's popularity. *Diamond Lil* was in such demand that West had to schedule two performances a day.[14]

By May 1948, British audiences began to peter out, and West returned to the United States, exhausted but renewed. She announced her return to films that summer and her intention to open a new play the following winter. Yet both projects evaporated. Instead, she appeared in Los Angeles County Court. Michael Kane and Edwin O'Brien, two writers hired in 1938 by Jim Timony to work on a *Catherine* script, had slapped her with a $100,000 plagiarism suit.

When the case came to trial at the end of August, West made the most of it. Each day, with Timony by her side, she appeared in striking apparel. For the first court session, she selected a white dress suit with a white scarf draped over her blond locks. For jury selection, she chose a red, white, and blue sailor dress accessorized by a yachting cap. During testimony requiring her to recite lines from *Catherine Was Great*, she appeared in black satin with long black gloves and a large black-and-white tricornered hat. At the end of one session, twenty-five Cub Scouts burst into the courtroom and swarmed around the star, begging for her autograph. She signed away, inscribing her photos, which she happened to have on hand, with "When you turn twenty-one, come up and see me sometime."

The trial stretched on for almost two months, during which Los Angeles was hit with record-breaking heat and unrelenting smog. Undeterred, fans often packed the courtroom or waited outside to see the famous star. They were not disappointed. Henry T. Moore, attorney for Kane and O'Brien, called West as his first witness. Moore asserted that she had not written the play and, beyond that, did not even understand some of it. "This French is what?" demanded the lawyer, referring to one line. "It's a matter of a sort of suggestive remark," West replied, examining the script through a bejeweled lorgnette. She referred the attorney to Larry Lee, her secretary since the late 1920s, for an explanation. "What does it mean?" Moore snapped at her. She only repeated, "It's a sort of suggestive remark." The attorney hammered away on historical detail, demonstrating that West did not even know what century Catherine the Great lived in. He pushed her to recite the litany of Catherine's lovers in chronological order. "I can't remember of 300 men which one came in order," she snapped back. "Neither can you. No woman could." Laughter filled the courtroom.[15]

A parade of witnesses passed. Timony admitted he had hired Kane and O'Brien, but only as research assistants. He pointed out that their script was incomplete; it was missing a third act. O'Brien testified that he was unable to make duplicates of the final scenes because he had run out of carbon paper. Moore fought on, highlighting similarities between his clients' script and West's Catherine Was Great. West's attorney insisted that she had been working on her script since 1933. Finally, on October 4, with a mound of evidence entered into the record, the case went to the jury. Four days later, they announced a deadlock seven to five in West's favor. The judge declared a mistrial. Mae declared a victory.[16]

At fifty-five, Mae appeared vigorous, but by the end of the trial, Timony, who was sixty-four, was visibly ill. Each day during the litigation, he remained faithfully by Mae's side in the sweltering Los Angeles heat. In his spare time, he was negotiating for her return to the American stage. By fall, he had rounded up two backers, Albert H. Rosen and Herbert J. Freezer, and sold them on the idea of reviving Diamond Lil in the United States. West knew Rosen fairly well; he was a veteran vaudeville theater manager. In recent years, with Freezer's help, he had purchased a small playhouse in Montclair, New Jersey, a perfect place to tryout Diamond Lil. In early October 1948, West departed for New York to recruit and rehearse new cast members. Timony, growing weaker, reluctantly remained behind in Los Angeles. Refusing to see a physician, he began dabbling in a new project, looking into business prospects in the growing desert town of Las Vegas.

Once in New York, West launched into preparing the play. She altered the script slightly, deleting a few old lines in favor of some of her films' most memorable dialogue, including "Goodness, what diamonds." Retaining her trademark "Frankie and Johnny," she added some new songs, among them "Come Up and See Me Sometime" and "A Good Man's Hard to Find." She offered cast members small salaries, relying on second-string performers. Old friends filled out the cast. For Gus Jordon, she selected Walter Petrie, who had played Bearcat Delaney in *The Constant Sinner*. She insisted that Rosen hire Billy Van and Jack Howard, two of the members of the original 1928 cast. Rosen recruited one of his friends, pianist David Lapin, to accompany West during her musical numbers.[17]

On November 29, 1948, *Diamond Lil* made her comeback in Rosen's Montclair playhouse. The crowd filled the theater to capacity; many fans and critics had journeyed from New York City to catch the return of the Bowery's most famous diva. From the minute Lil first swayed into Gus Jordon's Suicide Hall until her final "You can be had," the audience applauded and cheered. At the play's close, Mae received a standing ovation, making repeated curtain calls as the audience clapped, whistled, and shouted for more.[18]

Diamond Lil was back. West continued to play to sellout crowds for three weeks, breaking all of Montclair's box office records. She then moved on to an equally successful run in Philadelphia, and by mid-January she was playing packed houses in Baltimore. She had a full calendar, with bookings in Toronto, Rochester, Buffalo, and Syracuse before heading back to Broadway, where Rosen had secured the Coronet Theater for *Diamond Lil*'s homecoming.

But West's plans were abruptly cut short. On January 15, 1949, returning to her Baltimore hotel after an evening performance, she began to experience familiar abdominal pains. They grew so intense that her staff rushed her to a local hospital. Doctors declared her condition serious, speculating that she was suffering from either an obstruction or an inflamed appendix. They strongly recommended exploratory surgery. Mae stubbornly refused. Despite their pleas, she would not even consider it; ignoring doctors' warnings, she signed herself out of the hospital. Although she protested, Rosen canceled the rest of the Baltimore run as well as several other bookings.

West and company returned to New York. She claimed she summoned the Sri who again healed her. Yet cast members noted that she continued under a doctor's care; a physician was always available in the wings. After a brief rest, Mae determinedly forged ahead. On February 5, *Diamond Lil* celebrated her Manhattan homecoming. As in Montclair, Philadelphia, and Baltimore, opening night was a sellout. Mae claimed that this was the most memorable of all of her premieres. At her first entrance, the audience jumped to their feet and gave her a five-minute standing ovation. *Life* observed that New York had not seen such an outpouring since the grand dame of international theater Sarah Bernhardt made her farewell performance almost forty years before. On successive nights, Manhattanites continued to pack the theater, showering Mae with cheers and applause. It remained, according to most, a stunning spectacle, climaxed with West's rendition of "Frankie and Johnny" in her arresting scarlet gown.[19]

Even most critics were happy to have Lil back. While one who had seen the original maintained that *Diamond Lil* was "as feeble as it was in the first place" and another declared it "the silliest and most dilapidated play ever written," all agreed West's performance was sheer genius. The *New York Times* rhapsodized, "The snaky walk, the torso wriggle, the stealthy eyes, the frozen smile, the flat, condescending voice, the queenly gestures—these are studies in slow motion, and they have to be seen to be believed." Noting that the playbill proclaimed that "Miss West has long been acclaimed one of the greatest show-women of all time," reviewer Gilbert Gabriel remarked, "Without any impolite accent on the 'long,' I'll say Amen to that."[20]

Only a few performances into its Broadway run, *Diamond Lil* had sold out weeks in advance and was playing to standing room only crowds. What had started as a limited engagement now appeared ready for a long stay. To promote her homecoming, West agreed to appear on television on Saturday, February 26. She played a matinee that day, rushed back to her hotel, and, while changing, slipped on a bathroom rug and fell. X-rays revealed that she had fractured her ankle. Surgery was unavoidable, and Mae found herself wearing a cast. Clearly, *Diamond Lil* had to be postponed. Rosen refunded the advance tickets and assured the public that Mae West would be back soon.

West's ankle healed slowly. In May, after doctors removed her cast, Rosen immediately announced her return. But Mae demanded more time for recuperation, and in June, much to Rosen's frustration, she left New York City with her new lover, David Lapin, to convalesce in Los Angeles. She joked about her mishap, reaffirming her carefully cultivated image by denying that she had broken her ankle stumbling over a pile of men.

Even though the bathroom rug may have caused her injury, her recent medical history indicated a downturn in her health. It is possible that she was suffering from stress and exhaustion, not to mention the effects of wearing a corset again. However, it is also likely that Mae's health problems may have resulted from unstable blood sugar levels, for she was later diagnosed as diabetic. Of course, any public admission of illness was impossible. Mae West's image had to remain invincible and resilient. As she recuperated, *Life* praised her as "an American symbol, as beloved and indestructible as Donald Duck."

Again and again, *Diamond Lil*'s return was put off. Rosen grew anxious. West's comeback was in jeopardy of losing momentum, not to mention large box office receipts. A *New York Times* reporter interviewing her at the Ravenswood observed that she could stand only for short periods and used a cane to walk. Mae insisted that it was impossible to resume her role, that her performance required full mobility. She compared herself to a dancer whose delivery depended on "movement of her feet and the well-known motion of her hips."[21]

Some have asserted that West was purposefully stalling. Stanley Musgrove, later West's publicist and biographer, believed that Lapin held her back. He was domineering and had developed an antagonistic relationship with the rest of the company, including Rosen. But at this point in her life, it seems unlikely that West would have sacrificed her wants for any man. (And it was not long before she dumped Lapin.) While she was probably still on the mend, she was also toying with another opportunity. That year, film director Billy Wilder offered her a starring role in a comedy called *Sunset Boulevard*. She would play Norma Desmond, a silent film star who takes on a young lover and makes a victorious comeback on the modern screen. Eventually, West turned the part down: She refused to play an aging actress and likely realized retooling the part was impossible. Mary Pickford declined the role as well. Finally, Gloria Swanson accepted it, and Wilder transformed the film into a drama with Desmond as a tragic and delusional star, spiraling downward and murdering her young lover.[22]

Instead, in midsummer, with her ankle healed, West took *Diamond Lil* to the annual theater festival in the small, historic mountain town of Central City, Colorado. As the event's featured play, *Diamond Lil* became an instant smash. Demand for tickets was so great that it was held over for almost a month. After a brief, lucrative stopover in Detroit, *Diamond Lil* returned to New York on September 6 as popular as ever. Advance tickets again sold out and each night West received standing ovations. Police were always on hand to control the mobs lining up outside the stage door hoping to see her leaving the theater. Her nightly departure was a performance in itself. In full stage makeup and attired in her finest furs, gowns, and jewelry, West emerged from the stage door into the throng, greeting the crowd as she climbed into her limousine. As her driver slowly drove out of the alley, she cracked the limousine window, shook hands, signed autographs, and chatted with fans. Then, after the crowd dispersed, she would return, take off her makeup and gown, slip into slacks, and head to her hotel.

In January 1950, West took *Diamond Lil* on the road. Throughout the country, fans mobbed her, tickets for the play usually sold out, and audiences cheered her return. But the trip was not without its problems. On February 16, in Rochester, as she finished the second act, she collapsed onstage. Her physician, waiting in the wings, whisked her off to her hotel room. A publicist attributed her sudden illness to food poisoning at first but later announced that West was suffering from "sheer exhaustion." Determined that the show must go on, she returned the next evening; her doctor assured the press that she was in sound health. Despite her reported exhaustion, the cross-country tour continued.[23]

In Kansas City, Owney Madden, who had been exiled by the FBI to Hot Springs, Arkansas, slipped in to see *Diamond Lil* and reminisce about old times. Again, after each performance, she mingled with the audience, greeting the fans and signing autographs. An opinion poll in 1949 ranked Mae West along with Eleanor Roosevelt as "the best known women in the world." West credited her success and fame to the people who had stood loyally by her. Sounding much more like her earliest self, she professed, "I'm for the masses and the masses are, it seems, all for Diamond Lil."[24]

She also understood that they had played an important role in her transformation into an icon. Increasingly she was recognized as a "national institution"; critics described her as a "historical American phenomenon" and an "international legend." Absorbing their reflections into her star persona, *Diamond Lil*'s playbill proclaimed, "Miss West as Diamond Lil is as important a part of the American scene, the American way of life as is the rolling plains, the towering skyscrapers, the hot dog, and the atomic bomb." Beyond her links to Americana, she had become a symbol herself. According to John Mason Brown, "More than being a person or an institution, she has entered the language and taken her place in the underworld of the present's mythology." For the public, Mae West was no longer just a star. She had evolved into a signifier, both an agent and a symbol that communicated its own meanings, and she embraced the public acknowledgment of her status. She realized, even with some trepidation, that the public had intertwined Lil with Mae West and that her appeal rested in the fantasy's genuineness. "Diamond Lil and I are getting to be pretty inseparable," she told a reporter. "It even gets to be a little frightening, this constant association with a single part. But it is what Diamond Lil's public wants and who am I to keep it from them?"[25]

Throughout 1950 and into 1951, West continued to tour, with occasional breaks, with *Diamond Lil*. Wherever she appeared, the fans turned out. Critics marveled over the unusual hold that Mae West had on the public. *Diamond Lil* brought out not only old-timers but also young people, most of whom had never seen either her plays or her films. By 1950, an entire generation of Americans had grown up knowing who Mae West was, able to recite her witticisms, and familiar with what she signified, but few had seen the original Mae West in action. Banned by the Hays Office, *She Done Him Wrong* and *I'm No Angel* remained locked in a Paramount vault. Despite censors' attempts to combat West's pernicious influence, *Diamond Lil*'s legend persisted and Mae West endured.

What started as a *Diamond Lil* revival soon became a Mae West renaissance. In 1949, Sheridan House, hoping to cash in on her renewed popularity, reissued her two novels, *Diamond Lil* and *The Constant Sinner*. Decca Records released a two-volume set of her songs. After more than twelve years of exile, radio lifted its ban, and in early 1950 West returned not once but twice to guest-star on *The Chesterfield Supper Club*, hosted by Perry Como. In a plug for the sponsor, when asked about Chesterfields, she replied, "Well, I'd say, Chesterfields are um, Um, UM." She also played Little Red Riding Hood, on her way to Grandma's house, merrily singing "Frankie and Johnny" and the famous blues tune "How Come You Do Me Like You Do."[26]

Attempting to ride the wave of West's renewed popularity, Paramount petitioned the Hays Office to allow the rerelease of *She Done Him Wrong* and *I'm No Angel*. Their request was flatly denied; Joe Breen warned, "No good will accrue to the industry among the right-thinking people with a release of a Mae West picture." While contemporary critics found it laughable that West had been considered so controversial, in the censors' view she remained extremely dangerous. Instead, the studio rereleased two milder vehicles, *Belle of the Nineties* and *Goin' to Town*.[27]

It is not surprising that Mae West and *Diamond Lil* enjoyed a renaissance in the late 1940s and early 1950s. As in the 1920s, many observers attributed her appeal to nostalgia, but this time theatergoers were longing not for the gay nineties but rather for the roaring twenties. One reviewer described Lil as "a taste of the twenties" and a product of prosperity and Prohibition, denying she had anything to do with the 1890s. Diamond Lil held court in the bawdy and sudsy atmosphere of Gus Jordan's saloon, calling forth the rowdiness of a simpler time, before depression, a second world war, and atomic bombs.

In the *Saturday Review*, John Mason Brown reported that although Americans "were supposed to be tougher now," Diamond Lil withstood the march of time. In a sense, her message in 1950 was as relevant as it had been in 1928. Lil returned to reflect the ambiguities of the times. She embraced but interrogated the material, caught in an eternal struggle between her diamonds and her soul. Lil advocates living life to its fullest "because when you're dead, you're dead. That's the end of it." She insists to Cummings, "I only know I'm here right now, and I'm going to get all the fun out of life I can." Lil's lust for the here and now seemed particularly timely in a senseless and unstable world where the clash of political ideologies and the threat of atomic annihilation made life seem precarious. But Diamond Lil, always certain and secure, always a winner and never a loser, shone as the hedonist who forgot about the past, conquered the present, and had no worries for the future. Lil, the American trickster, spoke across eras. "Only the Statue of Liberty has been carrying a torch for a longer time than Mae West," Brown wrote. "She, moreover, seems no more fatigued by maintaining her chosen attitude than does the iron lady down the bay with her eternally uplifted hand."[28]

Grounded in signification, Diamond Lil continued to allow spectators to decipher the performance to suit their needs. Reviewers' varied interpretations indicated Lil's lasting indeterminacy. The debate raged again: Was West joking? "Miss West has never asked to be taken seriously," surmised Brown. "If she is the high priestess of desire, she is also its most unabashed and hilarious parodist." But the New York Times's Brooks Atkinson was less certain, puzzled over Diamond Lil's "world of sex" with "very little sex in it." He demanded to know, "Is Miss West serious or is she kidding?" Lil's and Mae's allure was both real and symbolic; as a good trickster, she was both and neither, occupying the ether between extremes.[29]

Diamond Lil's (and Mae West's) successful perpetuation of female transgressiveness may have been one of her most attractive qualities for post–World War II female fans. During the war, American women had answered the country's call by taking on traditionally masculine roles, such as filling in for men in factories and volunteering for military service. After the conflict ended, American society reverted to traditional notions of female domesticity. To preserve jobs for men, postwar society bombarded women with messages encouraging them to return to homemaking and child rearing. Throughout American culture a backlash against the working woman appeared, epitomized by 1950s television sitcoms that depicted suburban mothers fretting over their children, fussing over their husbands, and worrying about the next family meal. In the midst of this revival of the cult of domesticity, Mae West, the signifier, offered an alternative and a challenge. She blazed on as a symbol of independent womanhood, doing battle with the male gender each night onstage. She refused to be a mother or wife, making it clear that the kind of cooking she was interested in did not happen in the kitchen.

How did West get away with such insubordination in the middle of a culture driven by conformity? She continued to rely on humorous indirection and contradictory messages. Lil was independent and sexually liberated but remained focused on men and their desires. Beyond this, Mae West was increasingly perceived of by many, and was beginning to assert herself, as a caricature. Always larger than life, she now appeared more exaggerated than ever. In part, this derived from real changes in her physique. Size-wise she was ever more robust and the severe theatrical makeup transformed her into a Super Diamond Lil. "Always and proudly an armful, Miss West is a bigger girl today than she used to be," remarked Brown. "But what devotee of the madame could object to there being more of her?" West's humor and overdetermined physical presence made her supercharged sexuality appear less threatening, less real.[30]

In November 1951, when ticket sales began to dwindle, West made a final appearance in New York City and closed *Diamond Lil*. When she returned to Los Angeles, she found that Timony had declined even further. He had been hospitalized in 1950 for heart failure and continued to suffer complications, yet he had remained her greatest champion. Despite his weakened state, he had begun planning a Las Vegas hotel and casino called "Mae West's Diamond Lil Casino and Restaurant." Additionally, he cheered Mae on as she began work on a new play that she called *Sextette*. The plot seemed particularly suited to her; it revolved around a recently married movie star who had to juggle five ex-husbands.

Unable to find a suitable venue for *Sextette*, West spent the summer of 1952 playing *Come On Up* with stock companies across the nation. She returned to Los Angeles in September and shortly afterward purchased a Santa Monica beach house designed by architect Richard Neutra. Mae decorated it in a traditional Westian style—white carpets, white and gold furniture, mirrors everywhere, a multitude of portraits of herself, and frescoes of male nudes adorning the walls. In one room, little monkeys, replacements for the long-lost Boogey, swung on small jungle-gym bars. For her bedroom, she purchased a large round bed to go beneath a mirrored ceiling surrounded by cupids. Hoping that the sea breezes would prove healthful to the ailing Timony, she claimed she invited him to stay at the beach house.

West insisted that as Timony declined, she could not leave him. He continued with his casino plans but was too incapacitated to oversee the now extensive Westian financial holdings. To complicate matters, the San Fernando Valley was in the midst of a housing boom, and as a primary property holder in that area, West stood to make a considerable amount of money. She consulted with her cousin Henry Doelger, the Northern California builder and developer. Slowly and shrewdly, she began to parcel off lots and sell them, increasing her fortune even more.[31]

It would seem logical that West would next attempt to break into the world of television. She had participated in almost every form of twentieth-century mass entertainment, and television was quickly supplanting film, theater, and radio as the nation's preferred diversion. While West's spicy reputation ran counter to the conservative trends of the TV networks, producers nonetheless began to approach her with ideas for the small screen. She rejected them all until, in 1953, her old friend William Le Baron proposed a series called *It's Not History, It's Herstory*. The show would feature

West playing famous historical figures, including Catherine the Great, Priscilla Alden, Marie Antoinette, Mme. Pompadour, Delilah, Cleopatra, and Pocahontas. When a *Los Angeles Times* reporter expressed skepticism that Mae could be toned down for television, both West and Le Baron insisted they "would make no effort to be on the sexy side." But later, Le Baron promised that West's material would be "real adult fare."

Overall, West's comments sounded more like those of the scholars of women and gender almost a generation later. She complained to *Theatre Arts* magazine that men rather than women had written history, distorting women's contributions to the past. She declared her television series would present a woman's perspective, an important corrective to history. "These pictures will not be written from the man's point of view," she explained. "They aren't history. They are a woman's story." While this series was intended to be humorous, at one level, West again was attempting to subvert patriarchal society.

The *Los Angeles Times* reporter, like several others, also sought West's opinion on the newest crop of sex symbols. She announced, "Marilyn Monroes may come and Marilyn Monroes will go, but Mae West will always be the standard by which they judge sex." Mae not only had absorbed her role as a symbol but also was in the process of promoting it, encouraging the public to read her as a signifier of sex. "All the new personalities coming up in the movies try to be sexy," she observed. "They turn themselves inside out striving for recognition. Me, I don't have to do a thing to be called sexy except stand up."[32]

While Le Baron and West worked on *Herstory*, Timony, as much as possible, pursued his dream of building his desert tribute to Diamond Lil. But both projects quickly folded. West's much publicized entrance into television was shelved. And on April 5, 1954, Jim Timony, a few months short of his seventieth birthday, died of a heart attack, ending all plans for West's resort hotel. The *New York Times* eulogized him as the man responsible for transforming West "from a relatively obscure singer and dancer into an internationally known prototype of the American siren." Mae West, and now Jim Timony in death, had both been completely overshadowed by Diamond Lil.[33]

As a fitting tribute to Timony, West did not give up completely on Las Vegas. The casinos were busily recruiting many of Hollywood's stars for floor shows in their nightclubs. Frank Sinatra, Dean Martin, Sammy Davis Jr., Danny Thomas, and even Marlene Dietrich all played Vegas. Mae decided to follow the pack. She visited the desert town, toured various casinos, and signed with the Sahara to appear at $25,000 a week. It was an unheard-of amount for Vegas. Now all she needed was an act.

West's muse came in the form of a muscleman. One afternoon, she received a call from an acquaintance, bodybuilder George Eiferman. Learning from him that the recently crowned Mr. America of 1954, Richard DuBois, wanted to meet her, she invited the men to the Ravenswood. Eiferman, DuBois, and ten other bodybuilders rushed over to her apartment. "There were only a dozen," she wrote, "but the room looked crowded." It was decided—the Las Vegas act would include a generous proportion of musclemen.[34]

As she assembled the act, she personally interviewed most of the nation's top bodybuilders, finally selecting a group of nine, including DuBois, Eiferman, and a quiet thirty-one-year-old former Mr. California, Chuck Krauser. She also recruited a male chorus line and convinced her old friend Louise Beavers, who had just finished starring as a maid in the TV series *Beulah*, to join the act.

To promote her Las Vegas opening, West did a series of interviews. Hedda Hopper was one of the first and innocently asked, "You had Cary Grant too, didn't you?" "Twice, dear," was Mae's response. "Had him twice." When a *Parade* reporter showed up unexpectedly early and laden down with camera equipment, he found West entertaining a group of society women. He claimed that Mae, much to her guests' surprise, commanded, "Take your equipment and get into the bedroom." Mae bragged to another interviewer that everyone read double meaning into whatever she said. At a Denver hotel, when struggling with two large trunks, she shocked the bell captain by demanding, "I want a boy—a big boy."[35]

The publicity made way not only for the famous sex signifier but also for West's subversive language play. The act was full of linguistic games. In many ways, it functioned as a review of her career, drawing from her vaudeville routines, films, personal appearance tours, and plays. Running almost forty minutes, it opened with male dancers in tuxedos performing a tribute to the legend of Mae West. As they finished, she made a grand entrance, corseted and gowned à la Diamond Lil and singing "I Like to Do All Day What I Do All Night." Attended by her black maid, Beulah, West offered a string of quips, some old, a few new, but most from a chaise lounge at center stage. When the phone rang, Beulah answered, "Miss West's suite." "Don't brag," Mae called out. "Just tell 'em I'm in." Beulah announces that four hundred men await her in the lobby and asks if they should be sent away. Mae, gazing into a mirror, remarks, "Don't be silly. There's enough for everybody."

Beavers exited and West prepared for the act's central feature, a muscleman contest. The nine bodybuilders, each representing a different nation, filed out wearing large white capes. They encircled Mae, reclining languidly on her chaise lounge, and on cue dropped their capes, revealing that they were clad only in skimpy white loincloths. Then each paraded before her as she remarked on their various "attributes." "I feel like a million tonight," she murmured. "But one at a time." After bantering with each muscleman, she declared a winner. It was always Mr. America.

The contest over, Beulah reappeared solo, professing admiration for Diamond Lil and a desire to be just like her. Then she introduced the finale: Mae West reemerged, delivered a monologue taken from *Diamond Lil*, and closed with "Frankie and Johnny."[36]

When West opened her act at the Sahara's Congo Room in July 1954, it was an immediate sensation. Her engagement, which lasted almost three weeks, topped all of the Sahara's attendance records. She was invited back for the winter holiday season and secured bookings in the best nightclubs around the country, including Chicago's Chez Paree and New York's Latin Quarter. Her New York engagement also broke records. It beat out *The Pajama Game* as the city's hottest show and was held over for seven weeks.

West's muscleman act proved she remained a cunning social critic. With it she produced her most blatant objectification of men, a total inversion of gender expectations. As the musclemen marched onstage, she announced, "I've got something for the girls — boys, boys, boys." As women had been scrutinized in beauty contests, a practice she had criticized in the 1920s with *The Wicked Age*, she now scrutinized men. Mae's musclemen existed only for the pleasure of the female spectator, encouraged to project herself into the Westian image. Mae had long understood the function of spectacle that scholars had only theorized about. "You'd be surprised how people sit there and think that's themselves up there," she remarked about audiences. She saw herself as a signifier for women and of womanhood, contending, "I'm the woman's ego, see." West's work compelled women to assume a male attitude, looking upon the exploited male body as an object to be possessed and dominated. In a traditional Westian dualism, the muscleman act both challenged and reinforced the presentation of gender in entertainment.[37]

Like West, the musclemen appeared as giant caricatures; she had picked them for their exaggerated physiques. Anxiously competing for Mae's approval, they reinforced the transformed Westian presence. As an older woman and more than ever perceived as a burlesque of womanhood, she could no longer enhance her image and desirability with men in tuxedos, a trick dating back to her Harry Richman days. Now, to emphasize her allure and undermine male domination, she selected men with bulging muscles whose masculinity was as exaggerated as her femininity.

With the muscleman act, she completely merged Diamond Lil with Mae West. No longer attempting to draw any lines, she became Mae West playing

Mae West unmediated by any third party or fictional character. Fans saw Mae West—who was Diamond Lil of course—in her boudoir with her trusted maid, entertaining a host of men. It was such an intimate blending of star and character that George Eiferman observed, "Of course, everything was done tongue-in-cheek, but Mae always played herself."[38]

Although the public was willing to accept the blending onstage, it still seemed reluctant to embrace a sixty-one-year-old woman as desirable and sexual. While the Mae West of the 1950s certainly appeared to be physically fit and remarkably strong, it became harder to appear "ageless." Columnist Earl Wilson visited her backstage in New York City and reported that when he quizzed West about her age, she looked "hurt." She continued to pronounce faith in mind power. "If you take care of your health and you're interested in positive thinking, you'll be okay," she told him. Yet he persisted, contending that a discussion of her age was a catchy angle for his article. She finally retorted, "Honey, why don't you just say, 'Good to the last drop.' "[39]

West's difficulty with aging resulted from her philosophy of power and gender relations. For her, the female body remained a woman's most potent weapon in the struggle between the sexes. In an effort to maintain that power as she aged, she had stopped denying links to her characters and reconstructed herself into an openly sexual older woman. She now tried to ignore age, replicating the Diamond Lil from days of yore, but creating the illusion became harder and harder. The signifier depended on the visual, and that image was shifting. West began maintaining that she was remarkably unchanged, relying on the idea that it is not what you see but how you see it.

Sometimes this approach worked. Some persisted in reading West as both enduringly tantalizing and rebellious. In 1956, a British journalist declared her superior to all contemporary sex goddesses, including Marilyn Monroe, Jane Russell, and Ava Gardner. "Ingenues, all of them and almost as antiseptic as the *Esquire* pin-ups," he wrote, praising West as "every inch a woman." *Variety* celebrated her sustained allure as well as her contradictory nature. Their reviewer observed that she "bares nothing, yet reveals everything." Equally supportive was *Ebony* magazine, the African-American community's counterpart to *Life*. It offered up earnest praise for West and co-star Louise Beavers. *Ebony* applauded the two for resisting the age discrimination that denied older women their sensuality, declaring that "the sexiest, most-talked-about and one of the highest paid acts this season . . . was a hilarious team of two grandma-aged show-women both nearing 60." Beavers assisted in perpetuating the illusory Mae West, telling *Ebony,* "Mae has always been a pal to me. She hasn't changed a bit in looks or personality since that first day I met her."[40]

Ebony's appraisal of West was high. It described her relationship with Beavers as "one of the strongest friendships in show business." It also obscured the line between reality and fantasy, contending that the "Las Vegas Act symbolizes [the] friendship of [the two] actresses." While it lamented that Beavers was onstage only six minutes during the act, it cited trade papers' praise for her contribution.

Although Beavers's role was limited, she was clearly an important element of West's act. Her character represented a summation of Mae's earlier and contradictory messages on race. As was typical for the Westian maids, Beavers's character, Beulah, served her mistress with devotion. She answered the phone and assisted Mae onstage. But, as *Ebony* observed, the banter between the two characters revealed that she also functioned as Mae West's "confidante." Most important, Beavers introduced the act's finale while imagining herself as Diamond Lil. This fantasy within a fantasy affirmed Diamond Lil's racial elasticity, suggesting that a black woman could project herself into the role just as readily as a white woman. It also was a covert reminder that Lil's roots were in black culture: She arose from the black character that preceded her. There was Mae West, one more time, singing and playing out "Frankie and Johnny."[41]

During the mid-fifties West alternated between touring with the muscleman act and with *Come On Up*. And her personal life took an upswing. As tour manager, she hired a former lover, wrestler Vincent Lopez. But Lopez proved to be every bit as possessive as Jim Timony; he threatened all the men in the act, warning them away from Mae. According to Eiferman, Richard DuBois, often West's escort, was angered by Lopez and eventually left the show. Soon another contender emerged, Chuck Krauser. He waited for a hiatus in Los Angeles and, after Lopez departed, sought Mae out at the beach house and professed his love. She was impressed: He was not only "the strong silent type" but had remarkable patience. By the summer of 1955, the two had become inseparable, and Krauser moved into Timony's old bedroom in the Ravenswood. West always preferred to sleep alone. "I require a full-size bed so that I can lie in the middle of it and extend my arms spread eagle on both sides without their being obstructed," she revealed.[42]

Krauser, whose real name was Chester Ribonsky, was a former navy man, merchant marine, and wrestler who had worked his way up the bodybuilder circuit. He was as loyally devoted as Jim Timony, but unlike Timony, Deiro, and even Frank Wallace, he made no attempts to manipulate or control her. Those who knew him remarked on his kindness and indulgence. He was no show business wheeler-dealer, but he was attuned to health and fitness and made sure that Mae followed a healthy regime. He not only appeared in public at her side but carefully protected and defended her in every way.

Krauser's protective nature generated some controversial publicity when the muscleman tour went east in late spring 1956. George Eiferman had recruited the current Mr. Universe, Mickey Hargitay, to join the show. West's requirements for those appearing in the act were strict; it was all work, and the musclemen were required to eat properly, work out, and rest between performances. The cast was prohibited any romances on the road. It was essential that the men in the act follow this rule, for their behavior offstage had an impact on West's star and fictive personas. In the blur of fantasy and reality, the bodybuilders who lusted after Mae West onstage desired her offstage as well. Although West had settled into a monogamous relationship with Krauser, the musclemen played a critical role in perpetrating her signified reputation as wanton and irresistible.

Hargitay defied this image in a fundamental way. He not only ignored West's prohibition of road-tour love affairs but violated it with, from her perspective, the most offensive of all choices. When the muscleman act reached New York City, he commenced a very public affair with actress Jayne Mansfield, even allowing himself to be photographed as she was being crowned Brooklyn's Blossom Queen. West reprimanded Hargitay, but he defiantly refused to end the affair. Angered by his insolence, she demoted him in the muscleman lineup. Mansfield's comments only inflamed the matter. "I've been always told to respect my elders," she remarked. "She's sixty-four, and if I look that good at sixty-four, I'll have no problems whatever."[43]

For West, Jayne Mansfield was particularly troubling. Like Marilyn Monroe, Mansfield was proclaimed a sex symbol. But West was rankled not so much by Mansfield's remarkable beauty as by her eagerness, unlike Monroe or Russell, to promote herself as a sex symbol. West viewed that title as exclusively hers and regarded anyone else who claimed such a status as an interloper. West lashed out at Mansfield, accusing the actress of stealing her image. Later, in an anonymous letter to Louella Parsons, West declared Mansfield "a phoney in all departments." At least one critic reviewing Mansfield's appearance in *The George Raft Story* agreed, describing her performance as "a high school Mae West."[44]

When the muscleman tour reached Washington, D.C., in June 1956, West called a press conference in her dressing room. According to Hargitay, she invited him to announce that he had ended his affair with Mansfield. Other sources indicated that West had intended to publicize changes in her lineup. Regardless, Hargitay showed up, telling reporters that he was being forced out because "he was no longer in Miss West's favor." As the accusations flew, voices grew louder. Within moments, Krauser had flattened Hargitay with a punch. West used the scandal to her advantage. What could better demonstrate her continued allure than two musclemen fighting over her?[45]

West also weathered another controversy. She found herself the target of *Hollywood Confidential*, one of Tinsel Town's most scandalous magazines. By the early fifties, the studios' power had declined, and stars could no longer rely on the protection provided by studio publicity departments and their cozy relationships with the media. *Hollywood Confidential* exploited the situation. Using call girls, the stars' neighbors and enemies, private detectives, phone taps, and other sources, they collected career-threatening information about Hollywood celebrities. Then the magazine sought payoffs to suppress its stories.

Apparently, West refused to be blackmailed. In November 1955, *Hollywood Confidential* ran a tell-all story entitled "Mae West's Open Door Policy" that featured a picture of Chalky Wright superimposed over her outstretched arms and also linked her to boxer William Jones. The article chortled that her "favorite color combination" was black and white and asserted that West had showered Wright with elaborate gifts, purchased a house for his mother, and financed his divorce. A subhead declared, "Chalky Wright came up to see Mae and stayed for a year."[46]

Publicly, West remained mum on the allegations. It was not unusual for stars to ignore *Hollywood Confidential*, for public denouncements only attracted more attention to the stories. But for Mae, the situation was even more complex, for the story cut to the core of her ambiguities about race and identity, linking her celebrity persona with the interracial love affairs that her fictional self had often flirted with in her fantasized world of stage and screen.

Although West remained silent, other celebrities, growing weary of *Confidential*'s threats, tried to fight with lawsuits. Their efforts failed. *Confidential*'s operations were spread across three states, making it impossible to prosecute the publishers. However, in the spring of 1957, the State of California took up the cause and charged *Hollywood Confidential* with criminal libel and the publication of obscene material. While the stars who had first taken action supported the state's case, others were less enthusiastic, fearing that a public trial would reveal damaging personal information. Their anxiety was not unfounded. When the case came to trial, attorneys representing Hollywood Research, *Hollywood Confidential*'s information-gathering agency, filed a witness list of over one hundred film celebrities. The defense insisted that they could prove their stories true if the stars and their friends were compelled to testify. On that list were Mae West and, reportedly, Chalky Wright.

Hollywood Confidential's trial began in early August 1957 and was marked by twists and turns, embarrassing revelations, and scandalous testimony. One former prostitute testified about an affair with Desi Arnaz, star of the popular *I Love Lucy* and husband of Lucille Ball. Francesca de Scaffa, reportedly an actress, testified that she had seduced Clark Gable just to get a story for the magazine. Most of the stars on the witness list, all subject to be called with only a two-hour notice, waited with apprehension. Several weeks into the open sessions, film industry representatives pleaded with the state to call off the trial. The Los Angeles district attorney snapped back, "Hollywood does not control justice in this state." When African-American cowboy star Herbert Jeffries appeared outside the courthouse, he summed up the performers' dilemma, telling reporters, "I don't know what side I'm supposed to be on. I'm down here to find out." West avoided testifying by supplying sworn depositions that she claimed proved *Confidential*'s story about her was false.[47]

Chalky Wright, who had signed a sworn statement refuting the rumors regarding his affair with West, was not there to back her up. Wright, who had retired from the ring in 1948 and was working in a bakery, had left his wife and moved in with his mother. On August 12, just as the *Hollywood Confidential* trial got under way, she found him dead in her bathtub. The LAPD immediately declared it an accidental drowning, postulating he had slipped and hit his head while bathing. West intimated he had been murdered.[48]

At the beginning of October, *Hollywood Confidential*'s case went to the jury. But jurors found themselves hopelessly deadlocked. Rather than retry the long and complicated case that threatened to drag Hollywood's aristocracy through more mud, the state made a deal with *Hollywood Confidential*. In exchange for a $5,000 fine and a promise to suspend publication of scandalous stories, the state agreed to drop charges against Hollywood Research.[49]

The scandal did little to impede West, and she continued to tour with either the muscleman act or *Come On Up*. In March 1958, she appeared on the televised Academy Awards show, singing "Baby, It's Cold Outside" with Rock Hudson. Critics raved that it was the evening's highlight; the *New York Times* commented, "Mae West and Rock Hudson stole this interlude, if not the entire show, with their suggestive singing." Additionally, with the assistance of author Stephen Longstreet, she began composing her autobiography. It was not surprising that at this juncture she elected to chronicle her past. Many celebrities from Hollywood's golden age, including Groucho Marx and Billie Burke, were writing autobiographies. Although West struggled to keep her image before the public through live performances, a memoir would reach many more people and keep her fresh in the American imagination. She entitled it *Goodness Had Nothing to Do with It*.[50]

West's book was not really an autobiography but rather a biography of a star named Mae West, a public persona that had evolved out of a fictional character (which had evolved out of a real person). Even Mae admitted that it was a tale of an invented heroine who always triumphed and never suffered failure. She told one acquaintance that her fans did not want to read about hard times, that they expected a story of successes and victories. *Goodness Had Nothing to Do with It* became a story of a woman who struggled for and against an identity and was finally compelled to embrace one.

The book, like most of Mae's work, was filled with conflicting messages, subtextually signifying some of the real West. She admitted her birth date was August 17, 1893, but claimed an image of agelessness, contending that her health consciousness—no drinking and smoking, proper sleep, a fat-free diet, exercise, and rubbing her breasts with cocoa butter—had enabled her to look and stay youthful. She transformed Tillie into a Bavarian heir to the Doelger Brewing fortune and her father (whose mother, she claimed, had three breasts) into a successful private eye and livery stable owner, a descendant of the elite Copleys of Boston. She countered the images of a privileged background with tales of gang brawls and her father desperately scooping up money thrown at her feet by appreciative audiences in her early days.

Throughout, West signified her link to her fictional character. Her life story cemented the star persona to Diamond Lil like nothing before. The autobiography served as a reference point from which the public could read Mae West, her work, and her world. (In later years, she often refused to answer interviewers' questions and simply referred them to her autobiography.) Her affirmation of her legendary sexual prowess was the most critical element in this final merging. Recapping an amazingly long list of lovers, she discussed each paramour's attributes. Those still alive or who had been married remained anonymous. Mr. D (Deiro) was passionately obsessed with her; Mr. X (Lapin) was characterized as "charming" and "sensitive." Timony was loyally fixated until the end. Most of her young and strong musclemen lusted after her, which in part, she asserted, caused the problems with Hargitay. With "Dinjo," whom she sneaked around with behind Timony's back during *Pleasure Man* rehearsals, she enjoyed intimacies "in dressing rooms, hallways, cars, backstage alone, dark, dusty, in an emptied theatre; even in a self-service elevator." Ted, a young boxer who had a part in the 1929 Chicago run of *Diamond Lil*, made love to her for fifteen hours straight.[51]

West confirmed that she was every bit as licentious as rumored. Even this carried multiple implications. Her confessions indicated deep ambivalence. One reviewer did conclude that she was "nothing but vivid flesh and torrid blood enhanced by candor, narcissism, experience, brains, independence, and a healthy bank account." But others came away with a different impression, noting her sterile descriptions of sex and her lovers. It may have been the most personal subtext of the book, revealing West's ongoing ambiguity about intimacy and men. The *New Statesman*'s Maurice Richardson remarked that she boasted of an "insatiable appetite for men, yet you never feel that she gets much pleasure out of any of her innumerable affairs."[52]

When it came to the rumored affair with Chalky Wright, West also offered mixed messages. As an affirmation of her whiteness, she adamantly denied that Wright had been her lover and portrayed *Hollywood Confidential* as a scurrilous publication. But interestingly, at the conclusion of her strident repudiation of *Confidential*'s assertions about her interracial affairs, she added:

> I did not change my way of life. I had harmed no one. I had a philosophy, an idea of how to live fully and in my way. I believed in it as fully and as strongly as I believed in being an American.[53]

It was a mysterious statement, seemingly unrelated to the Wright scandal. On the surface, it appeared to be an overall defense of her sexually liberated lifestyle, but it also reversed her preceding denial of interracial mixing. Concluding her discussion of Wright, it emerged as a covert admission that she had crossed the color line.

West's treatment of *Hollywood Confidential*'s rumors reveals her continued turmoil over the issue of race. Throughout her adult creative life, she had carefully negotiated between white racism and her own intimate cultural and personal affiliation with the African-American community. Like the rest of her work, her autobiography affirmed and challenged her whiteness. She credited Bert Williams, the blues, The Elite No. 1, and the shimmy as major inspirations for her performance style. But at the same time, she never once mentioned African-American friends and associates and even glossed over *The Constant Sinner*. As a fantasy, West's life story, which was in reality closely intertwined with issues of race, erased race.

West's autobiography was written during a time when race relations were in a flux. In 1954, in *Brown v. Board of Education*, the Supreme Court mandated the desegregation of public schools, a major victory for civil rights advocates. In 1956, the Montgomery bus boycott, led by Martin Luther King Jr., ultimately compelled the Court to outlaw segregation in public transportation. In many ways, it was a time of hope and promise, a more supportive environment for West to take an open stand against racism.

But she did not. In fact, her actions often seemed more in step with conservative white racial attitudes. When the muscleman act played the rigidly segregated Las Vegas, Beavers and later her replacement, black actress Billie Hayward, found that they were excluded from the local hotels and casinos. For Beavers, West rented accommodations in the African-American section of West Las Vegas. One troupe member claimed that West angered Beavers by sending her dresser to warn the African-American actress away from a friendship with one of the white male dancers, fearing it would hurt the act's chances in the desert city.

Yet such a dictate seemed inconsistent for a woman who had written and starred in *The Constant Sinner*, fought to get Duke Ellington for *Belle of the Nineties*, and defied the studio by lunching alone with Louis Armstrong. Perhaps her decline in power had forced her to become more wary, but she did publicly confront Las Vegas's white segregationist policies when Billie Hayward was injured in an automobile accident just outside the city limits; West demanded Hayward be taken to and treated at the nearest hospital, a whites-only facility.[54]

What held West back from becoming a vocal supporter for African-American equality? Perhaps it was pure opportunism: She may have feared, for whatever reason, that an openly anti-racist stance would hurt her career. On the surface, she appeared to be oblivious to the changes in race relations. The era's heightened attention to racial issues may have forced her into a more conservative mode, for the civil rights movement faced a backlash of vicious, violent, and sometimes deadly white racism. The racist atmosphere affirmed the frightening Westian fictional world where Money Johnson lost his life for his relationship with a white woman. West's speculation that Chalky Wright's death was murder may have been more than an attempt to cast aspersions on *Hollywood Confidential*. It may have indicated that fears of racist retaliation weighed heavily on her mind, that she, like Babe Gordon, had sacrificed a lover to protect her reputation. West really was "the constant sinner," defying the color line behind white society's back while upholding it in the open.

This internal conflict manifested itself in her autobiography. In many ways, *Goodness Had Nothing to Do with It* served as a reification traditional American values. West's self-portrait of scrappy determination and independence validated the American myth of success. Through hard work, self-reliance, and individualism, she had achieved wealth and fame. Additionally, she reinforced an image of sentimental patriotism. She mourned the fighting boys who had lost their lives in World War I as well as decrying Adolph Hitler and Soviet leader Joseph Stalin.

A metaphor for the autobiography itself, the book jacket that concealed the pink binding of *Goodness Had Nothing to Do with It* showed West surrounded by mirrors and reclining in her famous Ravenswood bed, admiring her own reflection. West's life story was a mirror reflecting Cold War America, in turmoil over societal divisions and struggling with its own identity. In a broader sense, it mirrored the images of those who peered into its pages. The trickster reflected back insecurities and fears, creating more chaos as she affirmed American society's assumptions and values.

The autobiography sold well, and before long a paperback version hit stores. To promote the book, in the fall of 1959 West agreed to appear on CBS's *Person to Person*, an interview show hosted by Charles Collingwood. On October 4, Collingwood showed up to film at the Ravenswood. When he questioned her about international relations, a timely Cold War topic, she quipped, "I've always had a weakness for foreign affairs." She then escorted him into her famous bedroom. When Collingwood inquired about the numerous mirrors above her bed, she explained, "They're for personal observation. I always like to know how I'm doing." But only hours before it was to air, network executives canceled the Mae West segment. A CBS spokesperson explained that they "felt that certain portions of the interview with Mae West might be misconstrued." When journalists sought her reaction to the cancellation, she professed shock. "The program showed my bedroom and bed and I was standing by it," she mused. "But I did wear a very sedate, dignified gown."[55]

West had better luck with her next appearance—on the Dean Martin show. The networks kept close watch on the prime-time variety shows, forcing her to work from an approved script. When she made her entrance, surrounded by a group of men, the orchestra blared a bawdy version of "Frankie and Johnny." As Martin stammered, she identified her escorts as "the cub scout patrol, uh, they're working on their merit badges." The audience roared with laughter as she fired off a round of Westianisms. When Martin prepared to duet with her on "I Can't Give You Anything but Love," he asked, "Are you ready?" She drawled, "Always."[56]

West's appearance was so successful that she scored a booking on comedian Red Skelton's show. Before she signed on, she made her appearance conditional on script approval and convinced the show's producer to allow her to insert her own dialogue. Finding her first script too risqué, the producer steered her through a rewrite to appease network censors. The show finally aired on March 1, 1960. In a mock interview about her book, she was introduced as the "woman who is an American Institution." She cautioned the interviewer to "use discretion, I understand the censor has a weak heart," and then slipped in probably one of the bawdiest comments to be heard on early television. When asked to describe men in her life who were offbeat, she replied, "Well, a smart girl never beats off any man."

The show closed with West delivering a song, "It's So Nice to Have a Man Around the House." But she became noticeably uncomfortable when Skelton inquired about the popularity of "Come up and see me sometime." Stumbling over her lines, she explained its fame derived from *Diamond Lil*: "Of course it was the way she said it and what she did when she said it that made it so famous." She had let a whole new generation, the savvy television generation of the 1960s, in on her secret, the power of signification—her trademark line echoing the black presence that had made her work so powerful.[57]

I Had Them All

Announcer: But you never let one man worry your slumbers.
　　You believed in the saying "There's safety in numbers."
Mae West: I was big-hearted. I had them all.
　　　　　　　—Mae West, *Masquers Tribute,* April 14, 1973

West's initial experiences with television left her dissatisfied. "I'm not too crazy about the TV scene because it places too many restrictions on my type of material," she wrote. "I don't like being censored, I don't think I deserve it." She had invitations to return to motion pictures, but her insistence on complete control shut down those possibilities. After being idle for almost a year, in the spring of 1961, West prepared for another comeback in the theater. While she was no longer a motion picture star, she could still play one on-stage. She dug out *Sextette* and reworked it for a national summer tour.[1]

West planned to premiere *Sextette* in early July at Chicago's Edgewater Beach Playhouse. She had written in a muscleman part for Chuck Krauser (renamed Paul Novak after the Hargitay scandal) and recruited Edith Head to design her gowns. But the production got off to a weak start. On a limited budget, she had to forgo understudies and could only afford one week of re-hearsals. On opening night, July 4, 1961, Mae came down with laryngitis and had to postpone *Sextette*'s debut. The production finally opened on July 7, with a prompter in the wings noisily feeding the cast their lines. The next day, during the evening's first performance, West's leading man, Alan Mar-shall, began complaining of severe back and chest pains. The second show was canceled, and he retreated to his hotel room. The following morning, he was discovered there, dead of a heart attack. With no one to fill in for Mar-shall, the next night the show's producer delivered the part himself, reading directly from the script. It took several days before West rounded up an-other actor to assume the role.

West remembered her audiences as understanding, but the critics were not so supportive. *Variety* rated the production poor. The *Chicago Daily Tribune*, while praising "the overpowering Walk, the eyes under long eyelashes which can light up a stage, the smile almost a sneer, and the solid mechanical punch lines, given out with hand on hip, eyes cast heavenward, and the old burlesque bump," nonetheless panned the play. The Edgewater's ticket sales dropped to an all-time low. West remained undaunted; she began reworking the script and trouped on to dates in the Midwest. By the time she opened at Miami's Coconut Grove in mid-August, *Sextette* was running in fine form. When she made her entrance on opening night, the audience gave her a long and hearty standing ovation. The *Miami Sun* declared *Sextette* a little "shocking" but "hilarious" and cheered West's endurance: "Age hasn't changed the picture one particle. Mae West is the best portrayer of a sexpot this reviewer has ever seen." West took out a full-page ad in *Variety* and ran a paste-up of *Sextette*'s positive reviews.[2]

Sextette continued to reinforce West's claim as a signifier of sexual rebelliousness. The play is set in Great Britain, where Marlo Manners, a famous American movie star, has just married Sir Michael Barrington, a wealthy nobleman. Although Barrington assures reporters that Marlo bears no resemblance to her "shocking" film characters, that she is "gentle . . . kind . . . reserved . . . almost—*demure*," within minutes he learns that he is husband number six. "Six is merely a number," Marlo assures him. Yet Barrington grows more anxious, especially when it becomes evident that Marlo's conniving manager, Dan Turner, is also in love with her. Turner constantly interrupts the couple and insists that Marlo make a screen test before departing on her honeymoon. Barrington hopes to convince Marlo to retire and devote herself to being his wife, but when he finds Turner alone with her in her bedroom, Barrington threatens divorce.

Things only get worse when Laslo Karolny, a passionate Hungarian film director and Marlo's fourth husband, turns up. As fate would have it, he has been selected to direct Marlo's screen test. To complicate matters even more, husband number five, Vince Norton, appears. He is a real surprise— a notorious gangster believed killed in a plane crash years before. He asserts that *he* is Marlo's true husband since she never divorced him. To prove his love, he has arranged for the return of her jewels, long ago lost in a robbery. But Scotland Yard shows up to arrest the gangster, and Marlo reveals she obtained a secret divorce from him. Barrington, deciding that he cannot live without her, whisks her away for a honeymoon in Italy. "You can't get away from destiny, so get with it," she advises him. "You and I will make *history* with this honeymoon."[3]

Marlo Manners perpetuated the blending of West's fictional and real selves for her audiences. With sly references to her well-known personal history, West cemented herself to Marlo. Manners is a movie star who, despite all Barrington's claims, turns out to be much like her spicy screen characters. She has enjoyed a vast number of lovers, and her desire for sex is insatiable as she moves from man to man. Laslo, who Marlo claims understands her better than anyone else, predicts that Barrington is just a passing fancy, that he too will suffer the fate of other husbands.

Like her other work, *Sextette* contained an array of conflicting messages. When Marlo first enters, she is gowned in an elaborate wedding dress. (Head had appropriately decorated it with West's symbol of mourning, pearls.) The image of Mae West in a white bridal gown was a travesty in itself, but Marlo further mocks marriage with her numerous, dispensable husbands. While she has ascended into the elite, marrying nobility, Vince Norton appears as a reminder of Marlo's underclass roots. West even slipped in a little racial confusion, concealed within Marlo's screen test. In this play within a play, Marlo becomes, ironically, a seductress of British nobility. The Earl of Crosswith, who has lusted after her from afar, follows her home, discovering she lives in the Limehouse district, London's Chinatown. He confronts her with his knowledge that she has been leading a "double life," assuring her that, nonetheless, he still loves her. "No man has learned my secret and been the same afterward," she warns him, revealing that men who follow her to Limehouse all suffer the same fate—suicide. He persists, and she cautions that "it isn't only your life, it's your soul that is in jeopardy."[4]

Reminiscent of *Klondike Annie*, Marlo's character lives among the Chinese in London's poorest neighborhood. Using the Limehouse setting, West again tries to exoticize her character (and her character's character), signifying she is a wicked and sinful woman. But in a twist, she upends assumptions about racial identity. It is not really clear what secret the Earl of Crosswith has discovered. Could it be only that this character within a character has crossed the color line? Or is it that she has passed for white, that her real roots are in the Limehouse district? West hints at the latter. Those lovers who uncover her "double life" all commit suicide. It is a deliberate inversion of the nineteenth-century "tragic mulatta" tales, in which a woman of color is driven by her forbidden love for a white man to take her life. Instead, in West's version, the white man kills himself as Marlo's racially indeterminate character lives on.

When West finished the *Sextette* tour, she returned to California. That August she turned sixty-eight, and after over fifty years of intermittent road trips, she was weary. She retreated to the Ravenswood, making occasional trips out to the beach house or to the San Fernando Valley to visit Beverly or John Junior, who was now married and had a son. At home, she surrounded herself with men—male housekeepers, butlers, and secretaries. Paul Novak, handsome and muscular, with a service revolver conspicuously jammed in his suit pocket, was her constant companion. Sometimes she was spotted dining at Perino's, one of Los Angeles's most famous Italian eateries, or at Man Fook Low, a downtown Chinese restaurant. Others remembered her happily stopping by Ships, a simple diner complete with toasters on the tables.

West continued to remain aloof from the Hollywood scene, withdrawing into her small circle of family and acquaintances. With more time to pursue her interest in spiritual matters, she invited close friends and family to her beach house or the Ravenswood for séances and demonstrations of psychic power. However, as time confirmed her status as an American legend, Hollywood's elite, who had previously snubbed her, became more hospitable. They began enticing her out with occasional honors. In April 1962, the Hollywood Friars' Club invited her to a testimonial roast for her former vaudeville partner Harry Richman. She became the first woman to be admitted to that exclusively male club. Although she declined to dine with the all-male crowd, she agreed to speak. After an introduction by comedian George Jessel, she swaggered across the stage to the podium to overwhelming applause. A hush fell over the audience. She remained silent. Surveying the room, she finally spoke: "This is what I've always dreamed of, wall to wall men." Richman rated her appearance "spectacular."[5]

Other honors came her way. In 1963, she received a star on Hollywood's Walk of Fame. The following year, the University of Southern California paid tribute to her at a special salute to famous film pioneers. That evening she first met the tribute's organizer, USC alumnus and Hollywood insider Stanley Musgrove. Gloria Swanson, who emceed the ceremony, introduced West by confessing, "I used to think I was something of a sex symbol until Mae West came along." According to Musgrove, West was the hit of the evening. She turned to Swanson and chuckled, "If there's anything you want to know, just ask."[6]

These tributes proved that Mae West remained firmly ingrained in the national consciousness. In fact, *My Little Chickadee* was released for television, providing many with their first and only taste of the cinematic West. In 1964, Paramount courted her for a role in an Elvis Presley film, *Roustabout*, sending studio executive Paul Nathan to meet with her at the Ravenswood. Relying on her longtime negotiation strategy, she insisted they discuss his proposition in her bedroom. When Nathan revealed that she would play a carnival owner who had an alcoholic lover and was about to lose her busi-

ness, she immediately dismissed him. "She is alert, sharp, eager to do a picture," Nathan reported. "But definitely not this one. She would probably like
to play it if Elvis played a small part *opposite* her."[7]

West did accept television producer Arthur Lubin's invitation to appear
on the popular sitcom *Mister Ed*. She had known Lubin for years; he had been
a Paramount production assistant in the 1930s and was an occasional guest at
her beach-house séances. He offered her what Paramount did not—a role as
Mae West. He even hired movers to bring in her own furniture for scenes in
her television-land boudoir and allowed her to rework her part.

Mister Ed focused on the mishaps of architect Wilbur Post, who is constantly placed in awkward situations by Mister Ed, his mischievous talking
horse. Ed talks only to Wilbur, leaving family, friends, neighbors, and clients
in a constant state of bewilderment over the architect's strange behavior. In
West's episode, which first aired in March 1964, she hires Wilbur to redesign her stables in French provincial for her Parisian horses. When Mae
telephones Wilbur, Ed answers, and she becomes determined to meet the
deep voice on the other end of the line. She arrives at the Posts', bawdy blues
blaring in the background, in an elegant black limousine attended by tuxe-
doed escorts. Her presence awes the Posts and their next-door neighbors,
the Kirkwoods, who have gathered to see the famous star. When they ask
her for her secret to youth, femininity, and beauty, she advises, "Dress like a
woman, look like a woman, act like a woman, feel like a woman."

Of course, Mae fails to locate Wilbur's handsome-voiced associate. But
when Ed hears of the pampered life her horses lead, he turns up on Mae's
doorstep pretending he is orphaned. She takes him in, and her groomers, all
musclemen, begin combing him and rubbing him down. But, discovering the
good life includes a bubble bath, he returns home, complaining to Wilbur,
"My name is Ed, not Edwina." Later, when Mae phones again, Ed informs
her that he is unable to "come up and see her" because the army has drafted
him. Mae hums, "I'll just have to start my own draft board."[8]

West's *Mister Ed* appearance sustained her image for yet another generation of television viewers. Unlike the *Red Skelton Show* or the *Dean Martin
Show*, *Mister Ed* drew a large number of children and teens. At the same time,
it affirmed her status as a signifier of sexual rebelliousness, a proud woman
who boldly pursues men and is admired by all for her sensuality. The Posts
and the Kirkwoods marvel at her agelessness, her ability to transcend time.
Indeed, West's gowns—one a flashy floral print—and her 1960s locks indicated that she was attempting to stay contemporary.

While West had some control over her dialogue, this episode essentially
remained the creation of the series' writers. The result was the immersion

of Mae West in the world of Mister Ed. Ed and Mae were a good match. They were both tricksters who wreaked havoc on a society they had little power over. *Mister Ed* was a nice transition for Mae, for the series reflected much of the changing nature of America.

By the sixties, young people and other groups were rebelling against the conservatism and conformist pressures of Cold War America. A counterculture, the hippies, evolved and challenged the values that the postwar world had held so dear. As the civil rights movement invigorated the struggle for equal rights among oppressed groups, many Americans began to question authority and fight for their rights. Additionally, as the Vietnam War escalated, young people protested U.S. involvement in that distant conflict. As a result, Americans were deeply divided; some embraced change, and others clung to tradition.

Although *Mister Ed* was a lighthearted comedy, it also reflected the turbulence of the times. Its basic premise revolved around power and conformity. Ed constantly contests Wilbur's authority and repeatedly forces him to deviate from his conformist ideals. Wilbur appears ordinary; he works hard, loves his wife, lives in a comfortable home, and is a successful businessman, but he puts most of his energy into hiding the fact that he talks to his horse and, even worse, that his horse talks back.

West's reputation as a cultural rebel made her a perfect guest star for *Mister Ed*. Just her presence perpetuated the challenge to conformity. Like Wilbur and Ed, she appeared idiosyncratic. She stood apart from the Posts and the Kirkwoods; she was richer, sexier, and smarter. But she was also eccentric, a powerful woman completely out of step with gender norms. She was willing to expend a considerable amount of money to treat her horses to human comforts. In the end, West was even too much of a nonconformist for Ed: Willing to defy all expectations of horses, he refused to permit his masculinity to be compromised by a bubble bath.

West's guest appearance on *Mister Ed* was a success. The show drew some of the highest ratings of its four-year run. Lubin scheduled her for a return performance, and she began working on a script that included a sequence set in the Old West. Her career seemed on the upswing. That August, she celebrated her seventy-first birthday at the hip Los Angeles nightclub the Peppermint Lounge, doing the twist.

While West was really beginning to enjoy her status as a legend, she confronted several crises. First, Paul Novak, growing weary of harassment from Beverly and John West, left Mae briefly. Although Mae warned him to "just remember, there ain't no swingin' doors on this place," she soon coaxed him home. But her personal troubles were far from over. Beverly's drinking had grown worse. She had twice married and divorced Vladimir Baikoff; supported by Mae, she spent most of her time at the San Fernando Valley ranch. The relationship between the two sisters remained uneasy. Unlike Mae's, Beverly's entertainment career never got off the ground. Publicly Beverly was loyal to Mae, but privately she blamed her sister for her failures, maintaining that her family had forced her to step aside to support Mae's ambitions. From Mae's perspective, Beverly had wasted her life on drink, and she had little patience for her lack of self-discipline. Yet she remained protective of her younger sister and finally convinced Beverly to spend five months in a treatment program. Although it helped, eventually Beverly returned to drinking. Stanley Musgrove, who first met Beverly in the late 1960s, was astonished to discover that she looked old enough to be Mae's mother.[9]

In addition to caring for Beverly, Mae wrestled with stressful litigation. In 1964, she filed a suit against Marie Lind, a Mae West imitator who billed herself as "the one and only Diamond Lil." As early as 1950, Mae had initiated legal action against Mae West impersonators. From her perspective, it was imperative for her to establish exclusive rights to the Diamond Lil persona. By the early sixties, she had grown more determined to completely control it. For Mae, it was not a question of money—she had plenty of that. But anyone who dared to mimic her undermined her unique identity, the distinctiveness that had become the essence of her performance and her public self. She was livid when a cigar manufacturer revised her trademark line, running advertisements with a sultry voice-over inviting, "Why don't you come up and smoke one sometime?"

In September 1964, West's case against Marie Lind came to trial in Los Angeles. Although Mae had earlier insisted that Diamond Lil was a real person, now she claimed that the Bowery queen was a purely fictional character. She presented early scripts and produced witnesses who testified that Diamond Lil was a product of her creative work. One even argued that Diamond Lil was synonymous with Mae West, that the two were interchangeable. West's representatives contended that Lind's act was not just an impersonation of a character but an appropriation of a personality. When Lind took the witness stand, she maintained that Lillian Russell had been known as Diamond Lil and that it was a generic name "that might apply to a dance-hall girl or saloon singer." But Lind was no match for West's high-powered attorneys. After listening to several days of testimony and reviewing *Diamond Lil* scripts, a judge granted West exclusive legal rights to Diamond Lil. In his decision, he noted that "a great deal of time, money and effort went into the creation of secondary meaning identifying Miss West by the name 'Diamond Lil.'" Mae West had finally achieved total oneness with her stage persona.[10]

It was not without cost. Shortly after the trial ended in mid-September, Mae collapsed. She was rushed to a hospital, where she registered under Beverly's name and underwent tests. After six days, she was released, diagnosed with diabetes. Still career-minded, West, with the help of Novak, kept her illness strictly secret. It led some to speculate that Mae was the victim of a heart attack; others claimed she was exhausted. In the film colony, it was rumored that she had suffered a breakdown. Attempting to maintain her resilient image, Mae insisted that it was just a virulent viral infection and that she still enjoyed boundless energy because, as a medical marvel, she possessed a "double thyroid." Yet it was clear that her health was not good, and privately Novak often had to nurse her through diabetic seizures. Her second *Mister Ed* appearance was canceled, and she turned down invitations to guest-star on *Gilligan's Island* and *The Hollywood Palace*. All social invitations were declined. It only contributed to the growing image of Mae as an eccentric. She recuperated at the Ravenswood with short trips to the beach house, where, it was rumored, the blinds remained shut all day and she walked on the beach after dark with Novak guiding her over the sands.[11]

That October, Mae received another jolt. Shortly after her release from the hospital, her brother, John, died suddenly of a massive heart attack. Both Mae and Beverly were devastated. A funeral service was held, and he was interred with Tillie and Jack in the Brooklyn family crypt. A month later, for the first time, Mae drew up a will, leaving most of her estate to Beverly and bequeathing $10,000 to Paul Novak; the rest was left to close friends, cousins, and charities. Shortly afterward Mae claimed that her brother's spirit visited her, hovering above her bed, his eyes filled with tears. She maintained that she looked away and without a word he disappeared. With a psychic's help, she interpreted his appearance as an expression of his remorse for disappointing her by failing to settle into a career. She insisted that she mentally assured him that she "was glad he lived his life as he wanted to."[12]

West's well-known belief in spiritualism combined with her reclusiveness and advancing age presented another challenge to her star image. Her illness had left her weakened, and photographs revealed that she had grown visibly older. And as Mae aged, she did so in a society that was more and more obsessed with youth. Thanks in part to the commercialization of youth culture, young people's fashions, language, and music were elevated as the norm. Journalists looking for good stories often exploited the youth angle. For Mae, it was going to be a struggle to keep up with the times.

In late 1964, West had recuperated enough from illness and grief to grant a couple of interviews. The first was with the *Saturday Evening Post*'s Lewis Lapham, who scored it through a mutual acquaintance who instructed him on proper Mae West interview etiquette: He must address her at all times as Miss West, must not mention the names of certain actresses or W. C. Fields, and must behave with utmost propriety, assuming the bearing of "an attentive young man teetering on the edge of reckless infatuation."

Lapham was happy to abide by her wishes, and after he made it past the entrance of her Santa Monica beach house, now overgrown with weeds, through the blinding whiteness of her living room, he was treated to a classic Westian performance in, of course, her boudoir. She began the interview herself, denouncing those who dared imitate her or claim the title of sex symbol. Lapham expressed total agreement. "Nothing but common drabs tricked up in tight skirts," he affirmed. West was pleased: "Young man, I see you understand a few things." In many ways, Lapham did understand her. His article, in the form of a letter to a doubting friend, argues that Mae West maintained an "overwhelming sexual force" despite her age. He speculated that she had never possessed the qualities identified with a classical definition of American female beauty and concluded that "Miss West achieves her effect by the force of her will." He believed that she was thoroughly aware of the "artifice" of her star persona, that it was the mechanism by which she had built and perpetuated the institution of Mae West.[13]

The next interviewer, acclaimed photojournalist Diane Arbus, came to the opposite conclusion. While Arbus acknowledged that West had been a symbol of sex, she portrayed the star as now sadly deceived. One of her photographs showed a seventy-one-year-old Mae West reclining seductively in her bed with one of her monkeys, which she reportedly often slept with. Arbus rejected West's verbal perpetuation of her image. West bragged, "I was once asked what ten men I'd like to have come up and see me sometime. Why ten? Why not a hundred, a thousand? Not all at once of course." Arbus refused to play along: She noted West's odd habit of referring to herself as "sexy Mae" and intimated that the aging actress was a little senile. In Arbus's view, West and her "mythical kingdom" were in decay. For many, Mae West, as an older woman, could not stand for rowdy sex and bold womanhood. American society would reject any seventy-one-year-old woman who tried.[14]

The contrasting views of Lapham and Arbus would follow Mae West for the rest of her life. Some testified to her eternal desirability; others held steadfastly that she was living in a pathetic fantasy world. But as before, many were not sure whether Mae West was serious or kidding. Since her early successes onstage, she had left her audiences uneasy, and now, using her star persona, she still made the public uncomfortable and uncertain. Every interaction continued to be a performance designed to challenge authority and assumptions. "All my life," she confessed to one reporter, "I've been a put-on."[15]

While West's health and advancing age did force her to curtail many of her activities, she looked to new avenues to keep alive the signifier that she had worked so hard to build. Hoping to appeal to the younger generation, she embarked on a recording career, this time focusing on rock and roll. In 1966, she made an album, *Way Out West*, which included songs by the Beatles and Bob Dylan. She also reprised the soul hits "When a Man Loves a Woman" and "Boom, Boom," which included the appropriately Westian lyrics "When I walk that walk, and when I talk that talk." That December, she followed with a holiday rock album called *Wild Christmas*, which included "Put the Loot in My Boot" and "Santa, Come Up and See Me."

Some disparaged these efforts, insisting that West was too old to rock and roll. While her albums failed to reach the top ten, they sold fairly well, and many noted that her voice was in fine form. When journalist Helen Lawrenson visited West at the Ravenswood in 1967, Mae produced a pile of fan letters, all from teenage boys or young men who she claimed had discovered her through her music. Entertainment reporter Kevin Thomas also came up to interview West about her foray into the rock scene. She argued that it was a logical trajectory, that rock and roll originated in ragtime (an indirect acknowledgment of rock's black roots). To prove the link she treated him to spontaneous versions of "Doin' the Grizzly Bear" and "My Maricooch a Make a da Hoochy Macooch," two numbers from her earliest days in show business. But she affirmed her determination to stay modern. "I like the new beat," she told him. "The kids have the right idea."[16]

In 1968, West recorded another album, *Great Balls of Fire,* with backing from music impresario Mike Curb. She demanded that the producer, Ian Whitcomb, use African-American musicians as her accompanists, but he refused. Instead, he recorded the instrumentals without her, later bringing her in to do her vocal tracks in a single session. In addition to a rendition of the Doors' "Light My Fire," which West complained was nonsense, she recorded "Rock Around the Clock" and "Happy Birthday 21." Whitcomb composed a song in her honor called "How Miss West Won World Peace," a bawdy Westian plan for ending the Cold War with the seduction of world leaders. When her recording session finished, she prepared to leave through the back door. But, learning that an African-American rhythm and blues band was waiting in the lobby to rehearse, she announced to Whitcomb, "I'll exit right through them, dear." As she did, Whitcomb claimed, the waiting musicians responded with a resounding "Amen." But it was a while before anyone got to hear the results of West's work that day. *Great Balls of Fire* was held up until Mike Curb became the head of MGM Records and finally ordered the company to release it in 1972.[17]

West's flirtation with the recording industry allowed her to perpetuate her status as a trickster and rebel. It was a crafty effort to signify her symbol by using her voice rather than her physical image. While her body, a key element of her performance, was no longer as mutable as it once had been, the voice was still strong and very Westian. Aware of the press's negative manipulation of her visual image, she began denying interviewers' requests to photograph her. The only images released to the public were carefully retouched portraits. For *Way Out West*, she posed among admiring young backup musicians, wearing a tight, gold evening gown. A publicity photo of her playing the guitar was worked over; her face wrinkle free, she sported a psychedelic print dress and a beehive hairdo. But for the most part, she relied on her now legendary voice and her unique language play. She was aided by the publication of a collection of her witticisms, entitled *The Wit and Wisdom of Mae West*. The book's opening pages assured readers:

> And 'neath the sun I've found but one
> Tradition I can trust:
> One thing that's sure and does endure
> Is Mae West's bust.[18]

In the mind's eye, the trickster defied age and lived on.

Slowly, West made remarkable progress in regaining her health, and Hollywood again began to approach her with offers. In 1965, producer Ross Hunter tried to recruit her for his *The Art of Love,* but when he refused to let her rewrite her part, she backed out. She turned down Italian director Federico Fellini, who offered her a part in *Juliet of the Spirits* and a role as the erotic witch mother in *Satyricon*. Those parts, she felt, were not suited to her character; they would not be useful in her struggle to maintain and signify her image.

In the meantime, West, now almost seventy-five, made a brief return to public performing. In February 1968, the USC film fraternity, Delta Kappa Alpha, honored her. Rather than taking the stage and answering questions from the audience as was customary, she arranged to appear in a brief skit. After the guests finished eating, the lights went up on the stage, revealing USC's star football players, including Ron Yary and O. J. Simpson, in a huddle. On cue, they parted, and there was Mae West stretched out on a white chaise lounge. Director George Cukor, an old friend who was acting as master of ceremonies, attempted to interview her about her early career. Instead, she "cut off the questioning and nodded to her piano player . . . and then started telling the story of Diamond Lil." She followed with "Frankie and Johnny" and received a standing ovation. Before exiting, she addressed the crowd: "I want to thank you for your generous applause—and your heavy breathing." "Roll me over," exclaimed entertainment reporter James Bacon, "I'm in love with Mae West all over again."[19]

West knew that she did not possess the endurance to return to the stage and held out hopes for a film comeback. She told Kevin Thomas of plans to transform *Catherine Was Great* into a rock opera. She also became determined to film a new version of *Diamond Lil*, this time in color. But she got the strongest support in Hollywood for her plans to bring *Sextette* to the screen. She began negotiations with several producers and Warner Bros. for the project. When she revealed her plans to ESP expert Richard Ireland, who had replaced the now deceased Jack Kelly as her spiritual adviser, he predicted that she would soon return to the screen but not in *Sextette*.

She interpreted it as a sign when the William Morris Agency informed her that Twentieth Century–Fox and producer Robert Fryer wanted her for a film based on Gore Vidal's bestseller *Myra Breckinridge*. Vidal's controversial novel focused on a gay film critic, Myron Breckinridge, who undergoes a sex change operation and, as the gorgeous Myra, seeks revenge against men and the film industry. West read a draft of the script and, assuming that Fryer wanted her to play Myra, turned him down, protesting, "I like my sexes stable." But at a Ravenswood meeting with Fryer and the film's director, Hollywood newcomer Michael Sarne, the producer graciously corrected her mistaken impression. They did not want her for Myra; they had envisioned her as Hollywood talent agent Letitia Van Allen. Again West balked. In Vidal's novel, Van Allen is beaten by a male lover and hospitalized. Mae was in no way going to play a victim of a batterer. Rather, "I might send him to the hospital," she opined.[20]

Fryer persisted. He offered her $350,000, top billing, a private dressing room decorated in white French provincial, and Edith Head as her costume designer. But what really sold West was Fryer's guarantee that she would have complete control over her dialogue. She signed on and soon changed the character's name to Leticia, contending that her friends might mispronounce the name, putting the emphasis "on the tit."[21]

By the summer of 1969, Twentieth Century–Fox was heralding *Myra Breckinridge* with a barrage of advance publicity. Even before the film went into production, West was granting interviews to promote it. Although she had not appeared in a movie in almost twenty-six years, she informed reporters, "It's a return, not a comeback. I've never really been away, just busy." Although she feigned ignorance about co-star Raquel Welch, cast as the transsexual Myra Breckinridge, she spoke glowingly of Michael Sarne, praising the director as "a very bright young man."[22]

Behind the scenes, however, almost everyone, including West, quickly became frustrated with Sarne. The director had decided to transform Vidal's complex satire of Hollywood and sexuality into a film script himself. In an effort to retain the novel's flavor, Sarne envisioned the project as avant-garde and planned explicit sex scenes and a pastiche of footage from old films as fantasy sequences. The result, in Mae's estimation, was baffling; she consistently complained that the script made no sense. Others involved in the project, including Welch and film critic Rex Reed, who had accepted the role of Myron, shared her opinion.

That August, before shooting began, Welch made friendly overtures to West, calling her on the phone to chat. In turn, West invited her up to the Ravenswood for a visit. She prepared the complete treatment for the young actress, considered by many to be Hollywood's hottest sex symbol. But moments before Welch arrived, the air conditioner blew a fuse. Stanley Musgrove, now working as West's publicist, and several assistants scurried to fix it. Mae rushed into her legendary bedroom, made the bed herself, and quickly picked up the rest of the apartment. When the Ravenswood switchboard announced Welch's arrival, Mae sequestered herself in her bedroom preparing for an entrance. Welch knocked, Musgrove took his place on a white sofa, Mae closed the bedroom door, and her butler let the Hollywood starlet in. After the usual suspenseful moments, Mae West swept into the room, shook Welch's hand, and offered her a drink. Welch requested spring water, West's favored beverage as well. She professed her admiration for the veteran actress's work and revealed her reservations regarding Sarne. While Mae too was concerned, she remained politely noncommittal.

Privately, as West revised her part, she grew increasingly impatient with Sarne's conception of the film. "As for the fantasy angle," she told friends at dinner one evening, "it's like someone tells you a story and you get all interested. Then they say, 'then I woke up and it was all a dream.' You want to smack 'em in the face." With the assistance of Musgrove and a screenwriter, David Giler, she remolded the plot and attempted to reconstruct Leticia Van Allen into the Mae Westian character. West's early drafts transformed Van Allen into a powerful female booking agent who worked from a casting bed, not a casting couch. After a vigorous romantic interlude, she puts one young beau in the hospital. As a subplot, Van Allen is also a popular recording artist; with old-fashioned Hollywood flourish, West sketched in several musical numbers. When Musgrove finally saw West's first drafts, he discovered that she had deleted several of Welch's scenes. Urging her to put them back, he suggested she consider Welch's character as a homosexual. He claimed that revelation reinvigorated West, at least for the moment. When her interest

flagged again, Fryer sent over a song for her to review, "Hard to Handle." She was
delighted to learn that she would be backed by an all-male African-American
chorus in ties and tails. But, still fearful of the racial climate, she cautioned
Musgrove, "They must never touch me—because of the southern senators."[23]

Yet Sarne was determined and as singleminded as West. Regardless of the
concerns expressed by Fryer, West, and the rest of the cast, he tenaciously
clung to his vision of *Myra Breckinridge*. His refusal to address their criticisms
only further alienated those involved in the film. In her dealings with him,
West, like others, found him arrogant and rude. In early September 1969,
Sarne came to the Ravenswood to discuss West's reconception of her role.
Although Fryer approved of her revisions, according to Musgrove, Sarne
"sniggered at them." West was outraged. As Sarne departed from her apartment and walked down the hall to the elevator, she mimicked him. Musgrove and Fryer found themselves laughing uncontrollably at her amazingly
on-target impersonation.[24]

Myra Breckinridge limped along under a cloud of dissension and discontent.
The atmosphere brightened briefly once the filming began. Sarne acquiesced to
West's changes and even sought Musgrove's guidance on handling the legendary
star. Musgrove instructed him to laugh at her jokes and compliment her appearance. When West arrived for her first day on the set in mid-October, Sarne, on
behalf of the entire cast and crew, presented her with a bouquet of white
roses, arranged in the shape of a large heart with her name across the middle.
Musgrove noted that, at least for the time being, West's presence had lifted
the cast's mood from "dreary anxiety" to "pleasant excitement."[25]

West promptly began preparing a scene in which Van Allen, arriving at
her white French provincial office complete with large round bed, strolls
past a long line of aspiring actors and breathes, "Get your resumés out,
boys." She felt it required her special attention, and she spent one entire day
sequestered in her dressing room auditioning over thirty young actors for
the scene. When she emerged, Rex Reed asked her what she had been doing.
"Well," she drawled, "we weren't playing Scrabble."[26]

It was not long before gloom again descended on the production. West's
elaborate changes in plot and dialogue clashed with Sarne's script, resulting
in more confusion and dissension on the set. Welch complained that West's
revised lines made her role as Myra even more incomprehensible. But Welch
also disagreed with Sarne's depiction of male homosexuality. "I don't think it
is a subject to be treated in a snickering way," she told one interviewer.

In many ways, pairing Welch with West was a mistake. Both women coveted the status of sex symbol. The twenty-nine-year-old Welch was regarded as a stunning beauty, and she was well aware that her marketability

relied on her sex appeal. For West, it went even deeper; desirability and allure were more than just commodities—they were instruments of power.
Unlike Welch, she had never enjoyed acknowledgment as a true beauty, but
she had spent a lifetime enacting it. As West had grown older she had resolved her greatest internal struggle, her quest for identity, by cementing it
to her celebrated image as a signifier of sex. When a journalist asked West
to discuss the differences between her public and private selves, she contended that "the public Mae West is more exaggerated for the screen. She's
pretty much the same as the private Mae West, who is less exaggerated."
West inevitably treated Welch as an interloper.

Welch was awed, frustrated, and angered by West. "I'm still on a four-
year-old studio contract and have no protection on this picture whatever," she
told an interviewer. "I'm the one with the head on the block." Although she
regarded West as all-powerful, Welch fought back. She resisted changes in
her dialogue and warned David Giler against tampering with her lines. She
discerned West's attempts to transform *Myra Breckinridge* into a Mae West vehicle. "Mae West is the inimitable Mae West and she has nothing to do with
the Leticia Van Allen in the book," Welch commented. "She is making an entirely separate picture from the one I'm making." Her actions succeeded in
angering not only West but also Edith Head. At Head's urging, West's contract had specified that when she shared scenes with other characters, she was
to appear exclusively in black-and-white gowns. The savvy designer knew
that the black-and-white contrast would make West stand out on the screen.
According to Head, Welch, at Sarne's direction, showed up in a black-and-
white gown to film a scene with West. Both West and Head were furious;
Welch eventually ended up in blue. According to Musgrove, Edith Head remarked during *Myra Breckinridge*'s filming, "God, I'm glad I drink."

As rumors circulated about the West-Welch feud, interviewers sought out
the two, attempting to fan the fire. Welch told *Look* magazine, "She looks
wonderful in person, and is a tiny little lady, absolutely minute." And she
lodged a stinging criticism: "If you can buy the fact that a seventy-seven-year-
old woman can sexually put a twenty-seven-year-old boy in the hospital, then
you can buy anything in this picture." When *Look* sought West's reaction, she
defaulted to classic Westian double messages. She contended, "You're never
too old to become younger," and insisted that she still enjoyed an active sex
life. When pressed about Welch, she had little to say except, "She's a sweet
thing. She has one or two little scenes in the picture, I believe."[27]

The division between West and Welch paled in comparison to the continuing tensions between the entire cast and Michael Sarne. As filming proceeded, the project became increasingly chaotic. In late spring 1970, with

Sarne undecided on an ending, $1.5 million over budget, and way behind schedule, the studio pulled the plug. They insisted that he wrap it up and begin editing the film for release.[28]

In June 1970, *Myra Breckinridge* was finally ready for the big screen. The studio, believing that the film would receive a positive reception in progressive San Francisco, sent it there for a trial run. According to West, who declined to attend, the crowd cheered her each time she appeared on the screen. Sarne, who had already deleted much of her material, was infuriated. When he returned to Los Angeles at three the next morning, he began reediting the film. West's circle insisted that he was so angered by her scene-stealing that he cut much of her work completely out. Reportedly, he dumped the footage in a trash bin on the Fox lot. When Fryer discovered Sarne's deed, he demanded the director restore her scenes. Sarne followed orders at least to a point: He claimed that some of the discarded film had already been hauled away and lost forever.

The reedited film made two debuts, one in Hollywood and another at New York City's Criterion Theater. West and most of the cast opted for the Manhattan opening. Ads for the film's debut beckoned, "You Gotta See It to Believe It!" Appropriately, capturing the difference between the symbols conveyed by Welch and West, they showed the two side by side. Welch held an outstretched baton and wore a red, white, and blue bikini and white boots. Mae posed, as she had done over thirty years before, as the Statue of Liberty draped in Old Glory. With Welch, everything was revealed; with Mae, what lay beneath Liberty's red, white, and blue gown as she lifted her torch high into the air was left to the imagination. On one level, Welch appeared as the cheerleader for messages long signified by Mae West.[29]

On opening night, June 23, 1970, a mob of 2,000 spectators packed the streets around the Criterion. When Welch arrived, the crowd pressed against the wooden police barricades, chanting her name. When West arrived, pandemonium broke lose. As she stepped out of a black limousine, the mob surged and "splintered the barriers trying to reach her." Fans rushed toward the legendary actress, and aides hustled her into the theater.[30]

Unfortunately but not surprisingly, the critics did not share the opening night crowd's enthusiasm. Almost universally, *Myra Breckinridge* received hostile notices. The *New York Times*'s Vincent Canby decried the loss of the novel's biting satirical tone and proclaimed that the film only demonstrated "the lengths to which today's moviemakers will go to try to be different and dirty." He also balked at West, claiming that she possessed "the figure of a cinched-in penguin and a face made of pink-and-white plaster in which little holes have been left for her eyes and mouth." While others agreed that the film was both meandering and obscene—it received an X rating—several contended that West's appearance was its highlight. Another reviewer complained that she was not on the screen nearly enough and noted that when she did appear "she sweeps in regally, sumptuously gowned and coiffed, and intoning amusing lines."[31]

In general, the public, many of whom had been drawn to *Myra Breckinridge* by West's return to the screen, found the film distasteful and poorly produced. One moviegoer declared it a "witless mélange of street dirt," and even the hip generation embracing the sexual revolution of the 1960s turned away from the film. Within a few weeks of its release, it was clear that *Myra Breckinridge* was a box office disaster. Twentieth Century–Fox withdrew it, and Michael Sarne found himself a Hollywood outcast. Even West, who in old Hollywood style had kept her disagreements with the film's director private, publicly criticized the picture. In an interview just after the premiere, she expressed reservations. "I'm not too sure about *Myra Breckinridge*," she remarked. "They didn't use enough of me or my material until the budget had been run up high." Later, she was even more to the point, suggesting that audiences were "disturbed, confused, and irritated" by the film. "He should have had a narrator explain what it was all about," she insisted, "or distributed 'A Guide to the Confused' pamphlets."[32]

Despite *Myra Breckinridge*'s failure, the movie rekindled so much interest in Mae West that one journalist labeled it a "Mae West revival." Shortly after the film's debut, she released a new edition of her autobiography, updating her fans on her achievements since 1959. Most major newspapers and magazines sought her out for interviews. In addition to repeating over and over the life story of an independent, ambitious, and always victorious star, she also held forth on a variety of timely issues. She deplored the Vietnam War but refused to endorse any particular politician or party. She praised young people but insisted to one journalist that the unrest and societal divisions were a part of a "conspiracy." To the chagrin of a Twentieth Century–Fox publicist, she endorsed the left. "Communists have done a lot of good things," she contended. "You can't tear them down. They're the ones who got old age pensions, money for the poor, unemployment so they can at least live." The studio representative interjected, "She means socialism, not Communism." West just silently nodded.[33]

It was an odd confession from a woman who had shied away from the left during the Cold War and, in the early sixties, had led Lewis Lapham to conclude that she was "right of Goldwater." But Mae often reversed her positions, always leaving an element of uncertainty. Mae's glowing appraisal of Communism may have been calculated to unnerve the studio's publicist or the interviewer; it also may have represented her attempt to mirror the times. With the escalation of the Vietnam War, the hostility toward the left had eased, especially among the younger generation, whom Mae saw as her newest and most loyal supporters. The radicalism of the 1960s, in particular with more attention to class, had created an atmosphere that embraced many of the attitudes that she had long communicated subversively through her work. While she had backed away from those themes after World War II, by the 1960s, with sectors of society rebelling against the Cold War climate, Mae found that her symbol was becoming ever more popular. Her endorsement of the contemporary slogan "Make love not war" seemed to give it all the more meaning. Mae affirmed, "There should be more loving and less fighting."

West also embraced her reputation as a liberated woman. She seemed firmly aware that scholars had begun debating her image and were divided over her relationship to feminism. On the one hand, West rejected feminism. Believing it undermined a woman's feminine qualities, her most powerful weapon in the battle between the sexes, she flatly declared, "I don't consider myself a feminist." At the same time, she proclaimed support for the women's liberation movement. "Liberation was always in the back of my mind," West told a reporter. Emphatically, she insisted that her lifelong goal had been to elevate women, to portray characters that made them feel proud as well as powerful. "I'm always for the woman lifting the woman up," she claimed. What prevented many feminists of the day from fully embracing Mae West was her continued reliance on female desirability as her major attribute in the struggle against patriarchy. But Mae exploited her own philosophy as an opportunity to perpetuate her rebellion, to continue the subversive pranks she had always played. The trickster could be almost eighty and still enjoy sex. "Age has nothing to do with sex," she insisted. "Sex is a frame of mind, and let me say I've got a very good mind." In an instant, within the same interview, she insisted that she had not changed since she was twenty-six (or, as she often claimed, twenty-sex). She consistently befuddled and disappointed those who hoped to claim her as an icon of liberated womanhood. But in Mae West's world, nothing could stand still; everything had to be in flux.[34]

In addition to embracing her symbol as the liberated woman, she emerged as a vocal supporter of the modern gay struggle. While she clung to her antiquated notion that gays were men with women's souls, she pleaded for tolerance and understanding. "The gay boys—looks like they're gonna take over," she remarked proudly to several reporters, reflecting on the escalation of the gay rights movement. She boasted that *The Drag* and *The Pleasure Man* were sympathetic treatments of homosexuality that had offered employment to numerous gay performers. When the *Los Angeles Times* ran a story claiming that she had called musclemen "fags," she immediately responded with a scathing letter. "Never in my life have I used the word *fag*," she wrote. She denied that she had speculated on "body builders' sexual orientation" and claimed she knew, from personal experience, that many musclemen were definitely straight.

West was aware that the gay community comprised some of her most loyal followers. Dating back to her early career, she had been celebrated as an icon in gay culture. With the growing struggle for gay rights, her popularity had soared in that sector. Her appeal extended beyond her exaggerated image of femininity; West's famous witticisms and her blunt and bold expressions of sexuality were celebrated not only by women but also by gay men. Just after the premiere of *Myra Breckinridge*, the *Gay News*, which had sent a reporter to cover Mae's press conference, reprinted a long list of her Westianisms verbatim. "If you were in a hospital bed, who would you want in the next bed?" someone asked. "Well," she responded, "I'd want a man there."[35]

Many speculated on the relationship between West's style and gay camp. She vociferously maintained that the boldness of camp originated in *her* brazen portrayal of womanhood. She remained supportive of gay rights but resisted categorizing her performance style in what was essentially a male tradition. Of course, in her early career West had borrowed from gay performers, but by this point they had also absorbed much from her. Her image of strength, sensuality, and womanishness was an empowering symbol for both women and gay men struggling for equality in a world dominated by heterosexual men. Still, West became incensed at being constantly compared to female impersonators and characterized as camp. At a benefit for Tom Bradley, who would soon become Los Angeles's first African-American mayor, actress Martha Raye kissed West on the cheek and praised her as "the queen of us all." Mae was gracious but later speculated that Raye's comment was "a crack." Stanley Musgrove began withholding articles from West that referred to her style as camp.[36]

At the same time, Musgrove realized the potential for publicity carried by West's relationship to camp and drag. In his personal papers, he saved a script that he helped author for *Rona's Reports*, radio spots on Hollywood happenings delivered by columnist Rona Barrett, a friend of Mae's who shared her interest in spiritualism. Barrett announced that a new pornographic film called *Dinah East* had gone into production. Reportedly, the film was about a starlet who is killed in an automobile crash; an autopsy reveals that she was a he. Barrett noted that the film was based on the old rumor that Mae West was really a man. She also teased listeners with the scoop that when West died, a secret that had been hidden for many years would be revealed.

Mae reveled in the mystery that surrounded her and in interviews reinforced an indeterminacy. She gleefully bragged that her participation in *Myra Breckinridge* would again revive the debate over censorship. In another interview, she supported stricter censorship. "Right now, I think censorship is necessary," she contended. "The things they're doing and saying in films right now just shouldn't be allowed." When discussing the sexual revolution, she often declared herself its foremother; in other instances, she suspiciously asserted that "somebody" was "pushing" the new sexual permissiveness. West continued to play with dualisms, often leaving her interviewers confused as she contradicted herself within a few sentences. Some wrote it off to age. Others maintained she was as sharp and as puzzling as always.[37]

In many ways, Mae was more alive than ever. She had finally successfully transformed the entire world into her stage, the one place where she truly felt comfortable and in control. Interviewers flocked to the Ravenswood, deferentially seeking out the Hollywood legend. They were rarely disappointed, for Mae entertained them one and all. One politely asked, "If you had your life to live over again, would you do anything different?" "No," she replied, "I'd do everything, only more of it."[38]

Although West had embraced the media as a perfect forum in which to continue her work, she had not abandoned hope for another return to the screen. She appeared to be in robust health, but her advancing age made it increasingly difficult to pursue this goal. Hollywood, more than ever entranced by youth, was reluctant to back a Mae West project. As she slowed down, she was forced to relinquish more and more oversight of her career to Stanley Musgrove. His inclusion in her inner circle directly affected the nature and direction of her work during her final years. Interviews were something she could control, but the complicated and rigid nature of the entertainment industry required an energetic expert like Musgrove.

Musgrove was widely respected and well connected in show business. He maintained a partnership with Robert Wise, the famous director of *The Sound of Music* and *West Side Story*. In addition to his insider status, Musgrove also had a clear understanding of the star's ego. Unlike Sarne, he was not confrontational and sought to appease performers like Mae West by appealing to their vanity. When dealing with Mae, he proceeded gingerly, quickly discerning her likes and dislikes, knowing what to say and what not to say. In many ways, he insulated her. He continued to keep press coverage he determined upsetting away from her and even hid unflattering photographs. Musgrove's approach may have been manipulative, but it was not an uncommon tactic for handling top names like Mae West, who could be temperamental, unreasonable, and easily angered.

While on the surface Musgrove appeared attentive and willing to work within West's rigidly structured world, he often grew frustrated with her. In his view, she was, even for a star, abnormally self-centered and moody. She often harangued him on the phone for hours. Additionally, like others, he perceived her as startlingly self-deceived and was appalled at her declarations of her eternal youth and extraordinary talent. He dreaded her incessant bragging about her past and found her repetition of stories so boring that he once cut short an interview she was giving to a graduate student writing a dissertation on vaudeville. Forced to endure a dinner with Mae at George Cukor's house where they listened to *Great Balls of Fire*, he confided to his log, "I'd heard most of it several times and I'm sure I looked bored and tired."[39]

Musgrove's reaction to *Great Balls of Fire* may have had something to do with Mike Curb's association with the album. During the filming of *Myra Breckinridge*, Musgrove and Wise were planning a television special entitled *A Night with Mae West*. But so was Curb, who hoped to use it to promote her album. As a result, both parties put considerable effort into courting West for their respective projects. She refused to commit to either one. Musgrove enlisted the support of Edith Head, who agreed to draw up some costumes for his proposed special. He generated scripts only to have Mae reject them as "too old-fashioned." One day when he showed up at the Ravenswood, she presented him with her own script, which he found outrageously vulgar. He panicked when he read in the *Los Angeles Times* that she was going ahead with Curb's special. When Musgrove confronted her, West reassured him; she would do his first and Curb's second. But with the negative reception of *Myra Breckinridge*, Musgrove's plans collapsed. His sponsor, the Singer Sewing Machine Company, fearing it might be linked with the disastrous X-rated movie, pulled out. Before long, Curb's plans fizzled as well.

Regardless, Musgrove stood by West, almost as if he were playing the role of one of her faithful but scheming managers. In turn, Mae, completely in character, was aware of his machinations and plotted to get the most out of him. She never completely trusted him; when he made phone calls, she secretly listened in from her bedroom extension, then later quizzed him about what he had said. For Musgrove, it was an emotional roller coaster. He was well aware that she was suspicious of him, and her behavior toward him was completely unpredictable. Sometimes she subjected him to angry outbursts, and other times she treated him like a confidant. Her moods changed within seconds. Paul Novak had never seen her cry, she once insisted to Musgrove. When Musgrove expressed astonishment that she never cried, she snapped back, "I didn't say that, I said Paul hadn't seen me cry." She also claimed that she was not in love with the former muscleman and that he was no more than a good friend. Musgrove remained distrustful of her and ascribed her contradictory behavior and admissions to her eccentric nature.

West's approach was calculated to keep Musgrove off guard. The element of surprise allowed her to control him. She once sternly warned him, "Don't you ever go against anything I say." For Mae, men were never to be trusted and were always to be manipulated. Her relationship with Musgrove carried not only professional but also personal objectives. It reaffirmed her identity and served as another engagement in her ongoing war against patriarchy.[40]

Despite his Hollywood savvy, Musgrove found West continually baffling. It was difficult for him to appreciate the subtleties of her merged personal and professional selves. Material he wrote for her, which she often rejected, lacked the nuanced multiplicity of meanings that had been the hallmark of her work. His later biography of Mae depicted her as a delusional and embittered woman who treated everyone the same way she treated him. But West's personal assistant, Tim Malachosky, who joined her entourage in 1970, viewed her as kind, unflappable, and generous—evidence that not every member of her inner circle was forced to submit to her bristling temper. While Mae remained a contradiction, even in her personal life, it seems that Musgrove never understood her; he never went beyond the surface. Additionally, Musgrove's log of his interactions with West and her associates contained racial and homophobic slurs indicating that he did not always share her open-mindedness. Ideologically, Musgrove and West were incompatible, but it was his professional hand that guided her through the final years of her life.[41]

Musgrove also thought West's involvement in spiritualism and the psychic world was a little wacky, yet her interest in such matters continued to grow. As *Myra Breckinridge* drew her back into the public eye, she began inviting more people to séances and demonstrations of ESP at her beach house. The wide-ranging guest list included fans, Hollywood notables, some of those involved in *Myra Breckinridge*, and Hollywood reporters. Nevertheless, Mae remained exceptionally shy and extremely protective of her private world. When longtime acquaintance Sidney Skolsky attended a session, he noted that Mae graciously received each guest, directing him or her to the living room, yet for most of the evening, she silently watched from behind a partition in the dining room. Even at her own parties, she chose to be alone and observe the festivities from a safe distance.[42]

While West maintained a protective distance from acquaintances and show business people, she thrived on the attention she received from the public. And the Mae West revival rolled on. One journalist noted an active

Mae West fan club and reported that West maintained a scrapbook of recent fan letters. Although *She Done Him Wrong* and *I'm No Angel* had remained banned for thirty-five years, the resurgence of interest in West (and the demise of the Hays Office) compelled Paramount to release them once again. Soon she became a topic in film history courses, and she received even more honors. In late 1969, the Academy of Motion Picture Arts and Sciences staged a tribute to her, with a thousand members according her a standing ovation. "If you told me twenty-five years ago that Mae West would receive a standing ovation in the citadel of the motion picture academy," Skolsky wrote, "I would have looked at you funny." In the fall of 1970, USC voted her Sweetheart of Sigma Chi. The following year UCLA named her Woman of the Century, applauding her for breaking down barriers for women. Harvard's Hasty Pudding Club also saluted her. Even the Venice Film Festival offered a formal recognition of her contributions to film.[43]

On April 14, 1973, she received one of Hollywood's greatest honors. The Masquers Club, one of the film colony's oldest fellowships of performers, declared it "Mae Day" and honored her with the George Spelvin Award. The affair proved that Mae West, who was only five months away from her eightieth birthday, was in excellent shape. Testimonial speeches credited her with saving Paramount from bankruptcy and heralded her as "the only woman with whitecaps in her waterbed." Mae waived the traditional acceptance speech; instead, with a ragtime piano blaring in the background, she took the stage and entertained the crowd for almost thirty minutes. She opened with a soliloquy of the saga of Diamond Lil and followed with a version of "Frankie and Johnny," spoken à la Bert Williams. While the audience listened to her album *Great Balls of Fire*, she took a short break. She then reappeared with "a little song I wrote while the jury was out" and launched into a tune about *The Pleasure Man*. For her finish, she appropriately returned to her black roots, wrapping the evening up with the African-American blues ballad "After You're Gone." As Mae sang, "You'll miss the best girl you've ever had," the crowd went wild. And to everyone's astonishment, she finished, as she had at the peak of her vaudeville days, with a shimmy. The audience stomped their feet, hooted, cheered, whistled, and applauded. It was a remarkable encore. It would be her last live performance.[44]

I Wrote the Story Myself

I wrote the story myself. It's all about a girl who lost her reputation but never missed it.

　　　　　　　　　　　—Mae West, *Wit and Wisdom*, 1967

Of course, Mae West, now an octogenarian, had no intention of
retiring. She told one writer, "I've got so much energy, I look
great, I want to work. Work is very important to a woman like
me." Although there were few professional opportunities, she
became sought-after socially. Through Musgrove, she met Blanche Seavers, a
wealthy USC trustee, and philanthropist Sybil Brand, both of whom often
entertained her as a dinner guest. She dined with Bette Davis and Greta
Garbo, both awed by her presence and strength. But she still preferred the
company of her inner circle, a tight-knit group that included Tim Malachosky, Stanley Musgrove, and longtime friend and fan Dolly Dempsey, who
had known Mae since 1935. Sometimes Mae went shopping with Edith
Head. But she was almost inseparable from Paul Novak; when he shopped
for groceries, she rode along, waiting in the limousine with a secretary. Instrumental in keeping the legend alive, he fixed her meals, chauffeured her
around, made sure she exercised daily, and carefully attended her career.[1]

West busied herself by producing, with assistance, two more books, both
published in 1975. With Larry Lee, who had worked for her in various ca-
pacities since 1929, she turned *The Pleasure Man* into a novel. She excised all
mention of drag queens, focusing exclusively on the roguish and abusive
Rodney Terrill. In the novel, Terrill appears much like *The Ruby Ring*'s Gloria or *The Hussy*'s Nona Ramsey; he can please any woman with his shifting
personality. But he was no projection of the Mae Westian character. As in
the play, he pays for his libertine affairs with a fatal castration. During his
murderer's trial, when an attorney enters into evidence the instruments
used to perform the inexpert surgery, the novel's narrator declares that the

women in the gallery "stared at the objects with fascinated horror." The gay theme may have disappeared, possibly a reflection of West's attempt to distance herself from camp, but the gender message remained loud and clear.[2]

With the aid of a ghost writer, she also completed *Sex, Health, and ESP*. She had consistently maintained that good health and mind power had allowed her to enjoy her legendary sex life. In her book she revealed that she rechanneled her sex drive into pure energy that propelled her through all tasks. She encouraged readers to strip off their clothes, lie in bed, think about sex, and, once the "urges" increased, set off to work. In addition to advocating healthy eating habits, she also shared her closely guarded beauty secret. She divulged that in 1928, during *Diamond Lil*'s run, she began to take a daily high colonic. At first, it was probably a matter of expediency; the Royale's bathroom was on the opposite side of the stage from her dressing room, making access impossible during the show. But she also believed that it purified the body of toxins. While it was unconventional by contemporary standards, West's generation believed that colonics, enemas, and laxatives were ways of maintaining good health. Although it contributed to her eccentric reputation, she had great faith in the benefits of this old-fashioned remedy.[3]

While she was working on her books in the summer of 1974, she received a visit from Robert E. Johnson, the editor of *Ebony* and *Jet* magazines, two of the African-American community's most popular publications. Johnson produced a laudatory article for *Jet* on West's support of the black community. She no longer shied away from racial issues, openly endorsing the African-American struggle for equality. In fact, in her recently updated autobiography, she boasted, "I'm proud of my efforts to advance blacks." Aware of recent criticism that her portrayal of black maids was derogatory, she insisted to Johnson that her work, while limited, offered an alternative to the traditional stereotypes. "I was the first film star to establish a rapport with Black maid characters in relationships that virtually were on a peer level," she told Johnson. "That's no big thing now, but it was considered radical thirty-four years ago." Johnson also interviewed several African-American performers and athletes who testified to her progressive racial attitudes. Furthermore, as she had done many times in the past, she highlighted the black roots of her performance. When discussing the shimmy, she offered Johnson a live demonstration, declaring, perhaps revealingly, "This was the Black people's dance . . . and if you ever saw it performed then you would know that no white person could create such a dance."[4]

West's performance for Johnson indicated that she now attempted to link not only her fictional character but also her star persona to the African-American presence. Curiously, she waited until the 1970s, when it was much safer, to finally become an outspoken advocate of civil rights. In the area of race, unlike class and gender, she remained tentative until the end of her life. West was secure in her womanhood and with her working-class background; of all the controversial topics she explored, race, for some reason, was the hardest one for her to come to terms with. Perhaps Mae, who borrowed so liberally from the African-American community, found herself the trickster tricked. As a white woman whose performance was so rooted in black culture, she could never achieve either blackness or whiteness. On the other hand, this interracialness, which upended the ideology of race and racism, may have been one of her greatest accomplishments.

West's conflicts over race and the autobiographical nature of her work attest to an ongoing and complex struggle with her racial identity. Throughout her life, she had seesawed between seeking and rejecting whiteness, between claiming and denying blackness. Her complicated relationship with race appears similar to that of those who pass, rejecting their African-American heritage to enjoy the privileges of white skin but all the while experiencing guilt, fear, and self-loathing. Although Mae West had come to play the total narcissist, a bold role for any woman—"I don't like myself, I'm crazy about myself," she chuckled during an interview—she appeared to have mixed feelings about herself. Whether enacting Frankie or in interviews displaying her likeness to her African-American maid, West seemed to be consistently daring society to confront a secret. But few were willing to accept the challenge. The trickster's ultimate deception was that the star who had become celebrated as the symbol of white female sensuality was not really white. Even Johnson helped perpetuate the game, entitling his article "Mae West: Snow White Sex Queen Who Drifted."[5]

West told Johnson that she hoped to bring *The Constant Sinner* to the screen with Sidney Poitier as her co-star. Certainly, that was impossible. But she did move ahead on *Sextette*. In early 1976, she lined up two producers, Dan Briggs and Robert Sullivan. They were only twenty-two years old, and neither had ever made a film, but Briggs was the son of a wealthy heiress who owned Las Vegas's Tropicana, and he had access to considerable funds.

It was imperative that the project move along expeditiously. West was entering her eighty-fourth year and beginning to age considerably. Several interviewers commented on her frailty. Some found her a little forgetful. During one interview she confused *Diamond Lil* with *Sextette,* and in another she declared her intention to write her autobiography. (Paul Novak always graciously corrected her.) From Musgrove's perspective, she was becoming increasingly paranoid. She confided to him that she believed Sybil Brand had put glass in her food at a banquet. She also alleged that Warren Beatty had lifted material from *The Pleasure Man* for his film *Shampoo*. Suspicious that someone had stolen one of her rings, she told Musgrove that she had forced Novak, Beverly, and one of her butlers to take polygraph tests.

Some of West's accusations could also have been designed to keep Musgrove in a constant state of confusion. Many of those who encountered her in these later years also found her remarkably keen-minded. Even Musgrove admitted that publicly she offered a stunning performance, seeming endlessly sharp and retaining her classic wit. After an outing to the theater, some members of Mae's party pressed her for an opinion. "I kept concentrating on making my mind wander," she declared with old Westian flair. "It [the play] made me realize there's less to life than sex."[6]

Eager to get *Sextette* off the ground, Musgrove, serving as West's liaison, began working with Briggs and Sullivan. To direct the film, they recruited Irving Rapper, a Hollywood veteran who had guided Bette Davis through the 1942 classic *Now, Voyager*. At Musgrove's suggestion, screenwriter Herb Baker came on board to update the script. Edith Head agreed to do West's wardrobe. African-American musician Van McCoy was selected as music coordinator, to compose and oversee West's numbers. Several noted performers were happy to sign up; a chance to work with Mae West was a once-in-a-lifetime opportunity. In addition to Dom Deluise, whom West called "Dan," Briggs and Sullivan recruited several rock stars, including Ringo Starr, Keith Moon, and Alice Cooper. Tony Curtis signed on to play one of Marlo Manners's husbands. The young producing duo also arranged for filming to take place on the Paramount lot.

In the meantime, West made a rare television appearance on Dick Cavett's *Backlot USA*. Musgrove paid Hollywood's Oriental Theater, which was going to be closed anyway, $250 to announce on its marquee, "Closed Tonight to Watch Mae West on TV." It might not have been necessary: West's performance was a sensation. Replete in Diamond Lil costume, she sang "Frankie and Johnny" and "After You're Gone," for which she received a standing ovation from everyone present for the taping. Cavett raved, declaring her "the eighth wonder of the world." The *New York Times* affirmed, "She is something—a wonderful, glamorous, talented and marvelously witty something—unto herself."[7]

But West focused most of her energy on *Sextette*. As a publicity stunt, her camp announced in *Variety* and the *Hollywood Reporter* that she was conducting a talent search to find a *young* unknown actor to play Sir Barrington. Although the press snickered at an eighty-four-year-old woman being romanced on the screen by a young man, over three thousand men lined up outside Paramount to audition for the part. After days of interviewing legions of young men, West declared none of them appropriate. She finally accepted, at Rapper's suggestion, actor Timothy Dalton. She decided he had a Cary Grant quality.

Almost from the beginning, problems beset the film. It was clear that Briggs and Sullivan were severely underexperienced. West's advanced age made it difficult for the young producers to recruit more backers. Even before a single scene was shot, the $1.5 million budget began to balloon. Additionally, Baker's script revisions did not go well; when Mae did not reject them, the producers did. Edith Head struggled through the entire process, livid when she discovered that the producers, to save money, had decided to use old gowns from West's previous films and plays. And even Head had trouble accepting the octogenarian as sensual. "You're trying to pass her off as a sex symbol," the designer reprimanded Musgrove. "You should be ashamed of yourself." Irving Rapper, who was almost eighty himself, proved another liability. According to the film's publicist, Peter Simone, during auditions for West's leading men Rapper yelled, "Where's Bette?"[8]

By the fall of 1976, West's patience with Briggs and Sullivan, who some believed were using her as an entrée into Hollywood, had grown short. Since they held the purse strings, however, there was little she could do except fume. Eventually, she compelled them to fire Rapper, but she rejected all other candidates for director, declaring them "old guys." Finally, Briggs and Sullivan invited English director Ken Hughes, who had worked on Disney's *Chitty Chitty Bang Bang*, to come to Hollywood to interview with her. Hughes had reservations about working with the elderly actress but was surprised to discover that West seemed delightfully competent. According to Hughes, he won West over and was immediately signed to a contract. Little did he know, Briggs and Sullivan had already put together a press release announcing that he had come on board.

Finally, on December 1, 1976, over forty-three years after West first swaggered onto a Paramount set, filming began on *Sextette*. The script was still being revised, and, to appease West, Baker added scenes with male gymnasts and bodybuilders, more musical numbers, and a walk-on part for George Raft. But almost immediately everything came to an abrupt halt. West rejected most of Baker's changes. Briggs and Sullivan complained that debts were piling up. "Well," she told Musgrove, "it's gonna cost them a lot of money because it don't play right for me."[9]

The debate over the script continued. Since scenes were being added and deleted on a daily basis, West was often caught off guard. Arriving on the set one day, she balked at a new scene in which Marlo weeps when she learns Barrington plans to leave her. At a story conference, she roared, "Mae West would never cry over a man. She would just yell, 'Next!' " She was deaf to arguments in favor of the scene. "Don't tell me," she warned. "I know what's good for me."[10]

Hughes also thought the script was weak and with West's blessings began revising it on his own. During the day he filmed, and each evening he re-worked the next scenes. It left no time for West to study the dialogue. But she trusted Hughes; she may have realized that he was the last hope for *Sextette*. She agreed to wear a tiny receiver concealed in her wig through which Hughes fed her lines he had written the night before. Rumors circulated that Mae's receiver picked up police transmissions and she called them out in-stead of her lines. Hughes later adamantly denied it.

Almost everyone associated with the production remarked on Mae West's amazing determination. They also noticed that time had caught up with her. When not shooting or issuing directives, she sat in a chair resting quietly. "But," remembered production assistant Sal Grasso, "the minute they hit the lights she became the magic we know." Hughes grew disappointed quickly. He found Mae forgetful and sometimes disoriented. She seemed un-able to follow his directions, especially when a scene required her to move from one spot to another. He tried marking white lines on the floor to make it easier for her, but with her eyesight failing, she was unable to see them. He arranged rows of sandbags to direct her across the set, but they were little help. Eventually he resorted to shooting her from the waist up, assigning a handsome young production assistant to crawl on the floor out of camera range and guide her around the set. She did not protest.

Hughes remained impressed by West's dedication to seeing the film to its finish. Although she did not begin work until early afternoon, she often worked late into the night. He claimed that one scene, in which she walked down a hall and entered an elevator, required seventy-four takes, which West endured without complaint. He also described what happened after the scene was finally completed: The crew broke into applause and packed up for the night; when Novak arrived to pick West up, she was nowhere to be found. After a frantic search, Hughes realized that she was waiting pa-tiently in the mock elevator, unaware the scene was wrapped. When they opened the door, West asked, "You wanna go again?"[11]

The filming of *Sextette* was carried out only by West's sheer will and forceful determination. Everyone, including Mae, thought that the produc-tion was severely flawed. Even Novak, after viewing the dailies, realized it was poor and insisted to Musgrove that the musical numbers were the film's final hope. In the end, Edith Head blamed director Hughes for cutting cor-ners, declaring, "The filming was a tragedy." Rod Dyer, who spearheaded

Sextette's promotional campaign, insisted that Mae West was the reason he survived. "That lady is still making them laugh," he told a reporter. "And the world could use a good joke."[12]

In March 1977, after more than twelve arduous weeks of filming, *Sextette* finished with a budget that had ballooned to over $7 million. As Hughes began editing the film, the production ran into yet another setback: Hollywood was rife with rumors that *Sextette* was a flop, and no studio was willing to distribute it. To drum up support, Briggs and Sullivan scheduled sneak previews in the spring and summer of 1977. The first was a private, star-studded screening on the Paramount lot. Next, they secured the Bruin Theater in Westwood, just outside UCLA's gates. The big advance publicity campaign drew a mob, many of them college students, who packed the streets around the theater. Inside, at the film's end, the audience gave West a standing ovation. Out front, she greeted fans and then climbed into her limousine. She turned to longtime friend Herbert Kenwith, who had served as the lighting director on *Come On Up* and the *Diamond Lil* revival, and remarked, "That was yesterday; now I must think of tomorrow."[13]

Briggs and Sullivan were not ready to move on. With debts in the millions, they were determined to put the film into theaters. After a year of failed attempts to secure a distributor, they decided to premiere and circulate the film themselves. West agreed to appear at its debut at Hollywood's Cinemadome. Just as they had done forty years before, fans filled the streets around the theater, hoping to catch a glimpse of the legendary actress. After the film, she took the stage and offered the public what would be her final thanks for their support.

The critics' response to *Sextette* confirmed what West already knew. Overwhelmingly, they gave it negative reviews. Several reviewers decried her appearance, contending that the cinematography only made her look worse. Another complained that her famous voice had grown "hoarse" and her trademark gait unsteady. *Variety* commented that "the best that can be hoped for *Sextette*, as far as West's reputation is concerned, is that it will be forgotten—soon." Many were appalled at her boldness, finding it outrageous that an eighty-four-year-old woman would surround herself with handsome young men and make rowdy allusions to her active sex life. The *New York Times* declared the film "embarrassing" and announced, "Granny should have her mouth washed out with soap, along with her teeth."[14]

As a whole, *Sextette* was declared a fiasco. After failing in their attempts to distribute the film, in 1979 Briggs and Sullivan signed with Crown International to circulate *Sextette*. But it was too late. With the passage of time and the negative reviews, interest in the film had faded. A show business insider sneered, "Who's gonna pay to see an eighty-five-year-old woman go to bed with a thirty-year-old man?" Others did come to West's defense. Several years later, scholar Carol Ward pointed out that West was being held to a double standard. It was acceptable, even humorous, for comedian George Burns to surround himself with beautiful young women, but it was absolutely intolerable for Mae West to do the same with gorgeous young musclemen. It was considered pathetic, not funny. Yet as bad as it was, *Sextette* stood, probably unintentionally, as one of Mae's most revolutionary pieces. As painful as it was to watch the aged Diamond Lil navigate through her scenes, she was challenging the very core of gender norms, especially those that robbed older women of sensual pleasure.

For Mae West's admirers, the *Sextette* debacle did not matter. *After Dark,* whose correspondent had visited West on the set, announced, "Mae West *is* Diamond Lil." When the magazine honored her with its Ruby Award at a banquet, five hundred fans lined up for autographs. Asked about her experiences on *Sextette*, Edith Head praised Mae as "a great lady and social force." Perhaps Ken Hughes appreciated West more than it had appeared. He maintained that the film was "a glorious failure, but somehow we emerged triumphant, substantiating that adage that 'the show must go on.' "[15]

After *Sextette*, West announced plans to film *Catherine Was Great*, but, growing more infirm, she was unable to carry it off. Instead, in August 1979, she celebrated her eighty-sixth birthday by signing a contract to do a series of radio commercials endorsing Poland Spring Water. Although West had rarely endorsed commercial products, this one was perfect; she had used it for years. "I've been drinking Poland Spring Water for about—hmm—20 years," she quipped. "Started when I was four." Since the commercials were radio spots, she would only have to use her legendary voice. Through her purring endorsement over the airwaves, she kept the Diamond Lil flame burning. "I'm just crazy about it," she murmured familiarly. "I invited the boys from Poland Spring to come up and see me sometime—and they did."[16]

West's public appearances were fewer and fewer. According to both Musgrove and Malachosky, she was growing weaker. Some days were better than others. On good days she attended to business and began consolidating her assets. She was rumored to be worth more than $10 million. However, she neglected to update her will and struggled with her mortality. In one of her final interviews, she told a writer, "I never think about death, dear." Actually, it seemed that Beverly was in far worse shape than her older sister. Mae agonized over Beverly, whose mental state had worsened considerably. Drinking again, Beverly had spells of violent hallucinations and at one point was discovered talking to pictures on a wall of the San Fernando Valley ranch house. She remained resentful of her famous sister, angrily insisting that she did not want to be buried in the family crypt. "I've had enough of her while I'm alive," she told one of Mae's butlers. "I don't want to be lying next to her dead."[17]

Mae had bad days too. She once asked Paul Novak to take her to her beloved mother. On occasion, she was unsure who he was. Yet she struggled on. At a dinner party in 1980, Musgrove claimed, Mae West suddenly took over and delighted guests with her *Diamond Lil* soliloquy and "Frankie and Johnny."

Shortly afterward, on August 10, 1980, a week before Mae had planned to celebrate her eighty-seventh birthday with a big bash, she fell getting out of bed. Novak helped her into the living room. Mae tried to speak but could not. She collapsed in tears. Language had been her greatest gift, her most potent weapon. No doubt, even she knew Mae West was dying.

She was taken to Hollywood's Good Samaritan Hospital, where tests revealed that she had suffered a stroke that left her tongue paralyzed. When the press besieged the hospital, Novak rose to the occasion. He announced that Mae West had sustained a concussion falling out of bed while dreaming of handsome actor Burt Reynolds. But before long, the word was out that West was severely ill.[18]

She passed her eighty-seventh birthday in the hospital, surprising her doctors by rallying. But on August 27, she suffered a diabetic reaction to the formula in her feeding tube. After doctors recalibrated it, she improved. Paul Novak, by her side twenty-four hours a day, tended to her needs, took her for walks, and even drove her out to the beach. She seemed responsive but disoriented. Then, on September 18, she suffered a second stroke that left her paralyzed on her right side. She developed pneumonia and hovered near death for several days. Somehow, she battled back and again improved. Novak consulted with stroke specialists, faith healers, and practitioners of alternative medicine. But Mae showed no more signs of progress. Finally, in early November after exhausting all possibilities, he took her home to the Ravenswood. He hired around-the-clock nurses and rented a hospital bed for Mae's legendary boudoir.

When Mae's limousine pulled into the Ravenswood's underground garage, she smiled. Novak, Malachosky, and Dempsey set up a routine, shuttling her between her bed and the living room. They played music for her and talked to her. Novak secured a copy of *She Done Him Wrong* and screened it for her at the apartment. Mae pointed at her image on the screen. It was there that Diamond Lil achieved immortality.

Even in the familiar surroundings of her cherished little two-bedroom apartment, Mae continued to decline. On the morning of November 22, one of the nurses roused Paul Novak to tell him that Mae had taken a turn for the worse. He found her feverish and struggling to breathe. He moved her to a white satin chair, hoping that would make her breathing less labored. Soon her personal physician arrived. He announced that nothing more could be done. Novak summoned a priest from the church just down the block, who gave Mae a blessing. Only a few minutes later, at 10:30 A.M., Mae West passed away. The brazen jezebel of American popular culture who had broken out of the tenements of Brooklyn to become one of Hollywood's most famous stars, not to mention one of America's most popular rebels, was gone.[19]

Across the nation and around the world, the wire services flashed the news—Mae West was dead. But Diamond Lil, the symbol Mae West had created, lived on. Each obituary recited the saga of Diamond Lil, the headlines blaring, "Mae West: Epitome of Witty Sexuality Dies" and "Mae West, Stage and Movie Star Who Burlesqued Sex, Dies at 87." The *Los Angeles Times* eulogized her as "a paradox, the ultimate sex parodist who wrote and delivered such lines as 'Goodness had nothing to do with it' and 'Beulah, peel me a grape.'" Newspapers around the world ran her most famous sayings, acquainting another generation with the Westian wordplay that had become ingrained in the American language. It indicated the pervasiveness of Mae's deployment of the African-American tradition of signification. The trickster's voice lived on to continue to challenge and upset society's conventions. The *New York Times* let her speak through her obituary, reprinting Mae's summation: "It isn't what I do, but how I do it. It isn't what I say, but how I say it, and how I look when I do it and say it."[20]

At Musgrove's urging, Paul Novak organized a private service. On the afternoon of November 25, one hundred of Mae's family, friends, and acquaintances gathered at Forest Lawn's Old North Church to memorialize Mae West. Beverly West had been drinking and was so distraught that she was unable to go into the chapel. She wept outside in her limousine. Inside, Mae lay in an open casket surrounded by whiteness—a white casket lined in white satin, dressed in her white pearl-trimmed wedding gown from *Sextette*. As the final contradiction, while mourners gathered, the organist disregarded the typical funeral airs in favor of Mae's most popular tunes, many of them the blues and including "My Old Flame," "I Wonder Where My Easy Rider's Gone," and, of course, "Frankie and Johnny." Producer Ross Hunter eulogized West, reminding the audience, "The Mae West character never wanted anybody to feel sorry for her and she wouldn't want them to start now." Now, in death, the character had completely overtaken her creator.[21]

That night Mae's body was flown home to Brooklyn, and the following morning Paul Novak and Dolly Dempsey arrived at Cypress Hills for the interment. Two priests and a bishop offered short prayers and blessed the casket.

Dempsey placed a small wreath on the top, and the cemetery staff slid it into the crypt that Mae had long ago reserved for herself, right above her mother. The two were reunited; Mae returned home after faithfully fulfilling Tillie's dreams.

Shortly before her death in 1981, Edith Head reminisced about her friend Mae West: "She always knew exactly what it meant to be a woman and how to get what she wanted. I think she died without a regret in the world." And while it was a fitting eulogy, ironically her life seemed better reflected in the words of African-American author James Weldon Johnson. In 1912, while Mae was still a vaudeville newcomer, he anonymously published a novel in which the central character, a black man, passes for white. The opening lines read, "I know that in writing the following pages I am divulging the great secret of my life." His life, like hers, was spent performing, and his assessment captured the essence of an undaunted trickster-hero like Mae West. "I know that I am playing with fire, and I feel the thrill which accompanies that most fascinating pastime; and, back of it all, I think I find a sort of savage and diabolic desire to gather up all the little tragedies of my life, and turn them into a practical joke on society."

Some say that you can still see Mae West's reflection in the mirrors at the Ravenswood.[22]

Really a Prologue

All my past is really a prologue. I go on and on . . .
—Mae West, *Goodness Had Nothing to Do with It*, 1959

Born in August 1893—"one of the hot months"—Mae West boasted that she "was a child of the new century" and that she "ran toward it boldly." Many have viewed Mae West as a paradox, a label she delightedly perpetuated. In the 1930s, at her popularity's peak, she announced in an interview, "I'm so ultramodern that I'm old-fashioned. That's the *real* truth of the matter." From earliest childhood, Mae lived in a swirling world of contrasts, constantly entangled in polarities and contradictions. In the Brooklyn of Mae West's youth, herds of deer still wandered its largest park while gangs of poor and working-class men and boys roamed its streets. The young Mae was raised in transitional places and times. Born on the cusp between two centuries, she became both the old and the new. Such dichotomies marked her entire existence.[1]

But just as she was nurtured on the bridge between the nineteenth and twentieth centuries, she has become a bridge between the twentieth and twenty-first. This later period witnessed a Mae West renaissance, a resurgence of public fascination with her life, movies, and plays. Videos of her films, recordings of her songs and live performances, a made-for-televison movie, documentaries on her life, and a compilation of her early plays appeared. Her image was reproduced on postcards, greeting cards, posters, tee-shirts, pens, and even address labels. Over a dozen books on her life and work were published, including insider accounts by members of her inner circle, popular biographies that perpetuated her image as a legendary sex goddess, and academic interpretations wrestling with the meaning of Mae West and her performance. Several parts of the country hosted revivals of *SEX* and *Diamond Lil*. By the year 2000, Mae West was, yet again, back on Broadway—in *Dirty Blonde*, a play celebrating her life and her fans.[2]

The sustained and growing interest in Mae West so many years after her death indicates that, for many Americans, she has continued to fulfill some fundamental needs (and desires). Some sectors have elevated Mae West to the status of feminist icon. Others, celebrating her connections to the gay community, have proclaimed her the queen of camp. When Mae West's posthumous comeback commenced in the 1980s, it coincided with a rising resistance to a climate of political and social conservatism. For many, she represented the antithesis of conservative trends, a hero for American masses. She was unique and had created a distinctive subversive persona that many related to and admired. "There is no other Mae West," observed journalist Steven Roberts before her death. "She is an institution, a living legend, as much a part of American folklore as Paul Bunyan or Tom Sawyer or Babe Ruth."[3]

Ascending to the status of a folk heroine/hero, Mae West, born of turn-of-the-twentieth-century paradoxes, became a beacon to those confronting the contradictions at the turn of the twenty-first century. She was more than, as one critic aptly characterized her, "a true sexual democrat" and, as many alleged, a singleminded profiteer. While she was unabashedly commercially driven, she also provided, and continues to provide, her audiences with stinging critiques of American society. As Mae West simultaneously embraced and rejected the dominant culture, her life, image, and performance became (and remain) a site for the reflection on, dialogue over, and resolution of the major tensions confronting Americans.[4]

It is Mae West's ability to oscillate between chaos and calm, as a trickster breathing order into disorder, that allows her voice to resonate throughout the years, giving her a timeless nature. As the trickster, she refused (and refuses) to claim a single identity; determined to create as much confusion as possible, she rejected and represented all extremes. Through her immersion in African-American signifying, Mae West reminds us that all polarities are really constructions of a society that operates to promote and preserve the status quo. By rejecting the divisions between black and white, man and woman, rich and poor, and self and other, she continues to challenge a society that thrives on fixity and certainties. She fits snugly into Russian writer Mikhail Bakhtin's contention that trickster figures fight for "the right to be 'other' in this world, the right not to make common cause with any single one of the existing categories that life makes available, none of these categories quite suits them, they see the underside and the falseness of every situation." In a way, West's paradox rested on a single question she posed over and over again: "Why does it have to be this *or* that?" It is a question that, while unsettling, is also comforting and empowering.[5]

Like all tricksters who represent the weak, disenfranchised, and oppressed, she triumphed (and continues to triumph) not through strength, power, and position but rather by her cunning, wit, and guile. She defied categorization, constantly transfigured and transfiguring, remaining perpetually unfixed and destabilized. At a dizzying pace, she disrupted the status quo, then reestablished order, only to create chaos once again. "The best way to behave," she advised, "is to misbehave."[6]

Like many tricksters, West also embraced the qualities of a shapeshifter, remaining indeterminate in her physical form, forever changeable. To an on-screen beau attempting to woo her with the old cliché "I've been places and seen things," she rumbled back, "I've been things and seen places." Yet there was an immutability in her mutability. As Steven Roberts observed, "Sometimes she was like mirrors in a barbershop: an almost infinite number of images, each reflecting the other, Mae West playing Mae West playing Mae West." At one level, he discerned her links to the topsy-turvy world of African-American tricksterism and signification. Mae West's world is even more like a carnival funhouse's Hall of Mirrors, and now her image is reflected everywhere. But most important, the subtext of that image, rooted in black traditions, demonstrates that degree to which American cultural roots are African. Mae West was and is a cultural agent that celebrates and perpetuates the African presence within American society.[7]

There lies Mae West's appeal; she functioned and continues to function as the American trickster-hero that now connects three centuries. Her audiences revel in her ability to speak the unspeakable and her crafty manipulation of the dualities of existence. For Americans of the Great Depression of the 1930s, when her mass appeal was first established, she provided hope that they too, despite their uncertain status, could triumph over hardships and dire conditions. And regardless of the shifts in American circumstances, her appeal remains basically the same. She speaks across the decades and now centuries, an empowering and reassuring presence. We continue to be drawn to her special talent of reflecting and mocking our norms, expectations, and anxieties. She urges us to think about who we were, who we are, and who we are going to be.

"There is no Mae West," once claimed a close associate. "It doesn't make any difference how often you see her or how much you talk to her, you never know her because, I tell you—there is no Mae West!" He was probably right. There probably never was a Mae West; rather there were and are Mae Wests. She can only be understood as the creator of converging and diverging figures, swaying through a hallway of mirrors. Her life story is a trickster's tale, the continuing and whirling evolution of three selves—a private person, a star, and a fictional character—the complex and intertwining personas that composed Mae West.[8]

Sources

Archival Sources and Abbreviations

The sole collection of West's writings is in the Manuscript Division, Library of Congress, Washington, D.C (LC), which contains drafts of most of her plays. The largest depository of materials on West is located at Margaret Herrick Library, Academy of Motion Picture Arts and Sciences (AMPAS), which houses the Paramount Collection (including her scripts, pressbooks, clipping files, and budget reports for her Paramount films), a biography file (MW/BF), the Sidney Skolsky Collection (SSC), and the Production Code Administration Censorship Files (PCA). Other archives that have information include Mae West Clipping File, British Film Institute, London, England (BFI); J. Walter Thompson Company Collection, Hartman Center for Sales, Advertising, and Marketing History, Special Collections, Duke University (Duke); *The Will Hays Papers*, edited by Douglas Gomery (Frederick: University Publications of America, 1988), microfilmed from collection at Indiana State Historical Society (Hays Papers); Special Collections, Theater Arts Library, Harvard University (HU); Municipal Archives, New York City (MA-NYC); Special Collections, Music Library, University of California, Los Angeles (ML); Mae West Clipping File (MW/MAD) and John Sumner Papers (Sumner Papers), State Historical Society of Wisconsin, Madison; Billy Rose Theater Collection, Performing Arts Research Center, New York Public Library, New York City (Rose); Stanley Musgrove Collection (SMC) in Archives of Performing Arts, University of Southern California; Shubert Archives, New York, New York (SA); Smithsonian Institution, Washington, D.C; Special Collections, Boston University; Special Collections, University of Iowa, Iowa City, Iowa (UI); G. Robert Vincent Voice Library, Michigan State University (VL MSU).

Other Source Abbreviations

BC: Birth Certificate
Census: United States Census, Population Schedules, Washington, D.C.
CF: Clipping File

Clipper: New York Clipper
DeC: Death Certificate
Examiner: Los Angeles Examiner
FBI: Mae West File, Federal Bureau of Investigation
Graphic: New York Evening Graphic
Lain's: Lain's Brooklyn City Directory
LAT: Los Angeles Times
News: New York Daily News
NYHT: New York Herald Tribune
NYT: New York Times
Lic.: Marriage License
MW: Mae West
Trow's: Trow's New York City Directory
VR: Variety
UCD: Uppington's Brooklyn City Directory

Notes

Chapter One

1. John Kobal, *People Will Talk* (New York: Knopf, 1985), 153; "Mae: The Star That Will Not Dim!" *Rona Barrett's Hollywood*, November 1970, 79; *Rona's Reports* Script, September 15, 1970, SMC; Gerald Early, "Understanding Afrocentrism," *Civilization* (July–August 1995): 31–39.

2. DeC, Mae West, November 22, 1980, Los Angeles, California; *Trow's, 1867,* 1072; DeC, John West, November 12, 1906, Brooklyn, New York, MA-NYC; Denis Hart, "Diamond Mae," *Daily Telegraph*, August 21, 1970, BFI; *Census 1870,* New York City, *1880, 1900,* Brooklyn, New York; Michael Cohn and Michael K. H. Platzer, *Black Men of the Sea* (New York: Dodd, Mead, 1978), 60; W. Jeffrey Bolster, *Black Jacks: African-American Seamen in the Age of Sail* (Cambridge: Harvard University Press, 1997), 177–179; Mae West, *Goodness Had Nothing to Do with It: The Autobiography of Mae West* (Englewood Cliffs: Prentice-Hall, 1959), 2; Celeste Terrell Barnhill, *Joseph West and Mary Jane Owen* (Greenfield: Mitchell Printing, 1930).

3. Hart, "Diamond Mae"; John West, November 15, 1906, Mary Jane West, August 26, 1909, Emma West, June 16, 1883, Interment Records, Linden Hill Methodist Cemetery, Ridgewood, New York; *Census, 1870,* New York City, *1900,* Brooklyn, New York; DeC, Edith [West] Elmore, June 22, 1894, DeC, Mary Jane West, August 22, 1909, Brooklyn, New York, MA-NYC; *Lain's, 1863–64,* 94; *1864–65,* 86.

4. Luc Sante, *Low Life: Lures and Snares of Old New York* (New York: Farrar, Straus & Giroux, 1991), 197; Herbert Asbury, *The Gangs of New York: An Informal History of the Underworld* (1927; reprint New York: Capricorn Books, 1970), 174, 232–239; *Census, 1870,* New York City, *1900,* Brooklyn, *1920,* Queens, New York; West, *Goodness,* 2; Ernest A. McKay, *The Civil War and New York City* (Syracuse: Syracuse University Press, 1990), 296. John Edwin West fails to appear in the 1890 U.S. Census of Civil War Veterans. *Trow's, 1867,* 1072.

5. West, *Goodness,* 3; Richard Meryman, "Mae West," *Life,* April 18, 1969, 69.

6. David R. Roediger, *The Wages of Whiteness: Race and the Making of the American Working Class* (London: Verso, 1991), 133–137; Noel Ignatiev, *How the Irish Became White* (New York: Routledge, 1995), 34–61.

7. *Lain's, 1874,* 812, *1882–83,* 1220; *Census, 1870, 1880,* Brooklyn, New York; DeC, John West, November 12, 1906, DeC, Emma West, June 15, 1883, Brooklyn, New York, MA-NYC; West, *Goodness,* 3; William L. Felter, *Historic Green Point* (Greenpoint: Green Point Savings Bank, c. 1919), 18, 28–33; *Sanbourne Fire Insurance Map,* 1887, vol. 9, p. 99.

8. West, *Goodness,* 2–3; Charles Samuels and Louise Samuels, *Once Upon a Stage: The Merry World of Vaudeville* (New York: Dodd, Mead, 1974), 102; *LAT,* August 25, 1934.

9. Son of Phillip and Christiana, Jacob Delker was born in July 1835 in Germany. Christiana was born in October 1838, also in Germany. Variations of her maiden name include Breuning and Bruner. *Census, 1900,* Brooklyn, New York; DeC, Jacob Delker, September 20, 1902, DeC, Matilda West, January 26, 1930, Lic, Carl Delker and Mathilde Misdorn, May 26, 1889, Lic, John West and Tillie Delker, January 9, 1889, DeC, Christiana Delker, October 15, 1901, all Brooklyn, New York, all MA-NYC; West, *Goodness,* 3.

10. Ruth Biery, "The Private Life of Mae West: Part Two," *Movie Classic,* February 1934, 21; Clipping, May 27, 1935, Scrapbook #5, SSC; George Eels and Stanley Musgrove, *Mae West: A Biography* (New York: William Morrow, 1982), 21–22; Roger Daniels, *Coming to America: A History of Immigration and Ethnicity in American Life* (New York: Harper Perennial, 1990), 146–157, 223–227; West, *Goodness,* 3; Will Anderson, *The Breweries of Brooklyn* (Croton Falls: Anderson, 1976), 41–43; *Lain's, 1886–87,* 267, *1891–92,* 152, *1892–93,* 892; *Census, 1900,* Brooklyn, New York; Edwin G. Burrows and Mike Wallace, *Gotham: A History of New York City to 1898* (New York: Oxford University Press, 1999), 823–824; *Sanbourne Fire Insurance Map, 1887,* vol. 9, pp. 8, 94; Hugo Ullitz, *Atlas of the Borough of Brooklyn, City of New York* (Brooklyn: E. Belcehr Hyde, 1904), vol. 3, p. 23.

11. West, *Goodness,* 6; Kobal, *People,* 161; *VR,* June 9, 1922; Meryman, "Mae West," 69; Daniels, *Coming to America,* 150–155.

12. Ruth Biery, "The Private Life of Mae West: Part One," *Movie Classic,* January 1934, in Carol Ward, *Mae West: A Bio-Bibliography* (Westport: Greenwood Press, 1989), 106; Kathy Peiss, *Cheap Amusements: Working Women and Leisure in Turn-of-the-Century New York* (Philadelphia: Temple University Press, 1986), 1–33; Christine Stansell, *City of Women: Sex and Class in New York, 1789–1860* (Urbana: University of Illinois Press, 1987), 123–126, 179–180; West, *Goodness,* 6.

13. Bert Prelutsky, "Going Up to See Mae West," *International Herald Tribune,* July 29, 1968, BFI; West, *Goodness,* 2–3.

14. Tyra Samter Winslow, "Diamond Mae," *New Yorker,* November 10, 1928, 27; Aileen St. John Brenon, "The Real Mae West," *New Movie Magazine,* c. 1934, MW/MAD; West, *Goodness,* 2–3, 6, 16–18, 108; Biery, "Part Two," 20–21, 70.

15. Meryman, "Mae West," 69; Lic, John West and Tillie Delker, January 9, 1889, BC, Katie West, August 23, 1891, DeC, Katie West, October 30, 1891,

DeC, John West, November 12, 1906, all Brooklyn, New York, all MA-NYC; Charlotte Chandler, *The Ultimate Seduction* (New York: Doubleday, 1984), 47. Stanley Musgrove kept a log while working for West. See Musgrove Log, August 5, 1975, SMC; Prelutsky, "Going Up."

16. Mae explained that she changed the original spelling: "I didn't like that 'y' hanging below the line." Chandler, *Ultimate*, 47, 49, 52; *Lain's, 1893–94*, 1362; *Census, 1900*, Brooklyn, New York; Musgrove Log, August 21, 1969, SMC.

17. West, *Goodness*, vi, 4–6; *Boston Herald*, April 30, 1934, MW/CF, HU; Biery, "Part One," 106–108; *News*, February 21, 1933.

18. Meryman, "Mae West," 69; "Because Mae West Isn't Diamond Lil," c. 1934, MW/MAD; West, *Goodness*, 5–6; *News*, February 21, 22, 1933.

19. Biery, "Part One," 108; Meryman, "Mae West," 69, 72; West, *Goodness*, 3–11, 16–18, 163–164; Elza Schallert, "Go West," *Motion Picture*, May 1933, 84. The Wests moved from Willoughby to Bleecker (1894), Driggs (1895), Humbolt (1897), and Conselyea (1900); *Lain's, 1893–94,* 1362, *1894–95*, 1435, *1895–96*, 1465, *1897–98*, 1660, *1898–99*, 1829; Hart, "Diamond Mae"; *Census, 1900,* Brooklyn, New York; Clipping, April 14, 1930, Scrapbook #4, SSC; Sante, *Low Life*, 220.

20. Biery, "Part One," 106–107; West, *Goodness*, 6, 7, 21–22; BC, Mildreth [Mildred] Katharina West, December 8, 1898; BC, John Edwin West, February 11, 1900, Brooklyn, New York, MA-NYC.

21. West, *Goodness*, 4, 12–13, 18–19, 26–27; Biery, "Part One," 106–108; Robert Johnson, "Mae West: Snow White Sex Queen Who Drifted," *Jet*, July 25, 1974, 40–48; *News*, February 21, 1933.

22. Eric Ledell Smith, *Bert Williams: A Biography of the Pioneer Black Comedian* (Jefferson, N.C.: McFarland, 1992), 24–39.

23. Henry Louis Gates Jr., *The Signifying Monkey: A Theory of African-American Literary Criticism* (New York: Oxford University Press, 1988), 29–56.

24. Ann Charters, *Nobody: The Story of Bert Williams* (New York: Macmillan, 1970), 135; Mel Watkins, *On the Real Side: Laughing, Lying, and Signifying— The Underground Tradition of African-American Humor That Transformed Culture, from Slavery to Richard Pryor* (New York: Simon & Schuster, 1994), 143, 157–194.

25. Watkins, *Real Side*, 76, 160–161, 298; West, *Goodness*, 14; Mae West, *The Wit and Wisdom of Mae West*, ed. Joseph Weintraub (New York: Avon Books, 1967), 71.

26. Chandler, *Ultimate,* 52–53; Smith, *Williams*, 16–17, 124–134, 139.

27. Johnson, "Snow White," 43.

28. George Haddad-Garcia, "Mae West, Everybody's Friend," *Black Stars*, April 1981, 62–64.

29. West, *Goodness*, 1, 8–10; Eileen Southern, *The Music of Black Americans: A History*, 2d ed. (New York: Norton, 1983), 308–330; Kobal, *People*, 158; Clipping, April 14, 1930, Scrapbook #1, SSC; Biery, "Part One," 106–108; Chandler, *Ultimate*, 50–51.

30. "Mae West Tells a Story: Her Own," c. 1948, MW/CF, HU; West, *Goodness*, 7–14; Chandler, *Ultimate*, 5; Robert W. Snyder, *The Voice of the City: Vaudeville and Popular Culture in New York* (New York: Oxford University Press, 1989), 99–100.

31. "Isn't Diamond Lil"; West, *Goodness*, 8–13, 26; Biery, "Part One," 108.

32. Jane R. Westerfield, *An Investigation of the Life Styles and Performance of Three Singer-Comediennes of American Vaudeville: Eva Tanguay, Nora Bayes, and Sophie Tucker* (Ph.D. dissertation, Ann Arbor: University Microfilms, 1988), 4–56; Biery, "Part Two," 20–21, 70–71; Charters, *Nobody*, 89; *Examiner*, April 26, 1935; *News*, February 21, 1933.

33. West, *Goodness*, 10–11, 14.

34. *News*, February 22, 1933; Andy Logan, *Against the Evidence: The Becker-Rosenthal Affair* (New York: McCall, 1970), 53, 60–64, 75; Asbury, *Gangs*, 340–342; *NYT*, July 19, 1912; Vina Delmar, *The Becker Scandal: A Time Remembered* (New York: Harcourt, Brace & World, 1968), 4–20, 44–45.

35. Julia Shawell, "Mae West Curves Herself a Career," *Pictorial Review*, February 1934, MW/MAD; West, *Goodness*, 13–21; *News*, February 22, 1933; Tom Baily, "The Life Story of Mae West," Paramount Studios, c. 1933, BFI.

36. "Mae West Says, 'I Have Loved, But . . . ,'" *Sunday Dispatch*, January 13, 1935, BFI; *News*, February 22, 1933; *New York Dramatic Mirror*, February 16, 1907; *Brooklyn Eagle*, May 1, 1904; West, *Goodness*, 13–16.

37. Edith Head and Jane Kesner Ardmore, *The Dress Doctor* (Boston: Little, Brown, 1959), 52; West, *Goodness*, 15–16.

38. "Isn't Diamond Lil."

39. West, *Goodness*, 14–16; Edward William Mamman, *The Old Stock Company School of Acting: A Study of the Boston Museum* (Boston: Trustees of the Public Library, 1945), 54–63; Baily, "The Life Story"; Shawell, "Mae West Curves"; *News*, February 22, 1933; Biery, "Part One," 108.

40. "Me and My Past," *Delaware Star*, September 9, 1935, BFI; Faye Dudden, *Women in the American Theatre: Actresses and Audiences, 1790–1870* (New Haven: Yale University Press, 1994), 6, 57–70.

41. West, *Goodness*, 14–16; 26; Jeremy P. Felt, *Hostages of Fortune: Child Labor Reform in New York State* (Syracuse: Syracuse University Press, 1965), 8, 57, 97–99.

42. Barbara Cohen-Stratyner, *Ned Wayburn and the Dance Routine: From Vaudeville to Ziegfeld Follies* (Madison: Society of Dance Scholars, 1996), 6–11; *VR*, September 9, 1942; West, *Goodness*, 16; Biery, "Part Two," 20–21, 70; Kobal, *People*, 162; Johnson, "Snow White," 44.

43. Susan Gubar, *Racechanges: White Skin, Black Face in American Culture* (New York: Oxford University Press, 1997), 3–7; Roediger, *Wages*, 123–125; West, *Goodness*, 19; Sophie Tucker and Dorothy Giles, *Some of These Days: The Autobiography of Sophie Tucker* (Garden City: Doubleday, Doran, 1945), 33–35; Janet Brown, "The 'Coon-Singer' and the 'Coon Song': A Case Study of the Performer-Character Re-

lationship," *Journal of American Culture* 7 (Spring/Summer 1984): 1–8; "Me and My Past"; David Keane, Press Release, Paramount, c. 1935, MW/BF.

44. West, *Goodness*, 19.

45. West, *Goodness*, 16; Brenon, "Real Mae."

46. Kobal, *People*, 161–162.

47. Biery, "Part Two," 20–21, 70–71; Chandler, *Ultimate*, 44; Karl Fleming and Anne Taylor Fleming, *The First Time* (New York: Simon & Schuster, 1975), 312–316.

48. Mae West, *Sex, Health, and ESP* (London: Allen, 1975), 8–9; Musgrove Log, August 16, 1969, SMC; Chandler, *Ultimate*, 43.

49. West, *Goodness*, 3, 16–18; Maurice Leonard, *Empress of Sex* (New York: Birch Lane Press, 1991), 18–19.

50. Meryman, "Mae West," 69; DeC, Julia [West] Weeks, December 24, 1893, Brooklyn, New York, DeC, Edith Elmore, Christiana Delker, Jacob Delker, John West [1906], Mary Jane West (see notes 2, 3, and 9 above), MA-NYC; *Census, 1910*, Brooklyn, New York.

51. Ned Williams, "The Men in Mae West's Life," *Hollywood*, June 1934, BFI; Biery, "Part Two," 20–21, 70.

52. *New York Post*, July 4, 1970.

53. West, *Goodness*, 22.

Chapter Two

1. West, *Goodness*, 21–25; *VR*, July 7, 1917; Shirley Staples, *Male-Female Comedy Teams in American Vaudeville, 1865–1932* (Ann Arbor: UMI Research Press, 1984), 99–101, 122–124, 143–148; *Examiner*, April 25, 1935; Chandler, *Ultimate*, 51, 57.

2. Biery, "Part Two," 70.

3. Robert C. Allen, *Horrible Prettiness: Burlesque and American Culture* (Chapel Hill: University of North Carolina Press, 1951), 197–240, 282–284.

4. *Examiner*, April 24, 1935; West, *Goodness*, 26–27; *Los Angeles Daily News*, November 28, 1936, MW/BF.

5. *VR*, September 30, 1911; *Examiner*, April 23, 24, 1935; *Clipper*, August 19, 1911; *Census, 1910*, Brooklyn, New York; Irving Zeidman, *The American Burlesque Show* (New York: Hawthorn Books, 1967), 11–13, 52–56.

6. *Examiner*, April 23, 1935; *Clipper*, June 3, September 2, 1911.

7. Brenon, "Real Mae"; West, *Goodness*, 28.

8. West, *Goodness*, 28; Fleming and Fleming, *First Time*, 317.

9. *I'm No Angel* (1933); West, *Goodness*, 28–29; *Examiner*, April 24, 1935; Kobal, *People*, 162–163; Lic, Frank Wallace and Mae West, April 11, 1911, Milwaukee, Wisconsin; Fleming and Fleming, *First Time*, 312–317; Musgrove Log, June 5,

1975, SMC; David B. Charny, "Mae's 'Husband' Describes the Day They Married," *Daily Mirror*, Robinson Locke Scrapbooks, Rose; *Time*, July 19, 1937, 62.

10. West, *Goodness*, 28–31; *New York Sun*, April 23, 1935, MW/CF, HU; *Time*, July 19, 1937, 62.

11. Clipping, October 1, 1933, MW/BF.

12. Charles Higham, *Ziegfeld* (Chicago: Regnery, 1972), 85–86; West, *Goodness*, 30–31; Lewis Erenberg, *Steppin' Out: New York Nightlife and the Transformation of American Culture, 1890–1930* (Chicago: University of Chicago Press, 1984), 137.

13. *NYT*, September 23, 1911; *Clipper*, September 23, 1911; West, *Goodness*, 32–36; Frank Condon, "Come Up and Meet Mae West," *Collier's*, June 16, 1934, 26, 42.

14. West, *Goodness*, 33–36; Biery, "Part Two," 70; *NYT*, September 23, 1911.

15. *Clipper*, November 11, December 2, 1911; *VR*, October 7, November 25, 1911; West, *Goodness*, 35–37; James Gardiner, *Gaby Deslys: A Fatal Attraction* (London: Sedgewick & Jackson, 1986), 30–56; Cecil Walter Hardy Beaton Sr., *The Book of Beauty* (London: Duckworth, 1930), 22–24.

16. *New Haven Morning Journal-Courier*, November 18, 20, 1911; *New Haven Evening Register,* November 17, 18, 1911.

17. *New Haven Morning Journal-Courier*, November 20, 22, 1911; *New Haven Evening Register,* November 20, 1911; Musgrove Log, August 21, 1969, SMC; *LAT*, August 31, 1969.

18. *New Haven Morning Journal-Courier,* November 20–24, 1911; *VR*, November 25, 1911, March 9, 1912; *New Haven Evening Register,* November 20, 1911.

19. Gardiner, *Gaby Deslys*, 58, 62–63; *VR*, November 25, 1911; West, *Goodness*, 37; Eels and Musgrove, *Mae West*, 44.

20. West, *Goodness*, 37–44; *VR*, March 9, 23, 1912; *New Haven Morning Journal-Courier*, February 24, 27, 1912; Staples, *Male-Female*, 59, 121.

21. West, *Goodness*, 41–44; *News*, April 15, 1938.

22. *Clipper*, April 20, 1912; *NYT*, April 12, 1912; *VR*, April 20, 1912; *New York Dramatic Mirror*, April 17, 1912.

23. *VR*, May 25, April 20, 1912, March 13, 1914.

24. *VR*, May 18, 25, 1912; West, *Goodness*, 44; *Clipper*, May 25, 1912; *Billboard*, June 1, 1912.

25. John Kobal, *Gotta Sing, Gotta Dance: A History of Movie Musicals* (New York: Exeter Books, 1983), 165; Marshall Sterns and Jean Sterns, *Jazz Dance: The Story of American Vernacular Dance*, 2d ed. (New York: Da Capo Press, 1994), 104–125; Brenda Dixon Gottschild, *Digging the Africanist Presence in American Performance: Dance and Other Contexts* (Westport: Greenwood Press, 1996), xiv, 1–2, 81–85.

26. West, *Goodness*, 44–45; *VR*, July 26, December 13, 1912, January 3, 1913; Manager's Report, December 30, 1912, Union Square Theater, New York City, Keith-Albee Records, UI.

27. Dana Rush, "Back of the West Front," *Photoplay*, February 1934, 60, 109–110; Charles Stein, *American Vaudeville Seen by Its Contemporaries* (New York: Knopf, 1984), 152; West, *Goodness*, 43–44; *VR*, March 13, 1914; Meryman, "Mae West," 69.

28. Manager's Reports, November 3, 1913, Columbus, Ohio, November 10, 1913, Philadelphia, Pennsylvania, Keith-Albee Records, UI; *Detroit News*, August 26, 1913; *San Antonio Light*, September 11, 1914; *VR*, March 13, 1914; West, *Goodness*, 47–48; John E. DiMelgio, *Vaudeville U.S.A.* (Bowling Green: Bowling Green University Popular Press, 1973), 87–95; "Route Lists," *Clipper*, February–December 1913; Winslow, "Diamond Mae," 26; Michael McDonald Mooney, *Evelyn Nesbitt and Stanford White: Love and Death in the Gilded Age* (New York: Morrow, 1976), 206–207.

29. Manager's Reports, November 3, 1913, Columbus, Ohio, November 10, 1913, Philadelphia, Pennsylvania, Keith-Albee Records, UI; *VR*, March 9, December 13, 1912; *New York Morning Telegraph,* October 1, 1913, Robinson Locke Scrapbooks, Rose.

30. *Clipper*, October 4, 1913, 6; *VR*, October 3, 1913; Manager's Report, November 3, 1913, Columbus, Ohio, Keith-Albee Records, UI; West, *Goodness*, 49.

31. Manager's Report, November 10, 1913, Philadelphia, Pennsylvania, Keith–Albee Records, UI; *New York Morning Telegraph*, October 11, 1913, Robinson Locke Scrapbooks, Rose; Sterns and Sterns, *Jazz Dance*, 210; *New York Tribune*, August 5, 1913; *San Antonio Light*, September 8, 1914.

32. *San Antonio Light*, September 6, 1914; *Examiner*, April 24, 1935; *Clipper*, October 4, 1913.

33. Eels and Musgrove, *Mae West*, 40–41.

34. *Detroit News*, August 24, 26, 1913; *Clipper*, August 23, 1913, 22; *Accordion News*, August 1935; West, *Goodness*, 52–54.

35. Biery, "Part Two," 70–71; *Examiner*, April 24, 1935; Nils Thor Granlund, *Blondes, Brunettes, and Bullets* (New York: McKay, 1957), 43; Joe Laurie Jr., *Vaudeville: From Honky-Tonks to the Palace* (New York: Holt, 1953), 69; *VR*, February 20, 25, 1914; West, *Goodness,* 52–60.

36. *Clipper*, January 9, 1915; West, *Goodness*, 54–60; Biery, "Part Two," 70–71; *VR*, December 25, 1914, January 9, 1915.

37. *VR*, August 20, 1915; "Route Lists," *Clipper,* April–September 1915.

38. *VR*, March 17, June 2, 1916; *Clipper,* January 8, March 18, 1916; Snyder, *Voice*, 76–77; Robert Sklar, *Movie-Made America: A Cultural History of American Movies*, 2d ed. (New York: Vintage Books, 1994), 33–86; *Pittsburgh Leader*, April 9, 1916; Laurie, *Honky-Tonks*, 252, 271–272.

39. West, *Goodness*, 54–61; Biery, "Part Two," 70–71.

40. *Accordion News*, August 1935.

41. *VR*, July 7, 1916; West, *Goodness*, 45–46; Musgrove Log, October 9, 1969, SMC; "Mae West Story," *Revival of America*, April 1976, SMC.

42. Musgrove Log, October 9, 1969, SMC; Eels and Musgrove, *Mae West*, 37–38; *VR*, November 16, 1916.

43. West, *Goodness*, 60–62; Biery, "Part Two," 70–71.

44. West, *Goodness*, 61–64, 66–67; Allan H. Spear, *Black Chicago: The Making of a Negro Ghetto, 1890–1920* (Chicago: University of Chicago Press, 1967), 129–201; *LAT*, July 2, 1970.

45. West, *Goodness*, 63; Houston Baker, *Blues, Ideology, and Afro-American Literature: A Vernacular Theory* (Chicago: University of Chicago Press, 1984), 4–7.

46. West, *Goodness*, 64; Johnson, "Snow White," 44; William Howland Kenney, *Chicago Jazz: A Cultural History* (New York: Oxford University Press, 1993), 9–11, 54; Sterns and Sterns, *Jazz Dance*, 12, 104–114, 235; Malcolm Oettinger, "Literary Lil," *Picture Play*, September 1933, 26, 62.

47. West, *Goodness*, 64; Sterns and Sterns, *Jazz Dance*, 235.

Chapter Three

1. West, *Goodness*, 6; *VR*, June 6, 1919; "While the Men," MW/MAD; Kirtley Baskette, "Has Mae West Gone High Hat?" *Photoplay*, July 1934, 39.

2. West, *Goodness*, 63; Lic, Mildred West and Serge Treshatny, January 29, 1917, Brooklyn, New York, MA-NYC; *NYT*, April 16, 1927; *VR*, May 4, 1917, April 7, 1954; *UCD*, *1905*, 1004, *1906*, 1086; *Clipper*, October 14, 1916; Brenon, "Real Mae"; Schallert, "Go West," 33; "Mae Takes a Day Off," James Timony CF, Rose.

3. *New York American*, June 30, 1935, Robinson Locke Scrapbook, Rose; *LAT*, July 22, 1942; *Time*, July 19, 1937, 63.

4. *New York Dramatic Mirror*, October 19, 1918; *NYHT*, October 5, 1918; *Clipper*, October 9, 1918; *VR*, October 11, 1918; Leonard Hall, "Look Out! Here's Mae West!" *Photoplay*, January 1933, 46, 108.

5. West, *Goodness*, 65–66; Sterns and Sterns, *Jazz Dance*, 190, 210, 232.

6. "Everybody Shimmies Now" (New York: Charles K. Harris, 1918), ML; West, *Goodness*, 65; Meryman, "Mae West," 72.

7. "Mae West Says 'I Have Loved, But. . . . '" *Sunday Dispatch*, January 13, 1935, and "Me and My Past," *Delaware Star*, September 9, 1934, BFI.

8. *NYT*, September 15, 1931; "Maid Tipped Her Off," c. 1934, MW/MAD; *News*, April 15, 1938.

9. *Theatre Magazine*, February 1919, 97; *Clipper*, December 11, 1918.

10. *VR*, September 19, 1919; *New York Dramatic Mirror*, September 18, 25, 1919.

11. *Clipper*, September 17, 1919; "Here and There," *Graphic*, October 23, 1931, *Constant Sinner*/CF, SA; *VR*, December 13, 1918, August 13, 1920.

12. *New York Dramatic Mirror*, November 6, December 25, 1919; *VR*, October 31, 1919; Jerry Stagg, *The Brothers Shubert* (New York: Random House, 1968), 184–186.

13. *Clipper*, August 11, 1920; *VR*, August 22, 1913, August 13, 1920.

14. *Census, 1920*, Queens, New York; Shawell, "Mae West Curves," 31; *NYT*, April 16, 1927; *VR*, February 9, 1927.

15. *VR*, March 11, 1921, April 22, 1921; *Clipper*, February 9, 1921; *Washington Post*, March 6, 1921.

16. *Clipper*, August 24, 1921; *VR*, August 26, 1921; Jon Tuska, *The Complete Films of Mae West* (New York: Citadel, 1972), 27–28; *Theatre Magazine*, November 1921, 308; Harold Atteridge, James Hussey, and Owen Murphy, *The Whirl of the Town / The Mimic World*, script; *The Mimic World* / CF, SA.

17. Mae West, *The Ruby Ring*, April 1, 1921, LC; Meryman, "Mae West," 66.

18. West, *Ruby Ring*, 12, 16.

19. Harry Richman with Richard Gehman, *Hell of a Life* (New York: Duell, Sloan & Pearce, 1966), 38–44, 93; Ruth Geri, "West of Broadway: A Reminiscence of Mae's Early Days by Harry Richman," *Hollywood*, October 1934, BFI; Milton Berle, *"B.S." I Love You: Sixty Funny Years With the Famous and Infamous* (New York: McGraw-Hill, 1988), 24, 227–228, 241; Musgrove Log, January 16, 1975, SMC.

20. Richman, *Hell of a Life*, 39–42; *Clipper*, July 12, 1922; *VR*, June 23, July 14, 1922; Geri, "West of Broadway"; West, *Goodness*, 73–74; "Former Partner of Mae West," "Mae Curves Pads," Scrapbook #1, Box 11, Harry Richman Papers, Special Collections, Boston University.

21. *News*, August 13, 1922; West, *Goodness*, 74–75; Program, *Ginger Box Revue*, July 28, 29, 1922, Rose; *VR*, August 4, 1922; *Stamford Advocate*, July 26, 1927; Southern, *Music*, 354; Geri, "West of Broadway."

22. *News*, August 13, 14, 1922; *VR*, August 11, September 1, 1922; *Clipper*, August 16, 23, 1922.

23. *Clipper*, August 23, 1922; *VR*, September 8, 1922; Richman, *Hell of a Life*, 33–35.

24. West, *Goodness*, 72, 77; Mae West, *The Hussy*, 1922, LC.

25. West, *Hussy*, I, i, 7–8.

26. Ibid., II, i, 34–35.

27. Ibid., I, ii, 22.

28. *VR*, January 19, 1923.

29. *VR*, April 26, 1923, 31; *Clipper*, April 25, 1923.

30. Richman, *Hell of a Life*, 34, 43–44; Granlund, *Blondes*, 90–91.

31. Mae West Non-Show Song File, ML; *NYT Magazine*, November 30, 1969.

32. *VR*, March 5, 26, 1924; Lic Application, Mae West and R. A. "Bud" Burmeister, March 22, 1924, Houston, Texas; *San Antonio Light*, March 23, 24, 1924; *VR*, September 10, 1924.

33. Ned Williams, "The Men in Mae West's Life," *Hollywood*, June 1934, BFI; Jacoba Atlas, "Mae: Image From a Cracked Mirror: Part II," *Los Angeles Free Press*, June 21, 1974; Chandler, *Ultimate*, 48.

34. *NYT*, October 30, 1926, April 17, 1927, April 18, 1929; *NYHT*, April 17, 19, 1929; *VR*, October 3, 1928, April 24, 1929; Kevin Thomas, "A Match Made in

the Cotton Club: Mae West and Owney Madden's 'Hot Romance'," *LAT Calendar*, December 23, 1984, 2.

35. Graham Nown, *English Godfather* (London: Ward Lock, 1978), 16– 49, 53–87; Asbury, *Gangs,* 344–355; Thomas, "A Match," 2; Stanley Walker, *Night Club Era* (New York: Stokes, 1933), 109–111, 240–242; Louise Berliner, *Texas Guinan: Queen of the Night Clubs* (Austin: University of Texas Press, 1993), 96–111.

36. Thomas, "A Match," 2; Eels and Musgrove, *Mae West,* 100–101; David Levering Lewis, *When Harlem Was in Vogue* (New York: Vintage Books, 1982), 208–209; Willie "the Lion" Smith with George Hoeffer, *Music on My Mind: The Memoirs of an American Pianist* (Garden City: Doubleday, 1964), 67, 135–137, 172; Barry Singer, *Black and Blue: The Life and Lyrics of Andy Razaf* (New York: Schirmer, 1992), 171–172.

37. Singer, *Black and Blue,* 257–258; Sterns and Sterns, *Jazz Dance,* 76, 147, 161–166, 268–271.

38. Perry Bradford, *Born With the Blues: Perry Bradford's Own Story* (New York: Oak Publications, 1965), 131–133; Clippings, February 2, April 4, 1930, Scrapbook #1, SSC.

Chapter Four

1. "Interview With Mae West," *Hollywood in the Thirties: Discussion and Question Transcripts,* December 1, 1969, 6, AMPAS; Meryman, "Mae West," 66; West, *Goodness,* 77–78.

2. NYT, July 29, September 13, 1926, March 31, 1927; VR, August 4, 1926; NYHT, March 18, 31, 1927; Meryman, "Mae West," 66; Musgrove Log, August 16, 1969, SMC.

3. NYT, January 26, July 17, 1926; Brooks Atkinson, *Broadway* (New York: Macmillan, 1970), 249; West, *Goodness,* 78–82; NYHT, March 31, 1927; Thomas, "A Match," 2; "Me and My Past."

4. Musgrove Log, November 18, 1969, SMC; Allen Churchill, *The Theatrical Twenties* (New York: McGraw-Hill, 1975), 212–213, 232; Edward Sammis, "The Strange Career of Mae West's Kid Sister," *Screenplay,* December 1933, 20, BFI; NYHT, March 31, 1927; West, *Goodness,* 85–86; VR, June 30, 1926.

5. West, *Goodness,* 83–88; NYHT, March 31, 1927; "Interview With Mae West," 8–9.

6. News, February 24, 1933.

7. NYHT, April 27, 1926; "Another New Play," April 28, 1926, SEX/CF, HU; VR, April 28, 1926; NYT, April 28, 1926; West, *Goodness,* 91.

8. "Discovering SEX," April 27, 1926, SEX/CF, HU; Mae West, *Three Plays by Mae West: SEX, The Drag, and The Pleasure Man*, ed. Lillian Schlissel (New York: Routledge, 1997), 41.

9. West, *Three Plays*, 68, 70.

10. Ibid., 74, 90, 92.

11. *NYT*, April 27, 1926; *New Yorker*, May 8, 1926, 26; *VR*, April 28, 1926; "Another New Play."

12. Robert Benchley, "All About Sex," *Life*, May 20, 1926, 20; *VR*, January 26, 1927; Zora Neale Hurston, "Characteristics of Negro Expression," in *Negro: An Anthology*, ed. Nancy Cunard (1934; reprint New York: Ungar, 1970), 30–31.

13. Elizabeth Yeaman, "Mae West Ascends to Theaterdom's Elite," BFI; Ann Douglas, *Terrible Honesty: Mongrel Manhattan in the 1920s* (New York: Farrar, Straus & Giroux, 1995), 38–41, 64.

14. West, *Three Plays*, 54–56; *New York Morning Telegraph*, February 1, 1927; Peiss, *Cheap Amusements*, 110–113.

15. *NYHT*, January 23, 1927; West, *Wit and Wisdom*, 87; *Graphic*, December 20, 1926.

16. *NYHT*, January 23, 1927.

17. West, *Three Plays*, 55–59, 85–86; "Discovering *SEX*"; *VR*, May 5, 1926.

18. West, *Three Plays*, 44–45.

19. Michael Taft, *Blues Lyric Poetry: An Anthology* (New York: Garland, 1983), 117.

20. Baker, *Blues*, 7.

21. "Discovering *SEX*"; *VR*, February 2, 1927.

22. John Sumner, "Padlock Drama," *Theatre Magazine*, May 1928, 11–12, 62. NYSSV, Executive Secretary Reports, April 1926, January 1927, Box 2; Sumner, Speech, February 2, 1929, Box 2; Author's League of America, "Program of the Joint Committee Opposed to Political Censorship," c. 1922, Folder 10, Box 3; Frederic F. Van De Water, "The Obscene Drama," Folder 4, Box 4; John Sumner, "Autobiography Draft," ms 1, pp. 11–13, Box 1; all Sumner Papers. *VR*, June 9, August 4, 1926, January 26, 1927; *NYT*, June 8, 1926; Percy Hammond, "Is There No 'Flit'?" *Constant Sinner*/CF, HU.

23. *New York Daily Mirror*, April 30, 1926, *SEX*/CF, Rose; *VR*, February 9, 1927.

24. *NYHT*, January 23, 1927, *SEX*/CF, HU; *VR*, May 5, 1926; "Discovering *SEX*."

25. George Walsh, *Gentleman Jimmy Walker: Mayor of the Jazz Age* (New York: Praeger, 1974), 5–12, 18–21, 97, 11; Nown, *English Godfather*, 34, 91; Oliver E. Allen, *The Tiger: The Rise and Fall of Tammany Hall* (New York: Addison-Wesley, 1993), 215–216, 227–230, 236; Kaier Curtain, *"We Can Always Call Them Bulgarians": The Emergence of Lesbians and Gay Men on the American Stage* (Boston: Alyson, 1987), 69–70.

26. Churchill, *The Theatrical Twenties*, 232, 234; NYSSV Executive Secretary Reports, October 1926, November 1926, Box 2, Sumner Papers.

27. *NYT*, April 28, 1927; Nown, *English Godfather*, 68–70, 76; Berliner, *Texas Guinan*, 109, 165, 182, 191; Whitney Bolton, "Critic Impressed by Mae West Role of Siren at Séance," *Philadelphia Inquirer*, May 4, 1969; Lewis Yablowsky, *George Raft* (London: Allen, 1975), 1–2, 15, 35–36, 240; Berle, *"B.S.,"* 25, 241–243.

28. Eels and Musgrove, *Mae West*, 65; *VR*, December 29, 1926; Smith, *Music on My Mind*, 137; West, *Goodness*, 91–92; C. Robert Jennings, "Mae West: A Candid Conversation," *Playboy*, January 1971, 76.

29. George Chauncey, *Gay New York: Gender, Urban Culture, and the Making of the Gay World, 1890–1940* (New York: Basic Books, 1994), 291–299, 304–321; West, *Goodness*, 92; Curtain, *We Can Always*, 18.

30. *NYHT*, September 13, 1931, *Constant Sinner*/CF, SA; *VR*, January 12, 26, 1927.

31. *VR*, January 5, 1927; NYSSV Executive Secretary Reports, January 1927, Box 2, and Van De Water, "The Obscene Drama," Box 4, Sumner Papers.

32. West, *Three Plays*, 97–100, 102, 116, 124; *VR*, January 26, February 2, 1927; West, *Goodness*, 95.

33. West, *Three Plays*, 132–134, 139–140.

34. *VR*, February 2, 1927; West, *Goodness*, 95; *NYT*, February 1, 1927.

35. *VR*, February 9, 1927; *NYT*, February 11, April 16, 1927.

36. *New York Morning Telegraph*, February 1, 1927; *VR*, February 2, 1927; Chauncey, *Gay New York*, 291–293.

37. *VR*, January 26, February 2, 1927; Curtain, *We Can Always*, 84–85, 102; Chauncey, *Gay New York*, 312–313.

38. Jack Hamilton, "Raquel Welch, Mae West: Talk About Men, Morals, and Myra Breckenridge," *Look*, March 24, 1970, 48; West, *Goodness*, 94–95.

39. Jennings, "Mae West," 78; Chauncey, *Gay New York*, 286–290.

40. West, *Three Plays*, 118, 133; Mae West, "Sex in the Theatre," *Parade*, September 1929, 13; Walker, *Night Club*, 101; Chauncey, *Gay New York*, 185–187.

41. *VR*, February 2, 9, 1927; *NYT*, February 1, 1927.

42. West, *Goodness*, 96–97; *NYT*, February 10, 17, 1927; Walsh, *Gentleman Jimmy*, 42–47; *VR*, March 2, 1927; Allen, *Tiger*, 235–254.

43. *NYT*, February 10–13, 1927; *News*, February 24, 1933; *VR*, March 2, 1927.

44. *VR*, March 16, February 22, 1927; *NYT*, March 11, 1927.

45. *VR*, March 16, 23, 30, 1927; *NYT*, March 21, 1927.

46. *VR*, March 30, 1927; *NYT*, March 31, 1927; *NYHT*, March 30, 31, April 2, 1927; West, *Three Plays*, 216–218; Bruce Gould, " 'Sex' on Trial," *New Republic*, April 20, 1927, 246–248.

47. *NYT*, April 1, 20, 1927; *NYHT*, March 30, 1927; *VR*, April 6, 1927; West, *Goodness*, 97–98.

48. *NYT*, April 1, 1927; *NYHT*, March 30, April 2, 1927.

49. "Clean Town," c. 1927, and *NYHT*, April 2, 1927, *SEX*/CF, HU.

50. *NYT*, April 6, 1927; *VR*, April 6, 13, 1927; *NYHT*, April 6, 1927.

51. *NYT*, March 18, April 6, 20, 1927; *VR*, April 13, 20, 1927; *NYHT*, April 6, 1927.

Chapter Five

1. Mae West, "Ten Days and Five Hundred Dollars: The Experiences of a Broadway Star in Jail," *Liberty*, August 20, 1927, 53–56; Samuel Roth, *Stone Walls Do Not: The Chronicle of a Captivity* (New York: Faro, 1930), vol. 1, pp. 133–134; *NYT*, April 20, 21, 28, 1927; Rush, "Back of the West," 110; Brenon, "Real Mae."

2. *NYT*, April 21, 28, 1927; West, *Goodness*, 100.

3. West, "Ten Days," 53–55; Clippings, c. 1928, MW/MAD; *News*, February 24, 1937.

4. West, "Ten Days," 54–55; Rush, "Back of the West," 110.

5. *NYT*, April 28, 1927; West, *Goodness*, 101–104; *VR*, November 9, 1927.

6. Mae West, *The Wicked Age* (1927), I, 3–4, II, III, 8, LC.

7. Stephen Rathburn, "The Wicked Age," MW/CF, HU; *NYT*, November 5, 1927; *VR*, November 9, 1927; *LAT*, April 9, 1933.

8. *VR*, November 16, 23, 1927; *NYT*, November 5, 15, 1927.

9. West, *The Wicked Age*, I, 4–5, 18.

10. Roth, *Stone Walls*, 21, 157–160.

11. *VR*, April 11, July 4, 1928; West, *Goodness*, 108–109; Douglas, *Terrible Honesty*, 378–379, 481; Marie Beynon Ray, "Curves Ahead," *Collier's*, October 7, 1933, 40; *NYT*, April 22, 1928; *Theatre Magazine*, September 1928, 30; Anonymous, "Memo Typescript," MW/Photograph File, HU; *News*, February 25, 1933.

12. "Memo Typescript"; "Concerning the Methods of Mae West," *Diamond Lil*/CF, HU; Kobal, *People*, 166; *VR*, June 13, 1928.

13. Gilbert Seldes, "The Theatre," *Dial*, June 1928, 531–532; West, *Goodness*, 110–111; *VR*, April 11, 1928.

14. Mae West, *Diamond Lil*, I, 5, 13–14, SA; "The Underworld Sensation, Mae West," Flyer, *Diamond Lil* Program File, HU; *VR*, July 4, 1928.

15. West, *Diamond Lil*, I, 19–21, 27, SA.

16. Ibid., II, 8, 13.

17. Ibid., II, 24, 28.

18. Ibid., III, 5–10, 13, 17–19.

19. Richard Lockridge, "The Return of a Native in Diamond Lil," *Diamond Lil*/CF, HU; *NYT*, April 10, 1928; *VR*, April 11, 1928; *NYHT*, April 29, 1928; John Mason Brown, "Valedictory to a Season," *Theatre Magazine*, June 1928, 393–394; West, *Goodness*, 111–113, Berliner, *Texas Guinan*, 129, 160.

20. Winslow, "Diamond Mae," 26–29; Eels and Musgrove, *Mae West*, 80; *News*, February 25, 1933.

21. West, *Goodness*, 111; *VR*, May 9, 1928.

22. *VR*, July 4, May 9, June 13, 27, July 18, August 1, 1928; Charles O. Vander, "Heard on Broadway," *Theatre Magazine*, September 1928, 30.

23. West, *Goodness*, 111; Richard Lockridge, "The Return of a Native," *Diamond Lil*/CF, HU.

24. Brown, "Valedictory," 394; *NYHT*, April 29, 1928; *NYT*, April 10, 1928; "Diamond Lil Opens," *Diamond Lil*/CF, HU; "Memo Typescript."

25. West, *Diamond Lil*, I, 7, 13, 27, SA.

26. Mae West, *Diamond Lil*, I, 26–28, LC [earliest draft].

27. West, *Diamond Lil*, II, 3, 13, 27–28, SA.

28. Jordon appears to be a composite of Sullivan and John McGurk, the real owner of Suicide Hall. Sante, *Low Life*, 119–120; Harold Zink, *City Bosses in the United States* (Durham: Duke University Press, 1930), 85–95.

29. West, *Diamond Lil*, I, 16, SA.

30. West, *Diamond Lil*, I, 31, III, 15, LC; West, *Goodness*, 106.

31. Sheldon Brooks, "I Wonder Where My Easy Rider's Gone," (Chicago: Will Rossiler, 1929), ML; "Diamond Lil Opens"; Angela Y. Davis, *Blues Legacies and Black Feminism: Gertrude "Ma" Rainey, Bessie Smith, and Billie Holiday* (New York: Pantheon Books, 1998), 3–41; Hazel Carby, "It Jus Be's Dat Way Sometime: The Sexual Politics of Women's Blues," in *Gender and Discourse: The Power of Talk* (Norwood: Albex, 1988), 227–242.

32. West, *Goodness*, 114–115; Tristram Potter Coffin, *The Female Hero in Folklore and Legend* (New York: Seabury Press, 1975), 169–173.

33. West, *Diamond Lil*, I, 20, III, 14, SA.

34. *VR*, August 22, 1928.

35. West, *Diamond Lil*, I, 27, SA; Ashton Stevens, *Actorviews* (Chicago: Covici–McGee, 1923), 113–118; George Davis, "The Decline of the West," *Vanity Fair*, May 1934, 82; West, *Three Plays*, 122.

36. Lemuel Fowler, "He May Be Your Man but He Comes to See Me Sometimes" (Chicago: Ted Browne Music, 1922); Bradford, *Born With the Blues*, 131–132.

37. Stark Young, "Diamond Lil," *New Republic,* June 27, 1928, 145–146.

38. Winslow, "Diamond Mae," 26–29; West, *Goodness*, 115.

39. *VR*, August 29, 1928; West, *Goodness*, 116–118, 125–127; West, *Three Plays*, 224, 231.

40. *VR*, September 19, 1928; "*Pleasure Man* Ends Wales Act Reign of Terror," *Equity*, April 1930, 9–10, *Pleasure Man*/CF, HU.

41. West, *Three Plays*, 145–170, 183–185, 200.

42. *VR*, October 10, 1928; Curtain, *We Can Always*, 132; Jeffrey Amherst, *Wandering Abroad: The Autobiography of Jeffrey Amherst* (London: Secker & Warburg, 1976), 82; *NYT*, October 2, 1928; "*Pleasure Man* Ends Wales Act Reign of Terror."

43. Gilbert Gabriel, "Last Night's First Night," October 2, 1928, *Pleasure Man*/CF, HU; *NYT*, October 2, 3, 1928, June 7, 1936; *VR*, October 3, 10, 1928.

44. Curtain, *We Can Always*, 136; *NYT*, October 4, 5, 1928; *News*, October 4, 1928.

45. *VR*, October 10, 1928.

46. *NYT*, October 5, 6, 19, 1928; NYSSV, Executive Secretary Reports, October 28, 1928, Box 2, Sumner Papers; "West Is Indicted," October 5, 1928, "The Prosecutor's Case," March 24, 1930, *Pleasure Man*/CF, HU.

47. West, *Sex, Health, and ESP*, 39; DeC, Matilda West, January 26, 1930, Brooklyn, New York, MA-NYC; Eels and Musgrove, *Mae West*, 90.

48. *VR*, October 3, December 19, 1928, April 24, 1929; *NYT*, April 17, 18, 21, 1929; *NYHT*, April 17, 19, 1929.

49. *VR*, January 23, May 1, 1929; West, *Goodness*, 133–135; West, *Sex, Health, and ESP*, 114–117.

50. *VR*, June 12, 19, 26, 1929; *Detroit News*, June 3, 5, 6–9, 1929.

51. West, "Sex in the Theatre," 12–13, 32; Gerald Weales, *Canned Goods as Caviar: American Film Comedy of the 1930s* (Chicago: University of Chicago Press, 1985), 50–51.

52. "Mae West as Teacher," *Outlook and Independent*, September 11, 1929, 55; *VR*, July 3, 1929.

53. *LAT*, December 23, 1929; *VR*, October 30, December 4, 1929, January 1, 15, 1930; West, *Goodness*, 141–142; West, "Sex in the Theatre," 13.

54. Resumé, Jason Joy, January 11, 1930, J.V.W. to Joy, April 22, 1930, Hays to Joy, April 22, 1930, *She Done Him Wrong*, PCA.

55. West, *Goodness*, 142; *NYHT*, February 1, 1930; DeC, Matilda West (see note 47 above); *Brooklyn Eagle*, January 27, 1930.

Chapter Six

1. West, *Goodness*, 142–143; DeC, Matilda West (see chapter 5, note 47); *Brooklyn Eagle*, January 27, 1930; Eels and Musgrove, *Mae West*, 91; Bernard Sobel, *Broadway Heartbeat: Memoirs of a Press Agent* (New York: Hermitage House, 1953), 266; Brenon, "Real Mae."

2. *NYT*, January 14, February 6, March 18, 19, 20, 1930.

3. *NYT*, March 20, 21, 22, 1930; "Prosecution's Case," March 24, 1930, *Pleasure Man*/CF, HU; West, *Three Plays*, 237.

4. *NYT*, March 22, 25, 27, 29, 1930; "Captain Coy," March 22, 1930, and "The Prosecution's Case," March 24, 1930, *Pleasure Man*/CF, HU.

5. *NYT*, March 29, 1930.

6. *NYT*, April 1, 2, 1930; West, *Three Plays*, 238.

7. "Mae West Fails to Testify," April 2, 1930, *Pleasure Man*/CF, HU; Berliner, *Texas Guinan*, 165.

8. *NYT*, April 4, 5, 16, 1930; "*Pleasure Man* Ends Wales Act Reign of Terror"; West, *Goodness*, 129.

9. Toni Morrison, *Playing in the Dark: Whiteness and the Literary Imagination* (New York: Vintage Books, 1992), 17; Joe Laurie and Abel Green, *Show Biz From Vaude to Video* (New York: Holt, 1951), 374; Berliner, *Texas Guinan*, 161–165; Yablonsky, *Raft*, 56–57; Chandler, *Ultimate*, 48.

10. Mae West, *Frisco Kate*, December 15, 1930, III, i, 3, 10, LC; *Brooklyn Standard Union*, February 1, 1930.

11. West, *Frisco Kate*, I, ii, 20.

12. Stagg, *Brothers Shubert*, 276–280; *VR*, December 27, 1930.

13. West, *Goodness*, 140–143; Oettinger, "Literary Lil," 26, 62; Lowell Brentano, "Between the Covers—II," *Forum*, February 1935, 97–99; George Thomas Kurian, *The Dictionary of American Book Publishing: From Founding Fathers to Today's Conglomerates* (New York: Simon & Schuster, 1975), 7.

14. Brentano, "Between," 97–99; Musgrove Log, September 2, 1969, SMC; *News*, February 26, 1933; Oettinger, "Literary Lil," 62.

15. Mae West, *The Constant Sinner* (New York: Macaulay, 1930; 4th printing 1931), 15.

16. Ibid., 167–168.

17. Ibid., 259.

18. Ibid., 305, 307, 313.

19. West, *Sinner*, 90; Biery, "Part One," 103.

20. West, *Sinner*, 76, 167–169, 266–267, 307.

21. Ibid., 160–165.

22. Ibid., 168–169, 305.

23. Ibid., 159, 168.

24. West, "Sex in the Theatre," 2–13, 32; West, *Sinner*, 177–178.

25. West, *Sinner*, 158; Johnson, "Snow White," 42.

26. West, *Sinner*, 159, 255, 261, 299–300.

27. Ibid., 228.

28. West, *Sinner*, 52, 92, 216.

29. Wallace Thurman, *The Blacker the Berry* (New York: Macaulay, 1929), 34, 87; Dorothy West, "Elephant's Dance: A Memoir of Wallace Thurman," *Black World*, November 1970, 77–85; Nathan Huggins, *Harlem Renaissance* (New York: Oxford University Press, 1971), 111–136, 158–189.

30. West, *Goodness*, 112–113, 141; Carl Van Vechten, *Nigger Heaven* (New York: Knopf, 1926); Huggins, *Harlem Renaissance*, 93–118.

31. West, *Sinner*, 174–175, 194.

32. Angelica Houston and Peter Lester, "Mae West: The Queen at Home in Hollywood," *Interview*, December, 1974, 12–14.

33. West, *Goodness*, 144.

34. *VR*, October 22, November 19, 1930, January 7, 1931; West, *Three Plays*, ii.

35. West, *Sinner*, i, ii, iv; West, *Goodness*, 144; *Publisher's Weekly*, March 7, 1931, 1136.

36. Other African-American cast members included Robert Rains, Herbert Brown, Marie Remsen, George Williams, and the black jazz band Dave Nelson's Hot Shots. *Billboard*, September 26, 1931; *Pittsburgh Courier*, October 17, 1931; *NYHT*, October 4, 1931. Contracts: Mae West (author) July 10, 1931, and Mae West (actor), August 20, 1931; Letters: Mae West to Joseph M. Gaites, July 10 and August 20, 1931; Memoranda: Adolph Kaufman to Lee Shubert and J. J. Shubert, August 25, 1931 and Treasurer to Norman Light, August 25, 1931; all *Constant Sinner* Files, SA.

37. "Tribute to Mae West," Friends of the USC Library, March 21, 1982, USC; Richard Grupenhoff, *The Black Valentino: The Stage and Screen Life of Lorenzo Tucker* (Metuchen: Scarecrow Press, 1988), 98–101; Eels and Musgrove, *Mae West*, 100–101; Douglas, *Terrible Honesty*, 102.

38. *NYT*, August 30, 1931; *Standard Union*, September 1, 1931, *Constant Sinner* Files, SA.

39. Joseph Wood Krutch, "In Defense of Mae West," *Nation*, September 30, 1931, 344; Mae West, *The Constant Sinner*, prompt book (1931), II, i, 4–8, II, v, 37, SA.

40. West, *Sinner*, prompt book, I, iii, 1, 6–7.

41. Ibid., I, v, 5; II, iii, 19; III, iii, 15.

42. *NYHT*, September 16, 1931; *Billboard*, September 26, 1931; *NYT*, September 15, 1931; *VR*, September 22, 1931; "Constant Sinner," *New York Journal, Constant Sinner* Files, SA.

43. Wilella Waldorf, "Mae West Returns," September 15, 1931, *Constant Sinner*/CF, HU; "Mae West's New Drama," *New York World Telegram* and "Mae West Stages a Tawdry Slumming Party," *New York American, Constant Sinner* Files, SA.

44. *Pittsburgh Courier*, October 17, 24, 1931; *New York Amsterdam News*, September 16, November 4, 1931; Eels and Musgrove, *Mae West*, 101.

45. NYSSV Executive Secretary Reports, November 1930, Box 2 and October 1931, Box 3, Sumner Papers; "Mae Frightens Play Judges" and "Mae West's Play Disrupts Censorship Board," *Constant Sinner* Files, SA.

46. *New York Graphic*, September 15, October 23, 1931, and Alice Hughes, "Mae West Can't Shop in Stores," *New York Telegram*, October 7, 1931, *Constant Sinner* Files, SA; *NYT*, September 15, October 4, 1931; *VR*, November 12, 1930; Chauncey, *Gay New York*, 51, 263, 266.

47. West, *Sinner*, prompt book, I, iii, 5; Stagg, *Brothers Shubert*, 276–285.

48. *Pittsburgh Courier*, December 5, 1931.

49. *Washington Evening Star*, November 24, 1931; *Washington Herald*, November 24, 1931; *Washington Post*, November 24, 1931; Grupenhoff, *Black Valentino*, 99–100.

50. *Washington Post*, November 25, 26, 1931; *Washington Evening Star*, November 25, 1931; *NYHT*, November 26, 1931, *Constant Sinner* Files, SA; *Billboard*, December 5, 1931; *Pittsburgh Courier*, December 12, 1931.

51. *NYHT*, November 26, 1931; Grupenhoff, *Black Valentino*, 100–101; *Billboard*, December 12, 1931.

52. *Illustrated News*, June 20, 1932, MW/BF; *NYT*, June 16, 1932; "George Raft Interview," *Mike Douglas Show*, June 24, 1974, VL MSU.

Chapter Seven

1. Adolph Zukor with Dale Kramer, *The Public Is Never Wrong* (New York: G. P. Putman's Sons, 1953), 267; *Cinema Digest*, July 25, 1932, 4–5.

2. *Illustrated News*, June 20, 1932; West, *Wit and Wisdom*, 27; *VR*, June 14, 1932; West, *Goodness*, 146–149; *Night After Night*, Paramount Budget Reports, AMPAS; *LAT*, June 20, 1932.

3. Edward Churchill, "So You Think You Know Mae West," *Motion Picture*, July 1935, 49.

4. Ruth Biery, "The Private Life of Mae West: Part Four," *Movie Classic*, April 1934, 90.

5. *LAT*, July 17, 1932; Madge Tennant, "Mae West: Broadway's Most Daring Actress Drops Into Hollywood," *Movie Classic*, c. 1932, BFI.

6. "Mae West Loves," April 16, 1933, MW/BF; Kirtley Baskette, "Mae West Talks About Her 'Marriage,'" *Photoplay*, August 1935, 39, 40; Berliner, *Texas Guinan*, 161–165, 175; *LAT*, December 5, 1933.

7. Zukor, *The Public*, 267–268; West, *Goodness*, 150–151; *Cinema Digest*, July 25, 1932, 5; *Night After Night*, Revised First Script, August 6, 1932, Paramount Script Files, and *Night After Night,* Budget Reports, August 25, 1932, AMPAS.

8. "Mae West Fight," September 14, 1932, MW/BF.

9. *Night After Night Pressbook* (1932), AMPAS; *Night After Night*, (1932).

10. *Night After Night* (1932).

11. Davis, "The Decline," 82.

12. *Night After Night Pressbook*, AMPAS; Raft, *Mike Douglas Show*.

13. Yablonsky, *Raft*, 88; West, *Goodness*, 157; *Illustrated News*, June 20, 1932; *Night After Night Pressbook*, AMPAS.

14. *NYT*, October 31, 1932; *Motion Picture Herald*, October 13, 1932; *VR*, November 1, 1932.

15. *NYT*, October 7, 1932; *VR*, November 1, 1932; James Robert Parrish, *The Paramount Pretties* (New Rochelle: Arlington House, 1972), 302–303; Kenneth Baker, "War Clouds in the West?" *Photoplay*, December 1933, 110; Tino Balio, *Grand Design: Hollywood as a Modern Business Enterprise* (Berkeley: University of California Press, 1995), 13–15.

16. "West Robbery," October 13, 14, 1932, *Herald*, December 4, 1933, *Citizen News*, January 1, 1934, all MW/BF; *LAT*, December 5, 1933.

17. Hays to Zukor, October 18 and November 22, 1932; Hays to H. W. Warner, October 19, 1932; Memorandum from JVW, November 11, 1932; Wingate to Hays, November 1, 11, 1932; Aide Memoire, undated; JPH to Colonel, November

5, 1932; Hays to Wingate, November 22, 1932; all *She Done Him Wrong*, PCA. *VR*, November 29, 1932; *LAT*, October 31, 1932; Jack Jacobs, "The Dandy Who Directed: Lowell Sherman," *Focus on Film* (Winter 1975/1976): 43–51.

18. Martin Quigley, *Decency in Motion Pictures* (New York: Macmillan, 1937), 49–70; *VR*, November 29, December 6, 1932. Memorandum from Maurice McKenzie, November 28, 1932; Wingate to Hurley, November 29, 1932; Hays to Wingate, December 2, 1932; all *She Done Him Wrong*, PCA.

19. West, *Goodness*, 160; *New York World Herald*, February 5, 1933.

20. Edith Head and Paddy Calistro, *Edith Head's Hollywood* (New York: Dutton, 1983), 20–23, 152; Head and Ardmore, *Dress Doctor*, 51–55.

21. Graham McCann, *Cary Grant: A Class Apart* (New York: Columbia University Press, 1996), 226; Dorothy Hertzog, "Is Mae West a Fizzle?" *Picture Play*, May 1934; 13–14; "Miss West Talks Shop," c. 1934, BFI; Kobal, *People*, 418; John Bright, "One of a Kind," *L.A. Weekly*, July 16–22, 1982.

22. *VR*, January 13, 1933; West, *Goodness*, 161. Wingate to Hurley, January 11, 1933, and Wingate to Hays, January 13, 1933, *She Done Him Wrong*, PCA. Balio, *Grand Design*, 13–15; I. G. Edmonds and Robert Mimura, *Paramount Pictures and the People Who Made Them* (New York: Barnes, 1980), 187; John Douglas Eames, *The Paramount Story* (New York: Crown, 1985), 37.

23. *She Done Him Wrong Pressbook* (1933), AMPAS; Hall, "Look Out!" 46, 108; "A Portrait in Dots," Press Release, Paramount, October 1933, BFI.

24. *VR*, December 20, 1932, 4; February 7, 14, 21, 28, March 14, 1933; *New York World Herald*, February 10, 1933.

25. Daily Reports, February 21, 23, 24, 1933, Hays Papers; *Sunday Dispatch*, January 6, 1935, BFI.

26. Ben Maddox, "Don't Call Her a Lady," *Picture Play*, April 1933, BFI; *VR*, February 14, 1933; *NYHT*, February 10, 1933; John Mason Brown, "The Constant Sinner: Mae West of Stage and Screen," *New York Evening Post*, March 25, 1933.

27. *NYT*, February 10, 1933, 12; *VR*, February 14, 1933; Daily Report, February 18, 1933, Hays Papers.

28. *She Done Him Wrong* (1933). Memoranda: Wingate to Hurley, November 29, 1932, January 11, 1933; to Hays, December 2, 1932; to Harry Cohn, March 2, 1933; all *She Done Him Wrong*, PCA.

29. *News*, February 20, 1933.

30. *Time*, May 11, 1936, 70; "Letters Condemning Mae's Influence," 1934, MW/MAD; Bradford, *Born With the Blues*, 132; *LAT*, October 19, 1933.

31. "Frankie and Johnny," *Rudy Vallee Show*, 1933, VL MSU.

32. Donald Bogle, *Toms, Coons, Mulattoes, Mammies, and Bucks: An Interpretative History of Blacks in American Films* (New York: Continuum, 1990), 45–46, 62–66.

33. Mae West and John Bright, "Ruby Red," First Script, November 8, 1932, A–32; *She Done Him Wrong*, Paramount Script Files, AMPAS.

34. Head and Ardmore, *Dress Doctor*, 54.

35. Chris Albertson, *Bessie* (New York: Stein & Day, 1972), 191; *Polly Tix in Washington* (Educational Films Corporation, c. 1933); Frank Rose, *The Agency: William Morris and the Hidden History of Show Business* (New York: HarperCollins, 1993), 66; Clipping, December 5, 1936, Scrapbook #5, SSC; *Life*, September 1933.

36. *News*, February 20, 1933; Jay Brien Chapman, "Is Mae West Garbo's Greatest Rival?" *Motion Picture*, July 1933, 28–29, 76.

37. Schallert, "Go West," 84.

38. Clipping, August 27, 1935, Scrapbook #5, SSC; Brenon, "Real Mae;" "Biography of Mae West," October 1933, and Tom Baily, "The Life Story of Mae West," c. 1933; Paramount Press Releases, BFI.

39. Kobal, *People*, 355; Condon, "Come Up," 42; Schallert, "Go West," 84; "I Was Tempted," April 1934; Maddox, "Don't."

40. "Me and My Past"; *I'm No Angel Pressbook* (1933), AMPAS.

41. Janet Frame, *An Autobiography* (London: Women's Press, 1990), 44; "Churches War Against Obscenity," *Literary Digest*, March 3, 1934; *Chicago Tribune*, July 8, 1934; *LAT*, October 13, 1933, pt. 2, p. 1; "particularly approve," c. 1933, MW/MAD.

42. Hughes, "The Minority Vote," MW/CF, HU; James Davies, "And Now, a Fresh Slant on Mae," *Screenland*, January 1934, 25, 97; Schallert, "Go West," 32–33.

43. Mae Tinee, *Chicago Tribune*, n.d., BFI; Biery, "Part Four," 41, 89; Cecilia Ager, "Mae West Reveals the Foundation of the 1900 Mode," *Vogue*, September 1933, 67, 86; *Herald Examiner*, April 9, 1933, MW/BF.

44. Ager, "Mae West Reveals," 86.

45. Ray, "Curves Ahead," 24, 40.

46. Ager, "Mae West Reveals," 67, 86; Schallert, "Go West," 32–33.

47. Patricia Keats, "Sex Is Beautiful: Mae West Sexplains It All," MW/MAD; Daily Report, February 21, 1933, Hays Papers; Hilary Lynn, "How 12 Stars Make Love," *Photoplay*, August 1933, 31; Virginia Maxwell, "It's the Caveman Within Us Calling for Mae," *Photoplay*, December 1933, 38–39, 102.

48. Maddox, "Don't"; *New York Sun*, February 20, 1933; Jennings, "Mae West," 76.

49. Schallert, "Go West," 32; "Defending Mae West," *Movie Classic*, December 1933, BFI; West, *Goodness*, 162–163.

50. Shawell, "Mae West Curves"; *VR*, November 19, 1924, March 28, 1933; Hertzog, "Fizzle"; *Citizen News*, May 2, 1934, MW/BF.

51. "Charity Work," August 27, 1933, MW/BF; Stanley Musgrove, *Mae West*, Draft, SMC; *Boston Herald*, August 12, 1934, MW/CF HU.

52. Maria Riva, *Marlene Dietrich* (New York: Knopf, 1993), 142, 151, 432, 434; Marlene Dietrich, *Marlene*, trans. Salvator Attanasio (New York: Grove Press, 1989), 103–104.

53. Clipping, August 31, 1933, Scrapbook #4, SSC; Eels and Musgrove, *Mae West*, 115, 133; "Mae West Loves," April 16, 1933, MW/BF; Biery, "Part One," 70; Riva, *Dietrich*, 343.

54. Zukor, *The Public*, 267; Daily Reports, July 7, 1933, Hays Papers; Clipping, June 17, 1933, Scrapbook #3, SSC.

Chapter Eight

1. *Albany Knickerbocker Press*, May 1, 1933, in Daily Report, February 21, 23, May 4, 1933, Hays Papers; West, *Goodness*, 164–165, 167; Zukor, *The Public*, 269; Schallert, "Go West," 33, 84.

2. Leonard J. Leff and Jerold Simmons, *Dame in the Kimono: Hollywood, Censorship, and the Production Code from the 1920s to the 1960s* (New York: Grove Weidenfeld, 1990), 30.

3. *VR*, April 25, 1933; *Denver Post*, May 14, 1933; John Callan O'Laughlin to Hays, April 10, 1933, Hays to Jack Warner, July 6, 1933, and John Stuart to Breen, June 1, 1933, Hays Papers; Clipping, July 11, 1933, Scrapbook #3, SSC; *LAT*, April 10, 1933.

4. Sidney Kent to Hays, *She Done Him Wrong*, PCA; Daily Reports: February 23, 24, 1933, Hays Papers; Gregory Black, *Hollywood Censored: Morality Codes, Catholics, and the Movies* (Cambridge: Cambridge University Press, 1994), 23–24.

5. Martin Quigley to Will Hays, August 4, 1932, Hays Papers; *Motion Picture Herald*, August 19, 1933; "The Girl I Went to See," January 15, 1934, BFI.

6. Wingate to Botsford, June 23, 1933, *I'm No Angel,* PCA.

7. Gladys DuBois, Ben Ellison, and Harvey Brooks, "No One Does It Like That Dallas Man"; Holman to McKenzie, June 21, 1933, Wingate to Botsford, July 5, 1933, and McKenzie to Wingate and Breen, June 23, 1933; all *I'm No Angel,* PCA.

8. Wingate to Botsford, June 23, July 11, 1933, and Wingate to Kelly, July 19, 1933, *I'm No Angel*, PCA; Edith Efron, "Television Should Be Censored!" *TV Guide*, August 15–22, 1970, 16–18; Tim Malachosky and James Greene, *Mae West* (Lancaster, Calif.: Empire, 1993), 32.

9. Mae West, *Goodness Had Nothing to Do With It* (New York: Manor Books, 1976, last edition), 285; Clippings, August 5, September 17, 1933, Scrapbook #3, SSC; Julia Lang Hunt, "Trials and Triumphs of a Hollywood Dress Designer," *Photoplay*, June 1936, 54, 86–88; Baskette, "Has Mae West," 110.

10. Wingate to Hart, September 16, 1933, and Hart to McKenzie, October 4, 1933, *I'm No Angel*, PCA.

11. Condon, "Come Up," 42; *LAT*, October 14, 1933; Premiere Program, *I'm No Angel*, October 12, 1933, *I'm No Angel* Production File, AMPAS.

12. "Perfect Day," February 1934, *New Movie Magazine*, MW/MAD; *LAT*, October 14, 1933, May 20, 1934; Riva, *Dietrich*, 367; Clipping, September 24, 1934, Scrapbook #4, SSC; West, *Goodness,* 152.

13. *I'm No Angel* (1933).

14. According to lore, West ad-libbed "peel me a grape" during filming. However, it is present in the preshooting drafts of the screenplay. *I'm No Angel,* June 19, 1933, Paramount Script Collection, AMPAS.

15. Wingate to Botsford, June 22, 1933, *I'm No Angel,* PCA; West, *Goodness,* 169.

16. Lion tamer Mabel Stark may have stood in for West in some scenes. West, *Goodness,* 164–166; Zukor, *The Public,* 269–274; Kobal, *People,* 160.

17. *Kansas City Star,* November 11, 1933; *NYHT,* October 21, 1933.

18. *Boston Herald,* August 12, 1934, MW/CF, HU; "Perfect Day," MW/MAD; "Charity Work," August 27, 1933, and Press Release, Paramount, c. 1934, MW/BF.

19. *Screenland,* January 1934, 62; *I'm No Angel Pressbook* (1934), AMPAS.

20. "Miss West in Her Victorious Course," n.d. and *Boston Herald,* October 28, 1933, MW/CF, HU; *LAT,* November 5, 1933; Mae Tinee, *Chicago Tribune,* n.d., BFI.

21. *NYT,* October 14, 1933; *VR,* September 29, 1933; William Troy, "Mae West and the Classic Tradition," *Nation,* November 8, 1933, 547–548.

22. Quigley, *Decency,* 35–36; "Letters Condemning Mae's Influence," MW/MAD; *Tampa Tribune,* October 24, 1933, in Daily Report, October 30, 1933, Hays Papers.

23. *LAT,* October 22, 1933.

24. *NYTH,* October 22, 1933; Daily Reports October 23, 26, November 3, 17, 1933, Hays Papers.

25. "West Asks Rolph," October 11, 1933, MW/BF; *LAT,* January 4, 1934; Sammis, "Kid Sister"; Nown, *English Godfather,* 119–120; West, *Goodness,* 178–179.

26. *LAT,* December 5, September 28, 29, 1933; Berliner, *Texas Guinan,* 186–189; *Post Record,* December 5, 1933, MW/BF.

27. *Examiner,* January 16, 1934; *LAT,* December 6, 1933; *Citizen News,* January 16, 1933; all MW/BF.

28. *LAT,* January 17, 1934; *Herald,* January 15, 1934; *Examiner,* January 17, 1934; *Citizen News,* January 15, 17, 1934; *Daily News,* January 18, 1934; all MW/BF.

29. *Daily Express,* April 1934, BFI; *LAT,* February 2, March 11, 1934; *Daily News,* February 3, 1934; *Herald,* January 19, 1934, MW/BF.

30. *LAT,* January 31, 1934.

31. "It Ain't No Sin," March 2, 1934, *Belle of the Nineties,* Paramount Script Collection; "It Ain't No Sin," Treatment, *Belle of the Nineties,* PCA; Clipping, September 22, 1934, Scrapbook #4, SSC.

32. Black, *Hollywood Censored,* 170–172, 181.

33. Jimmie Fidler, "Come-upped and Saw Mae West," and "Stamped for Change," MW/MAD; Gladys Hall, "The Crime of the Day in Hollywood," *Motion Picture,* January 1934, 28–29, 70.

34. *LAT,* September 23, 1934; Clipping, May 2, 1934, Scrapbook #4, SSC; West, *Goodness,* 175.

35. "It Ain't No Sin"; "Creole Man," *Belle of the Nineties,* PCA.

36. Breen to Botsford, March 12, 1934, *Belle of the Nineties,* PCA; Clippings, March 12, May 2, 1934, Scrapbook # 4, SSC.

37. "A Puritan" and "Frank, Humorous," MW/MAD; Hall, "Crime of the Day," 70.

38. Malachosky and Greene, *Mae West,* 59; Johnson, "Snow White," 40. "My Old Flame," "Troubled Waters," Duke Ellington Collection, Smithsonian Institution; West, *Goodness* (1976), 284–285; Breen to Botsford, March 7, 1934, and Hays to Zukor, March 28, 1934, *Belle of the Nineties,* PCA; Baskette, "Has Mae West," 39, 110–112; Clippings, March 12, April 9, May 2, 1934, Scrapbook #4, SSC; Charles Higham, *Hollywood Cameramen: Sources of Light* (Bloomington: Indiana University Press, 1970), 121–133.

39. "Jack West," March 18, 1934; "Mae West Brings Father to Hollywood," July 1, 1934; Paramount Press Release, c. 1934; *Herald,* May 2, 1934; *Citizen News,* May 2, 1934; *Post Record,* May 2, 1934; all MW/BF. Sammis, "Strange Career"; *LAT,* January 4, 1934; Clippings, April 23, 30, 1934, January 1, 1935, Scrapbook #4, SSC; Eels and Musgrove, *Mae West,* 141–43.

40. Anita Loos, *Kiss Hollywood Goodbye* (New York: Viking Press, 1974), 169–171; *NYT,* June 9, 1934; Hedda Hopper, *From Under My Hat* (Garden City: Doubleday, 1952), 303–304; West, *Goodness,* 245.

41. Black, *Hollywood Censored,* 174–176, 183; "Acceptions and Rejections," July 1934, Breen to Hays, June 2, 1934, Breen to Hammell, June 6, 1934, Memorandum from Breen, June 6, 1934, *Belle of the Nineties,* PCA; Clipping, June 25, 1934, Scrapbook #4, SSC;

42. Clippings, August 20, September 22, 1934, Scrapbook #4, SSC; Memorandum from Hays, July 15, 1934, *Belle of the Nineties,* PCA.

43. Breen to Hays, August 3, 1934, to Hammell, August 7, 1934, *Belle of the Nineties,* PCA; Clippings, August 20, 1934, Scrapbook #4, SSC.

44. Clippings, August 23, 1934, SSC; *Citizen News,* August 18, 1934; MW/BF; *LAT,* August 25, 1934.

45. *Belle of the Nineties* (1934).

46. *VR,* September 25, 1934; *NYT,* September 22, 1934; *Illustrated Daily News,* September 1934; *Motion Picture Daily,* August 20, 1934; *Belle of the Nineties Pressbook* (1934).

47. Lawrence Levine, *Black Culture, Black Consciousness: Afro-American Folk Thought From Slavery to Freedom* (New York: Oxford University Press, 1977), 159–160, 244.

48. *VR,* August 25, 1934; Davis, "The Decline," 46; *Bridgeport* (Connecticut) *Star,* October 9, 1934, Scrapbook, Ellington Collection, Smithsonian Institution; Gilbert Seldes, "Sugar and Spice and Not So Nice," *Esquire,* March 1934, 60.

49. "No One Really Knows Mae West," Paramount Press Release, c. 1935, MW/BF; *Belle of the Nineties Pressbook*; Oettinger, "Literary Lil," 26.

50. Haddad-Garcia, " Everybody's Friend," 63; *NYT,* June 9, 1934; Winter to Breen, n.d. and "Acceptance and Rejections," February and November 1934, *Belle of the Nineties,* PCA.

51. Winter to Breen, n.d., *Belle of the Nineties*, PCA; Will H. Hays, *The Memoirs of Will H. Hays* (Garden City: Doubleday, 1955), 412; William French, "What Price Glamour?" *Motion Picture*, November 1934, 29; *Boston Herald*, September 24, 1934, MW/CF, HU; *Illustrated Daily News*, September 1934; MW/BF; "Twenty Five Deep," October 1934, BFI.

52. *NYT*, September 30, 1934; *Boston Herald*, September 27, 1934, MW/CF, HU; Gilbert Seldes, "Two Great Women," *Esquire*, July 1935, 86, 143; Frank Walsh, *Sin and Censorship: The Catholic Church and the Motion Picture Industry* (New Haven: Yale University Press, 1996), 110.

53. George Kent, "The Mammy and Pappy of Us All," *Photoplay*, May 1934, 32–33, 100–103; Paramount Press Release, c. 1934, MW/BF; *Belle of the Nineties Pressbook*; Leo McCarey, "Mae West Can Play Anything," *Photoplay*, June 1935, 30–31, 126–127.

54. "Miss West Talks Shop," 1934, BFI; Helen Harrison, "The Man You Want: Mae West Gives You His Number," *Photoplay*, September 1934, 67; *LAT*, September 23, 1934.

55. Mae West, "That's All Brother," *Mae West Canned Laughter*, Audiocassette (Mind's Eye, 1985).

Chapter Nine

1. *LAT*, May 20, September 23, 1934, September 3, 1948.

2. Breen to Hammell, December 19, 1934, to Hays, January 2, 1935, *Goin' to Town*, PCA; *Citizen News*, September 26, 1934, MW/BF.

3. Breen to Hammell, January 16, 24, 1935, *Goin' to Town*, PCA.

4. *LAT*, January 7, 1935; *VR*, January 8, 1935; Dave Keene, Paramount Press Release, c. 1935, MW/BF; DeC, John West, January 6, 1935, Oakland, California.

5. *Goin' to Town*, Paramount Budget Records, AMPAS.

6. Press Release, c.1934, MW/BF; *NYT*, May 19, 1935; Clippings, November 13, 1935, Scrapbook #5, SSC; Hertzog, "Is Mae West."

7. Budd Schulberg, *Moving Pictures: Memories of a Hollywood Prince* (New York: Stein & Day, 1981), 486–487; Scott Eyman, *Ernst Lubitsch: Laughter in Paradise* (New York: Simon & Schuster, 1993), 225–239; West, *Goodness*, 190; *Goin' to Town*, Paramount Budget Records, AMPAS; Clipping, May 11, 1935, Scrapbook #5, SSC.

8. Hays to Zukor, February 8, 22, 1935, *I'm No Angel*, PCA; Clipping, December 11, 1934, Scrapbook #4, SSC; *Goin' to Town Pressbook* (1935), AMPAS.

9. *Time*, May 6, 1935, 54–55; *Examiner*, April 22, 23, 1935; *NYT*, April 22, 1935.

10. *Time*, May 6, 1935, 54–55; *LAT*, April 23, 1935; *Examiner*, April 24, 25, 1935; *New York American*, June 30, 1935, Robinson Locke Scrapbook, Rose.

11. *Time*, May 6, 1935, 54; *NYT*, May 12, 1935.

12. *VR*, May 29, 1935.

13. *Goin' to Town* (1935).

14. Breen to Hays, n.d., *Goin' to Town*, PCA.

15. *Motion Picture Daily*, October 12, 1935; Zaring to Breen, May 31, 1935, *Goin' to Town*, PCA; *NYT*, May 19, 1935.

16. *Hollywood Reporter*, April 23, 1935; *VR*, May 15, 1935; *NYT*, May 19, 1935.

17. *NYT*, May 11, 1935; *VR*, June 5, 1935.

18. *NYT*, May 11, 1935; Clipping, May 11, 1935, Scrapbook # 5, SSC; *VR*, May 15, 1935.

19. Robert Eichberg, "Mae West Marriage Question," MW/MAD; *Examiner*, April 24, 25, 1935; *LAT,* January 12, 1936; *NYT,* January 7, 15, 1937.

20. Baskette, "Mae West Talks," 38–40, 91; Clipping, August 27, 1935, Scrapbook #5, SSC; J. Eugene Chrisman, "An Open Letter to Mae West," *Motion Picture*, August 1935, 38, 79; *NYT*, August 11, 1940.

21. Anthony Quinn, *The Original Sin: A Self-Portrait* (Boston: Little, Brown, 1972), 210; Johnson, "Snow White," 42, 46, 48; *LAT*, December 4, 1936; West, *Goodness*, 254; Harry McCarthy, "Mae West's Open Door Policy," *Hollywood Confidential*, November 1955, 18, 19, 46–47.

22. Tamm to the Director [Hoover], October 8, 1935; Hoover to Dunn, October 8, 1935; Dunn to Hoover, October 13, December 10, 1935; "Suspect Released," *Evening Public Ledger*, October 8, 1935; Laboratory Reports; all FBI. "Retains Her Nonchalance," MW/CF, HU; *LAT*, October 8, 9, 1935.

23. Robert Parrish, *Growing Up in Hollywood* (New York: Harcourt, Brace, Jovanovich, 1976), 72–88.

24. Clippings, September 24, December 10, 1935, Scrapbook # 5, SSC; Raoul Walsh, *Each Man in His Time* (New York: Farrar, Straus & Giroux, 1974), 275–278; *VR*, September 25, November 6, 1935; West, *Goodness*, 181–182; Marion Morgan and George McDowell, "Hallelujah, I'm a Saint/How About it Brother," *Klondike Annie,* Paramount Script Collection, AMPAS.

25. Asian-American cast members for *Klondike Annie* included Soo Young (Fah Wong), Mrs. Wong Wing (Ah Toy), Wong Chung, (Tong member), Paul Fung (Tong member), and Tetsu Komai (Lon Fang). Call Bureau Cast Service, January 10, 1936, Production File, and Paramount Budget Reports, *Klondike Annie,* AMPAS.

26. Telephone, Hays and Hammell, June 26, 1935, and Hammell to Hays, June 29, 1935, *Klondike Annie*, PCA.

27. Memorandum from G. S., 1935, *Klondike Annie*, PCA.

28. Breen to Hammell, September 4, 1935, *Klondike Annie*, PCA.

29. *Klondike Annie* (1936).

30. Clipping, December 9, 1934, Scrapbook #5, SSC. C. Metzter Notes, December 31, 1935; Breen to Hammell, December 31, 1935; Staff Criticisms, February 7, 1936; Memorandum: Breen, February 10, 1936; all *Klondike Annie*, PCA.

31. *Klondike Annie Pressbook* (1936) and *Screen Book Magazine*, April 1936, n.p., *Klondike Annie*, Production File, AMPAS; *Motion Picture Herald*, February 15, 1936.

32. *VR*, March 18, 1936; *Klondike Annie Pressbook,* AMPAS; Hays to Breen, February 29, 1936, *Pittsburgh-Sun Telegraph*, February 22, 1936, and social worker's comments, *Klondike Annie,* PCA.

33. *Illustrated Daily News*, February 28, 1936; Malachosky and Greene, *Mae West*, 103–106.

34. James Thurber, "Redemption," *Stage*, April 1936, 46–47.

35. Breen to Hays, March 2, 1936, *Klondike Annie*, PCA.

36. Thurber, "Redemption," 47.

37. *NYT*, March 15, 1936; *Hollywood Reporter*, March 21, 1936; *Motion Picture Herald*, March 7, 14, 1936.

38. [Hearst] to Koblentz and all managing editors, n.d., *Klondike Annie*, PCA; *VR*, February 26, 1936; *Examiner*, February 28, 29, 1936.

39. West, *Goodness*, 186; *Motion Picture Herald*, March 7, 1936; *Illustrated Daily News*, February 28, 1936; *Time*, March 9, 1936, 44.

40. *Citizen News*, March 4, 1936; *VR*, March 11, 1936; *Examiner*, February 27, 1936.

41. Claude A. Shull to Paramount Studios, May 1, 1936, and Anonymous to Hays and West, *Klondike Annie*, PCA; James Skinner, *The Cross and the Cinema: The Legion of Decency and the National Catholic Office for Motion Pictures, 1933–1970* (Westport: Praeger, 1993), 17–19, 34, 50.

42. *Motion Picture Herald*, March 7, 1936.

43. West, *Goodness*, 190; *NYT*, March 15, 1936; *VR*, January 15, 1936; "There Is Unrest," MW/CF, HU.

44. John Kobal, "Mae West," *Films and Filming*, September 1983, 21–25.

45. *Citizen News*, February 25, 1936, and Louella Parsons, February 22, 1936, MW/BF; *LAT*, February 22, 25, 26, 1936; *NYT,* March 6, 1936; Clipping, February 19, 1936, Scrapbook #5 SSC.

46. Clippings, March 12, June 18, 1936, Scrapbook #6, SSC.

47. McKenzie to Hays, November 7, 1934, *Go West Young Man*, PCA.

48. Memoranda, JIB [Breen], February 13, 19, June 1, 1936, *Go West Young Man*, PCA; *Personal Appearance*, June 25, 1936, and *Go West Young Man*, Paramount Script Collection, AMPAS.

49. *Go West Young Man Pressbook* (1936), AMPAS.

50. *Go West Young Man* (1936).

51. *NYT*, November 19, 1936.

52. Notes, Breen, June 1, 1936, *Go West Young Man*, PCA; *Personal Appearance*, June 25, 1936, and *Go West Young Man*, Paramount Script Collection, AMPAS; *VR*, December 25, 1936.

53. *VR*, November 3, December 25, 1936; *New York Evening Journal*, November 19, 1936; *Indianapolis Star*, November 21, 1936; *NYT*, November 19, 1936.

54. *Motion Picture Herald*, November 14, 1936; Tuska, *Complete Films*, 127; Graham Greene, *Graham Greene on Film*, ed. John Russell Taylor (New York: Simon & Schuster, 1972), 124.

55. Madame Sylvia, "Is Mae West Skidding on the Curves?" *Photoplay,* November 1936, 48–49, 86, 88.

56. "Exclusive," *Screen Guide,* and Mae West to Lew Garvey, 1936, MW/MAD.

57. *Los Angeles Daily News*, November 28, 1936; *NYT*, December 15, 1935; *LAT*, February 28, 1936.

58. "Overstuffed," MW/MAD; *Time*, July 19, 1937, 62; Clipping, July 10, 1937, Scrapbook #6, SSC; *LAT*, May 9, 1937; *NYT*, July 8, 1937; *Look*, May 25, 1937, 26–29.

Chapter Ten

1. West, *Goodness*, 190–196; *LAT*, September 3, 1948.

2. Balio, *Grand Design*, 244; West, *Goodness*, 190–192; Head and Castro, *Edith Head's Hollywood*, 25.

3. Cohen to Breen, August 3, 1937, Breen to Cohen, August 6, 10, 1937, and Private Memorandum, JIB [Breen], August 10, 1937, *Every Day's a Holiday*, PCA.

4. "I wouldn't even lift my veil" survived until the early release. West, *Goodness*, 193. State Censorship Reports, January 13, 1938; Breen to Cohen, August 6, 10, 1937, September 1, 1937; Cohen to Breen, August 31, 1937; all *Every Day's a Holiday*, PCA.

5. Haddad-Garcia, "Everybody's Friend," 63.

6. Hoagy Carmichael with Stephen Longstreet, *Sometimes I Wonder: The Story of Hoagy Carmichael* (New York: Da Capo Press, 1976), 274.

7. *Every Day's a Holiday* (1937).

8. Breen to Cohen, August 6, 1937, *Every Day's a Holiday*, PCA.

9. "Mae West has learned," *Every Day's a Holiday,* PCA; *Every Day's a Holiday*, Yellow Script, Paramount Script Collection, AMPAS.

10. Breen to Cohen, September 1, November 24, 1937, *Every Day's a Holiday*, PCA; Yellow Script, Paramount Script Collection, AMPAS.

11. *Every Day's a Holiday Pressbook* (1937).

12. *NYT*, December 12, 1937, January 19, 1938; *Motion Picture Herald*, December 25, 1937; J. Walter Thompson Agency to Oboler, December 11, 1937, Duke; West, *Goodness*, 193–195; *LAT*, November 12, 1964.

13. *Chase and Sanborn Hour*, Script, December 12, 1937, Duke.

14. Ibid; *Evening Star*, December 18, 1937; *NYT*, December 18, 1937; *Time*, December 27, 1937, 30; *Congressional Record*, 83, pt. 1, 75th Congress, 3rd Session, January 14, 1938, 560–563; *Motion Picture Herald*, December 25, 1937.

15. "Nationwide Protests," *Every Day's a Holiday*, PCA; *Motion Picture Herald*, December 25, 1937; *LAT*, November 12, 1964.

16. *NYT*, December 25, 26, 1937, January 15, 16, 1938.

17. *Motion Picture Daily*, December 21, 1937, *Indianapolis Star*, January 15, 1938, *NYHT*, January 27, 1938, all *Every Day's a Holiday*, PCA; *NYT*, January 27, 30, 1938.

18. Clipping, May 12, 1938, Scrapbook #6, SSC.

19. Sidone Gabrielle Colette, *Colette at the Movies* (New York: Ungar, 1975), 62–64.

20. West, *Wit and Wisdom*, 92–94; Charles Fox, "Personality: Mae West," *Film*, March/April 1956, 19; "Glamour Under Fire," *Business Week*, May 14, 1938.

21. Clipping, May 16, 1938, Scrapbook #6, SSC; *New York Post*, March 15, 1939, "Personal Appearance," MW/MAD; Eels and Musgrove, *Mae West*, 187–196; *NYT*, April 22, 1938; West, *Goodness*, 196; *VR*, January 5, 1938; Parrish, *Paramount Pretties*, 577–578.

22. *NYT*, April 17, 1938; Clipping, May 12, 1938, Scrapbook # 6, SSC; "Six Shows a Day" and "Mae's Tour," MW/MAD; *Boston Herald*, April 27, 1938, MW/CF, HU.

23. *New York Post*, March 15, 1939; Irwin F. Zeltner, *What the Stars Told Me: Hollywood in Its Heyday* (New York: Exposition Press, 1971), 54–58.

24. West, *Goodness*, 196–198; *Memo From David O. Selznick*, ed. Rudy Behlmer (New York: Viking, 1972), 178.

25. *New York Post*, March 15, 1939; Frank Vreeland, *Foremost Films of 1938: A Yearbook of the American Screen* (New York: Pitman, 1939), 17.

26. *New York Post*, March 15, 1939.

27. W. C. Fields, *W. C. Fields by Himself: His Intended Autobiography*, ed. Ronald J. Fields (Englewood Cliffs: Prentice-Hall, 1973), 324–353.

28. Listening Post to Joseph Breen, September 8, 1939, *My Little Chickadee*, PCA.

29. *Boston Globe*, September 29, 1994; Meryman, "Mae West," 70.

30. Breen to Pivar, September 26, 1939, October 23, 31, 1939, *My Little Chickadee*, PCA; Fields, *W.C.*, 347–349.

31. *My Little Chickadee* (1939)

32. *NYT*, November 12, 1939, March 7, 1940; *Boston Globe*, August 18, 1939, MW/CF, HU; Fields, *W.C.*, 359.

33. *My Little Chickadee*; Harold Clurman, "Mae West," *New Republic*, February 21, 1949, 28.

34. *Hollywood Reporter*, February 7, 1939; *NYT*, March 16, 1940; *VR*, February 7, 1939.

35. Delight Evans, "An Open Letter to Mae West," MW/MAD; *My Little Chickadee*.

36. West, *Sex, Health, and ESP*, 110; Clipping, January 8, 1940, Scrapbook #6, SSC; "Spy Picture," *Boston Post*, 1942, MW/CF, HU.

37. *NYT*, March 16, 1940; *Time*, December 13, 1943, 94, 97.

38. "My Little Chickadee," *Life*, February 19, 1940, 64–65; "Never Grows Old!" 1943, MW/MAD.

39. *Time*, December 13, 1943, 97; Donald R. Morris, "Why Don't You Come Up?" *American Heritage*, September 1992, 34–35; Kirk Douglas, *The Ragman's Son* (New York: Pocket Books, 1989), 104–105.

40. Rosen to Tamm, March 30, 1943, FBI; *NYT*, February 21, 1940, October 21, 1942; *LAT*, August 5, 1943; *VR*, October 19, 1966.

41. West, *Goodness*, 209–211; Press Release, c. 1934, Paramount Studios, MW/BF; *Belle of the Nineties Pressbook;* Johnson, "Snow White," 40, 42, 45–46; West, *Sex, Health, and ESP*, 116–122.

42. West, *Sex, Health, and ESP*, 123–149; West, *Goodness*, 211–215; Meryman, "Mae West," 72; Jennings, "Mae West," 82.

43. West, *Goodness*, 193, 219, 221; *Time*, December 13, 1943, 97.

44. West, *Goodness*, 219–220; Breen to Ratoff, July 19, 1943, *Heat's On*, PCA.

45. *Heat's On* (1943); West, *Goodness*, 219–220; Malachosky and Greene, *Mae West*, 161; Eels and Musgrove, *Mae West*, 199.

46. *NYT*, November 26, 1943; *Time*, December 13, 1943, 94, 97; *VR*, December 1, 1943; *Chicago Defender*, July 31, 1943; Jim Pines, *Blacks in Films: A Survey of Racial Themes and Images in American Films* (London: Studio Vista, 1975), 57.

47. West, *Goodness*, 220; *Heat's On* (1943).

48. *NYT*, July 18, 1943.

49. Mr. Blackwell with Vernon Patterson, *From Rags to Bitches: An Autobiography* (Los Angeles: General Publishing Group, 1995), 71–74; Kate Sprochnle, "Theatre," *Mademoiselle*, October 1944, 166, 229; West, *Goodness*, 222–223.

50. Art Cohn, *The Nine Lives of Michael Todd* (New York: Random House, 1958), 189; "Mae West Tribute," USC, 29–31; Downing to Bill, November 13, 1944, Downing Collection, HU; West, *Goodness*, 224.

51. Eels and Musgrove, *Mae West*, 212–219; Cohn, *Nine Lives*, 188–195; Steven Roberts, "76—And Still Diamond Lil," *NYT Magazine*, November 2, 1969, 80.

52. *New York Post*, March 15, 1939, MW/MAD.

53. Cohn, *Nine Lives*, 188–195; Michael Todd Jr. and Susan McCarthy Todd, *A Valuable Property: The Life Story of Michael Todd* (New York: Arbor House, 1983), 119–122.

54. Mae West, *Catherine Was Great,* April 10, 1944, I, i, 6, 10, LC; Handwritten lines in playbill, *Catherine Was Great*, October 8, 1944, *Catherine Was Great*/CF, HU.

55. West, *Catherine*, I, ii; West, *Wit and Wisdom*, 22.

56. West, *Catherine*, I, I–v.

57. West, *Catherine*, III, v.

58. "Catherine Was Great," *Life*, August 21, 1944, 71–72; *New Yorker*, August 12, 1944, 38; *NYT*, August 3, 1944; Joseph Wood Krutch, "Furtherest West," *Nation*, August 12, 1944, 194; *News*, August 3, 1944.

59. West, *Goodness*, 222–225; "Admirers Are Legion," MW/MAD; Sprochnle, "Theatre," 166; Downing to Bill, November 13, 1944, HU.

60. Krutch, "Furtherest West," 194; *New Yorker*, August 12, 1944, 38; West, *Goodness*, 197; *New York Post*, March 15, 1939; Sprochnle, "Theatre," 229.

61. West, *Catherine*, II, iv, 1; II, i, 4, iii, 6; III, i, 3; Cohn, *Nine Lives*, 190; *San Francisco Chronicle*, September 1, 1972.

62. *Boston Post*, January 24, 1945; *Christian Science Monitor*, January 23, 1945; Stark Young, "What Maisie Knows," *New Republic*, August 21, 1944, 219–220.

63. Playbill, *Catherine Was Great*, October 8, 1944, *Catherine Was Great*/CF, HU; West, *Wit and Wisdom*, 21.

64. Mikhail Bakhtin, *Rabelais and His World,* trans. Helen Iswolsky (Bloomington: Indiana University Press, 1984), 3; Brentano, "Between Covers," 97–98; *NYT*, March 12, 1936.

65. West, *Catherine*, II, i, 6.

66. *Boston Herald*, January 23, 1945.

67. West, *Goodness*, 227; Todd and Todd, *Valuable Property*, 122.

Chapter Eleven

1. West, *Goodness*, 227–228; Arlena Gibson, "Go West, Young Man," *Village Voice*, August 29, 1989, s7–s8.

2. Mae West, *Come On Over/Embassy Row* [*Come on Up*], February 28, 1946, III, 23, 27, LC.

3. West, *Come On*, II, 13.

4. Thomas Schatz, *Boom and Bust: The American Cinema in the 1940s* (Berkeley: University of California Press, 1997), 34.

5. Berle, "*B.S.,*" 241–242.

6. West, *Come On*, II, 5–6.

7. *LAT*, February 16, 1947; West, *Come On*, I, 4–6, 14.

8. Gibson, "Go West," s7–s8; West, *Goodness*, 228–229; *Theatre World, 1945–46*, 135; *1946–47*, 132–133.

9. West, *Goodness*, 229.

10. *LAT*, February 9, 11, 1947.

11. Tuska, *Films*, 164; *Theatre World, 1946–47*, 132; West, *Goodness*, 228; Eels and Musgrove, *Mae West*, 222.

12. *Mirror*, September 18, 1947, *Graphic*, September 17, 18, 1947, BFI; West, *Goodness*, 229–231.

13. Malakosky and Greene, *Mae West*, 181; *Mirror*, December 30, 1949, BFI; West, *Goodness*, 231.

14. "Review," January 26, 1948, *Diamond Lil*/CF, HU; *Sunday Express*, January 25, 1948, BFI; West, *Goodness*, 231–232; Lawrence Lader, "Come Up'n See Her," *Pageant*, February 1950, 57–62.

15. *LAT*, August 25–28, 1948; Malachosky and Greene, *Mae West*, 189; *Standard*, April 24, 1948, BFI; West, *Goodness*, 234–235.

16. *LAT*, September 1–3, 1948.

17. West, *Goodness*, 236, 244; *Theatre World,* 1948–49, 185; Eels and Musgrove, *Mae West*, 188–189, 227–229; Clippings, c. 1950, December 12, 1953, BFI.

18. *NYT*, November 28, 30, 1948; West, *Goodness*, 237.

19. *Tribune*, February 5, 1949, *Diamond Lil*/CF, HU; *NYT*, January 16, 17, 21, 1949; "America's Favorite Hussy," *Life*, May 23, 1949, 104; West, *Goodness*, 237; Lader, "Come Up'n," 59.

20. Howard Barnes, "Personal Triumph," January 7, 1949, *Diamond Lil*/CF, HU; *New York Post*, February 7, 1949; *NYT*, February 7, 1949; Gilbert Gabriel, "Westward Wow!" *Theatre Arts*, May 1949, 26.

21. "America's Favorite Hussy," 104; *NYT*, February 28, May 19, June 8, 1949; Lader, "Come Up'n," 57–62; West, *Goodness*, 238–241.

22. Eels and Musgrove, *Mae West*, 229–231, 239–240; Kevin Lally, *Wilder Times: The Life of Billy Wilder* (New York: Henry Holt, 1996), 186–189.

23. *NYT*, September 7, 1949, February 17, 18, 1950; West, *Goodness*, 241; Eels and Musgrove, *Mae West*, 234–238.

24. *NYHT*, December 5, 1948; *NYT*, January 21, 1950; Thomas, "A Match"; Helen Lawrenson, "Mirror, Mirror on the Ceiling: How'm I Doing?" *Esquire*, July 1967, 72.

25. John Mason Brown, "Mae Pourquoi," *Saturday Review,* October 8, 1949, 50; *New York Post*, February 7, 1949; Playbill, *Diamond Lil*, Plymouth Theater, January 30, 1951, *Diamond Lil* Program File, HU.

26. *Mae West on the Air: Rare Recordings* (Sandy Hook Records, 1985); West, *Goodness*, 241–242; *Newsweek*, January 16, 1950, 46; Brown, "Mae Pourquoi," 50–51.

27. Breen to Luraschi, September 2, 1949, Luraschi to Breen, September 6, 1949, *I'm No Angel*, PCA; *NYT*, September 7, 1949.

28. *New Republic*, February 21, 1949, 28; Mae West, *Diamond Lil*, 1964, II, ii, 14, LC; Brown, "Mae Pourquoi," 50.

29. Brown, "Mae Pourquoi," 50; *NYT*, February 7, 1949.

30. Brown, "Mae Pourquoi," 50–51; *New York Post*, February 7, 1949.

31. West, *Goodness*, 242, 244; Clipping, c. 1950, "Mae West Will Receive," BFI; "So I Went Up to See Mae West," *Popular Photography*, July 1966, 32–33.

32. *LAT*, September 13, 1953; *Theatre Arts*, October 1953, 89; West, *Goodness*, 243–244.

33. *NYT*, April 6, 1954; *VR*, April 7, 1954.

34. West, *Goodness*, 245–247; West, *Goodness* (1976), 253–254; Linda Henry, "Beauty and the Beef: Bodybuilding Legend George Eiferman," *Muscle and Fitness*, May 1994, 144–147, 200, 205.

35. Kaplan, "Mae West No Gamble," BFI; *VR*, July 28, 1954; West, *Goodness* (1976), 253–255; "Sexiest Night Club Act," *Ebony*, November 1954, 103–106.

36. "Sexiest Night Club Act," 103–106; Henry, "Beauty and the Beef," 144–147; West, *Goodness*, 248; *VR*, July 28, 1954.

37. "Sexiest Night Club Act," 103–106; Earl Wilson, "Mae West Finding Years No Handicap," MW/BF; Meryman, "Mae West," 62; West, *Goodness*, 248–250; *VR*, July 28, 1954.

38. Henry, "Beauty and the Beef," 146.

39. Wilson, "Finding Years."

40. Fox, "Personality," 19; Tuska, *Films*, 173; "Sexiest Night Club Act," 103–106.

41. "Sexiest Night Club Act," 103–106.

42. West, *Goodness*, 245–252, 263; West, *Goodness* (1976), 253–256.

43. Jocelyn Faris, *Jayne Mansfield: A Bio–Bibliography* (Westport: Greenwood Press, 1994), 17; *Washington Post*, June 8, 1956; Henry, "Beauty and the Beef," 147; Eels and Musgrove, *Mae West*, 246.

44. "Sex Legend's Apartment Sale," *Collector*, November 1994, 20; Faris, *Jayne Mansfield*, 1–14, 88.

45. *Washington Post*, June 8, 29, 30, 1956; "Guilty of Universe Assault," c. 1956, MW/MAD; West, *Goodness*, 252–254; West, *Goodness* (1976), 259–261.

46. McCarthy, "Mae West's Open Door," 18–19, 46–47.

47. *NYT*, May 5, July 30, August 1, 4, 1957; *LAT*, August 12–14, 19, 20, 1957; West, *Goodness*, 254–255.

48. West, *Goodness*, 255.

49. *LAT*, August 13, 1957; *NYT*, August 13, 1957; *NYT*, November 8, 13, 1957.

50. Alan Arnold, "Often, It's Written by the Star," *Saturday Review*, November 28, 1959, 23–24; *NYT*, March 27, 1958.

51. West, *Goodness*, 52, 123, 132–133, 237, 268; Eels and Musgrove, *Mae West*, 17.

52. *NYT*, October 11, 1959; Maurice Richardson, "Showbiz Dames," *New Statesmen*, October 29, 1960, 56–57.

53. West, *Goodness*, 255.

54. Eels and Musgrove, *Mae West*, 246–248; "Sexiest Night Club Act," 103–106; Johnson, "Snow White," 42, 46.

55. *NYT*, October 16, 1959; *Book Review Digest*, 1960, 1423.

56. "Dean Martin Show," c. 1959, *Mae West on the Air*.

57. "Red Skelton Show," March 1, 1960, *Mae West on the Air*.

Chapter Twelve

1. West, *Goodness* (1976), 262.

2. *Chicago Daily Tribune*, July 8, 10, 1961; West, *Goodness (1976)*, 264–266; *Miami Sun*, August 13, 1961; *VR*, c. 1961, SMC.

3. Mae West, *Sextette*, May 5, 1961, I, ii, LC.

4. Ibid., I, i, 19–20.

5. Richman, *Hell of a Life*, 42–43; West, *Goodness* (1976), 276–278; Leo Guild, "The Strange Dark World of Mae West," *People*, October 11, 1964, BFI; Kobal, *People*, 156; Lewis H. Lapham, "Let Me Tell You About Mae West," *Saturday Evening Post*, November 14, 1964, 76–78; Musgrove Log, August 21, 29, 1969, January 16, 1975, SMC.

6. Eels and Musgrove, *Mae West*, 261.

7. Rose, *The Agency*, 271.

8. "Mae West Meets Mister Ed," *Mister Ed*, March 15, 1964; "Mister Ed Barges Into a Boudoir," *TV Guide*, February 29–March 6, 1964, 20–21; Eels and Musgrove, *Mae West*, 260–261; Malachosky and Greene, *Mae West*, 234.

9. *LAT*, July 15, 1999; Lapham, "Let Me," 76; Malachosky and Greene, *Mae West,* 238; Musgrove Log, October 9, 1969, March 27, May 15, 1973, SMC.

10. West, *Goodness* (1976), 266–272; Malachosky and Greene, *Mae West*, 237.

11. Diane Arbus, *Diane Arbus Magazine Work*, ed. Doon Arbus and Marvin Israel (New York: Aperture, 1984), 58–61; Guild, "The Strange Dark"; Charles Krauser v. Estate of Mae West, Superior Court of California, County of Los Angeles, June 22, 1981.

12. West, *Sex, Health, and ESP*, 148–149; Will: Mae West, November 7, 1964, Los Angeles, California.

13. Lapham, "Let Me," 77–78.

14. Arbus, *Magazine Work*, 58, 61.

15. *VR*, April 17, 1968.

16. Kevin Thomas, "Mae West, Like Rock 'n Roll Music, Is Still Deeply Rooted in Ragtime," *Washington Post*, January 1, 1967; Lawrenson, "Mirror, Mirror," 75.

17. Ian Whitcomb, " 'Come Up and Rock With Me': My Adventures With Mae West," *Let It Rock*, March 1973, 18–22.

18. West, *Wit and Wisdom*, 9, 121.

19. West, *Goodness* (1976), 274–276; *VR*, February 21, 1968; Eels and Musgrove, *Mae West*, 266–267; *NYT*, August 10, October 13, 1968.

20. Jennings, "Mae West," 74; Hamilton, "Raquel Welch," 44–48; West, *Goodness* (1976), 276–278; Thomas, "Like Rock"; *NYT*, October 17, 1968.

21. Musgrove Log, August 13, 1969, SMC; West, *Goodness* (1976), 278–279.

22. *NYT*, August 14, 1969; Musgrove Log, August 21, 1969, SMC.

23. Musgrove Log, August 16, 20, 21, 31, September 2, 8, 17, November 8, 1969, SMC; *NYT*, August 14, 1969; West, *Goodness* (1976), 279–283.

24. Musgrove Log, August 15, September 8, 1969, SMC.

25. Musgrove Log, September 10, 15, October 17, 29, 1969, SMC.

26. "Mae West and the Men Who Knew Her," *A&E Biography*, 1994; Musgrove Log, October 13, 1969, SMC; *Myra Breckinridge* (1970).

27. Hamilton, "Raquel Welch," 47–50; Musgrove Log, October 15, 17, 27, 1969, SMC; *LAT*, May 21, 1981.

28. *NYT*, November 23, 1969; West, *Goodness* (1976), 280.

29. *LAT*, July 2, 1970; Eels and Musgrove, *Mae West,* 275; West, *Goodness* (1976), 279; Malachosky and Greene, *Mae West*, 274.

30. *NYT*, June 24, 25, 1970; *Evening Standard*, June 24, 1970, BFI.

31. *NYT*, July 5, 1970; *Time*, July 6, 1970, 70.

32. *NYT*, June 25, July 19, 1970; West, *Goodness* (1976), 282–283.

33. *New York Post*, July 4, 1970; *LAT*, February 10, 1971.

34. West, *Goodness* (1976), 286; Meryman, "Mae West," 62; "Mae West: The Star That Will Not Dim!" 79; *NYT*, August 25, 1976; Atlas, "Mae," 7, 20; Malachosky and Greene, *Mae West*, 252.

35. *Gay News*, July 20, 1970; Jennings, "Mae West," 76; *LAT*, November 17, 1975.

36. Musgrove Log, November 13, 1969, August 27, 1971, SMC.

37. Efron, "Television," 16–18; *NYT*, June 25, 1970; *Rona's Reports,* Script, September 15, 1970, SMC.

38. *Gay News*, July 20, 1970.

39. Musgrove Log, August 13, 14, 21, October 6, 21–26, 1969, November 17, 1976, SMC.

40. *Hollywood Reporter*, April 26, 1968; Musgrove Log, October 31–November 6, 8, 1969, December 10, 1969, and George Kirgo, "A Night With Mae West," Script, May 14, 1968, SMC.

41. Malachosky and Greene, *Mae West*, 281–308.

42. James Bacon, "The Photographic Memory of Mae West," *Examiner*, January 19, 1970; Sidney Skolsky, "Week in Review," *Hollywood Citizen News*, January 19, 1970; *VR*, January 19, 1970.

43. *Hollywood Citizen News*, December 4, 1969; *LAT*, February 10, 1971, May 10, 1972; *International Herald Tribune*, July 29, 1968, BFI.

44. *Mae Day: The Masquers Club Salutes Mae West* (Dionysus Empire, 1998); *VR*, April 25, 1973.

Chapter Thirteen

1. William Scott Eyman, "Mae West: Hollywood Isn't Dead, It's Just Taking a Siesta," *Take One,* September/October 1972, 21; Eels and Musgrove, *Mae West*, 261, 264–265, 283–284, 296; Malachosky and Greene, *Mae West*, 250, 312.

2. Mae West, *The Pleasure Man* (New York: Dell Books, 1975), 242.

3. West, *Sex, Health, and ESP*, 13–18, 68–69.

4. West, *Goodness* (1976), 284–286; Johnson, "Snow White," 40–48.

5. *Washington Post*, November 28, 1977; Johnson, "Snow White," 40.

6. Musgrove Log, January 20, March 25, May 19, June 10, 1975, SMC; Alan Cartnal, "They Done It Wrong," *New West*, January 16, 1978, 44–47; *Sunday Times*, June 6, 1976, *Times Sunday Review*, August 27, 1976, BFI.

7. Musgrove to Oriental Theater, April 1976, SMC; Arthur Ungar, "What Do You Say to a Legend (Mae West)?" *Christian Science Monitor*, April 2, 1976; Eels and Musgrove, *Mae West*, 290; Musgrove Log, August 25, 1976, SMC; "Mae West Tribute," USC.

8. Cartnal, "They Done," 44–48; Musgrove Log, June 15, October 6, November 17, December 5, 10, 1976, SMC; *NYT*, August 25, 1976.

9. Musgrove Log, October 5, 6, December 4, 5, 1976, SMC; Ken Hughes, "Acting Had Nothing to Do With It," *LAT Calendar*, February 23, 1997.

10. Patrick Pacheco, "Ladies and Gentlemen—The Lady, the Lions, and Her Amazing Sextette," *After Dark*, May 1977, 48–52.

11. Cartnal, "They Done," 46–47; *Sunday Express*, January 29, 1978, BFI; Hughes, "Acting," 29.

12. Cartnal, "They Done," 47; Musgrove Log, December 13, 1976, SMC.

13. "Mae West and the Men Who Knew Her"; Malachosky and Greene, *Mae West*, 330–331; Eels and Musgrove, *Mae West*, 303; *Sextette* (1979).

14. *Washington Post*, October 31, 1979; *NYT*, June 8, 24, 1979; Eels and Musgrove, *Mae West*, 303–308; Malachosky and Greene, *Mae West*, 332–333.

15. Pacheco, "Ladies and Gentlemen," 48; Cartnal, "They Done," 48; Hughes, "Acting," 29; Ward, *Bio-Bibliography*, 48.

16. *Sunday Express*, January 29, 1978, BFI; *Washington Post*, August 24, 1979.

17. Musgrove Log, May 19, September 26, 1974, SMC; Henry Thody, "Mae West Making a Sizable Return," *Sketch*, August 22, 1968, BFI; Eels and Musgrove, *Mae West*, 285–287; *Boston Herald*, August 3, 1979, MW/CF, HU.

18. Eels and Musgrove, *Mae West*, 308–309.

19. Eels and Musgrove, *Mae West*, 309–312; Malachosky and Greene, *Mae West*, 340–342; DeC, Mae West, November 22, 1980, Los Angeles, California.

20. *LAT*, November 23, 1980; *NYT*, November 23, 1980; *VR*, November 26, 1980.

21. Eels and Musgrove, *Mae West*, 312–315; Malachosky and Greene, *Mae West*, 343.

22. Head, *Edith Head's Hollywood*, 152; James Weldon Johnson, *The Autobiography of an Ex-Colored Man* (1944; reprint New York: Penguin Books, 1990), 1; *Hollywood's Legendary Homes* (American Movie Classics, 1999).

Chapter Fourteen

1. *I'm No Angel* (1933); West, *Goodness*, 1–2; Schallert, "Go West," 32–33, 84.

2. *NYT*, June 4, 2000.

3. Roberts, "Diamond Lil," 64.

4. Roger Ebert, "When I'm Good, I'm Very Good, but When I'm Bad, I'm Better," *TV Guide*, May 1, 1982, 50–52.

5. Mikhail M. Bahktin, *The Dialogic Imagination,* trans. Caryl Emerson and Michael Holquist (Austin: University of Texas Press, 1981), 159.

6. West, *Wit and Wisdom,* 110.

7. *I'm No Angel* (1933); Roberts, "Diamond Lil," 72.

8. Biery, "Part Two," 20.

Bibliographical Essay

Throughout her over eighty years in show business, Mae West's life and career were chronicled, at various times, in the media, public records, popular histories, and academic studies. What follows is a selection of the major sources that provided the foundation for her life story.

While some have disputed the authorship of works bearing West's name, she clearly had a major hand in their creation. Playscripts are edited in her handwriting. Additionally, her publicist, Stanley Musgrove, noted that she drafted scripts by hand. Scripts for West's plays in the Library of Congress Manuscript Division include *Catherine Was Great* (1944), *Come On Over/Embassy Row* (1946), *Diamond Lil* (draft 1928, 1964), *The Drag* (1927), *Frisco Kate* (1930), *The Hussy* (1922), *The Pleasure Man* (1928), *The Ruby Ring* (1921), *SEX* (1926), *Sextette* (1952, 1961), and *The Wicked Age* (1927). Three of these plays are reprinted in *Three Plays by Mae West: SEX, The Drag, The Pleasure Man,* ed. Lillian Schlissel (New York: Routledge, 1997). The Shubert Archives holds *Diamond Lil* (final draft, 1928) and *The Constant Sinner* (1931).

West's books are *The Constant Sinner* (4th printing of *Babe Gordon*, New York: Macaulay, 1931), *Diamond Lil* (1932; reprint New York: Sheridan House, 1940), *Goodness Had Nothing to Do With It: The Autobiography of Mae West* (Englewood Cliffs: Prentice-Hall, 1959; New York: Manor Books, 1976), *The Pleasure Man* (New York: Dell Books, 1975), *Sex, Health, and ESP* (London: Allen, 1975), and *The Wit and Wisdom of Mae West,* ed. Joseph Weintrab (New York: Avon Books, 1967). West also authored "Ten Days and Five Hundred Dollars: The Experiences of a Broadway Star in Jail," *Liberty,* August 20, 1927, and "Sex in the Theatre," *Parade,* September 1929.

MCA/Universal currently holds the rights to West's Paramount films and rereleased them on video in 1993. They are *Night After Night* (1932), *She Done Him Wrong* (1933), *I'm No Angel* (1933), *Belle of the Nineties* (1934), *Goin' to Town* (1935), *Klondike Annie* (1936), *Go West Young Man* (1936), and *Every Day's a Holiday* (1937). West's other films are *The Heat's On* (Columbia Pictures, 1943), Columbia Tristar Home Video 1993 reissue; *My Little Chickadee* (Universal Studios, 1939), MCA/Universal Home Video 1993 reissue; *Myra Breckinridge* (Twentieth Century–Fox, 1970); and *Sextette* (Crown International Pictures, 1979), Rhino Home Video 1997 reissue.

357

Other audio and visual material related to West includes the made-for-TV movie *Mae West* (ABC, May 2, 1982) and the documentary "Mae West and the Men Who Knew Her" (*A&E Biography*, 1994). The UCLA Film and Television Archives holds "Mae West Meets Mister Ed" (*Mister Ed*, March 15, 1964, CBS). West's recordings include *Canned Laughter* (Mind's Eye, 1985), *Great Balls of Fire* (MGM Records, 1972), *Mae Day: The Masquers Club Salutes Mae West* (Dionysus Empire, 1998), *Mae West on the Air: Rare Recordings* (Sandy Hook Records, 1985), *Mae West on the Chase and Sanborn Hour* (Radiola Records, 1990), *Way Out West* (Tower Records, 1966), and *Wild Christmas* (Dragonet, 1966).

There have been numerous studies of West's life and work. Accounts from two members of her inner circle include the contemptuous Stanley Musgrove and George Eels's *Mae West: A Biography* (New York: Morrow, 1982) and the laudatory Tim Malachosky and James Greene's *Mae West* (Lancaster, Calif.: Empire, 1993). Of the most recent, Maurice Leonard's *Mae West: Empress of Sex* (New York: Birch Lane Press, 1991) and Emily Wortis Leider's *Becoming Mae West* (New York: Farrar, Straus & Giroux, 1997) perpetuate the image of West as sex symbol. Ramona Curry's *Too Much of a Good Thing: Mae West as a Cultural Icon* (Minneapolis: University of Minnesota Press, 1996), Marybeth Hamilton's *When I'm Bad, I'm Better: Mae West, Sex, and American Popular Entertainment* (New York: HarperCollins, 1995), and Pamela Robertson's *Guilty Pleasures: Feminist Camp From Mae West to Madonna* (Durham: Duke University Press, 1996) are scholarly investigations of West's relationship to gay performance. They build upon earlier works by Parker Tyler (*The Hollywood Hallucination* [New York: Simon & Schuster, 1970]) and Susan Sontag ("Notes on 'Camp,' " in *Against Interpretation and Other Essays* [New York: Delta, 1967]). Jon Tuska's *The Complete Films of Mae West* (New York: Citadel, 1972) and Carol M. Ward's *Mae West: A Bio-Bibliography* (Westport: Greenwood Press, 1985) are excellent resources on West's career.

In the 1930s, newspapers, national magazines, and fan magazines (especially *Photoplay* and *Motion Picture*) frequently featured West. Key early articles include Thyra Sumner Winslow's "Diamond Mae," *New Yorker,* November 10, 1928, and Ruth Beiry's "The Private Life of Mae West," *Movie Classic,* January–March, 1934. Later interviews with West are in Diane Arbus, *Diane Arbus Magazine Work* (New York: Aperture, 1984); Charlotte Chandler, *The Ultimate Seduction* (Garden City: Doubleday, 1984); Anne Taylor Fleming and Karl Fleming, *The First Time* (New York: Simon & Schuster, 1975); and John Kobal, *People Will Talk* (New York: Knopf, 1985). Also see C. Robert Jennings, "Mae West: A Candid Conversation," *Playboy*, January 1971; Lewis H. Lapham, "Let Me Tell You About Mae West," *Saturday Evening Post*, November 14, 1964; Helen Lawrenson, "Mirror, Mirror, on the Ceiling: How'm I Doing?" *Esquire*, July 1967; and Steven Roberts, "76—And Still Diamond Lil," *New York Times Magazine*, November 2, 1969.

Context for West and her family's New York roots can be found in Edwin G. Burrows and Mike Wallace, *Gotham: A History of New York to 1898* (New York: Oxford University Press, 1999). On Brooklyn, see William L. Felter, *Historic Green Point* (Greenpoint: Green Point Savings Bank, c. 1919) and Grace Gleuck and Paul Gardner, *Brooklyn: People and Places, Past and Present* (New York: Abrams, 1991). In addition, New York politics is discussed in Oliver E. Allen, *The Tiger: The Rise and Fall of Tammany Hall* (New York: Addison-Wesley, 1993) and George Walsh, *Gentleman Jimmy Walker: Mayor of the Jazz Age* (New York: Praeger, 1974). New York's subcultures and underworld are explored in Herbert Asbury, *The Gangs of New York* (1927; reprint New York: Capricorn Books, 1970); Christine Stansell, *City of Women: Sex and Class in New York, 1789–1860* (Urbana: University of Illinois Press, 1987); Timothy J. Gilfolyle, *City of Eros: New York City, Prostitution, and the Commercialization of Sex, 1790–1920* (New York: Norton, 1992); Luc Sante, *Low Life: Lures and Snares of Old New York* (New York: Farrar, Straus & Giroux, 1991); and Alvin F. Harlow, *Old Bowery Days: The Chronicles of a Famous Street* (New York: Appleton, 1931). Also see George Chauncey, *Gay New York: Gender, Urban Culture, and the Making of the Gay Male World, 1890–1940* (New York: Basic Books, 1994) and Ann Douglas, *Terrible Honesty: Mongrel Manhattan in the 1920s* (New York: Farrar, Straus & Giroux, 1995).

For appraisals of West's relationship with the black community, see George Haddad-Garcia, "Mae West, Everybody's Friend," *Black Stars*, April 1981; Robert Johnson, "Mae West: Snow White Sex Queen Who Drifted," *Jet*, July 25, 1974; and "Sexiest Night Club Act," *Ebony*, November 1954. Henry Louis Gates Jr.'s discussion of the African-American tradition of signifying in *The Signifying Monkey: A Theory of Afro-American Literary Criticism* (New York: Oxford University Press, 1988) provides groundwork for understanding West's subversive humor. For general discussion of African-American history, culture, and signification, see Roger D. Abrahams, *Singing the Master: The Emergence of African-American Culture in the Plantation South* (New York: Penguin Books, 1992); Nichols Lemann, *The Promised Land: Black Migration and How It Changed America* (New York: Grove Weidenfeld, 1990); Lawrence W. Levine, *Black Culture and Black Consciousness: Afro-American Folk Thought From Slavery to Freedom* (New York: Oxford University Press, 1977); and Mel Watkins, *On the Real Side: Laughing, Lying, and Signifying: The Underground Tradition of African-American Humor That Transformed Culture, From Slavery to Richard Pryor* (New York: Simon & Schuster, 1994). Examinations of African-American music and dance are Brenda Dixon Gottschild, *Digging the Africanist Presence in American Performance: Dance and Other Contexts* (Westport: Greenwood Press, 1996); William Howland Kenney, *Chicago Jazz: A Cultural History* (New York: Oxford University Press, 1993); Eileen Southern, *The Music of Black Americans: A History* (2d ed., New York: Norton, 1983); and Jean Stearns and Marshall Stearns, *Jazz Dance: The Story of American Vernacular Dance* (2d ed., New York: Da Capo Press, 1994).

Houston Baker's *Blues, Ideology, and Afro-American Literature: A Vernacular Theory* (Chicago: University of Chicago Press, 1984) provides a theoretical framework for the blues as a rebellious force. For African-American women and blues, see Hazel Carby, "It Jus Be's Dat Way Sometime: The Sexual Politics of Women's Blues," in *Gender and Discourse: The Power of Talk* (Norwood: Ablex, 1988); Angela Y. Davis, *Blues Legacies and Black Feminism: Gertrude "Ma" Rainey, Bessie Smith, and Billie Holiday* (New York: Pantheon Books, 1998); and Daphne Duval Harrison, *Black Pearls: Blues Queens of the 1920s* (New Brunswick, N.J.: Rutgers University Press, 1988).

West was strongly influenced by the Harlem Renaissance. Core works on that period are Nathan Huggins, *Harlem Renaissance* (New York: Oxford University Press, 1971); David Levering Lewis, *When Harlem Was in Vogue* (New York: Vintage Books, 1982); and George Hutchinson, *The Harlem Renaissance in Black and White* (Cambridge: Harvard University Press, 1995). Key participants are examined in Arna Bontemps, ed. *The Harlem Renaissance Remembered* (New York: Dodd, Mead, 1972); Bruce Kellner, *Carl Van Vechten and the Irreverent Decades* (Norman: University of Oklahoma Press, 1968); and Eleanore Van Notten, *Wallace Thurman's Harlem Renaissance* (Amsterdam and Atlanta: Rodopi, 1994). Marianna Torgovnick, *Gone Primitive: Savage Intellects, Modern Lives* (Chicago: University of Chicago Press, 1990) discusses primitivism, which was popular not only among Harlem Renaissance figures but within American society in general.

For analysis of racial identity and the representation of African-Americans in U.S. culture, see Janet Brown, "The 'Coon-Singer' and the 'Coon Song': A Case Study of the Performer-Character Relationship," *Journal of American Culture* (Spring/Summer 1984); Laura Doyle, *Bordering on the Body: The Racial Matrix of Modern Fiction and Culture* (New York: Oxford University Press, 1994); Shelley Fisher Fishkin, *Was Huck Black? Mark Twain and African-American Voices* (New York: Oxford University Press, 1993); George Fredrickson, *The Black Image in the White Mind: The Debate on Afro-American Character and Destiny, 1817–1914* (Middletown, Conn.: Wesleyan University Press, 1987); Susan Gubar, *Racechanges: White Skin, Black Face in American Culture* (New York: Oxford University Press, 1997); Noel Ignatiev, *How the Irish Became White* (New York: Routledge, 1995); Eric Lott, *Love and Theft: Blackface Minstrelsy and the American Working Class* (New York: Oxford University Press, 1995); Toni Morrison, *Playing in the Dark: Whiteness and the Literary Imagination* (New York: Vintage Books, 1992); David R. Roediger, *The Wages of Whiteness: Race and the Making of the American Working Class* (London: Verso, 1991); Alexander Saxton, *The Rise and Fall of the White Republic: Class Politics and Mass Culture in the Nineteenth Century* (London: Verso, 1990); and Werner Sollors, *Neither Black nor White yet Both: Thematic Explorations of Interracial Literature* (New York: Oxford University Press, 1997).

West was nurtured and performed in almost all forms of late nineteenth- and early twentieth-century popular culture. General discussions of public amusements include Lewis A. Erenberg, *Steppin' Out: New York Nightlife and the Transformation of American Culture, 1890–1930* (Chicago: University of Chicago Press, 1984); David Nasaw, *Going Out: The Rise and Fall of Public Amusements* (New York: Basic Books,

1993); Kathy Peiss, *Cheap Amusements: Working Women and Leisure in Turn-of-the-Century New York* (Philadelphia: Temple University Press, 1986); and Stanley Walker, *The Night Club Era* (New York: Stokes, 1933). Discussions of boxing are in Gerald Early, *Culture of Bruising: Essays on Prizefighting, Literature, and Modern American Culture* (Hopewell: Ecco Press, 1994); Elliot Gorn, *The Manly Art: Bare-Knuckle Prize Fighting in America* (Ithaca: Cornell University Press, 1986); and Jeffrey Sammons, *Beyond the Ring: The Role of Boxing in American Society* (Urbana: University of Illinois Press, 1988).

Discussions of early burlesque are Robert Allen, *Horrible Prettiness: Burlesque and American Culture* (Chapel Hill: University of North Carolina Press, 1991) and Irving Zeidman, *The American Burlesque Show* (New York: Hawthorn Books, 1967). For vaudeville, see John E. DiMeglio, *Vaudeville USA* (Bowling Green: Bowling Green University Popular Press, 1973); Joe Laurie Jr., *Vaudeville: From the Honky-Tonks to the Palace* (New York: Holt, 1953); Joe Laurie Jr. and Abel Green, *Show Biz From Vaudeville to Video* (New York: Holt, 1951); Charles Samuels and Louise Samuels, *Once Upon a Stage: The Merry World of Vaudeville* (New York: Dodd, Mead, 1974); and Robert Snyder, *The Voice of the City: Vaudeville and Popular Culture in New York* (New York: Oxford University Press, 1989).

Stock companies provided West with training. Useful early works are Marian Spitzer, "Ten-Twenty-Thirty: The Passing of the Popular Priced Circuit," *Saturday Evening Post*, August 22, 1925; Edward William Mamman, *The Old Stock Company School of Acting: A Study of the Boston Museum* (Boston: Trustees of the Public Library, 1945); and Arthur Ruhl, "Ten-Twenty-Thirty," *Outlook*, August 19, 1911.

West first garnered national attention on Broadway. Discussions of New York theater include Brooks Atkinson, *Broadway* (New York: Macmillan, 1970); Gerald Bordman, *American Musical Revue: From* The Passing Show *to* Sugar Babies (New York: Oxford University Press, 1985); Louis Botto, *At This Theatre: An Informal History of New York's Legitimate Theatres* (New York: Dodd, Mead, 1984); Allen Churchill, *The Theatrical Twenties* (New York: McGraw-Hill, 1975); Brooks McNamara, *The Shuberts of Broadway: A History Drawn From the Collections of the Shubert Archive* (New York: Oxford University Press, 1990); and Jerry Stagg, *The Brothers Shubert* (New York: Random House, 1968). For a useful study of women in early theater, see Faye Dudden, *Women in the American Theatre: Actresses and Audiences, 1790–1870* (New Haven: Yale University Press, 1994). Kaier Curtin's *"We Can Always Call Them Bulgarians": The Emergence of Lesbians and Gay Men on the American Stage* (Boston: Alyson, 1987) explores the representation of homosexuality in theater.

Robert Sklar, *Movie-Made America: A Cultural History of American Movies* (2d ed., New York: Vintage Books, 1994) provides a general history of U.S. film, the venue that propelled West to international fame. On studio politics, see Neal Gabler, *An Empire of Their Own: How Jews Invented Hollywood* (New York: Doubleday, 1988) and Thomas Schatz, *The Genius of the System: Hollywood Filmmaking in the Studio Era* (New York: Holt, 1988). Studies concentrating on film during the 1930s include Tino

Balio, ed., *Grand Design: Hollywood as a Modern Business Enterprise* (Berkeley: University of California Press, 1995); Andrew Bergman, *We're in the Money: Depression America and Its Films* (New York: New York University Press, 1971); and Henry Jenkins, *What Made Pistachio Nuts? Early Sound Comedy and the Vaudeville Aesthetic* (New York: Columbia University Press, 1992).

West receives extensive attention in works on censorship: Gregory Black, *Hollywood Censored: Morality Codes, Catholics, and the Movies* (Cambridge: Cambridge University Press, 1994); Gerald Gardner, *The Censorship Papers: Movie Censorship Letters from the Hays Office, 1934 to 1968* (New York: Dodd, Mead, 1987); Leonard J. Leff and Jerold Simmons, *Dame in the Kimono: Hollywood, Censorship, and the Production Code from the 1920s to the 1960s* (New York: Grove Weidenfeld, 1990); James Skinner, *The Cross and the Cinema: The Legion of Decency and the National Catholic Office for Motion Pictures, 1933–1970* (Westport: Praeger, 1993); and Frank Walsh, *Sin and Censorship: The Catholic Church and the Motion Picture Industry* (New Haven: Yale University Press, 1996).

Laura Mulvey's theory of spectatorship in *Visual and Other Pleasures* (Bloomington: Indiana University Press, 1989), which contends that Hollywood films by male directors permit men to project themselves into the male protagonists that subjugate female characters, has strongly influenced studies of women's images in film. Other explorations of women and cinema include Molly Haskell, *From Reverence to Rape: The Treatment of Women in the Movies* (New York: Penguin Books, 1973); Lea Jacobs, *The Wages of Sin: Censorship and the Fallen Woman in Film, 1928–1942* (Berkeley: University of California Press, 1995); and Marjorie Rosen, *Popcorn Venus: Women, Movies, and the American Dream* (New York: Avon Books, 1973).

Sources on race and film include Daniel Bernardi, ed., *The Birth of Whiteness: Race and the Emergence of the U.S. Cinema* (New Brunswick: Rutgers University Press, 1996); Donald Bogle, *Toms, Coons, Mulattoes, Mammies, and Bucks: An Interpretive History of Blacks in American Films* (New York: Continuum, 1990); and Thomas Cripps, *Slow Fade to Black: The Negro in American Film* (New York: Oxford University Press, 1993).

General theoretical works exploring cultural rebellion include Mikhail M. Bahktin, *The Dialogic Imagination*, trans. Caryl Emerson and Michael Holquist (Austin: University of Texas Press, 1981); Mikhail M. Bahktin, *Rabelais and His World*, trans. Helene Iswolsky (Bloomington: Indiana University Press, 1984); and Stuart Hall, "Encoding/Decoding," in *Culture, Media, Language* (London: Hutchinson, 1980). For historical overviews of aspects of the twentieth century, see Lynn Dumenil, *Modern Temper: American Culture and Society in the 1920s* (New York: Hill & Wang, 1995); Frederick Lewis Allen, *Only Yesterday: An Informal History of the 1920s* (1931; reprint New York: Perennial Library, 1964); Terry Cooney, *Balancing Acts: American Thought and Culture in the 1930s* (New York: Twayne, 1995); and William Chafe, *The Unfinished Journey: America Since WWII* (New York: Oxford University Press, 1991).

Index